RUSSIA AND THE NEW WORLD DISORDER

# BOBO LO

CHATHAM HOUSE
*London*

BROOKINGS INSTITUTION PRESS
*Washington, D.C.*

*Russia and the New World Disorder* may be ordered from:
BROOKINGS INSTITUTION PRESS
c/o HFS, P.O. Box 50370, Baltimore, MD 21211-4370
Tel.: 800/537-5487; 410/516-6976; Fax: 410/516-6998
www.brookings.edu

*Library of Congress Cataloging–in-Publication data*

Lo, Bobo, 1959–
  Russia and the new world order / Bobo Lo. — 1st [edition].
    pages  cm
  Includes bibliographical references and index.
  Summary: "Examines the interplay between Russian foreign policy and a complex global environment, contrasting the Kremlin's view of a declining West and resurgent Russia with the world Moscow actually faces, which is defined by a new disorder that challenges core Russian assumptions and puts a premium on adaptability"—Provided by publisher.
  ISBN 978-0-8157-2556-5 (hardcover : alk. paper)—ISBN 978-0-8157-2609-8 (pbk. : alk. paper)—ISBN 978-0-8157-2557-2 (ebook : alk. paper)  1. Russia (Federation)—Foreign relations. 2. World politics—21st century. I. Title.
  JZ1616.A5L62 2015
  327.47—dc23                                    2015011246

9 8 7 6 5 4 3 2 1

The paper used in this publication meets minimum requirements of the American National Standard for Information Sciences—Permanence of Paper for Printed Library Materials: ANSI Z39.48-1992.

Typeset in Minion and Univers Condensed

Composition by Oakland Street Publishing
Arlington, Virginia

Printed by R. R. Donnelley
Harrisonburg, Virginia

*To the one true politician in our family*
*the incomparable and beloved*
*Siriol*

# Contents

# Part III: Possibilities

# Acknowledgments

In *The Second Coming* (1919), W. B. Yeats wrote of an anarchic world in which "the ceremony of innocence is drowned; the best lack all conviction, while the worst are full of passionate intensity." Our times are, of course, immeasurably less destructive and more prosperous than a century ago. Yet they too reflect much of the cynicism, fatalism, and irrational passions described by Yeats. Today, it is as challenging as ever to stay true to the spirit of analytical enquiry, while retaining a sense of optimism amid the tide of events.

In this enterprise I have benefited hugely from the support of a wonderful band of family and friends. First among these is my darling wife, Siriol, without whom this book would have been mere nothingness. She has been at once a source of inspiration, a tower of strength, and a giver of perspective. She has offered vital suggestions to several drafts of the manuscript; tolerated the unspeakable mess of my infamous horizontal filing system; and managed a wide assortment of author neuroses. She has been—and is—incredible. Somewhat less incredible, but hugely entertaining and even (at times) lovable have been our two dogs, Lyosha and Riley. Without them, this book might have been completed a little sooner, but certainly much less enjoyably.

Such has been the pace of events in Russia and the world around it that this book has gone through numerous iterations. In an often tortuous process, many people have offered invaluable suggestions and corrected ghastly errors. I am especially indebted to Duncan Allan, John Besemeres, Ian Bond, Rodric Braithwaite, Laurence Broyd, Richard Connolly, Mary Dejevsky, Brian Fall, Thomas Gomart, Sam Greene, Janet Gunn, Phil Hanson, Hiski Haukkala, Kate Horner, Natasha Kuhrt, Ole Andreas Lindeman, Ed Lucas, Orysia Lutsevych, Marie Mendras, Andrew Monaghan, James Nixey, Craig Oliphant, Anthony Phillips, Alex Pravda, Gene Rumer, Bob Service,

James Sherr, Angela Stent, Kyle Wilson, and Andrew Wood. I have also benefited greatly from the considerable insights of Fiona Hill, Victor Larin, John Lough, Lilia Shevtsova, Dmitri Trenin, Jörg Wuttke, Yang Cheng, and Zhao Huasheng.

In Frank Capra's *It's a Wonderful Life*, the angel Clarence reminds the hero that "no man is a failure who has friends." By this criterion, I have been truly blessed. My friends have stood by me through thick and often thin, and I am more grateful than I can say for their generous gift. Thank you Lyn and Bruce Minerds, Linda Kouvaras and Richard Ward, Stephen Shay and Nicola Cade, Lizzy Fisher, Glenn and Agnes Waller, Berit Lindeman, Hilde Svartdal-Lunde, Bob Nurick, Emily Gale, Ros and Simon Harrison, Herbie Flowers and Claire Lacey, Karine Georgian, Nick and Natasha Murray, Ursula and Jon Harper, James and Alison Lonsdale, Guy Chazan, Ros Hanson-Laurent and Joe Laurent, Simon Tilford, Riitta Heino, and Vera Trenin.

I want to pay tribute to two wonderful former colleagues and friends from the Centre for European Reform. Clara O'Donnell and Philip Whyte passed away tragically young, but achieved great things in their short lives. In contrasting ways, they showed extraordinary courage in the face of crippling illness and awful fortune—one working creatively to the very end, the other seizing the opportunity to travel the world and absorb different experiences. It was a great honor and privilege to be able to call myself their friend, and I shall miss them terribly.

I would like to thank Chatham House and Brookings for their efforts in bringing this book to publication. Margaret May, in particular, has defied the logic of (semi-)retirement to transform a rough manuscript into something presentable. Not for the first time, I owe her a huge debt. Ľubica Polláková has done sterling work in organizing the practicalities of translating an ambitious project into reality, while Caz Hattam performed the laborious task of footnote checking with great diligence and alertness. I am grateful to Janet Walker at Brookings for pushing the whole process to rapid completion, and to Sese-Paul Design for their beautiful cover.

Finally, I would like to thank members of my extended (but close) family, above all Hugh and Helen Jones, who have been endlessly kind and supportive. This writer, at least, has never had to starve, while savoring the pleasures of cricket at Lord's and Cardiff, and one of the best wine cellars in the Welsh valleys.

# Abbreviations and Acronyms

| | |
|---|---|
| ABM | Anti-Ballistic Missile treaty (1972) |
| AIIB | Asian Infrastructure Investment Bank |
| APEC | Asia-Pacific Economic Cooperation group |
| ARF | ASEAN Regional Forum |
| ASEAN | Association of Southeast Asian Nations |
| BAM | Baikal-Amur Mainline |
| bcm | billion cubic meters |
| BRICS | Brazil, Russia, India, China, and South Africa group |
| BTC | Baku-Tbilisi-Ceyhan pipeline |
| CAGP | Central Asia–China gas pipeline |
| CBM | confidence-building measure |
| CIS | Commonwealth of Independent States |
| CMEA | Council for Mutual Economic Assistance |
| CNPC | China National Petroleum Corporation |
| CPSU | Communist Party of the Soviet Union |
| CSCAP | Council for Security Cooperation in the Asia-Pacific |
| CSTO | Collective Security Treaty Organization |
| CTR | Cooperative Threat Reduction program |
| CWC | Chemical Weapons Convention |
| DCFTA | Deep and Comprehensive Free Trade Area |
| DPR | Donetsk People's Republic |
| DPRK | Democratic People's Republic of Korea |
| EaP | Eastern Partnership |
| EAS | East Asia Summit |
| ECHR | European Court of Human Rights |
| EEC | Eurasian Economic Commission |
| EEU | Eurasian Economic Union |

| | |
|---|---|
| ENP | European Neighbourhood Policy |
| ESPO | East Siberian–Pacific Ocean oil pipeline |
| EurAsEC | Eurasian Economic Community |
| G-8 | Group of Eight |
| G-20 | Group of Twenty |
| GECF | Gas Exporting Countries Forum |
| GUUAM | Georgia, Ukraine, Uzbekistan, Azerbaijan, and Moldova (group) |
| ICBM | intercontinental ballistic missile |
| ICC | International Criminal Court |
| IMF | International Monetary Fund |
| INF | Intermediate-range Nuclear Forces treaty |
| INSOR | Institute of Contemporary Development |
| IOC | international oil company |
| IS | Islamic State |
| ISAF | International Security Assistance Force |
| KEDO | Korean peninsula Energy Development Organization |
| LNG | liquefied natural gas |
| MAP | Membership Action Plan (NATO) |
| MED | Ministry of Economic Development |
| MFA | Ministry of Foreign Affairs |
| MOD | Ministry of Defense |
| MoU | Memorandum of Understanding |
| NDN | Northern Distribution Network |
| NGO | nongovernmental organization |
| NRC | NATO-Russia Council |
| NSR | Northern Sea Route |
| ODIHR | Office of Democratic Institutions and Human Rights |
| OPEC | Organization of Petroleum Exporting Countries |
| OSCE | Organization for Security and Cooperation in Europe |
| P5 | Permanent Five members of the UN Security Council |
| PCA | Partnership and Cooperation Agreement (EU) |
| PfP | Partnership for Peace (NATO) |
| PLA | People's Liberation Army (China) |
| PLAN | People's Liberation Army Navy |
| PPP | purchasing power parity |
| R2P | "responsibility to protect" |
| RATS | Regional Anti-Terrorist Structure |
| RFE | Russian Far East |
| RIAC | Russian International Affairs Council |
| ROC | Russian Orthodox Church |
| ROK | Republic of Korea |

| | |
|---|---|
| RRF | Rapid Reaction Force |
| SCO | Shanghai Cooperation Organization |
| SES | Single Economic Space |
| SLBM | submarine-launched ballistic missile |
| SORT | Strategic Offensive Reductions Treaty (2002) |
| START | Strategic Arms Reduction Treaty (2010) |
| TANAP | Trans-Anatolian Natural Gas Pipeline |
| TAP | Trans-Adriatic Pipeline |
| TAPI | Turkmenistan–Afghanistan–Pakistan–India pipeline project |
| UNCLOS | United Nations Convention on the Law of the Sea |
| UNGA | United Nations General Assembly |
| UNM | United National Movement (Georgia) |
| UNSC | United Nations Security Council |
| UNSCR | United Nations Security Council Resolution |
| USRBC | U.S.-Russia Business Council |
| VTsIOM | Vserossiiskii tsentr izucheniya obshchestvennogo mneniya (All-Russian Center for the Study of Public Opinion) |
| WMD | weapons of mass destruction |
| WTO | World Trade Organization |

# Prologue

The weak get beaten.

VLADIMIR PUTIN, SEPTEMBER 4, 2004

## The Shock of the Old

The Russian annexation of Crimea in March 2014 was an act both revolutionary and regressive. It was revolutionary in that, for the first time in more than half a century, one European state had seized territory from another by force of arms. In the process, Moscow appeared to shake the very foundations of the post-1945 international system, and signal the end of post–cold war accommodation with the West. There was a new "order" in the world, even if no one quite knew what its rules were or how it would turn out.

At the same time, the Kremlin's actions were a throwback to an era that many had assumed had gone for good. The most pertinent comparison here is not with the cold war or some idealized conception of the international community, but with Russia shortly after Vladimir Putin succeeded Boris Yeltsin in the Kremlin. The prominent scholar Dmitri Trenin wrote then of Russia's evolution from geopolitics to globalization in response to new realities—the end of empire and of cold war rivalry, the ascendancy of economic and technological power, and the emergence of an interdependent world in which the primacy of nation-states was much weakened. Geopolitics remained relevant, but now needed to be viewed within the "broader context of Russia's post-communist, post-imperial transformation."[1]

Today there is a very different narrative in Moscow. Globalization, or at least Western-led globalization, is out, while geopolitics has returned as the main organizing principle of Putin's foreign policy. The dominant theme is of the reversion to the traditional, the familiar, and the indigenous. At home the Kremlin is energetically pursuing a Russian "national idea" based on conservative political and social values, free of the contaminating influence of Western liberalism.[2] Internationally it is leading a resurgent nationalism that openly defies U.S. leadership and challenges the legitimacy of many existing global norms and institutions. The feelings of inferiority that once characterized Russian elite attitudes have given way to a new militancy and, in public at least, aggressive self-confidence.

The Ukraine crisis exemplifies this change of mood and approach. It also highlights how differently Russia and the West see the world. Such polarization extends well beyond mere policy disagreements. It reflects conflicting views about the nature of international politics, the rules of global governance, and so-called "universal" values. It emerges out of clashing historical narratives, and reveals schisms on such basic questions as definitions of success, power, and greatness. It is symptomatic of the gulf in perceptions that Western leaders should accuse the Kremlin of conducting a nineteenth-century foreign policy,[3] while Moscow charges the United States and Europe with failing to come to terms with a twenty-first-century post-Western order.

## Russia and the New World Disorder

It is easy to forget amid the drama of human tragedy and escalating tensions in Ukraine that the Kremlin's actions arise out of a particular context. They are at once a microcosm and a reaffirmation of Putin's larger vision for Russia and its place in international society. They highlight critical trends in Russia's domestic development, its relations with the West, and the conduct of foreign policy. They pertain not only to a troubled past and volatile present, but also to a wholly unclear future.

This book sets out to answer three questions of fundamental importance. First, *what challenges does a world in the midst of unprecedented and accelerating change present to Russia?* Much of the intellectual debate in Moscow (and elsewhere) has centered on the "decline of the West" and the concomitant emergence of the BRICS countries (Brazil, Russia, India, China, and South Africa). There is an implicit assumption that "the rise of the rest" and the "shift of global power to the East" are historical inevitabilities.[4] In the Kremlin's interpretation of the "polycentric system of international relations,"[5] Russia stands as an independent center of power, the geopolitical and civilizational pivot between East and West.[6] In this world, the great powers dominate more than ever,[7] the nation-state is back as the basic building block of international relations, competition is everywhere, and military strength provides the key to real power and influence.

Yet a global environment more fluid and unpredictable than at any time since the fall of the Berlin Wall poses enormous challenges to *all* countries—large and small, strong and weak, the emerging along with the well established. This *new world disorder* casts doubt on the validity of many of Moscow's assumptions. Thus military might is exposed as counterproductive in advancing national interests, while soft power of various kinds remains surprisingly influential. The United States has lost much of its authority, but no other country has shown the will, let alone capacity, to assume the responsibilities of leadership. State actors dominate international politics, yet the influence of the great powers is constrained by the growing assertiveness and capabilities of smaller nations. Most of all, past pedigree and a sense of entitlement are no longer enough to secure Russia a privileged status in the international system. In the new world disorder, performance, including an ability to embrace change, has become everything.

The tension between these two worlds, the perceptual and the actual, leads to a second question: *how is Russian foreign policy responding to the demands of the new world disorder?* Putin acknowledges that Russia must operate in a "rapidly changing world, a world that has become more open, transparent, and interdependent."[8] But what does this mean in practical terms? To what extent, if any, do such external (and internal) realities shape Moscow's approach toward issues of global governance, the post-Soviet neighborhood, engagement with Asia, and interaction with the West?

It is obviously unrealistic to expect an early transformation in today's climate. The feeling of crisis is thick in the air, and the emphasis is very much on preservation, not reinvention. But it is useful to consider whether the Kremlin is beginning to rethink, or at least modify, core foreign policy principles. For example, does the much-trumpeted "turn to the East" represent a progressive shift away from the historical Westerncentrism of Russia's elite? Or is it a variation on old-fashioned strategic balancing, whereby partnership with China serves primarily as leverage against the United States and Europe?

There is a vital distinction to be made here between tactical dexterity and strategic adaptation. It is one thing for the Kremlin to react in agile fashion to discrete events and opportunities, such as the vacillation of the Obama administration over Syria, or the Maidan revolution in Kyiv. It is quite another to respond flexibly and imaginatively to broader trends that are often difficult to grasp—the diminishing influence of the major powers in global governance; the lust for sovereignty among the ex-Soviet republics; strategic diversification in the Asia-Pacific region; and growing Russia-fatigue in Europe. In these circumstances, the natural reflex is one of denial, and to seek instead a new Westphalian order through a modern-day Concert of Great Powers.[9]

Finally, *what are Russia's prospects in a post-American century?*[10] Moscow assesses these positively, seeing Russia not only as a permanent great power, but also as one of the principal beneficiaries of global shifts.[11] But there are many in the United States, Europe, and indeed outside the West who believe that it is destined to decline—left behind not only by the advanced nations of the West, but also by a dynamic East. Such contrasting judgments are often driven by normative biases and wishful thinking. Nevertheless, they raise important questions about Russia's future trajectory. What is the potential for Moscow to develop a new foreign policy for a new world (and a new Russia), and how might this look? Or does the Kremlin's belief in the timeless character of international politics rule out reform for the foreseeable future? What are the likely consequences of such conservative thinking and the consolidation of a "besieged fortress" mentality?[12]

The stakes are high indeed. One of the central arguments of this book is that a Russia able to redefine itself as a modern power will be a leading player in the twenty-first century, exerting a critical influence in many areas of international politics, economy, and society. Conversely, an unreconstructed Russia could end up as one of the principal casualties of global transformation—backward at home, marginalized from decisionmaking, and increasingly vulnerable to the ambitions of others. As the influential economist Vladimir Mau has warned, Russia might suffer a fate similar to that of sixteenth-century Spain, which in just over a hundred years declined from being the leading power in the world into a regional backwater at the periphery of Europe, sapped by a combination of expensive foreign adventures and domestic atrophy.[13] Worse still, it could end up like China in the late Qing dynasty, slowly disintegrating as a result of the stubborn failure to comprehend, let alone adjust to, the world around it.[14]

## Context, Performance, Possibilities

### Context

This book is divided into three parts. Part I looks at the context of Russian foreign policy. This means, in the first instance, the domestic factors that influence decisionmaking (chapter 1). In recent years it has become commonplace to emphasize the fusion of domestic politics and foreign policy, and to regard the latter as essentially an extension of the former. There is also the conventional Western wisdom that a country's political system and values determine its attitude to the outside world. Thus democracies are said to be more committed to positive-sum cooperation than authoritarian regimes, which tend to adopt narrowly self-interested, assertive, and even aggressive positions.[15]

Such simplifications, however, underestimate the complexity of the domestic/foreign policy nexus, which in Russia assumes various forms. The linkage is apparent at the most basic level in the political culture and modus operandi of the Putin elite. Although this elite is by no means monolithic, there are considerable commonalities within it, especially when it comes to foreign policy. The relationship between the domestic and the foreign in Russia is reflected too in the enduring influence of structural factors: geography; issues of history and historical memory; civilizational and ideological biases; and perceptions of identity. Finally, there are more mundane but no less important factors, such as immediate political imperatives, financial interests, societal pressures (nationalism, democratic sentiments, religious and social conservatism), as well as the impact of specific events, such as the anti-Putin protests of 2011–12.

The second facet of context is external (chapter 2). Preconceived ideas about the inherent nature of international politics, as well as more recent judgments about the rise and decline of major powers, form the intellectual basis of Putin's foreign policy. They go to the heart of perceptions of Russia as an independent global actor and regional leader. They feed notions of indispensability, uniqueness, and entitlement. And they encourage a generally upbeat view of Russia's prospects, as one of the winners in the transition to a new multipolar order. Above all, they reinforce the conviction that success depends on strengthening the fundamentals that have sustained Russia during better times, such as having a clear sense of national purpose, maintaining an unapologetic face to the world, and building up the capabilities to back all this up.

At the same time, regional and global circumstances intrude on the practice of foreign policy. The Kremlin faces a constant struggle in reconciling its vision of Russia's place in the world with meeting the challenges posed by the new world disorder. It seeks to create new realities and reaffirm old "truths," yet finds itself under severe pressure from trends over which it has little control, but which have major consequences for Russian interests. In this environment, the Kremlin's hankering for order and structure struggles against the untidiness of international politics, marked by the elusive (and changing) nature of power, the demise of leadership across the board, and the emergence of a world that is simultaneously inclusive and fragmented.

## Performance

Part II of the book takes the discussion from the contextual to the policy-specific. It analyzes the Putin regime's response thus far to four major challenges presented by the new world disorder: (1) to redefine Russia as a global actor and contributor to international public goods; (2) to recalibrate its influence in post-Soviet Eurasia; (3) to engage more productively in the Asia-Pacific region; and (4) to stabilize relations with the West. There is arguably a fifth imperative, beyond the immediate scope of this book, which is to develop the domestic capabilities—good governance, technological modernization, genuine rule of law—that would enable Russia to operate more effectively within the international system.

The area of global governance (chapter 3), more than any other, highlights the tension between the perceptual and the actual in Russian policymaking. On the one hand, the Kremlin plays up Russia's "indispensable" role, whether over Ukraine, Syria, the nonproliferation of weapons of mass destruction (WMD), or global energy security. On the other hand, Moscow has minimal influence on many of the most important issues on the contemporary global agenda, such as a new financial architecture and economic rebalancing.[16]

This disjunction is compounded by the contradiction between Putin's desire to promote Russia as a good international citizen and his conviction in what might be called the "divine right of great powers." When, for example, Moscow talks up the UN's "central and coordinating role" in world politics,[17] it interprets this in a very particular way—as the rationale for collective leadership by the five permanent members (P5) of the UN Security Council—in other words the recognized great powers. In similar spirit the "democratization of international relations" entails the dilution of American power (and consequent elevation of Russian influence), not the emergence of a multilateral system in which smaller nations have significant input into decisions. For the Kremlin global governance has little intrinsic value, but is seen largely in instrumental terms. It talks up the importance of "fundamental international legal norms and principles," not because it wishes to implement universal human values, but for just the opposite reason—to protect the sovereign rights of national governments, no matter how egregious, against the intrusion of a larger supranational (read: Western) morality.

Perhaps the most difficult of Russia's foreign policy challenges is to recalibrate its influence in the post-Soviet space from that of imperial master to post-imperial power (chapter 4). All empires struggle to adjust to decline, and Russia is no exception—as events in Ukraine have shown. A post-imperial mindset does not come readily to leaders who spent their formative years in the Soviet Union and were accustomed to Moscow managing affairs in the most distant republics. The collapse of the Soviet Union was a shocking experience in every sense, reflected in Putin's notorious claim that it was the "greatest geopolitical catastrophe of the [twentieth] century."[18] Inevitably, the end of empire is associated with defeat and humiliation, reinforced by the historical conflation of Russia with the USSR, and by the traumas of the 1990s.

While there is general understanding that the Soviet Union cannot be put back together, Moscow believes that it has a legitimate right of influence, and sometimes intervention, in the former Soviet republics.[19] It sees this as a function not only of history, but also of continuing political, economic, social, and cultural ties—what Foreign Minister Sergei Lavrov has termed "civilizational commonality (*obshchnost*)."[20] Well before the annexation of Crimea, Putin had demonstrated heightened patrimonial activism, not only in the Slavic core of Ukraine and Belarus, but also in the larger Eurasian space through the development of the Customs Union.

Set against such ambitions, however, are realities the Kremlin can hardly ignore. The most important is that the ex-Soviet republics have been independent for more than two decades, and have become increasingly jealous about preserving their sovereignty. Moscow therefore faces a difficult choice: either it recasts its approach to factor in the changing dynamics in these countries, including tolerating the presence of other external parties, such as the European Union and China. Or it insists on its "rights" and risks damaging the very relationships—and influence—to which it attaches such importance. The unfolding of the Ukraine crisis from late 2013 illustrates how badly things can go wrong when this delicate balance is disrupted.

One of the most publicized themes of the post-2008 period has been that of Russia's "turn to the East"—not just expanding ties with China, but treating the Asia-Pacific region as a major theater of security and economic engagement (chapter 5). Again the disconnect between the perceptual and the actual is stark. Moscow talks a big game, highlighting Russia's emergence as a "Euro-Pacific" power, geopolitical balancer between the United States and China, and economic and civilizational bridge across Eurasia.[21] However, it has struggled to make good on such grand ambitions. Notwithstanding several major energy deals, Russia's footprint on the Asian continent remains shallow, and few there believe that it has much to contribute beyond natural resources and weapons.

Historically the biggest obstacle to advancing Russian interests in Asia has been the Kremlin's tendency to view engagement in instrumental terms—as an element of global strategy, rather than as a priority direction in its own right. While there is recognition, in principle, of the need to pursue more committed policies in and with Asia, old habits die hard. Moscow's focus remains overwhelmingly centered on the major Asian powers, above all China, and its interest in broader issues of regional security-building and economic integration is superficial at best. Meanwhile, the continuing backwardness of Russia's eastern regions undermines its quest for acceptance and influence in an increasingly contested part of the world. To translate the "turn to the East" into reality will require a reorientation from the current overweening emphasis on geopolitics to a more economically driven strategy.

Over the past two decades Russian and Western policymakers have failed to bring stability to an interaction that has lurched between extremes of optimism and disillusionment, but whose general trend has been negative (chapter 6). The Ukraine crisis has seen relations plummet to a new low, and it is difficult to envisage even a partial normalization anytime soon. On top of enduring historical mistrust, sharp policy differences, and divergent perceptions and values, Moscow is inclined to overestimate the extent of Western weakness.[22] The global economic downturn, the struggles of the eurozone, and the failings of the Obama administration have encouraged brinkmanship in the Kremlin[23] and accentuated a highly transactional attitude toward cooperation. Overconfidence has also skewed the conduct of other areas of Russian foreign policy, such as the partnership with China.

The challenge for Moscow with the West is to pursue a more strategically consistent course based on a balanced appreciation of modern-day realities and Russia's long-term interests. This means neither pursuing a "pro-Western" foreign policy at the expense of neglecting Asia and other parts of the world—as during the early Yeltsin period—nor succumbing to exaggerated notions about the irrevocable decline of the West. A more practical approach would proceed from the understanding that the main threats to Russia in the twenty-first century do not come from U.S. missile defense or the European Union's underwhelming Eastern Partnership, but from instability in neighboring countries, WMD proliferation, and transnational crime. The getting of such wisdom, however, is contingent on breaking down the zero-sum mentality that has long colored views of the United States and developing a more sophisticated understanding of contemporary European dynamics.

## Possibilities

The third and final part of the book looks to the future, considering first how a more effective Russian foreign policy might take shape (chapter 7). Many Western observers dismiss the prospects for change out of hand, particularly while Putin continues to dominate Russian politics. This pessimistic assessment stems from the belief that a sense of "great power-ness" (*derzhavnost*) and empire has always been in the DNA of Russia's rulers, and has since been supplemented by a rampant nationalism and militant traditionalism. While the Kremlin may sometimes be more accommodating at an operational level, its strategic outlook will remain thoroughly conservative and reactionary.

It is difficult to be optimistic in light of recent events. The reinvention of Russian foreign policy would require an attitudinal revolution within the elite and among the wider population—a revolution whose remit would scarcely be limited to international relations. Even before the crisis in Ukraine, the political will to embrace change was conspicuously lacking. Many of Moscow's moves, such as the attempts to beef up the BRICS as a counter-Western political alliance, misread the world in which Russia must function. A more significant obstacle still is Putin's fear that reform—in foreign as well as domestic policy—could undermine the very foundations of his system. The unintended consequences of the Gorbachev and Yeltsin years have reinforced a deep conservatism.

Nevertheless, it would be foolish to rule out change on the basis of crude national stereotyping and historical determinism. Circumstances can and do alter perceptions. A geopolitically driven foreign policy may become unattractive, including to an elite brought up in a culture of military power, realpolitik, and national greatness. Mounting economic and social pressures, intra-elite fissures, and unfavorable external trends (slumping commodity prices; an increasingly assertive China) could establish a context in which today's improbable becomes tomorrow's possible and even necessary. Such a transition would be aided by the realization that, in the longer term, clinging to an obsolescent model of governance would jeopardize not only Russia's status, but also its prosperity and even sovereignty. In conditions where once unquestionable trumps, such as nuclear weapons, have lost much of their clout,[24] decisionmakers could choose instead to mobilize Russia's formidable soft power potential: as a primary contributor to global energy and resource security; as a stabilizing influence throughout much of the Eurasian continent; and as a source of still considerable intellectual capital to the world.

The book concludes with four scenarios for 2030 (chapter 8): (1) "soft" or semi-authoritarian stagnation; (2) hard authoritarianism; (3) regime fracturing; and (4) "second-wave" liberalism. The purpose of these scenarios is not to predict the future, which is a hubristic and generally fruitless endeavor, but to suggest some of the pathways along which Russian foreign policy might travel over the next ten to fifteen years. Many existing assumptions are likely to be challenged and quite possibly refuted. For instance, under the hard authoritarian scenario Russia's relations with the West could revert to a surprising if uneasy equilibrium, while there is a corresponding deterioration in ties with China. Or a liberal regime in Moscow may not necessarily bring about the positive changes in Russian foreign policy that many in the West hope for, but see a return instead to the awkward and often recriminatory interaction of the Yeltsin period.[25] In the end, the only real certainty is that Russia faces extraordinarily taxing times ahead. How its policymakers respond to a vast array of domestic and external challenges will be crucial to its future in an ever more disorderly century.

# Part I
# Context

# one
# The Domestic Context of Russian Foreign Policy

In Russia there is no law. There is a pillar, and on that pillar sits the crown.
                                                        ALEXANDER PUSHKIN

It has become axiomatic that a country's conduct of international relations reflects the influence of domestic factors. Indeed, the link is so strong that one might turn to Carl von Clausewitz's famous maxim to argue that diplomacy is merely the continuation of domestic politics by other means.[1] Yet such generalizations also invite misunderstanding and misrepresentation. They may reinforce crude national stereotypes, tendentious readings of history, and deterministic views of the future. And they are often misused to justify actions that are anything but pragmatic or logical.

These problems are especially evident in the case of Russia. Few countries have been subject to mythmaking on such an industrial scale. Many observers, foreign and Russian, surround it in a cloud of mysticism, in effect agreeing with the nineteenth-century poet Fyodor Tyutchev that "Russia cannot be understood by the mind alone . . . in Russia, one can only believe."[2] This has led to a host of trite simplifications and sometimes outright falsehoods—about the "Russian soul," the "strong leader,"[3] the alleged unreadiness and dislike of its people for democracy,[4] and Russia's timeless identity as a great power. It has also encouraged a self-serving, relativistic attitude along the lines that since Russia is so very different, it cannot be expected to behave like a "normal" nation.

On the other hand, there are those who treat Russian foreign policy as if domestic influences and considerations were of little relevance. They proceed from a (Western) moralist perspective, talking up universal values, common threats and challenges, and shared interests, only to discover that Moscow's perspectives and priorities often differ substantially from their own. When reality hits home, disappointment leads to accusations of bad faith and double-dealing. The Obama administration's reset policy exemplified these failings (see chapter 6).

Before discussing Russia's interaction with the new world disorder, it is critical to understand the different elements that constitute the domestic context of its foreign policy. They amount to an amalgam of ideas, interests, and instincts, whose influence varies, not only from issue to issue, but also according to time and circumstance. Taken together, however, they are the foundation of a particular attitude toward the world and Russia's place in it.

The most immediate of these elements is policymaking—that is, the mechanics of who makes policy and how they develop and implement it. This, in turn, ties into the question of political culture. It is not enough to identify the decisionmakers; we also need to know where they are coming from. What influences lead them to think and act the way they do? It has become almost de rigueur to emphasize the connection between authoritarianism at home and an adversarial foreign policy. This chapter argues, however, that deeper structural factors, such as geography and history, are much more influential in shaping Russia's approach to the world.

At the same time, foreign policy is not just the product of long-term realities, but is buffeted by unforeseen events. There is a tendency to exaggerate the inexorability of larger trends. Yet if history teaches us anything, it is that nothing is inevitable. Putin's conduct of foreign policy reveals strong predispositional influences. But it is also the "accidental" and unstable result of contemporary political conditions, economic outcomes, and social pressures. These establish realities that may frequently be short-lived, yet exert a powerful influence on decisionmakers at critical moments.

## Policymaking

Analysts have become so accustomed to using generic terms such as "Russia," "Moscow," and the "Putin regime/elite" that they tend to give little thought to what they mean by them. Partly this is an issue of practicality; some generalization is unavoidable in order to communicate information coherently. But it also tacitly acknowledges that in many cases it is impossible to delve much deeper. Trying to understand the inner workings of decisionmaking is a challenging enterprise even in relatively transparent political systems. It is especially so in an environment where there is such a strong culture of secrecy and informal networking, as in Putin's Russia.[5]

In effect there are two broad policy milieus—the real and the virtual. The latter is what outsiders see. This is the world of public policy statements, such as the Foreign Policy Concept, the Concept of National Security, and the Military Doctrine. Such documents present sweeping visions of Russia's destiny, unequivocal expositions of basic principles, and upbeat assessments of important relationships. They can be important in highlighting trends in Russian foreign policy, but offer few clues as to how it is actually made. Indeed, they convey a misleading clarity and certainty of thought.

By contrast, the real policy world is exclusive and almost invisible. This is where the big decisions are made. The vast majority of the political class plays little role, and public input is minimal. A particular order comes from the Kremlin, but without exceptionally privileged access it is often impossible to know who influenced whom, what, and how. It is often a case of "those who know don't tell, and those who tell don't know."

There is consequently a substantial element of guesswork involved in trying to understand the mechanics of Russian foreign policy. The difficulties are compounded by the fact that decisions rarely, if ever, reflect an "objective" national interest (whatever that means), but are made by individuals with their own particular biases, prejudices, and vested interests. As the commentator Igor Torbakov has noted, "The line between what is generally understood as *national interests* and . . . *group interests* is completely blurred in Russia."[6]

## The policy landscape

Nevertheless, there is much to learn even from a brief review of major actors and decisionmaking processes. One way of doing this is to distinguish between different policy functions: decisionmaking; ideational inspiration; implementation; and rationalization. Although there is considerable overlap between these functions, each represents a distinct dimension with its own exponents.

The most important function is *decisionmaking*, and this is reflected in the identity of those responsible for it. They include, most obviously, President Putin, but also other senior regime figures, such as the chairman of Rosneft, Igor Sechin, Prime Minister (and former president) Dmitry Medvedev, Head of the Presidential Administration Sergei Ivanov, and Secretary of the Security Council Nikolai Patrushev. Of course, whereas Putin is the supreme decisionmaker, the influence of the others is fairly limited—both because they are subordinate to him and because their areas of responsibility and interest are narrower. Thus Sechin's role in foreign policy focuses largely on the energy sector, in particular oil cooperation with China and Arctic development. Although as chairman of Rosneft he was the prime mover behind the cooperation agreements concluded with ExxonMobil in 2012 and CNPC (China

National Petroleum Corporation) in 2013, there is little evidence of any larger impact on the bilateral relationships with the United States and China.[7]

*Ideational inspiration* is not normally associated with policymaking, given the latter's emphasis on bureaucratic institutions and processes. However, its effect on Russian foreign policy has been considerable; ideas matter, even in a society notorious for its cynicism. In the first instance, they inform a general philosophical outlook. Putin has acknowledged the influence of nationalist thinkers such as Konstantin Leontiev and Ivan Ilyin on his view of Russia and its place in world civilization.[8] Ideas also feed into strategic culture. The thinking of Yevgeny Primakov (foreign and later prime minister under Yeltsin) has underpinned much of Putin's pursuit of a multipolar order, the vision of Russia as an independent center of global power, and notions of geopolitical balancing. Primakov may no longer be closely involved in policy circles, but his ideas have actually become more influential in recent years.[9] Finally, ideas shape concrete policies. Igor Rogachev, who served a remarkable thirteen years as Russian ambassador in Beijing from 1992 to 2005, was central to the development of a Sino-Russian partnership. Although he died in 2012, his legacy endures.

*Implementation* is a much underestimated area of foreign policy. It lacks glamor, and those who carry out decisions—principally the Ministry of Foreign Affairs (MFA)—tend to be dismissed as actors of little consequence. In fact, while the MFA and organizations such as the Ministry of Defense (MOD) are rarely the instigators of policy initiatives, they retain substantial preventative powers. Their restraining influence is especially important in discussions about strategic disarmament and missile defense.[10] The highly technical nature of these subjects ensures a high level of dependence by the leadership on specialist expertise and advice. Likewise, the Ministry of Economic Development (MED) plays a leading role in foreign economic and trade policy. Without its close involvement, projects such as the Eurasian Union and Russia's World Trade Organization (WTO) accession would not have gotten off the ground. These examples underline the reality that without effective implementation there is no policy*making*.

The last function, *policy rationalization*, is difficult to pin down. It amounts to more than the public diplomacy performed by the MFA's Information Department, or the skewed news coverage of media outlets such as RT and Rossiya Segodnya[11] (which in tone and content are similar to Fox News in the United States). It also goes beyond the standard formulations found in public policy documents, such as the Foreign Policy Concept. Instead, it might be described as the "intellectualization" of foreign policy—the explanation and justification of Russian positions to an outside, predominantly Western, audience. Its chief exponents include English-speaking Duma deputies such as Alexei Pushkov and Vyacheslav Nikonov, respectively chairman and deputy chairman of the International Affairs Committee; and Sergei Markov, co-chairman of the National Strategic Council of Russia. Revealingly, all three worked as journalists or in think tanks, or both, before they entered formal political structures.

### The supreme decisionmaker

The current policy landscape is centered on individuals and their networks rather than formal institutions. This is demonstrated above all by President Putin. No single person in the six decades since the death of Stalin has been so intimately identified with power and policy in Russia.[12] Such is his domination that he has engendered his own "ism." Putinism has emerged as a hybrid of centralized political power, economic rent-seeking,[13] social materialism, conservative morality, and an assertive international posture. In this connection, the comparison that is sometimes made with Charles de Gaulle undersells the extent to which Putin has become synonymous with political Russia.[14] For all that de Gaulle towered above his contemporaries, he nevertheless had to operate under far greater democratic and institutional constraints.

Putin's personal stamp is most apparent in the way decisions are made. Although a strong culture of secrecy existed in Soviet and Tsarist times, this has been systematically reinforced over the past fifteen years following a period of relative openness under Gorbachev and Yeltsin. There are very few people involved in decisionmaking, and the content of their deliberations is almost hermetically sealed. Putin operates on the principle that "fewer is better"—at once more cohesive, more secure, and more effective. The mechanics of his response to the 2014 Ukrainian revolution are instructive here. There was no wide, much less public, consultation process. Neither Kyiv nor Western capitals, and almost no one in Moscow, had any inkling as to how he would respond to the overthrow of Viktor Yanukovych.[15] This meant that when he did decide to act—embarking on the annexation of Crimea, and initiating separatist actions in eastern Ukraine—Russia's "enemies" were confounded. The surprise was near-total, enabling the Kremlin to sustain the diplomatic as well as military initiative.

It follows from this closed style of decisionmaking that Putin exerts a crucial influence on individual policies. Unsurprisingly, this is most apparent in priorities to which he assigns the greatest importance: Ukraine, Eurasian integration, Russia's energy ties, and the handling of international crises, such as the Syrian conflict. It is Putin who determines the fortunes, on the Russian side, of key relationships with the United States, Europe, and China. The political rapprochement with Europe in 2000 (after Kosovo), the post-9/11 "strategic choice" in favor of Washington, and the steady expansion of ties with Beijing all owed a tremendous amount to his direct involvement. Equally, the deterioration of relations with the United States and, to a lesser extent, Europe during 2004–08 was fueled by his anger over Western participation in the color revolutions in Georgia and especially Ukraine, and aversion to American "unipolarity."[16] Putin's personal sense of *obida* (offense) at U.S. support for the public demonstrations against him in late 2011 and early 2012 was the single most important reason behind the hardening of Russian policy toward Washington.

The Putinization of Russian foreign policy has never been more evident than in relation to Ukraine. For the past decade Putin has involved himself directly and repeatedly in its affairs. In the run-up to the Ukrainian presidential elections of December 2004, he visited Kyiv on several occasions to support Yanukovych, but above all to oppose the Western-leaning Viktor Yushchenko.[17] Although Putin had previously worked with Yushchenko when the latter was Ukrainian prime minister,[18] he decided that a functional relationship between them was impossible. The subsequent Orange Revolution was therefore not only a setback for Russian foreign policy, but also a personal humiliation. Similar considerations were in play following the 2014 Maidan revolution. Russia's strategic interests suffered a major blow with the political demise of Yanukovych, but no less important was Putin's embarrassment at the unexpected turn of events. In the circumstances, he felt that he had no option—*as a man* as well as a national leader—but to strike back. His credibility and legitimacy, not to mention his self-esteem, were on the line.

There are parallels here with the 2008 Georgia war. In both cases Moscow had substantive policy concerns that contributed to the likelihood of conflict, such as the expansion of Western influence in the post-Soviet space, and its perceived impact on the regional balance of power. In both cases Putin was personally invested in outcomes to an exceptional degree. In 2008 his loathing for Georgian President Mikheil Saakashvili gave him added incentive to teach Tbilisi a lesson. In 2014 he risked becoming a diminished figure at home and abroad unless he reacted vigorously to the change of power in Kyiv. Most important of all, in Ukraine as in Georgia the victory of Russian arms became portrayed as Putin's personal triumph—not just over hapless regional (and domestic) adversaries, but also over a shocked West.[19]

Putin's individual contribution has been critical in shaping Russia's energy diplomacy. His long-time interest in the geopolitics of energy explains his determined opposition to the EU's Third Energy Package (see chapter 3) and other projects to reduce European dependence on Russian gas, such as alternative pipelines circumventing Russia. Likewise, Gazprom's charmed existence is due almost entirely to his personal patronage. He has resisted calls to break up the company, which has become synonymous with poor performance—both because Gazprom serves the rent-seeking interests of the elite and because Putin regards it as a vital instrument of geopolitical influence (see below). More concretely, Putin has occasionally intervened to finalize an energy deal. One instance was the thirty-year gas supply contract between Gazprom and CNPC during his May 2014 visit to Shanghai. The deadlock in price negotiations looked set to continue before a last-minute compromise was reached—an outcome that would have been impossible without his direct involvement.[20]

All that said, Putin's reach or level of interest in foreign policy should not be exaggerated. There are many areas where his role is superficial or nonexistent. Anecdotal accounts suggest, for example, that he has very little involvement in managing Russia's G-20 agenda, and the often highly technical issues associated with global rebalancing and a "new financial architecture."[21] On nuclear disarmament and WMD proliferation Putin adheres firmly to the principle of strategic parity with the United States, but leaves the details of how this is to be achieved to the specialists in the MFA and MOD. Similarly, he is committed to realizing the vision of a powerful Russia in the world, but is not directly engaged in issues of military reform and procurement.

Like any top manager Putin delegates everyday decisionmaking to trusted subordinates. In foreign energy cooperation, particularly with China and the United States, the key player is Igor Sechin; on Syria it is Foreign Minister Sergei Lavrov; in defense matters it is Defense Minister Sergei Shoigu; and on the G-20 agenda it is First Deputy Prime Minister Igor Shuvalov. Crucially, though, Putin has the final say on the big decisions that are ostensibly taken by others. He approved the agreement between Rosneft and ExxonMobil; the decision to go to war with Georgia (even though he was in Beijing watching the Olympics); and, most likely, the controversial call to abstain on UN Security Council Resolution (UNSCR) 1973 regarding the NATO no-fly zone over Libya.

This last decision has been the subject of controversy, with some claiming that then president Medvedev followed his own line against the wishes of (Prime Minister) Putin.[22] Such an account, however, runs against the grain of recent Russian policymaking. It is improbable that Medvedev would have made the critical decision to abstain without at least tacit endorsement from his nominal subordinate but actual boss. Putin may have had reservations about abstention, but would have taken other considerations into account, such as the utility of sustaining the improvement in Russia's relations with the

United States and Europe.[23] Of course, this calculus soon became redundant, leading later to the revisionist view that abstention had been a grievous blunder. The Kremlin PR machine moved quickly to absolve Putin of any responsibility, and to blame Medvedev instead[24]—an illustration of the classic get-out clause, "the good Tsar let down by his venal [or incompetent] subordinates."[25]

Such episodes underline that Putin's contribution to Russian foreign policy is not limited to matters of substance. Putin the symbol has become as important as Putin the decisionmaker, whether it is in running rings around a slow-footed Barack Obama over Syria, or in seizing the initiative in Crimea and eastern Ukraine. His public self-confidence and unapologetic demeanor have become metaphors for a buoyant Russia—a far cry from the weak, humiliated nation of the 1990s, led by a disoriented Yeltsin. Unsurprisingly, the attempt during 2004–08 to create a second personality in the form of President Medvedev was always going to be difficult to sustain. In the hyper-personalized world of Putin's Russia, there can only be one icon—which is why Medvedev has cut a sometimes forlorn and humiliated figure.[26]

### The personalization of policy

Putin stands at the apex of a tall and thin pyramid of personalized power. Institutions still matter, but much less so than during the Brezhnev era (1964–82), when the scourge of "departmentalism" (*vedomstvennost*) often paralyzed decisionmaking.[27] While the Putin system is scarcely a model of efficiency, its ability to get things done is considerably greater than that of its predecessors. This is particularly the case in foreign policy, where there are fewer interested parties than in domestic affairs, and which benefits from being an area of broad elite consensus. Compared with the often bitter disagreements over economic reform, it has been largely free of acrimony or serious controversy. Russia's destiny as a great power and unique civilizational identity are accepted as self-evident truths, while resentment of Western policies and actions is evident across the political spectrum. It helps too that the wider population shares these sentiments (see below).

In Putin's Russia individuals make institutions, not institutions the individual.[28] This is not only true of the president himself, but also of other senior figures. Sechin's influence comes not from being chairman of Rosneft, but from having been Putin's closest colleague for two decades, ever since he was chief of staff to the then deputy mayor in St. Petersburg in the early 1990s. The influence of Alexei Kudrin on Russia's approach to international financial institutions owed something to his incarnation as a long-serving (2000–11) and very successful finance minister. But more important still was his friendship with Putin going back to their St. Petersburg days, when Kudrin was the other deputy mayor. Tellingly, although he was sacked by Medvedev in September 2011, Kudrin's continuing close ties with Putin mean that he retains some influence on economic policy.

It also works the other way around. Whereas well-connected individuals can drive policy, those without such "gifts" are unable to achieve meaningful outcomes. The process of Russia's accession to the WTO was so protracted because, among other reasons, there was no supporter powerful enough to push it through the various political and technical hoops. It was only when Putin gave his full backing to membership in 2010–11 that serious progress began to be made.[29] It has been much the same story with Russia's relations with the non-Western world. The Westerncentric bias of the political elite has meant that a "geographically balanced" foreign policy has been a rhetorical conceit rather than genuine aspiration. The exception to the rule, the "strategic partnership" with China, has happened because Putin and Sechin (on the energy side) have been personally committed to it.

The primacy of personalities over institutions applies also in instances where individuals who are not personally close to Putin may have impressed him by their competence and, no less important, toughness. A case in point is Sergei Lavrov. Already Russia's longest-serving foreign minister since Andrei Gromyko, he clearly enjoys Putin's trust and confidence.[30] Unlike his predecessor, Igor Ivanov, who was very much a pure executor of decisions, he is more involved in developing policy, notably on Syria.[31] Although Putin claimed personal credit for the initiative in September 2013 to remove chemical weapons stockpiles, Lavrov's fingerprints were everywhere—most evident in the idea of trading progress on chemical disarmament for a de facto American guarantee of no military action against President Bashar al-Assad.

One of the features of policymaking under Putin is that influence may wax and wane as individuals gain and lose favor. When Medvedev was sitting in the Kremlin, he was nominally in charge of foreign policy—a function traditionally associated with the institution of the presidency. Despite this advantage, his influence declined steadily over the course of his presidential term. During 2008–10 he was an important player in the U.S.-Russia reset. He was able to gain some traction in Moscow for his initiative on a "new European security architecture." He was prominent over Libya, and launched the so-called "partnership of modernization" with the European Union.

By late 2010–early 2011, however, his influence and standing were on the slide. In part this was the result of unfavorable external circumstances—the Arab Spring, growing tensions with Washington, and the lack of Western interest in his proposals for Euro-Atlantic security. But his fading fortunes also had domestic causes. These included the competing political interests of key players such as Sechin and Sergei Ivanov,[32] his own unimpressive public persona, and Putin's determination not to countenance any other center of power, however nascent. This last consideration was decisive in ensuring that Medvedev's influence on foreign policy had been virtually nullified by the time Putin announced his impending return to the Kremlin in September 2011.

### Complex decisionmaking

In contrast to the concentration of power at the top, Russian society has become increasingly diverse. This, in turn, has meant that policymaking can be messy in areas where there are domestic interests in play, as in the case of WTO accession. One reason why Putin took so long to throw his weight behind the bid was his fear that opening up parts of the economy to foreign competition could undermine his support among key constituencies. The issue was not so much direct pressure from the public or from special interests, but his uncertainty as to whether WTO membership was worth the political price that might have to be paid in, say, single-industry cities and towns (*monogoroda*). This led to prevarication and policy fluctuations, and, in the final stages of WTO negotiations, intense bargaining to protect vulnerable sectors, such as the auto industry and agriculture (see chapter 3).

The complications arising from a more variegated society are present, too, at the level of elites. One should avoid speaking in overly schematic terms about the influence on foreign policy of the *chekisty* (security and intelligence figures), the military, or big business. Although members of particular groups share a professional background, they are ultimately individuals, motivated by personal self-interest more than by corporate solidarity or an abstract national interest. Sometimes they will work to a common objective, such as building up Russia's security and military establishment. But at other times the enemy or target may be one of their own.[33] An example here is Rosneft's determined campaign to undermine Gazprom's near-monopoly of gas exports, which has acquired an added edge from the personal tensions between Sechin and Gazprom chief Alexei Miller.

In this case, as in others, policy outcomes may be an untidy compromise between different parties and their agendas. Such divisions are replicated across the Putin system. The Soviet tradition of cumbersome administrative bargaining has been eroded by Putin's political dominance, but it is still influential. As the Australian scholar Stephen Fortescue has observed, throughout the Putin era there has been a constant tension between "consultation and sign-off" (*soglasovanie*) and "hands-on management" (*ruchnoe upravlenie*).[34] This is especially pronounced in domestic policy, where the stakes are higher and the issues more contentious, but it is also relevant to the management of foreign relations.

Crucially, though, such intra-elite tensions do not challenge core foreign policy assumptions; differences are personal and interests-based, not ideational. Nor do they contradict the central reality of Russian politics, which is that all big decisions go through Putin in some form or other.[35] One of the Obama administration's more unfortunate misperceptions during the reset was the belief that there were two distinct policy camps in Moscow: a progressive, Westernizing wing led by Medvedev and a reactionary, conservative establishment under Putin. Yet without Putin's say-so there would have been no positive Russian response to the reset.

## Political Culture

Political culture is an elusive phenomenon with many dimensions. It encompasses institutional habits, such as personalized decisionmaking. It may describe allegiance to particular principles, for example, centralized government. It is often associated with different types of regime; thus, authoritarian states and liberal democracies give rise to contrasting political cultures. And it is also used in a looser sense, referring to a set of instincts about human existence and the way of the world. Moreover, political culture is not a static phenomenon, but is susceptible to changing internal and external conditions.[36]

The elusiveness of political culture makes it difficult to judge its influence on foreign policy. However, this has hardly deterred people from trying. Democratic peace theory, for instance, is based on the premise that democracies are inherently more peaceful than non-democracies, and so do not wage wars against each other. Their political culture is said to encourage benign and positive aims: boosting economic growth and international trade, improving global governance, and promoting universal norms and values.

Authoritarian regimes, on the other hand, are allegedly inclined toward more aggressive foreign policies. Their preoccupation with maintaining tight political control at home translates, in the international arena, into an emphasis on military capabilities, vigorous power projection wherever possible, and asserting status. Such attitudes do not necessarily result in confrontation, since authoritarian regimes may be pragmatic (or fearful) enough to eschew the risks of overtly threatening actions. But their underlying political culture conditions their behavior nevertheless.

In the case of Russia, it is sometimes claimed that the winner-takes-all nature of domestic politics encourages a combative and paranoid mindset.

Just as Putin and leaders before him have had to struggle to hold on to power, so they believe that a "forceful" foreign policy is the only possible course in a dog-eat-dog world. In other words, their survivalist instincts at home set the tone for the conduct of foreign policy.[37]

### Authoritarian peace and insecurity

The evidence to support such propositions is mixed. The collapse of the USSR was remarkable for its relative absence of conflict,[38] while Putin's growing authoritarianism during his second presidential term (2004–08) did not engender an obviously militarist foreign policy. Georgia was the first time Russia had waged war on another sovereign state since the demise of the Soviet Union. (Indeed, the rarity of such action in the past may have caused Tbilisi to underestimate Moscow's resolve.) Over the past two decades Russia has been involved in far fewer conflicts than the United States, which has undertaken military action in Iraq, Afghanistan, Libya, Bosnia-Herzegovina, Kosovo, and Somalia. Although there are good reasons for this, not least the fact that the United States possesses vastly greater force projection capabilities than any other country, it would be absurd to claim that Moscow has behaved more aggressively than Washington during this period. And there are many European countries that have been more involved than Russia in wars beyond their borders.[39]

All that said, the consolidation of authoritarianism has seen a revival of Lenin's "besieged fortress" syndrome. Following the killing of 334 people at School Number One in Beslan in September 2004, Putin not only blamed international terrorism for the outrage, but also held the West responsible for its allegedly compliant attitude toward Chechen insurgents.[40] The bogey of a conspiring West arose again in the aftermath of Ukraine's Orange Revolution, following the popular demonstrations against Putin's return to the presidency during 2011–12,[41] and, most acutely, in response to the Maidan revolution and Western sanctions against Moscow.[42]

It has been suggested that the annexation of Crimea and Russia's subsequent actions in eastern Ukraine were motivated in large part by the authoritarian requirement for a "short, victorious war." By late 2013 economic growth had stalled, and there was the imminent prospect of a prolonged recession. This threatened the stability of the Putin system and pushed the Kremlin to tap into other sources of legitimacy, such as popular nationalism and anti-Westernism.[43] The toppling of Yanukovych offered a perfect occasion to distract public attention from the deteriorating situation at home.

This theory is, however, unconvincing. A direct correlation between authoritarian rule and an adversarial approach to international relations is difficult to prove, given other plausible explanations. The hardening of Russian foreign policy over the past decade can just as easily be portrayed as a logical, if ill-advised, reaction to perceived *external* threats: the loss of Ukraine as a strategic buffer and sphere of influence; Western "encroachment" into the post-Soviet neighborhood via EU and NATO enlargement; and U.S. missile defense plans. In the 1990s, President Yeltsin, a figure regarded by many in the West as the embodiment of Russian democracy, reacted no less allergically to NATO enlargement, missile defense, and Western military intervention over Kosovo. This opposition did not translate into armed responses, but largely because of Russian impotence, not acceptance.[44]

Conversely, Putin's first presidential term, during which he tightened his political grip, saw a marked improvement in relations with Europe and the United States.[45] He clearly believed then that he could insulate cooperation with the West from developments in Russian domestic politics. And even when relations with Washington began to sour in the lead-up to the U.S.-led invasion of Iraq, his reaction was more restrained than that of French President Jacques Chirac and German Chancellor Gerhard Schröder—both U.S. allies. Putin also responded calmly to Washington's unilateral withdrawal from the 1972 Anti-Ballistic Missile (ABM) Treaty, and to the impending accession of the Baltic states to NATO.

### "The mind of the chekist"

Much has been written about the *chekist* mindset and its influence on domestic politics and foreign policy under Putin. Its defining features are said to include militarism, secrecy, professional and moral likemindedness, consequentialism (the ends justify the means), and anti-Americanism.[46] Yet it is problematic to separate out a *chekist* mentality from Russian political culture writ large. For one thing, as noted earlier, representatives of the intelligence agencies do not constitute a monolithic group. Not only do they compete with one another for rents, privileges, and access to Putin, but they also display a range of attitudes and opinions.[47]

Another difficulty is that even if one were to recognize such a thing as "the mind of an intelligence officer" (or, relatedly, a military mindset), this is likely to have been formed not only by professional upbringing, but by deeper societal influences as well. When U.S. Senator John McCain looked into Putin's eyes and saw KGB,[48] the object of his contemplation was actually much more complex. Individuals are the product not just of their immediate circumstances, but also of their wider environment and accumulated life experience.

Fiona Hill and Clifford Gaddy suggest that Putin's political conservatism may have been reinforced by the fact that he "missed" *perestroika* because he was serving in the late 1980s as a counterintelligence officer in the Soviet consulate in Dresden, East Germany. Yet as they acknowledge, there is more to Putin's wary view of the world than missing out on Gorbachev's reforms or operating within the narrow confines of the KGB. His regret at the passing of the USSR arose out of a larger sense of Russia's physical and historical identity, an identity he felt had been betrayed by the shortcomings of the Soviet system, the incompetence of its rulers, and the machinations of the West.[49]

From this comes a deep hankering for order. It is not just the authoritarian in Putin that leads him to support the Assad regime, or to abhor the grassroots democracy movements of Kyiv's Maidan and the Arab Spring. It is a visceral fear of instability and what it may mean for the system he has constructed, and for Russia's position in the world. In this, he and other intelligence officers, past and present, are far from being alone. Such anxieties resonate among the population at large.[50]

In attempting to understand the influence of political culture on foreign policy, we should therefore eschew deterministic, normatively driven theories that regard authoritarianism (or an intelligence background) as inherently incompatible with a sensible approach to international relations. There are plenty of examples that prove otherwise, notably China in the decade after the 1997 Asian financial crisis, just as there are liberal democracies that have pursued unwise and aggressive policies. Instead, we should look beyond the narrow confines of the Putin system and its principal actors to examine long-term structural influences, such as geography and history.

### The importance of geography

Of the many drivers of Russian foreign policy, geography is the most self-evident. It is geography that has defined Russia as one of the world's leading powers since the mid-eighteenth century. Covering more than ten percent of the earth's land mass and stretching almost the length of Eurasia, Russia retains a near-global presence by virtue of size alone. This has fostered the belief that it has a direct stake in developments from Europe to Northeast Asia and the Pacific, and from the Arctic to the wider Middle East. And it has ensured a globalist perspective on international affairs in general.

Russia's vastness has also been critical in establishing and reinforcing its identity as an empire. "Empire" and "imperialism" are pejorative terms these days, so it is unsurprising that policymakers in Moscow should deny the existence of an imperial mentality. Nevertheless, they see Russia as possessing a special status and aura—no longer an empire in the traditional sense, but certainly more than an "ordinary" nation-state. This translates into a powerful feeling of strategic entitlement, one that demands equal consideration from even the strongest nation in the world, the United States.[51]

Along with physical size and extent comes a self-identification based on multiplicity, ubiquity, and exceptionalism. The Russian Federation comprises more than a hundred distinct nationalities, several of the world's major religions, and multiple civilizational traditions. Russia is not European or Asian, Christian or Muslim; it is *all* those things, a civilization unto itself. Successive rulers—in Tsarist, Soviet, and post-Soviet times—have exploited the transcending nature of Russian identity for concrete ends. Thus Putin holds up Russia as a European civilization when engaging with the EU; emphasizes its Eurasian identity and "Asian-ness" when talking about the shift of global power to the East; highlights Russia's large Muslim community (15 percent of the population) when looking to project influence in the Middle East and Central Asia; and has in the past portrayed Russia as America's key transatlantic partner.[52]

A multiplicity of identities reinforces the idea of Russia's "specialness." As the journalist Konstantin von Eggert once put it, "all peoples are unique, but Russians think they are more unique than the others."[53] This feeling of exceptionalism operates in both an offensive and defensive mode. On the one hand, it provides a quasi-moral basis for involvement in any regional or global issue, and for Russia to be a member of virtually every significant international body. On the other hand, it serves to resist the intrusion of subversive foreign ideas, such as Western democratic liberalism. Since Russia simultaneously partakes of many civilizations, it is not bound by any single one of them, but may pick and choose as it sees fit, thereby preserving its independence. When Putin speaks of pursuing a path of development that takes into account Russia's particular circumstances and traditions,[54] he is, in effect, using geography as an instrument of legitimation. The notion of *spetsifika*—literally meaning "specificity," but really implying a combination of "specialness" and exceptionalism—supplies the intellectual and moral justification for the regime to function according to its own rules.

At the same time, geography has complicated Russian foreign policymaking. The advantages of physical reach are counterbalanced by the disadvantages of overextension. The small size of Russia's population—143 million in 2013—relative to its huge territory has been a constant source of anxiety to Moscow since the conquest of Siberia in the early seventeenth century. As Russia morphed from Muscovy into the world's largest land empire, it acquired new vulnerabilities and anxieties as well as new opportunities. The conquered lands were sparsely populated, and difficult and costly to defend. During the Soviet period the Far East became one immense fortified camp, a European redoubt in an alien and hostile environment.[55]

This insecurity persists today as a result of several factors, including the depopulation of the Russian Far East (RFE),[56] Russia's demographic decline for much of the last two decades, and the degradation of defense capabilities over the same period. In short, geography has nourished a security outlook dominated by threat perceptions and geopolitical calculus.

There are two other elements of geography that have contributed to Russian political culture. One is the location of resources. As Russians are fond of pointing out, their country possesses the full Mendeleev (periodic) table of elements. This has not only shaped its economic development, but also encouraged a view of natural resources as critical to Russia's persona as a great power. Such attitudes have been accentuated in the post–cold war period. Russia's position as the world's leading producer and exporter of energy, precious metals, and other commodities has become the main (and sometimes only) reason why many countries wish to engage with it. And although there is a strong aversion to ending up as a "raw materials appendage" to the West and now China,[57] the availability of such riches remains critical to perceptions of national power.

Second, the uneven distribution of Russia's population, with barely 30 million people living east of the Urals, has ensured a thoroughly Western-centric outlook. This is apparent in every dimension of public life: political structures and processes, economic orientation, social and cultural norms, and national self-identification, It is testament to the enduring power of geography that even during the worst periods in relations with the West, Russians have preferred to live, study, work, and invest in Europe and the United States. This geography is the foundation of a Russian foreign policy that, for all the talk about a reorientation to the East, is still fixated on the West.

### The impact of history

History—and historical memory—plays a crucial and multidimensional role in Russian foreign policy thinking: as the source of atavistic fears and humiliation; as the basis for national pride and assertiveness; and as an instrument of legitimation.

*History and insecurity.* Russia has enjoyed few periods of sustained peace and stability, but the last century has been extraordinarily turbulent by any standards. During this time it has suffered two world wars, absorbing colossal human and material losses; seen two empires collapse; experienced unspeakable levels of domestic repression; and at virtually no stage enjoyed a comfortable relationship with its neighbors or the wider world. It would be surprising indeed if these historical circumstances had not resulted in an abiding sense of insecurity.

The most existential fear is that of losing sovereignty and territorial integrity. This is a natural reaction to having been subject to repeated invasion: the Mongol onslaught in the thirteenth century, followed by three centuries of occupation (the "Mongol yoke"), Napoleon's invasion in 1812, and Hitler's devastating offensive in June 1941 and the ravaging of vast tracts of the western Soviet Union. At other times Russia has been attacked and occupied by Poles, Swedes, Turks, and Persians.

But historical insecurities also assume psychological forms, and these are arguably more influential still. The breakup of the Soviet Union into fifteen independent republics was traumatic not because it heralded the further disintegration of Russia or threatened economic penury and social anarchy. Although there were justified fears on these counts, for Putin and his associates—and many ordinary Russians—the real disaster was the transformation of the world's second superpower into an impotent also-ran. Virtually overnight everything they had taken for granted had been turned on its head and invalidated.

The troubles of the 1990s underlined these feelings of disorientation and insecurity. They revealed deep divisions within the body politic, hugely dysfunctional governance, military weakness (brutally exposed in Chechnya), failing economic performance culminating in the 1998 financial crisis and default, and acute social demoralization. In foreign affairs the "new Russia" was reduced to the status of supplicant to the West—constantly scrabbling around for money, while being endlessly criticized and patronized. Meanwhile, NATO expanded into areas that Moscow had controlled for decades. This expansion did not pose a physical threat, but it drastically altered the dynamic of Russia's international relations. One-time allies and client-states deserted *en masse*, presenting it with an unpalatable choice: either integrate with the West on the latter's terms or face growing isolation and backwardness. Given the circumstances, the Russian elite and public could not help but feel profoundly anxious about the future.

The return of political stability and economic growth under Putin alleviated this mood, but did not dispel it. Putin's frequent references to the need for a strong Russia owe much to a strategic culture in which hard power is paramount (see chapter 2). But they also reflect a darker view of a world in which security is invariably fragile, and enemies and threats are never far away. In this, history plays a hugely important role, not just in influencing the overall context and mood of policymaking, but also in the formulation of individual policies. For example, the "strategic partnership" with China has gained considerable impetus from the Russian fear of ending up on the wrong side of the strategic triangle—as occurred in the early 1980s, when the

Soviet Union faced a hostile Reagan administration in the United States and an unfriendly Chinese leadership under Deng Xiaoping, as well as mounting economic problems.

Such insecurities are closely bound up with a national humiliation complex that has deep roots. Originating in the Mongol occupation, this has been a near-constant of Russian attitudes toward the outside world. In the seventeenth to nineteenth centuries it was apparent in a feeling of backwardness relative to the rest of Europe, and was a primary motivation behind Peter the Great's determination to open a "window to the West."[58] In the post–cold war period the national humiliation complex has become enshrined in the belief that the West set out to abase Russia by exploiting its (temporary) weakness. According to this view, the economic "shock therapy" prescriptions of the early 1990s were designed to undermine it from within, while NATO took advantage of the Soviet collapse to absorb the former Warsaw Pact countries.[59]

The ongoing crisis over Ukraine fits snugly within this narrative. The Kremlin's allegation that NATO aims to bring Ukraine into its fold is a self-serving falsehood. What is real, however, is that Moscow sees resolution of the crisis in zero-sum terms: triumph or humiliation. The West, and specifically the United States, cannot be allowed to get away with the removal of a key Kremlin ally—both because of the geopolitical implications for Russia and because it would represent a national humiliation of the first order.

This complex is roughly analogous to China's "century of humiliation" (1842–1949), which was characterized by successive regime failures, foreign invasion and occupation, and socioeconomic disintegration.[60] In China, the century of humiliation has become a parable about the costs of weakness and virtues of strength. Russia's modern Time of Troubles[61] in the 1990s was much shorter, lasting barely a decade, while the collapse of the Soviet Union came largely from within. Nevertheless, the motivational aspect is similar. When Putin reiterates Stalin's slogan that the "weak get beaten,"[62] he is tapping into the view of many that Russia cannot trust in the good intentions of others, but must concentrate on building up its own strength. This includes consolidating political authority, tightening state control over the "commanding heights of the economy," maintaining social order, and enhancing its military capabilities.

*History as triumph.* Given these insecurities, it may seem odd that Putin and others should be so keen to trumpet Russia's importance to the world. However, what comes across sometimes as over-confidence and triumphalism reflects a history that has boasted great victories and achievements, along with tragedy and disaster. Russia has lost many battles, but few wars. Moreover, it has succeeded in reversing most of its defeats. It was overrun by the Mongols, but later expanded its empire to the farthest reaches of Asia. It suffered humiliating setbacks against Napoleon, but occupied Paris and led the restoration of absolute monarchies throughout Europe. It was devastated by Hitler's invasion, but raised the Soviet flag over the Reichstag. This pattern of eventual victories has imbued successive generations of rulers with the belief that Russia generally finds itself on the right side of history, even if it must undergo huge torments in the process.[63]

It also underpins the apparent complacency about Russia's shortcomings. Sometimes, of course, the attitude is precisely that. But often it reflects faith that solutions will somehow be found and Russia will again emerge successfully from its troubles. Events in recent years have tended to reinforce this view. The diplomatic isolation Moscow experienced following the 2008 Georgia war soon gave way to the U.S.-Russia reset and rapprochement with Europe. The global financial crisis only briefly interrupted a pattern of consistent economic growth since the late 1990s. The opprobrium heaped on the Kremlin over its support for Assad turned into gratitude for Russia's role in initiating the removal of chemical weapons from Syria. And its vigorous response to the overthrow of Yanukovych is seen in Moscow as critical in preserving Russian influence in Ukraine. In this last instance much of the political class acts on the assumption that the West, sooner or later, will be forced to accept Putin's realities.

This "winning" mentality—or, more accurately, belief in eventual success—has another aspect relevant to Russian political culture. Confidence in its essential rightness has meant that the leadership is hypersensitive to any suggestion of inferiority. It is insulted by the claim that the West won, and Russia lost, the cold war,[64] and the lack of credit Moscow has received for achieving a relatively peaceful post-Soviet transition. It is especially disturbed by the implications of such messages. The West's appropriation of victory in the cold war is viewed as a plot to justify unfair treatment of Russia, one that takes the form not only of ill-warranted criticisms about its domestic politics, but also of attempts to marginalize it in the Euro-Atlantic space and meddle in its neighborhood.[65]

*History as legitimation.* In a country where history plays such a central role in public consciousness, it is to be expected that its rulers should attach primary importance to the cultivation of national narratives. This is exemplified by the debate over Stalin. To most foreigners (and some Russians) he was a monster who caused the extinction of tens of millions of his fellow citizens, enslaved Eastern Europe, and was largely responsible for the onset of the cold war. In Russia, however, his reputation is much more positive; the Chinese Communist Party's official evaluation of Chairman Mao as "70 percent good,

30 percent bad" might equally be applied to Stalin. Many Russians credit him with establishing the Soviet Union as a global power and developed industrial society. They hold him up as the great leader who crushed Nazi Germany and saved the Motherland. And they view him as the ideal of the strong ruler, harsh certainly, but the only possible kind for a country that would otherwise descend into chaos and be picked off by foreign powers.[66]

Stalin's intimate association with Russian national greatness means there is little political (or popular) will to arrive at a full reckoning of his crimes. To do so might be to admit that many of "his" achievements are tainted, above all the Soviet Union's victory in the Great Patriotic War. While there is an obvious distinction to be made between the Soviet people's heroism and the tyranny of Stalinism, in practice de-Stalinization has often been conflated with a liberal Western conspiracy to delegitimize Russian achievements. Accordingly, Moscow has condemned "attempts to rewrite history" and "revise the outcomes of World War II."[67] It has taken the view that to subject such events to critical scrutiny, let alone admit fault, could encourage others to take advantage of Russian "weakness," and undermine its own legitimacy in the process. It is telling that Putin has reacted to the worsening crisis in relations with the West by defending the 1939 Molotov-Ribbentrop Pact, and comparing it favorably to the appeasement of Hitler by Neville Chamberlain and Edouard Daladier at Munich a year earlier.[68] It is also revealing that the human rights organization Memorial, founded to remember and rehabilitate the victims of Stalin's purges, is threatened with imminent closure—ostensibly on technical grounds, but really because it challenges the Kremlin's narrative and is therefore seen as an agent of Western influence.

## Political Conditions

The evidence of the post-Soviet era suggests that the impact of domestic politics on Russian foreign policy is more apparent in the *manner* in which it is conducted than in its content or orientation. A country in uncertain transition is rarely consistent in the pursuit of objectives, whereas one that enjoys stability and prosperity has a more secure basis on which to develop and implement long-term plans. During the 1990s, political uncertainty, economic crisis, and a loss of national self-confidence resulted in a disorganized and incoherent Russian approach to external relations. The Yeltsin administration veered erratically between seeking integration with the West and pursuing ambitions of strategic balancing and a new multipolar order. Decision-making became almost entirely ad hoc and reactive.[69]

The nexus between domestic political conditions and foreign policy has also been a feature of the Putin years. For much of this period there has been a fair measure of stability and optimism, and the Kremlin has presented an assured, if sometimes overconfident, face to the world. But at times when it has felt under domestic pressure, its anxiety has translated into a febrile approach, particularly vis-à-vis the United States. As a result, far from proceeding in linear, deliberate fashion, Putin's foreign policy has witnessed several major fluctuations.

### Political consolidation

Putin's first presidential term (2000–04) was notable for the recentralization of political power and an impressive economic recovery. The existence of a "Putin consensus"[70] at home translated into the steadier management of foreign policy, centered on the mending of ties with the West post-Kosovo.

His second term (2004–08) saw a sustained downturn in relations with the United States, and strident reactions to developments in the post-Soviet space, in particular the Orange Revolution. On the home front, however, Putin benefited from the consolidation of his personal authority, and rapid economic growth supported by the boom in global energy and other commodity prices.[71] Thus empowered, he pursued an ever more assertive approach in foreign affairs. His (in)famous speech at the February 2007 Munich Security Conference was partly the result of mounting exasperation at Western policies, but also stemmed from the belief that he had little to lose by calling out Washington and its NATO allies.[72] A Russia growing at 6–7 percent per annum, with vast financial reserves and no public debt, could ride out Western retaliation— especially since the Bush administration was pressing ahead anyway with missile defense deployment and NATO enlargement.

Putin's confidence was boosted by elite and public approval of his approach. Differences were largely limited to matters of detail and degree. There was no divergence on core principles, such as the reassertion of Russia's claims as a great power and as the leading actor in the post-Soviet space, and there was plenty of admiration for the energy Putin brought to the task. During this time ideational consensus was supplemented by institutional discipline—a significant change from the Yeltsin era, when there was open discord between various parts of the foreign policy establishment.

### The end of certainty

The years of the Putin-Medvedev tandem (2008–12) witnessed the reemergence of uncertainty. The global financial crisis had the effect of demystifying the Putin system, throwing the spotlight on a stagnant polity, endemic corruption, the absence of rule of law, and growing economic inefficiencies. It challenged lazy assumptions about guaranteed prosperity and stability. Discomfited by the slump in growth from 8 percent in 2008 to –7.9 percent in 2009 (the worst of any G-20 country), the regime found itself under pressure to maintain the Putin "social contract"—rising incomes and higher living standards in return for the population's acquiescence.[73]

The economy soon recovered, but Moscow's earlier bullishness gave way to a more cautious and nuanced attitude, evident in the functioning of the tandem itself. The latter was essentially a political show designed to convey the impression of a more diverse and accountable leadership. Yet the fact that Putin invested serious effort in this elaborate pretense reflected an appreciation that his system could no longer simply coast along.[74]

In foreign policy too there was a shift away from complacency. Dissenting voices began to be heard about the costs of deteriorating relations with the United States and Europe, and about Russia's vulnerability in the international system.[75] The magnitude or impact of these criticisms should not be exaggerated; by and large the Putin foreign policy consensus held firm. But Moscow's receptiveness to Western initiatives, such as Obama's reset initiative and the EU's "partnership for modernization," pointed to greater self-awareness and a concern to mitigate the vulnerability it felt in the wake of the global financial crash.

### Political crisis and reaction

The nexus between domestic politics and foreign policy was never more evident than following the anti-Putin demonstrations of late 2011 and early 2012. Most immediately, the shock felt by the regime, and Putin personally, gave rise to a series of highly emotional responses. Putin accused the United States of directly interfering in Russia's internal affairs, including funding and organizing the opposition. This reaction went well beyond the scope and tenor of previous attacks against Western governments. It indicated a level of insecurity not seen since Putin first entered the Kremlin in January 2000. The much-cited analogy with the Orange Revolution is apposite—to a point. Putin viewed this as a cautionary tale about the dangers of allowing a grass-roots, or indeed any other, democratic movement to challenge the established order. However, whereas in 2004–05 he was able to quarantine Russia from events in Ukraine, in 2011–12 everything was so much closer, and the threat to his rule seemed far more serious.

Putin's anti-Americanism also contained substantial elements of calculation. It recognized that many of the pillars of legitimacy the Kremlin had taken for granted—dominant political control, elite consensus, economic growth, and broad public support (or compliance)—were crumbling, and that new sources of legitimacy would have to be found and old ones revived. In these circumstances the distinction between domestic and foreign policy evaporated. Attacking Washington was no longer part of managing the United States, but became an extension of domestic politics by other means. The risk of a new crisis in bilateral relations paled into insignificance compared with the imperative of preserving power at all costs. Accordingly, Putin's 2012 presidential campaign played up "foreign policy" to a greater degree than in any other election in Russia's history, fingering the United States as all-purpose bogeyman—arrogant superpower abroad and subversive influence inside Russia. In adopting anti-Americanism as a tool to claw back lost authority, Putin was acting in the tradition of previous rulers, such as Tsar Nicholas I, Lenin, and Stalin, who exploited the idea of a Russia besieged by enemies abroad and traitors within.

The merging of domestic and foreign policy was also apparent in the distancing of the Putin elite from Western-led norms, and the reversion to "traditional values." This was partly a reaction to the discrediting of Western institutions as a result of the global financial crisis, a process that had been under way for some time. But the anti-Putin protests accelerated the normative shift away from the West. No longer able to rely on a materialist "social contract," Putin looked to a national moral renaissance that might supply him with a new and deeper form of legitimacy.

### Asserting the new "normal"

During 2012–13 Putin recovered much of his previous swagger. The protests lost momentum, the liberal opposition became demoralized, and popular figures such as Alexei Navalny were persecuted and marginalized. The regime reasserted its dominance of political life, and expanded into new areas, such as social media.[76] The clear and present danger that had appeared to threaten its survival receded. In this calmer atmosphere, the connection between domestic politics and foreign policy became looser for a brief time. The Kremlin felt better able to compartmentalize different baskets of issues; it could consolidate its grip on power and ideological discourse at home, while engaging with the outside world on its own terms.

But such "normality" is by its very nature fragile. Recent events in Ukraine have exposed the artificiality of separating the foreign from the domestic. As noted earlier, the Kremlin's forceful response was not motivated by a conscious desire to divert attention from its defective management of the economy, since it would scarcely have annexed Crimea had Yanukovych managed to cling on to power. However, Putin recognized that a compliant approach toward regime change in Kyiv could have critical consequences for his own popularity and credibility. He felt he needed to reaffirm that he was strong, that Russia was very much a great power, and that the West could not take liberties at its (and his) expense. The lure of domestic approbation, centered on the image of a besieged yet indomitable Russia, proved irresistible, and easily trumped concerns about the consequences for relations with the West.

This very nexus precludes an early softening of Kremlin policy. For as long as the Russian public attributes the problems of a plummeting ruble, stagnating incomes, and rising inflation to the actions of Western governments rather than the shortcomings of its own, Putin will pursue an uncompromising course. In this he acts on the presumption that Russians are well used to enduring great hardship and making huge sacrifices, but will never forgive weakness in those who rule them.[77]

## Economic Factors

The issue of regime confidence, and its relationship to foreign policy, is intimately tied to the condition of the Russian economy. Economic factors are at once sources of power, vulnerability, and engagement, and in recent years their influence on foreign policy has increased markedly.

### The state of the economy

The most obvious impact is in supplying the wherewithal to pursue national interests abroad. During the 1990s successive crises destroyed Russia's standing as a serious international actor. In the following decade, by contrast, rapid growth offered a launch-pad for an active foreign policy. The effect was not only material but also psychological. Whereas under Yeltsin Russia's misfortunes had fostered a mood of demoralization, under Putin a flourishing economy became emblematic of a power on the way up.

Throughout the Putin era, there has been a clear correlation between the state of the economy and the handling of foreign policy. Putin's first presidential term was a period of significant reforms and impressive growth. However, it was not yet clear whether this success was sustainable or whether it reflected a bounce-back following the 1998 financial crash and the fourfold devaluation of the ruble. Global oil prices were rising, but still at a modest rate. Cautious optimism tempered by uncertainty about Russia's longer-term prospects was conducive to a judicious foreign policy, largely free of excess.

By Putin's second term, these doubts had more or less disappeared. The Kremlin believed that the economy would continue to grow rapidly and for the foreseeable future. Oil prices quadrupled between January 2004 and July

2008;[78] Russia paid off its last remaining foreign debt in 2006; and global energy demand soared as a result of the booming Asian economies. Moscow saw no reason to listen to Western homilies about human rights and democracy when European and American companies were queuing up to access Russia's resources. For the Kremlin it was a good time to assert Russia's independence without worrying too much about possible downsides.

The global financial crisis dampened this hubris. The very factors—high global energy and commodity prices—that had underpinned regime confidence now became sources of vulnerability. After the price of Urals crude fell from US$129 to US$38 per barrel during 2008–09, the government was forced to spend a third of its gold and foreign currency reserves to keep the economy afloat,[79] and to turn to the Chinese for urgent credit to bail out Rosneft and Transneft.[80] The crisis demonstrated that Russia, far from being independent, relied heavily on the West—a U.S.-led international financial system and trade with the European Union. By exposing the myth of Russian economic exceptionalism, it ensured that Moscow would be amenable to improving relations.

But the crisis also conveyed other messages. First, Western economic leadership and moral authority had been seriously weakened. Second, although Russia had suffered during 2009, its subsequent recovery was notably faster than that of the leading Western economies—a point Putin never tired of reiterating. The eurozone countries, in particular, struggled to emerge from recession. Third, to minimize the fallout from future problems in the global economy, Russia would need to diversify its commercial ties beyond the West, and especially to the Asia-Pacific region.[81]

The diverse and contradictory influence of economic circumstances on foreign policy is evident today. With the onset of recession, Moscow would like to maintain partnerships with Western companies, and to quarantine these as much as possible from political disagreements. It understands too that for some years yet the United States will dominate the global economy, and the EU will remain Russia's principal source of foreign trade. But it is acutely aware that close dependence on the West exposes Russia to forces beyond its control, and makes it vulnerable to pressure from Western governments. The latter's sanctions in the wake of the Crimean annexation have aggravated these concerns.

Russia's economic fragility has increased the pressure to give substance to its "turn to the East" (chapter 5). This is not about choosing a mythical "China model" in preference to Western-style capitalism, but about spreading the economic and geopolitical risk. The Kremlin recognizes China's growing footprint in the global economy and the importance of expanding bilateral economic ties. Yet it is no less averse to relying on Beijing than it is to dependency on Brussels, Berlin, or Washington.

Ultimately the big lesson of recent years is that domestic economic performance is integral to Russia's capacity to sustain an independent foreign policy, and to the long-term stability of the Putin system. The Kremlin's strategic task is to translate this self-evident reality into positive policy outcomes. For the time being, though, its attention is focused almost entirely on the political exigencies of the conflict in Ukraine and the crisis in relations with the West. In this fraught context it has resorted to the usual survivalist expedient of blaming Russia's economic difficulties on malign outside forces.[82]

## Economics as power projection

Much has been written about the "energy weapon"—the exploitation of energy exports and pipelines for geopolitical ends. Until the 2014 Ukraine crisis, this was the most high-profile issue in Russia-EU relations, and it has played a vital role in policy toward the post-Soviet space (see chapter 4). But the regional geopolitics of energy is only part of the story. More significant still is the comfort that the Putin regime derives from Russia's pivotal position as a *global* energy producer and exporter. Energy and other strategic resources, such as gold, platinum, and aluminum, are seen as the twenty-first-century equivalent of the Soviet Union's nuclear arsenal—the guarantor, along with military might, of Russia's international influence and status.[83] This helps explain why, despite frequent talk of diversification, the economy has become increasingly reliant on natural resources. (The contribution of energy exports to the federal budget has grown from under 10 percent at the beginning of the Putin era to about half in 2013.)[84] The Kremlin is more concerned to play to Russia's comparative advantages than to pursue what it sees as the somewhat abstract aim of a "balanced" economy.[85]

The use of economic tools to project power is not limited to energy. In the post-Soviet neighborhood (including the Baltic states) and central and eastern Europe, Russian investments in banking, finance, manufacturing, and transport have grown. In many instances, the motivations are principally commercial. But it would be naïve to disregard the geopolitical dividend. While Russian companies are not mere instruments of the Kremlin, their participation in these often fragile economies can and does serve wider purposes.

In several of the ex-Soviet republics Russia's position as a leading source of trade and investment translates into a political influence similar to that enjoyed by the United States in Latin America from the 1950s to the 1970s. And even in countries where Russia is just another outside player, substantial economic participation ensures that its noneconomic interests are taken into greater account. It is no coincidence that Cyprus is Russia's most enthusiastic supporter within the EU, or that Hungary and the Czech Republic have been relatively sympathetic toward Moscow in recent years. The Kremlin recognizes that cultivating the corporate sector *in any country* maximizes its chances of influencing politicians. In Germany, for example, Angela Merkel's coalition government abhors many aspects of Russian domestic and foreign policy, yet for a long time was constrained by a powerful industry lobby broadly sympathetic toward Putin. The same is true in France and, to a lesser extent, the United Kingdom. During the Ukraine crisis French manufacturers and British energy and financial firms worked hard to counter or at least soften Western sanctions against Moscow.[86] Conversely, the modest level of business ties with the United States is a major reason why Russian interests have so little traction with the American political establishment.

### The personalization of foreign economic policy

Russia's foreign economic policy bears the mark of competing domestic interests and priorities. Indeed, in no other area of external relations is the distinction between private and public interest so blurred. Putin's energy diplomacy, in particular, serves the vested interests of the ruling elite. The case of Gazprom illustrates this well. It has become obvious that the company is in desperate need of reform. Its business model is obsolete; its export monopoly has weakened Russia's negotiating positions with foreign customers; and it operates in a virtual universe of permanently high prices and no shale revolution.[87] The sensible response to these problems would be to restructure the company and allow other firms, such as Novatek and Rosneft, to compete with it in exporting gas. Yet Putin has been averse to meaningful reform, in part because of Gazprom's importance as a source of rents to the elite.[88] He has vigorously defended it in the face of the EU's Third Energy Package and the European Commission's anti-trust suit (see chapter 3). Economic efficiency may be desirable, but keeping the elite happy is critical to the survival of the Putin system.[89]

Paradoxically, the best chance of Gazprom reform comes from competing interests within the ruling circle. One of Putin's closest confidants, Gennady Timchenko, is the leading shareholder in Novatek, while Igor Sechin is the driving force behind Rosneft's campaign to expand into the gas sector. Their individual priorities will be much more influential than any Western actions or a theoretical "Russian national interest" in determining Moscow's energy politics.

## Foreign policy and the modernization agenda

Russia's modernization agenda has been something of a weather vane for its relations with the West. It has featured prominently whenever these have been more or less positive, and disappeared during times of strain. In Putin's first presidential term, major reforms in tax, land ownership, and conditions for small and medium-size enterprises coincided with efforts to reach out to the West, initially to Europe and then to the United States.[90] During the years of the tandem, an upturn in cooperation with the West went hand in hand with a renewed, if largely rhetorical, emphasis on modernization. By contrast, Putin's second presidential term saw him talk up Russia as a global energy power, while tensions escalated with Washington and Brussels. And after his return to the Kremlin in March 2012, the demise of the modernization agenda accompanied a sharp downturn in relations with Washington.

Historically the reform agenda in post-Soviet Russia has been framed in terms of matching up to Western norms and standards. These might be interpreted in ways that were peculiarly Russian, as in the notion of "sovereign democracy" promoted by Kremlin ideologue Vladislav Surkov from 2006.[91] Nevertheless, the basic message remained: the West represented the benchmark. Recognizing this did not indicate pro-Western feeling so much as an appreciation that Russia had to emulate the West in key aspects if it was to "catch up and surpass" it.[92] Modernization was the ticket to international competitiveness; the choice was to "modernize or be marginalized."[93]

However, since late 2011 when Putin signaled his intention to stand for a third presidential term, the notion of modernization has been substantially redefined—that is, when it has been mentioned at all. The Kremlin sees "modernization" as, at best, a resource to support the political status quo. This is not to say that it has no interest in addressing corruption, the lack of rule of law, and poor governance. But these efforts are relevant only insofar as they strengthen existing power relations and the stability of the Putin system. In foreign policy this approach translates into a desire to import Western technology on a purely business basis, without any political conditionalities.

Moscow has come to view "Western-style" modernization as both subversive and an infringement on Russian sovereignty. It blamed Washington for the Rose and Orange Revolutions in 2003–04, and its determination to avoid a repeat scenario in Russia in 2011–12 saw it clamp down not just on the anti-Putin opposition, but also on many of the norms and values that, for the West, are intrinsic to true modernization. The 2014 Ukraine crisis confirmed this trend. Meanwhile, economic modernization has been caught in the political crossfire. A more open and competitive economy would threaten the rent-seeking interests of the elite, and it is a similar story with combating the institutionalized corruption that is at the heart of the Putin system.

Faced with these tensions, Putin has responded in ways that make little distinction between domestic and foreign policy. In prioritizing "stability" over reform, he reminds his audiences of the impact of Western policy prescriptions during the Yeltsin years, and of the continuing problems of eurozone countries. He expounds on Russia's traditions and the need to preserve the country's independence. He questions the viability of Western liberal capitalism in light of the global financial crisis and the rise of China. Above all, he emphasizes it is the Kremlin, and no one else, that will decide what Russia needs and under what terms.

## Social Forces

Although Putin has moved politics in a steadily more authoritarian direction, Russian society has become more diverse and demanding. The clichéd portrayal of an anaesthetized people is out of date, and its long-term support for the regime cannot be guaranteed. The changed social dynamics are reflected less in direct action such as the protests of 2011–12 than in a more generalized discontent about the government's failure to combat corruption and provide decent public services.[94]

So far, however, this discontent has been limited to domestic affairs. The Russian population has shown little interest in foreign policy, and has supported the Kremlin in any case. It enthusiastically approved the annexation of Crimea, and has been highly receptive to Putin's account of developments in eastern Ukraine and relations with the West. More generally it buys into the official narrative of a wronged Russia. A 2012 Pew Global Attitudes survey found that 73 percent of respondents believed that Russia deserved more respect from "other countries," in other words the West.[95] Subsequent Western sanctions have only strengthened such sentiments.

This synergy means that social forces have had relatively little impact on foreign policymaking. Such influence as exists is concentrated in three main areas: nationalism, religion, and public mores. These are not game-changers—at least not yet—but buttress an already strong institutional and philosophical conservatism within the Putin elite.

### Nationalism

Nationalism in Russia comes in various guises. There is the official nationalism that stresses Russia's great power identity and indigenous political and social traditions. There is an ethnic nationalism, which revolves around the idea of "Russia for the Russians"—*Russkie* (ethnic Russians) instead of *Rossiyane* (citizens of the Russian Federation). And then there is an ultra-nationalism that is virulently xenophobic, and that expresses itself in violence against ethnic, religious, and sexual minorities.

By far the most important of these variants is *official nationalism*. During the post–cold war period, many regimes in central and eastern Europe have sought alternative sources of legitimacy to fill the ideological void left by the demise of communism. Nationalism, with its roots in a country's geography and history, and simplistic messages, is a ready candidate. That said, in the first decade of the Putin era it was understated, with none of the extremism that infected the regime of Slobodan Milošević in Serbia during the 1980s.

But since late 2011 the climate has changed. Putin's resentment over Western criticisms of his return to the presidency, and his desire to refresh his popular legitimacy, have led him down the nationalist route. Thus in response to the protests of 2011–12, Putin promoted a retro vision of Russian national values, in which he assumed the position of defender of the faith against the corrupting influence of foreign ideas. He fed on popular anti-Western sentiment (including among some of the protestors), and accused the liberal opposition of colluding with outside forces to betray Russia.[96]

Official nationalism has acquired a more aggressive dimension that goes beyond the usual reiteration of Russia's "rights" in the international system. This raises the specter of territorial revisions on the basis of concepts such as Novorossiya ("New Russia"),[97] and arrogates to Moscow the right to intervene forcibly on behalf of expatriate Russians, especially those living in the post-Soviet neighborhood. The ongoing Ukraine crisis has highlighted this new strain.

At the same time, for Putin nationalism is a resource to be used selectively. There is an implicit understanding that it can be difficult to manage and is potentially destabilizing. He has been especially anxious to ensure that nationalism, of one kind or another, is not allowed to derail key priorities—political control, social order, and geopolitical influence. The government has from time to time tolerated ultra-nationalist violence, particularly when perpetrated against "people of Caucasian nationality" (*lyudi kavkazkoi natsionalnosti*)—Chechens, Ingush, Dagestanis, and others. But it has also ensured that occasional pogroms are not allowed to coalesce into a larger, more coordinated movement.

The Kremlin's contradictory attitude toward popular nationalism is illustrated by a couple of examples. In 2003 it created a nationalist party, Rodina ("Motherland"), to tap into nationalist constituencies at the Duma (parliamentary) elections. The ruse succeeded almost too well, with the party coming from nowhere to gain nearly 10 percent of the popular vote. By 2007, however, it had disbanded and its charismatic leader, Dmitry Rogozin, was packed off to Brussels as ambassador to NATO, where he could annoy Western governments instead of worrying the Kremlin.

The rise and fall of the Nashi youth movement is similarly instructive. It was originally set up to counter the contagious influence of grassroots democracy following the Orange Revolution in Ukraine. There were some parallels with Komsomol, the youth arm of the Communist Party of the Soviet Union (CPSU), in that it was intended to inculcate the values of the ruling system into young people, and to encourage their activism in support of it. Unlike Komsomol, however, Nashi's value was short-lived. Although it was deployed to harass foreign embassies,[98] influential figures in Putin's circle became unimpressed by its utility and increasingly concerned by its lack of discipline. Nashi's fate was sealed when the unsympathetic Vyacheslav Volodin replaced its principal advocate, Vladislav Surkov, as deputy chief of staff of the Kremlin administration in December 2011.[99] The organization was effectively disbanded in 2012, and the government concentrated its efforts instead on a mass campaign for "patriotic education" in schools.

Putin's top-down approach has ensured that unsanctioned forms of nationalism have had little impact on foreign policy. Thus, while he pays lip service to the problem of illegal migration, he recognizes that enforcing tight controls on the more than ten million workers from ex-Soviet republics would exacerbate Russia's growing labor shortage. It would also weaken Moscow's leverage across the post-Soviet space; the free movement of goods and labor is critical to the viability of the Eurasian Economic Union and to Putin's ambitious plans for Eurasian integration. Although a recent crackdown (late 2014) suggests a new responsiveness, the real deterrent to illegal migration is likely to be the recession in Russia, which makes it a much less attractive destination for migrant workers.[100]

The determination to exploit and mobilize nationalist sentiments, rather than be driven by them, is evident elsewhere. Until February 2014 Putin ignored public pressure to effect the reunification of Crimea with Russia, aware that this would negate efforts to build a symbiotic relationship with Kyiv. Once Yanukovych was overthrown, however, he shifted to a different calculus. Crimea was absorbed into the Russian Federation with breathtaking speed, while the Kremlin actively encouraged Russian ultra-nationalist paramilitary elements to destabilize eastern Ukraine.

Moscow's willingness to turn the nationalist tap on and off is demonstrated by its approach to the United States. The strongly anti-American tenor of official pronouncements during the 2012 presidential campaign gave way in the following year to a milder approach—still critical, but couched in more moderate language. However, following events in Ukraine, the United States resumed its position as public enemy number one, a status that seems likely to last for some time.

Such manipulation can backfire. There is a danger that popular nationalism, once loosed, may be difficult to control. But in some areas the Kremlin's management of nationalism has worked out quite well. Sino-Russian partnership has benefited from determined efforts to alleviate anti-Chinese sentiment among the Russian population,[101] and hose down the once contentious issue of Chinese "illegal migration" in the Russian Far East. Putin has also ensured that Islamophobia is a nonfactor in Russia's interaction with Muslim countries. Importantly, he has not surrendered to fears that Russia is losing its Slavic and Orthodox identity as a result of the higher birth-rates in predominantly Muslim areas of the Russian Federation (such as the North Caucasus and Tatarstan).

### Religion

Although Putin and other senior figures attend church services and are often seen in the company of religious leaders, religion itself has little influence over Kremlin decisionmaking, and even less in foreign affairs. There are occasional exceptions; the Kremlin has always respected the Orthodox Church's opposition to a papal visit. But the church is an instrument rather than a driver of policy. For Putin its chief value is as a legitimating symbol, highlighting Russia's (and his own) virtues in contrast to a spiritually and morally bankrupt West.

Orthodox Patriarch Kirill is especially useful to this purpose. He supplements Kremlin efforts to tap into a constituency that is politically and socially conservative, while emphasizing the distinctiveness of Russia's identity and values to an international audience. Kirill has also played a leading role in promoting closer ties with Ukraine and Georgia, an important consideration in countering pro-European tendencies in those countries. (The Sunni grand mufti in Kazan performs a roughly analogous function, boosting Russia's Islamic bona fides, particularly in Central Asia.)

The current relationship between church and state bears some similarities to the Tsarist era, notably the reign of Nicholas I (1825–55) when Orthodoxy (*pravoslavie*) was one of the three pillars along with autocracy (*samoderzhavie*) and nationhood (*narodnost*). However, it also resembles the very unequal interaction of Soviet times. The church's situation is far more secure and prosperous today, but its impact on policy is much less than under Tsarism. It serves at the pleasure of the Kremlin, in return for which it is handsomely rewarded.

Suggestions, therefore, that it acts as a malign influence on Russia's relations with the West are wide of the mark. The well-documented problems here have much more secular and concrete causes. The church is not responsible for the "turn to the East" or Putin's Eurasian Union. On the contrary, Kirill's ecumenical diplomacy has meant that relations with the Roman Catholic Church are better than they have been for decades.[102] While the Orthodox Church is scarcely a progressive force in Russian society,[103] its brand of conservatism has had little discernible influence on public attitudes toward Putin or the outside world. Opinion surveys routinely confirm that it is the most trusted institution in the country, but also that most people believe it should stay out of politics.[104]

*Public mores*

The influence of public mores on foreign policy is very limited. Although a strong social conservatism has occasionally complicated Russia's relations with the West, its effect on specific policies has been peripheral and fleeting. Such conservatism was not responsible, for example, for the disproportionate punishment meted out to the members of the Pussy Riot punk band for their performance protest at Christ the Savior cathedral in February 2012. The Kremlin claimed to be responding to public outrage. But in reality it exploited the incident to justify a more general clampdown on public dissent, and to discredit the anti-Putin opposition across the board. In rejecting U.S. and European criticisms of the verdict, Putin framed the argument as the West impinging on Russia's sovereignty, disrespecting its values, and corrupting its people. In other words, morality, like nationalism and religion, is a policy tool, to be used and managed as the regime sees fit.

Likewise, homophobic attitudes in Russian society have not forced the government to introduce anti-gay legislation; they have just made it easier to carry out repressive measures against its political opponents. The behavior of law enforcement agencies is frequently in breach of Russia's obligations as a member of the Council of Europe, and is criticized by European politicians, NGOs, and media. But homosexual rights as such are a marginal preoccupation for the Kremlin and, dare one say it, for Western governments as well— except on high-profile occasions such as the Sochi Winter Olympics.

## The Nature of the Domestic–Foreign Policy Nexus

Four main sources of domestic influence have played a decisive role in Putin's foreign policy: individual actors and their personal predilections; political culture shaped by long-term structural factors, such as geography and history; concrete political and economic interests; and circumstances and events.

Individuals are key to decisionmaking in all regimes, from the authoritarian to the democratic. But there are few countries where they are more important than in present-day Russia. While Putin is far from being master of all he surveys, his personal influence is felt at every level of domestic and foreign policy. Sometimes this takes the form of direct involvement in particular issues. At other times it is more indirect or muted. But either way, Putin has reinforced the template whereby individuals, not institutions or big ideas, are paramount. Moreover, this personalized model is not limited to him alone but is replicated at all levels of power.

At the same time, individuals are not self-standing entities but products of their environment and upbringing. They introduce to policymaking all kinds of baggage—memories, preconceptions, biases, instincts—that together form what might loosely be described as a political culture. The impact of this culture, however, cannot be reduced to oversimplifications about the alleged predispositional influence of an authoritarian or liberal mindset. The experience of the Putin period suggests that there is no automatic link between domestic authoritarianism and an adversarial foreign policy. Longer-term geographical and historical influences are far more relevant—Russia's physical immensity, the Westerncentrism of its political elite, the multiplicity of identities, and an abiding sense of insecurity.

But even these influences are by no means absolute, fixing once and for all the character of Moscow's engagement with international society. While Putin is influenced by Russia's physical and historical context, he also exploits this in the service of less lofty aims, such as holding on to power and defending the interests of the elite. Having recourse to history is in some ways the modern-day equivalent of the medieval *Dieu le veult* ("God wills it")[105]—enlisting God on one's side. Concepts such as Russia's "permanent national interests" are more useful to the Kremlin as legitimating devices than as the intellectual foundation for decisionmaking.

Contrary to accepted wisdom, different conceptions of historical destiny and national identity may arise under the influence of changing circumstances.[106] Indeed, this has happened several times in Russia's past, fundamentally altering the principles and practice of its foreign policy. Under Peter the Great and Catherine the Great, Russia transformed itself from a quasi-oriental and introspective backwater into a mainstream European power. Two centuries later Stalin presided over its rise as a global power. And in the 1980s Gorbachev challenged the notion that Russia can only function within an adversarial paradigm.

If there is any permanence in Russian foreign policy, it lies in the continuing primacy of tangible political and economic interests. Without these, ideas are mere abstractions. It is Putin's determination to consolidate his authority that gives real purpose to the notion of Russia as an independent center of power, one that brooks no "interference" from subversive outside forces. Thus opposing Western moral interventionism in the Middle East is motivated principally by the fear of democratic contagion. And the Kremlin's defense of Gazprom makes little sense until one recalls that the company serves as a cash-cow for a rent-seeking class on whose loyalty the Putin system depends.

The most variable domestic drivers of Russian foreign policy are events. The influence of such uncontrollables is extremely powerful, yet difficult to grasp. They disrupt seemingly linear trends, and rarely lead to clear-cut outcomes. They ensure that foreign policy is not only the continuation of domestic politics by other means (as suggested at the beginning of this chapter), but also a never-ending exercise in responding to unpredictable developments—the new world disorder. The economic slump of 2009 discredited the narrative of Russia's seamless resurgence as a global power and pushed the regime to adopt a more calibrated, less hubristic approach to foreign relations. Conversely, the anti-Putin protests of 2011–12 radicalized the context of Russia-U.S. interaction. The Kremlin's shock at the turn of events led it to ramp up anti-Americanism to levels not seen since the Georgia war—supplementing excoriating rhetoric with a series of measures targeted specifically at Washington.[107]

The interconnectedness of actors, culture, interests, and events suggests that the emergence of a new type of foreign policy in Russia will be highly problematic. As the Ukraine crisis has shown, the stars are not aligned in favor of change. The conservative and survivalist persona of Putin himself; a political culture dominated by historical insecurities and mythologies; the vested interests of the elite; and a reactionary reflex in the face of events—all point to the reaffirmation of traditional principles of power and policy. If there is to be change, it is unlikely to come from internal factors alone. The external context will be crucial, and it is to this we now turn.

# Two Worlds

> Where there is no common Power, there is no Law: where no Law,
> no Injustice. Force, and Fraud, are in warre the two Cardinall vertues.
>
> THOMAS HOBBES, 1651

Few countries have a greater need than Russia to engage effectively with international society. It has the largest number of direct neighbors, including the world's fastest growing power in China. It is the leading global supplier of energy and natural resources, which remain key to its stability and prosperity. And its self-identification as a great power is predicated on the capacity to influence others and its external environment. At the same time, few countries possess such a tradition of introspection and suspicion toward foreigners. Lenin may have popularized the expression "besieged fortress," but this phrase reflects much more atavistic instincts. When Peter the Great broke open Russia's "window to the West," he was overriding several centuries of isolationism and obscurantism.[1]

The tension between the necessary and the instinctive continues to influence Russian attitudes in the early twenty-first century. The Kremlin speaks of Russia needing to adapt to a world in transition, one that is increasingly globalized and interdependent.[2] However, its instinctive response to the pressures Russia faces in a postmodern century is to fall back on what it knows—conservative political and social values at home and classical interpretations of great power diplomacy abroad.

The issue for Moscow is not whether to engage with the outside world, but how. The previous chapter discussed the various elements—actors, political culture, interests, and circumstances—that have favored an essentially defensive mindset. Yet Putin's choice is much more than just an extension of domestic imperatives and priorities. It is also conditioned by his perceptions of contemporary international politics, and assessment of Russia's prospects as a regional and global actor. As with the domestic context, long-term structural influences coexist here with the erratic impact of external events and "strategic shocks."

Over the past decade, Putin has attempted to reconcile a traditional worldview (*mirovozzrenie*) with an interests-based approach to external relations. To this purpose, he has pursued the vision of a "global multipolar order," articulated by Yevgeny Primakov in the second half of the 1990s. As noted in the Prologue, this is the world as Moscow would like it to be. There are many unknowns and risks, but also strategic opportunities. It is a world in which Russia may prosper—provided, of course, that it adheres to the principles and interests that have guided its foreign policy during periods of success. For the Putin elite, the uncertainties of the international environment provide added arguments for the consolidation of power and authority. The choice, in foreign as well as domestic policy, is not "adapt or stagnate," but "preserve and stabilize."

It is one thing, however, for the Kremlin to attempt to mold the world according to its preconceptions, quite another to respond effectively to realities that contradict these on an almost daily basis. The real world is characterized by radical and often unpredictable shifts, and by fluidity rather than structure (let alone "order"). As such it presents an altogether different set of challenges from those imagined by the regime. Its principal message is that only those states that embrace change will prosper. For Russia, this means moving on from a historical sense of entitlement to redefining itself as an international actor of stature on the basis of performance.

## The World According to Moscow

It should be stated at the outset that there is no single Russian worldview. In a diverse, highly educated, and argumentative society, there are multiple views of the world, just as there are different understandings of the "national interest." Given that the subject is Putin's foreign policy, the focus here is on the assumptions, perceptions, and ambitions of the ruling elite. Although this elite is by no means monolithic, as already noted, there are nevertheless a number of commonalities and continuities that, together, constitute an identifiable worldview.

It is helpful to break this down into three parts. The first centers on strategic culture. Many years ago, the international relations theorist Jack Snyder defined this as "the body of attitudes and beliefs that guides and circumscribes thought on strategic questions, influences the way strategic issues are formulated, and sets the vocabulary and perceptual parameters of strategic debate."[3] Here strategic culture refers to the Kremlin's take on what might be described as "the way of the world"—the nature, habits, and framework of international behavior. The emphasis is less on formal regulation than on unwritten, but well understood, rules of the game: a world defined as much by competition as cooperation; the primacy of hard power; the centrality of the great powers; and the abiding importance of geopolitics.

The second part focuses more directly on the Russian elite's understanding of the international system, centered in the notion of a post-Western multipolar order or polycentric system. This aspect of Moscow's worldview is to some extent a recasting of the old Leninist question, *kto kogo*—"who will beat whom"—or, in today's context, who's up and who's down. It is shaped by perceptions of the decline of the West, the rise of the rest, and the shift of global power to the East. If strategic culture establishes the general philosophical bases for Russian foreign policy, then readings of the international system influence specific aspirations and policy responses.

Finally, any discussion of "the world according to Moscow" comes down to the question of where Russia fits in international society, today and in coming decades. The Kremlin continues to see Russia as a global power and regional hegemon. But how does it view the implications of such ideas, and to what extent is it able to reconcile these with the goals of "normality" and "international community"? How optimistic are Putin and other senior figures that Russia will indeed be one of the winners in a post-Western world order, or does their confident exterior mask mounting insecurities, most notably about the rise of China? What are their expectations about the possibilities and limits of Russian power?

## A Neo-Hobbesian Vision

There is a certain irony in the worldview of a seventeenth-century English political philosopher capturing much of the spirit of Putin's foreign policy. Thomas Hobbes's ultra-realist interpretation of international politics reflected the turbulence of his times, which saw him experience at first hand the English Civil War and the overthrow of King Charles I, and, from afar, the Thirty Years' War that devastated the European continent. The "state of nature" or anarchical world he described seems utterly at odds with the highly globalized and institutionalized environment of the early twenty-first century.[4]

Yet if today's global context differs in fundamental respects from seventeenth-century Europe, Russian policymakers nevertheless proceed from several of the premises that informed Hobbes's thinking. The first, and most important, is that the world is an alien and often hostile place, in which the strong prosper and the weak get beaten. For all the talk about interdependency and "win-win" solutions, it has always has been divided into winners and losers. Consistent with this view, few Russians believe, for example, that the United States and China can both thrive in the emerging international system.

Closer to home, Moscow exulted in the victory over Georgia in August 2008, not just because President Mikheil Saakashvili had been crushed, but because Russia had enjoyed a rare triumph over the United States, which in turn had suffered a very public humiliation.[5] This zero-sum mentality applies even when the outcome is negative-sum. At the height of the global financial crisis, there was considerable gloating at the troubles of the U.S. economy, despite its contagion effect on Russia.[6]

A second Hobbesian principle evident in Moscow's thinking is an abiding conviction in the primacy of hard power. While the waging of major wars is far less conceivable in a nuclear age, military strength remains central to Russian conceptions of great power-ness (*derzhavnost*).[7] The continuing attachment to a large standing army in the face of growing demographic constraints; the retention of a huge nuclear arsenal and emphasis on "strategic parity"; and substantial spending increases on the buildup of conventional and nuclear forces—all these reflect a security culture steeped in classical understandings of power. In the eyes of Putin and much of the political elite, military strength represents the ultimate guarantee of the world's attention and respect.[8]

Conversely, the Kremlin's approach to soft power is more akin to "soft coercion."[9] This is characterized by the surgical exploitation of weaknesses (for example, corruption) in the governance of neighboring states; the cultivation of inter-elite business networks;[10] the funding of political parties sympathetic to Moscow;[11] and the dissemination of propaganda through mass media outlets. Such methods resemble more closely the "active measures" (*aktivnye meropriyatiya*) pursued during the Soviet era[12] than they do the Western liberal notion of influence through example.[13] Most of all they arise out of the realist belief that true power comes from the ruthless deployment of political, economic, and strategic assets. Putin's handling of the Ukraine conflict exemplifies this thinking.[14]

A third feature of Moscow's worldview is the dominance of major powers in the international system. Although multilateral institutions play a vastly greater role than in seventeenth-century Europe (when they were nonexistent), Moscow sees contemporary politics in plutocratic terms, defined principally by the relations—sometimes cooperative, but frequently competitive—between sovereign actors. "Sovereign" in this context describes those few states that, in the Kremlin's view, are able to exercise genuinely independent choices—the United States, China, and Russia—plus other players with significant influence in selected areas, such as the leading Europeans (Germany, France), India, and Brazil.[15]

Smaller states and multilateral organizations are seen as objects or instruments of great power diplomacy, rather than as serious actors with proper agendas. When Moscow speaks about the "democratization of international relations," it understands this in very narrow terms—as the devolution of power from the former hegemon, the United States, to a group or "Concert" of Great Powers, including Russia. Although small states may sometimes be involved in international decisionmaking, this is regarded as rare and unnatural. Such elitist attitudes are the main reason why Putin—and Yeltsin before him—has never understood the institutional and political culture of the EU. They also explain why Moscow refuses to believe that Saakashvili attacked South Ossetia in 2008 without Washington's prior approval. The idea that a small state could embark on such a foolhardy venture of its own volition remains inconceivable.[16]

In keeping with a view of the world as an unforgiving place dominated by the major powers, there is little truck with the Western liberal claim that geopolitics is anachronistic.[17] Seen from Moscow, American actions since the fall of the Soviet Union have demonstrated that old-fashioned power projection continues to matter very much, even if it is coated with a normative veneer. Russian policymakers routinely accuse Washington of exploiting notions such as "promoting stability,"[18] democracy, and human rights, to hide ulterior geopolitical and commercial agendas. Thus in the 1990s it took advantage of Russian weakness to dominate the Euro-Atlantic security space through the enlargement of NATO. And over the past decade it has funded grassroots movements in Russia's neighborhood and the Middle East. The Russian political elite believes that the United States—whether under a Democratic or Republican administration—remains wedded to expanding its influence wherever possible, and using all available means.[19]

None of this implies that states cannot cooperate with one another. They can, must, and do. But the effectiveness of such interaction is determined, ultimately, by national strength and weakness. A strong state is in a position to promote and defend its interests; a weak one is not. The conclusion of successive generations of leaders—from Peter the Great, through Stalin, to Putin—is that Russia must look to its own interests and capabilities in order to prosper. It cannot rely on the benign intentions of others, weak international institutions, or woolly notions of shared norms and values.

## The Multipolar Order

In the Kremlin's eyes the international system is defined by multipolarity. This is a commonly misunderstood and distorted concept, susceptible to diverse interpretations. Curiously, the first Russian to use the term publicly was Yeltsin's liberal foreign minister, Andrei Kozyrev, who was widely pilloried as a stooge of the West.[20] He conceived of a multipolar world in cooperative terms—different powers working together to manage the post–cold war order. Today, however, the mainstream Russian interpretation is the one first promoted in the 1990s by Yevgeny Primakov, Kozyrev's successor as foreign minister. This vision is similar in that it imagines a world dominated by the interaction between different poles. But it could hardly be more different in spirit. As Primakov himself observed, the rationale behind a multipolar world order is to "counterbalance" the otherwise overweening influence of the sole superpower, the United States. It is a geopolitically motivated construct, centered in the principle of the balance of power. While it does not preclude cooperation with the United States, the main thread running through it is one of soft containment through a "consensus of the rest"—that is, the other poles in the international system.[21]

There are two other noteworthy aspects. For Moscow, multipolarity is less about establishing a new order than resurrecting the old. Its inspiration is the Concert of Europe, developed at the Congress of Vienna in 1815. The cast of characters is very different, but the underlying principles are the same. The great powers determine the arrangements and rules of international politics, and, crucially, abide by them. No single power may be allowed to threaten the status quo or assume disproportionate power—for Napoleonic France in the nineteenth century, read the United States today, and China in the future. Smaller states know their place, and frame national policies with due regard for the interests of the major powers. The latter do not interfere in one another's domestic affairs. And security—or at least their security—is collective and indivisible.

Multipolarity is also normative. Under Putin it has acquired a civilizational aspect that contradicts Western ideas of moral universalism. Russian statements refer approvingly to Samuel Huntington's theory of the "clash of civilizations."[22] Just as there are several centers of global power, so there are various civilizational "poles." The motivation here is to assert a cultural and moral relativism—and sovereignty—in the face of the pressure exerted by Western-led liberal values. The 2013 Russian Foreign Policy Concept thus juxtaposes "global competition . . . on a civilizational level," with "an increased emphasis on civilizational identity."[23] In proposing a "dialogue between civilizations," Moscow is stating unequivocally to the West that "our values are just as good as yours"—different, but in no way inferior.

There is the question of how far the Putin regime believes its multipolar rhetoric, or whether this serves mainly instrumental purposes. The answer is that it subscribes to the principle and feasibility of a multipolar order, but uses rhetoric to accelerate its emergence. It operates on the assumption that if enough major powers assert that the world is multipolar, the more quickly this will come to pass—an example of influencing perceptions to establish new realities. The development of the BRICS process plays a key role in this respect. Notwithstanding the lack of commonalities between its members, this group is the embodiment of the "multipolar world order" that Moscow desires.

Judging the sincerity of the Russian commitment to multipolarity also depends on how one defines the term. The Kremlin is not so naïve as to equate multipolar with equipolar; it still regards the United States as the leading power in the world. Moscow's understanding of multipolarity is more nuanced. It recognizes the existence of multiple centers of power, which are unequal yet independent, and which exert significant influence in their own particular spheres of influence (or, to use a slightly less loaded term, spheres of interest). While the United States continues to lead the Western world, China is emerging as the major player in the Asia-Pacific region (and, eventually, in world affairs), South America is dominated by Brazil, and South Asia by India. In the case of Russia, its enduring influence in post-Soviet Eurasia substantiates its claim to be a truly independent center of global power.

The terminology of multipolarity has shifted lately toward an emphasis on "polycentrism." The 2013 Foreign Policy Concept speaks of the transition to a "polycentric system of international relations" as a result of "profound changes in the geopolitical landscape." It is not entirely clear what has prompted this linguistic adjustment, although there are several possible explanations. One is that "multipolar order" is a somewhat hackneyed term, wheeled out by Boris Yeltsin and Chinese President Jiang Zemin in 1997, and since then often associated with barren strategic competition. "Polycentrism" sounds fresher, and more readily encompasses the civilizational dimension mentioned above.[24] That said, the importance of the name change should not be exaggerated. Just as there is no practical difference between the original Chinese concept of "peaceful rise" and its subsequent incarnation "peaceful development,"[25] so the distinction in Russia between multipolarity and polycentrism is nominal. Tellingly, Putin continues to speak of the former both as a desirable goal and as modern-day reality.[26]

### The shift of global power to the East

The Kremlin has become much more confident about the prospects of a new multipolar order since the global financial crisis. It identifies two interlinked phenomena: the decline of the West and the rise of the rest. Together they amount to what is routinely described as the shift of global power to the East. This position is summed up in the Foreign Policy Concept: "The ability of the West to dominate the world economy and politics continues to diminish. Global power and development potential is now more dispersed and is shifting to the East, primarily to the Asia-Pacific region."[27] This shift is multidimensional, encompassing politics, economics, military power, and normative influence.

*The decline of the West.* In subscribing to the fashionable theory of Western decline, the Russian political elite means principally the erosion of American global leadership. Europe's fall from grace has been more drastic, since the Second World War and following the financial crisis, but it is the fate of the United States that most interests policymakers. Although culturally and economically Moscow has always looked to Europe, its strategic and security focus—consistent with a neo-Hobbesian view of the international system—has long centered on the world's sole superpower.

Russians see a besieged America that is struggling in the face of growing external challenges, a dysfunctional political system, and a heavily indebted economy. They believe that it is less able and willing to lead, and that the concept of a U.S.-led Western alliance has become tenuous following the conflicts in Iraq and Afghanistan. They detect a loss of self-confidence, and mounting anxiety in the face of China's rise.[28]

At the same time, this America is raging against the dying of the light. Washington has moved to counter China's growing presence in the Asia-Pacific region through its "pivot" or "rebalancing" to Asia—reinforcing alliances with Japan, South Korea, and a number of Southeast Asian states and strengthening its strategic relationship with India. Moscow anticipates that Sino-American rivalry will become more intense as the United States strives to maintain its leading position in the world. Crucially, in this struggle few Russians are prepared to write it off completely; they expect it will remain a superpower, if no longer *the* superpower.[29]

Attitudes toward Europe are more dismissive. The global downturn and the eurozone crisis have confirmed the view that it is clapped out as a political force, crippled by liberal excess, and unable to respond effectively to the challenges of a dynamic global context.[30] There is a sense, more specifically, that the EU's European project is in deep trouble—a view strengthened by the rise of anti-Brussels sentiment in a number of European countries.[31] If there is to be a "Europe" in the future, Moscow believes, then it is likely to function on a very different basis. It will increasingly be dominated by a few key states, such as Germany and France, and characterized by widening divisions—between East and West, a well-run "north" (Germany and the

Nordic countries) and dysfunctional "south" (Greece, Spain, Portugal), and bigger and smaller states.[32]

In Russian eyes Europe's failures have undermined the very idea of "the West." The global financial crisis has not only damaged the credibility of the Bretton Woods financial institutions (the International Monetary Fund and World Bank), and democratic capitalism more generally, but also the West's *moral* authority. The conflation of Western and universal values that has held sway since the end of World War II is no longer tenable, and has given way to the reassertion of sovereign norms, and the "renationalization of world politics."[33] Supranational concepts born of the Western liberal order, such as the "responsibility to protect" (R2P) and the universality of human rights, have become delegitimized and unenforceable.

*Rise of the rest.* Just as the decline of the West is understood principally as that of the United States, so Russian views about the rise of the East center on China. No other country better exemplifies for Moscow the transformation of the international system. It not only heralds a change in global leadership (even if this takes some decades to be consummated), but also a different way of viewing, and managing, the world—one based on the existence of multiple centers of power and influence.[34]

The Kremlin sees China's rise as instrumental in shifting the center of global gravity from the Euro-Atlantic to the Asia-Pacific region. Beijing plays a pivotal role in efforts to develop more equitable international mechanisms, whereby the non-Western powers have enhanced roles.[35] China's emergence has also resulted in a security environment that is more complex and demanding. This is a function both of the modernization of its military and of the strategic responses of others to its expanding footprint. Finally, China is at the vanguard of a global normative revolution, as Western-led conceptions of universal values give ground to competing models of development.[36]

For Moscow the rise of the rest is more than simply an objective trend in international relations. It is an ideational project, driven by the assertion of national sovereignty against the political, economic, and normative hegemony of the West. The non-Western powers have a strong interest in working together to determine the rules of the international system—all the more so since the United States and Europe are no longer able to impose their vision of global governance on others.

The rise of the rest and decline of the West are mutually reinforcing elements in Putin's neo-Hobbesian vision. It is striking that the zero-sum calculus long associated with Soviet leaders has scarcely been diluted by more than two decades of globalization. In place of the ideological divide between communism and capitalism, the Kremlin now sees a contest between authoritarian traditionalism and democratic liberalism. Political engagement, economic interdependence, and human contacts between Russia and the West are immeasurably greater than during the cold war. But the competitive gene is as strong as ever. Indeed, against the backdrop of international relations that are "increasingly complex and unpredictable,"[37] globalization has had a multiplier effect. Competition these days is occurring on so many more fronts, involving a larger cast of players, and assuming ever more diverse forms.

## A World of Opportunity

Over the past two decades, there has been much discussion in the West and Russia about the latter's transition from superpower and empire into "normal" nation-state. The difficulty, however, is in establishing what is "normal." Normal in Europe means political pluralism, functioning institutions, strong rule of law, a balanced economy, vibrant civil society, and free media. But the Putin regime interprets "normal" somewhat differently. While it would like some of the "normalcy" of the West, such as high living standards, it proceeds from the primary assumption that Russia's natural condition is to be a great power; only on this basis can it (and its people) flourish.[38] This attitude is unsurprising. When one looks back at the sweep of Russian history, there have been very few periods since Peter the Great when it has not been a major power. In the past century one can point only to the years between the October 1917 revolution and Stalin's mass industrialization in the early 1930s. Even during the troubled 1990s Russia continued to see itself as such.

### Global actor and regional leader

It follows from this that the Kremlin cannot imagine Russia in any other terms than as one of the leading players in the world. Yet it also appreciates that a major power today differs in important respects from those of the past, including the Soviet Union. At the outset of his presidency Putin conceived of Russia as a "modern great power." In the post–cold war world it was no longer sufficient just to have vast territory, thousands of nuclear weapons, and a huge standing army—essential though these were. A modern great power also had to be politically stable, economically prosperous, and technologically advanced.[39] It had to be able to employ different forms of power in flexible fashion.

In this connection Putin sees no contradiction in projecting Russia's image as a geopolitical power while renovating its influence to the requirements of an international system where economic and other nonmilitary forms of influence have grown in importance. Moscow talks up the usual trumps, such as territorial extent and P5 membership, while exercising military power where it deems this appropriate. But it also points to Russia's pivotal position as a major supplier of energy and other strategic resources, and its still considerable intellectual capital.[40]

Another constant in Kremlin thinking is the insistence that Russia should be treated as a *permanent* great power, almost regardless of its domestic and international fortunes. A strong sense of entitlement has characterized its strategic culture for the past 300 years. Such attitudes extend across the political spectrum; it was the liberal Kozyrev, after all, who claimed that Russia was "doomed to be a great power."[41] This sense of destiny translates into a demand for "respect" (*uvazhenie*) by others, meaning the respect due *by right* to one of the world's elite. Institutionally, such recognition is reflected in Russia's membership in various exclusive "clubs"—the P5, the BRICS, the Middle East Quartet (the United States, the European Union, Russia, and the United Nations), the Korean Six-Party process, and previously the G-8. But more often respect is a state of mind rather than something quantifiable. It is measured by the extent of Western acceptance of Russia's "special" interests in the post-Soviet space, of its privileged place in international decisionmaking, and of its right to manage its domestic affairs free from "interference."

One of the corollaries of being a global actor is to be the dominant player in one's neighborhood, what Leon Aron called the "regional superpower."[42] As events in Ukraine have shown, this feeling remains very strong— unsurprising given that less than twenty-five years ago much of the neighborhood belonged, either directly or indirectly, to the Soviet empire. Although Russia is no longer in a position to exercise hegemonic power or demand "exclusive" rights of engagement, it still sees itself as the regional leader in a space extending from Ukraine in the west to the Central Asian republics in the east. This will be discussed in more detail in chapter 4, but it is worth emphasizing here that regional primacy is critical to the vision of Russia as a center of global power. Just as the United States leads the West, and China "heads" Asia, so Russia's credibility is seen to be contingent on dominating its part of the world.

### A Russia independent and unique

For Putin Russia's persona as a major power is predicated on its "independence." This term has a number of meanings. It can denote self-reliance, as in reduced dependence on Western governments and organizations, which are consequently unable to exercise significant leverage on Moscow. It can mean nonalignment and the rejection of "bloc-based" politics. And it has become closely associated with a "multi-vectored" foreign policy, and the pursuit of external relations on a "geographically balanced" basis, leaning neither East nor West.

Ultimately, though, independence is about preserving national sovereignty against those who would seek to deny or limit it. This goal has become synonymous with the regime's ceaseless pursuit of domestic and international legitimation. In much the same way as Putin embodies the state, so the interests of the regime have become indistinguishable from those of Russia itself. Consistent with this logic, external criticism of Putin's policies, particularly on domestic matters such as the rule of law, democratization, and human rights, is viewed as an assault on Russian sovereignty.[43]

In an uncertain world the identification of Russia as an independent center of global power has become more vital than ever to the Kremlin. It serves defensive purposes—containing liberal influences at home and resisting Western intervention in conflicts such as Syria. It also propagates Russia's "unique" persona as an autonomous international actor. There are various reasons why a post-Soviet Russia has not been integrated into Europe, the Euro-Atlantic community, or the Asia-Pacific region. But the most compelling is that it has not actually wanted integration, but rather cooperation and association. For real integration entails limitations on independence, the pooling of sovereignty, and the dilution of national "special-ness" (*spetsifika*). This makes sense for smaller and weaker states, but is extremely difficult to swallow for a country with the great power traditions of Russia.[44] The attitude of the political elite is that if Russia cannot lead (or co-lead), then neither will it follow.[45]

## The indispensable power

Since the reign of Catherine the Great (1762–96), Russia's leaders have underlined its indispensable role in first European and later global affairs. In the mid-eighteenth century Russia intervened in the Seven Years' War to support the Austrian Empire against Prussian expansionism. During the Napoleonic wars Tsar Alexander I's victories turned the course of history and saved Europe for autocracy. And in World War II the Soviet Union was crucial to the defeat of Hitler. The theme of indispensability is also reflected in the mystical notion of Russia as a civilizational and physical barrier protecting Europe against the barbarian hordes of the East.

This iconography has remained largely intact. In the Kremlin's eyes, a resurgent Russia is, by virtue of size, history, and potential, an indispensable player in global affairs. This self-belief takes various forms. In the first instance, it is enshrined in the conviction that there cannot be true security without Russia. This applies not only to its neighborhood, but also in general. Following his successful intervention over Syria's chemical weapons in September 2013, Putin argued that throughout history Russian participation had been decisive in securing a lasting peace—as at the 1815 Congress of Vienna, and again at Yalta in 1945. Conversely, its nonparticipation had been a major reason for the failure of the Versailles Peace Conference in 1919 and the subsequent march to World War II.[46] Most recently Putin has asserted that Western attempts to sidestep Russia over Ukraine have contributed hugely to that country's destabilization.[47]

The premise of indispensability underpins Moscow's strong attachment to concepts such as strategic nuclear parity. Its chief preoccupation here is less existential—the fear of obliteration—than in preserving its influence in the international order. For its nuclear arsenal is the one area where Russia remains America's equal (and China's superior), and as such represents for many the most reliable guarantee of its continuing status as a global power.

It is important to differentiate here between the desire for recognition and a willingness to assume concrete responsibilities. The Kremlin understands implicitly that Russia is not a global player on the same level as the United States (or the Soviet Union), and that in any case it is hardly advantageous to become embroiled in areas where it has little or no stake. What it seeks is acknowledgment of a *right of interest* in any issue it chooses, and of the principle of Russian indispensability. Thus it is more important that Russia be a member of the Middle East Quartet than that it should seek to influence the peace process. It is a similar story with the Korean Six-Party talks, the G-20, Asia-Pacific Economic Cooperation (APEC), and other forums. In the end, the value of "indispensability" comes not from being expected to deliver results—indeed, this is an unwelcome burden—but from others accepting Russia's importance and greatness as incontestable truths.

### Geopolitical balancer and bridge between civilizations

The Putin elite sees Russia as essential to the geopolitical equilibrium of the international order, the natural balancer between East and West, and, more specifically, between the United States and China. This self-appointed role derives from Russia's location in the Eurasian heartland, and from a history of strategic triangularism between Moscow, Beijing, and Washington.[48] Although such balancing appeared to become obsolete with the end of the cold war, the deterioration of relations with the United States during the 1990s encouraged a renewed push to position Russia as the global swing power.[49] Yeltsin's courting of the Chinese leadership, and the call for a "new multipolar order for the twenty-first century" in opposition to American "unipolarity,"[50] was directed to this purpose.

Although the Sino-Russian relationship has since acquired more of an intrinsic rationale (see chapter 5), geopolitical balancing remains central to Putin's foreign policy thinking. It has evolved from a philosophical abstraction into something more concrete, impelled by the "shift of global power to the East." This is reflected, for instance, in the coordination of Russian and Chinese efforts to oppose the removal of Assad.[51] Such balancing is intended both to resist specific actions seen as detrimental to Russia's interests, and to enhance its international stature by constraining American power more broadly. It functions on the zero-sum premise that what is bad for Washington is, more often than not, good for Moscow.

Russia's assumed identity as a balancer is not limited to grand calculus, but is geographically ubiquitous. In East Asia it is evident in efforts to promote itself as a counterweight vis-à-vis the United States,[52] and in occasional balancing between Beijing and Tokyo. Across Asia it is implicit in the Moscow–Beijing–New Delhi trilateral framework. And globally it is embodied by the BRICS.

In a less overtly competitive vein, the old idea of Russia as a bridge between Europe and Asia has been revived in the context of China's "New Silk Road."[53] This represents a form of soft balancing, but with the important distinction that the main thrust is less to hedge against others than to promote a "dialogue between civilizations" in which Russia plays a pivotal role by virtue of its geographical location, historical antecedents, and close ties with Europe, Central Asia, and China.[54] Like geopolitical balancing, however, it serves the purpose of positioning Russia as the indispensable power.

## The "lonely power"

There are obvious advantages to possessing several identities: a strong feeling of independence, a legitimate interest in many regional and global issues, and freedom of maneuver. But multiplicity also has its downsides. One such is that Russia's self-identification is spread very thinly, which means that it finds it difficult to commit properly to engagement with Europe or Asia. The leading Sinologist Victor Larin has written of an "East-West dilemma," in which consciousness of the need to engage more with Asia is counterbalanced by an enduring cultural and emotional attachment to Europe.[55] Other observers speak of "conflicted" identity, and of Russia being a "torn" country.[56]

The consequence of this ambivalence is that it has struggled to be accepted by others. Putin has long described Russia as a European civilization, yet many in Europe view it as an outsider, at best a peripheral presence on the continent. It is physically part of Asia, but is not regarded by local elites as Asian—culturally, politically, or economically.[57] And its ambitions to be a bridge between Asia and Europe are rarely taken seriously.

The tension inherent in the phenomenon of "semi-belonging," or partial exclusion, continues to influence Russia's self-perceptions and approach to international relations. At times it behaves as the "lonely power"[58]—on the one hand, imbued with a powerful sense of exceptionalism and righteousness; on the other hand, anxious that others will fail to grant it the respect it deserves. This has been a leitmotif of its relations with the West throughout the post–cold war era. And notwithstanding the 2012 APEC summit in Vladivostok, it is also the source of unease about its prospects in the Asia-Pacific region.[59] While the Putin elite rejects any suggestion that Russia is isolated, there is a tacit realization that it must work harder than most to position itself in the international system. Here Russia bears some resemblance to another high-profile "outsider," Turkey, which is an active player in Europe and the Middle East, but which struggles to gain full acceptance in either.

### A Russia on the up

It is often said that Moscow has a better idea of what it does not want than of what it does.[60] It opposes a unipolar world dominated by a hegemonic power; dislikes Western-led moral interventionism; and is hostile to the "encroachment" of the United States and Europe in the post-Soviet space. In fact, such objectives suggest that the Kremlin has a pretty good idea of what it wants. It seeks to facilitate an external environment that supports the legitimacy and stability of the Putin system.[61] It aims to secure international "respect"—if not support, then at least acquiescence—for Russia's interests in the post-Soviet neighborhood. And it is committed to promoting Russia as one of the world's leading powers, while maintaining foreign policy independence and strategic flexibility.

Seen from Moscow, current international trends have improved its chances of achieving these aims. There is genuine belief that, together with China, India, and other non-Western powers, Russia stands to gain from the vacuum left by the decline of the West. It will become more influential over the longer term, and this will enable it to renegotiate the rules of engagement with the United States and Europe. There are risks, of course. One is the arrival of a potential new hegemon in the form of China. This could become all the more alarming, given the vulnerability of resource-rich but population-poor regions in Eastern Siberia and the Russian Far East. Another unwelcome development would be the emergence of a Sino-American world order that would relegate Russia to secondary status. Xi Jinping's idea of "a new pattern of great power relations" with the United States would, if realized, heighten such fears.[62]

But the Kremlin appears to have banished such unpleasant thoughts for the time being. Concern about the asymmetry of the economic relationship with Beijing is outweighed by America's visible discomfiture with China's rise, satisfaction with Sino-Russian cooperation, and faith that China will need Russia for a long time to come—as a supplier of vital natural resources and as a good neighbor.[63] Indeed, their common opposition to grassroots democracy, American "unilateralism," and Western normative influence fosters hopes of a long-term strategic accommodation, and perhaps something more than that. As for a possible Sino-American order, this is a marginal preoccupation at best. The mainstream view is that the United States and China are set on a course of growing rivalry, enhancing Russia's opportunities to play the part of geopolitical balancer.[64]

The ongoing Ukraine crisis appears to challenge such optimism, not only estranging the Putin regime from the West, but also making it more beholden than ever to Beijing. However, there is little sign that the Kremlin's confidence has been dented. On the contrary, it believes that the crisis has proved it right about the weakness of U.S. global leadership, European frailties, the rise of the non-Western world, and Russia's ability to look after itself.[65] Although Russia faces a hard struggle to maintain its position as one of the world's leading powers, this enterprise is regarded as both feasible and necessary. Moreover, success depends on staying the course—not being intimidated or seduced into change by the West, but remaining true to its own traditions and strengths.

## Return of the New World Disorder

Putin's conduct of foreign policy is, however, coming under mounting pressure from regional and global trends. Far from there being a new multipolar order (or polycentric system) based on the dominance of a few major powers, the international environment is one of confusion and iconoclasm—in other words, a new world *disorder*. This disorder is characterized, among other things, by the changing nature of power, the demise of international leadership, the diminishing relevance of collusive great power arrangements, and the growing inclusiveness, but also fragmentation, of international politics. It is a world whose fluidity demands a radically different mindset from policymakers—adaptation and even reinvention, rather than containment and consolidation.

*Defining the new world disorder*

Over twenty years ago, the American political scientist Ken Jowitt wrote, in the wake of the collapse of communism, that the world was entering an era of unpredictability, a "new world disorder." Jowitt's thesis rebutted the triumphalist claim of Francis Fukuyama that history was "coming to an end" with the final victory of Western democratic liberalism.[66] He argued instead that the world was moving from a "Joshua period," with its relative certainties and clear boundaries, to a "Genesis environment"—"increasingly unfamiliar, perplexing, and threatening: in which existing boundaries are attacked and changed."[67]

Today's global landscape differs in many respects from the one Jowitt described. Yet some of the phenomena he identified remain pertinent. Politically, the world has become more chaotic, not more ordered. Traditional security threats have given way to myriad new challenges. Power and influence are elusive commodities. The number of active international players has increased exponentially, all with their particular interests that sometimes coincide, but often do not. There is growing uncertainty about the rules and norms governing international behavior. And the current globalized world is also one that is becoming ever more disaggregated.

A caveat should be added at this point. "Disorder" is a relative—and relatively peaceful—concept.[68] It stands in contrast to such overused terms as "order" and "international community."[69] It does not herald a return to some primordial chaos or large-scale confrontation. Indeed, notwithstanding the sharp deterioration in relations between Russia and the West and the advent of "new wars," the current period is arguably still one of the most peaceful in the modern (post-1500) era.[70]

Jowitt also qualified his Genesis analogy by admitting to a little creative exaggeration—the post-communist environment was not completely "without form and void."[71] Equally, the contemporary international context is by no means formless. There are rules, structures, and processes, according to which most state actors function most of the time. To mention just one example, the rules relating to freedom of navigation, as set out in the UN Convention on the Law of the Sea (UNCLOS), are on the whole well observed. Instances of rogue behavior by states are rare, and even most non-state actors adhere to what might be called "civilized" practice. (Terrorist organizations and criminal networks are exceptions, but they form only a tiny proportion of the total web of non-state and societal interactions.) The main reason why Moscow's annexation of Crimea provoked such shock and dismay in Western capitals was that it marked such a radical departure from the post–World War II norm.

Nevertheless, despite its relative lack of conflict the world has become messier, and the conduct of international relations more challenging. Compared with the more static systems of the past—the Westphalian order of the seventeenth and eighteenth centuries, the Concert of Europe in the nineteenth century, the cold war bipolarity of the twentieth century, and the period of post–cold war dominance by the West—there is little by way of common understanding. Established hierarchies and "truths" are breaking down. The new world disorder is by its very nature in constant flux, and defies easy summation. Its leitmotif is contradiction—or rather multiple contradictions: the reassertion of Westphalian concepts of sovereignty in opposition to supranational ideas of global governance; the relative decline of the major powers, alongside the growing weakness of multilateral institutions; unprecedented interconnectedness, but also resurgent nationalism, protectionism, and introspection.

### Russia and the new world disorder

The mainstream narrative in Moscow—and in many other parts of the world[72]—is that a hitherto dominant West is the principal casualty of global transformation. Reality, however, is somewhat different. Although the United States and Europe face tremendous challenges, it is Russia that is especially vulnerable to the adverse effects of disorderly change. We should consider why this is so in general terms, before examining several specific dimensions of the new world disorder and its implications for Russia.

In the first place, the current international environment presents decisionmakers in Moscow with unexpected challenges and counterintuitive choices. For more than three centuries, since Peter the Great (1682–1725) first dragged Russia into Europe, they have operated within a largely predictable and comprehensible framework. From the eighteenth century until the outbreak of World War I, the Tsarist Empire was an integral member of the European system of great powers. During the cold war, the Soviet Union represented one half of a bipolar world. And for much of the post–cold war period Russian foreign policy has functioned on the basis of a ready (if unpalatable) reference point in the shape of the United States' global primacy. Today, however, what passes for the international system has never been more unclear, nor have the demands of decisionmaking been more complex.

Second, Russia's domestic condition and foreign policy influence are based on a very narrow range of resources and capabilities. Its heavy dependence on energy and commodity exports makes it more vulnerable than most to strategic shocks, such as the U.S. (and now global) shale revolution, or large price fluctuations. In late 2014 the plummeting value of the ruble, record levels of capital flight, and rising inflation were a direct consequence of external factors, above all the fall in global oil prices and the severely restricted access of Russian enterprises to Western credit finance.

Third, Putin's response to uncertainties at home and abroad is to seek refuge in tradition, rather than address the need for wide-ranging modernization. In domestic affairs, this means a conservatism that harks back to the authoritarian stasis of Tsar Nicholas I.[73] In foreign affairs the emphasis is on the retro constructs of Great Power ("Concert") diplomacy, geopolitical balancing, and spheres of influence. The Kremlin has no interest in strategic adaptation; it believes that the onus is on others to adjust to Russia.

Fourth, Russia is institutionally and politically more fragile than the great majority of Western countries. Much is made of the Russian people's historical tolerance for pain. However, in recent years their expectations (and impatience) have grown substantially—a fact that the authorities understand only too well. The harshness of Putin's reaction to the protests of 2011–12 testifies to the extent of his anxiety on this point. This in turn raises questions about the extent of elite and public resilience to the potentially seismic effects of major shifts in the international system—if not today, then certainly in the longer term.

Fifth, Putin's Russia is more isolated than any Western country. It may be more "independent" than most, but it has very few regional or international support mechanisms. Even in the most optimistic incarnation of a Eurasian Union, it could not expect significant assistance from the other ex-Soviet republics in times of trouble. There is growing cooperation with China. But as chapter 5 shows, theirs remains a relationship driven by concrete interests rather than a broader likemindedness. As such it is susceptible to changing priorities and loyalties.

None of this is to suggest that Russia will implode soon or is doomed to terminal decline. The point, however, is that its margin for error—or bad luck—is smaller than most. To prosper, Russia needs many things to go right, and little to go wrong. As the commentator Sergei Karaganov wrote in 2011, "Hopefully, the luck will not fail this country before society and its ruling class wake up and start conducting a sensible policy to revive the nation and the country . . . we Russians know perfectly well that we are not always lucky."[74]

### The changing nature of power

There are many dimensions of power in the postmodern world: military might, economic strength, technological advancement, cultural influence, and normative power.[75] There is also the well-known distinction between hard and soft power—between influence through coercion and pressure, and influence through persuasion and attraction—although the boundaries are often blurred.[76] Power may be of a long-term character, or the product of a temporary concatenation of circumstances. The influence of energy- and resource-exporting countries such as Russia varies according to fluctuations in global commodity prices. Another important distinction is between active and preventative power. All countries, including the United States, struggle to prosecute an active agenda. But most countries retain some capacity to obstruct the objectives of others. Russia is an excellent illustration of this. It is unable to dominate the post-Soviet space as it once did, yet it retains considerable capacity to destabilize sovereign states and make life difficult for other external actors.

Amid the confusion of different dimensions of power, one can nevertheless discern some critical shifts. One is the diminishing value of *military might*. Such a statement may seem implausible given developments in Ukraine. But paradoxically Russian "successes" have exposed the shortcomings of the use of force, and of hard power in general. The takeover of Crimea in February 2014 was a stunning operation that achieved all its immediate objectives. Yet the strategic consequences of the Kremlin's actions have been almost uniformly negative for Russian interests. The administration in Kyiv will be hostile for the next few years at least, while popular support for Ukraine's pro-European (and pro-EU) orientation has been significantly strengthened.[77] Kazakhstan and Belarus have become more protective about their national sovereignty, which will constrain the development of Putin's Eurasian Union. The Americans and Europeans are taking a much closer interest in Ukrainian affairs. NATO has rediscovered a sense of purpose, and is reinforcing its military presence in front-line members such as Poland and the Baltic states.[78] And Russian strategic dependence on China is at a historical high. Russia's actions also have aggravated its macroeconomic situation, led to a dramatic increase in capital flight, discouraged foreign and domestic investment, and severely restricted the access of its major companies to credit finance. Putin himself faces a major conundrum. Having staked so much on victory, he could yet be forced either to climb down or to escalate to a more direct confrontation with the West. In either event the outcomes would be more uncontrollable and dangerous than he ever anticipated.

Putin appears to tacitly recognize some of these realities, in particular that military power alone can achieve little. The use of proxies and the resort to covert, deniable operations in southeast Ukraine—so-called "hybrid warfare"—point to a reluctance to deploy Russia's armed forces in significant numbers. Putin knows that such intervention would be colossally expensive, sucking up vast resources at a time of recession in Russia, and counterproductive in realizing his vision of "a Russian-Ukrainian world."[79] The difficulty, however, lies in extricating himself from this imbroglio without suffering a potentially catastrophic loss of face.

During the cold war, military might was sometimes (although not always) effective because it was the dominant form of power and recognized as such. In today's world, however, occasions such as the 2008 Russia-Georgia war are at best partial exceptions to the rule that military means are ineffectual or counterproductive in projecting long-term influence. Even where protagonists appear completely mismatched, the stronger side faces huge problems in converting seemingly irresistible power into desired outcomes. There are also unintended consequences. The U.S.-led wars in Iraq and Afghanistan demonstrated that the use of force can have a severely self-harming effect. And just as the United States saw its international standing plummet during the 2000s, so Russia's influence in Ukraine (and Europe) is at its lowest ebb in over two decades.

*Economic strength*, by contrast, has become all-important. Without it countries are unable to assert lasting influence, while leaving themselves vulnerable to domestic instability and outside exploitation. This has been one of the striking lessons of Russia's experience in the post–cold war era. But economic power, too, is patchy and fragile, a reality underlined by the global financial crisis. The United States is an economic superpower, yet finds itself in hock to the Chinese and its own excesses.[80] China has enjoyed an average of 9 percent GDP growth since the late 1980s, but remains a middle-level economy—technologically backward in most sectors, environmentally exposed, and with 250 million people living on less than two dollars a day.[81] Russia has the third-largest gold and currency reserves in the world, but has become an international anti-model—a byword for non-modernization (and even de-modernization), uncompetitiveness, and chronic corruption.

Economic means are considerably more effective than military might in projecting power. But their utility in this respect is constrained by significant caveats. The United States has found that its enormous financial power is insufficient to arrest the relative decline of its influence in many parts of the world. China is an economic behemoth, but is discovering that money can buy only so much; all countries, it seems, wish to expand commercial ties with Beijing, but many of them are wary of too close an engagement—and dependence. For Russia a preponderant economic strength in post-Soviet Eurasia is by no means an unmitigated blessing. Such power encourages its neighbors to diversify their external relations at the same time as maintaining parasitic ties with Moscow.

We are living at a time of permanent and accelerating *technological revolution*, in which those who live on past achievements and glories are doomed to fall behind. This is not merely about accessing the technology needed to develop individual industries, or putting the country's best and brightest through swish business schools. It involves an attitudinal transformation across the whole of society. For what matters most is not a country's present level—whether it is a major power, advanced economy, or developing country—but the hunger and capacity to better itself. This was the basis of America's emergence as a global power in the early twentieth century, and it is the foundation of Chinese success today. However, nothing threatens the standing of the United States and Europe so much as a failure to adapt to changing conditions and requirements. This too is Russia's great challenge.

Economic strength and technological capacity underpin the growing *ascendancy of soft power*. The most influential powers in today's world are those whose strengths lie principally in this area. The United States remains the sole superpower because it has the largest economy, the most advanced technology, and the most persuasive cultural and normative influence. Its military might arises squarely out of its economic and technological advantages, and in some respects represents a source of vulnerability. Thus overstretch in Iraq and Afghanistan has exacerbated America's economic difficulties, in particular by creating a massive public debt.[82] Equally, China's rise to global prominence is almost entirely a function of its economic transformation, not its military power.[83] Like Moscow and Washington, Beijing has discovered that the use of hard power has significant drawbacks. In the South China Sea, the activities of the PLA (People's Liberation Army) Navy have led ASEAN member-states to make common cause against Chinese interests, while the escalation of tensions with Japan over the Senkaku/Diaoyu islands has given impetus to U.S. "rebalancing" toward Asia.[84]

One reason for caution in assuming the long-term decline of the United States is that its vast wealth, high living standards, and substantial political and social freedoms continue to be seen as attractive by much of the developing as well as developed world. The so-called Washington consensus may have been badly tarnished, but there is a long way to go before other countries supersede America's soft power. Even when China becomes the world's largest economy by GDP in the next few years, its per capita income will still be five times lower than that of the United States, and its material quality of life correspondingly inferior.

At the same time, soft power has become more uneven in its impact—or perhaps its limitations are now better understood. As Joshua Cooper Ramo has pointed out, you can wear American brand clothing (but made in China!), watch Hollywood blockbusters, send your children to American and European universities, and yet still strive to undermine U.S. political, security, and economic interests.[85] China has shown that embracing Western consumerism does not mean subscribing to liberal democratic values; sometimes, the opposite is true. In a disorderly world, most countries have developed a certain skepticism and resistance toward even the most seductive of blandishments. Not only will they not be told, they will often not be persuaded.

This applies, too, in relation to Russia. Its popular culture—movies, TV shows, music—retains enormous appeal in the ex-Soviet republics. But this does not mean that their peoples wish to join the Russian Federation or to be an appendage of a "Russian world" as envisaged by the Kremlin. The case of southeastern Ukraine—as Russian-speaking and Russian-acculturated as they come—has highlighted that the most receptive of audiences still puts a high price on independence and freedom of action.[86]

### The end of leadership and the decline of the great powers

Ever since Oswald Spengler predicted the end of Western civilization in the aftermath of World War I, one of the principal narratives of international politics has been the West's struggle to maintain its primacy.[87] Over the past century this debate has waxed and waned according to the level of Western confidence. Little more than a decade ago the story was one of Western ascendancy. Fukuyama's theories about the "end of history" and the triumph of liberal democracy were reflected not only in the claim that the West had won the cold war, but also through the dissemination of neoliberal economic prescriptions (aka the "Washington consensus"), the success of the U.S.-led coalition in the Gulf War, and the enlargement of NATO and the EU. Even the devastating blow of 9/11 did not appear to disrupt the mood of triumphalism. At the beginning of 2002 few predicted an impending crisis of the West.

The question then is whether the Kremlin is right to claim that the world is witnessing the long-term decline of the West and the end of U.S. global leadership. The answer depends on what benchmarks are used. If one compares the situation today with the 1990s, the case for decline seems incontestable. The United States faces greater challenges to its authority than at any time since the end of the cold war. It self-evidently struggles to manage conflicts (Iraq, Afghanistan) where the enemy comes in unconventional forms—insurgencies, terrorist groups, and transnational criminal networks. It has shown no demonstrable ability to effect a solution to the Syrian conflict. The financial crisis has exposed the weaknesses of the leading Western economies. And the promotion of Western political values has suffered several high-profile setbacks. A growing number of countries are resisting the pressure to democratize, and when there has been democratization, the outcomes have often been unpalatable to Western governments—as in Iraq with the growth of Iranian influence, in Gaza where the openly anti-Israeli Hamas enjoys considerable popular support, and in Egypt where the country's first free elections in more than six decades resulted in the victory of the Muslim Brotherhood.

However, if we think back to the 1970s the challenges to U.S. authority and Western values were more numerous and formidable than they are today. Not only was there an entire rival system in the form of the Soviet Union and its satellite and client states, there was also a myriad of nonaligned but unfriendly actors: a truculent China; a defiant India; and an Arab world buoyed by the oil price spikes of 1973 and 1979. The American economy accounted for a greater share of global GDP then, but as the oil crises showed, Washington's capacity to dictate to others was strictly limited. U.S. President Richard Nixon, a ferocious anti-communist, was so concerned about the decline of American influence that he initiated and sustained a strategic rapprochement with "Red" China from 1971.[88]

Many Russian observers home in on the all too obvious weaknesses and blank spots in U.S. power, while underestimating how dominant and multidimensional this continues to be. By any serious criterion, the United States is much the most powerful country on the planet. Its military capabilities are superior to those of the rest of the world combined. Despite the financial crisis, it continues to dominate the global economy;[89] it remains the supreme technological power,[90] and its cultural and normative influence is unparalleled. Tellingly, young people from all over the world look to live, study, and work in America, rather than in China, India, or Russia.[91]

It is also lazy to view international politics as a zero-sum game, in which the decline of certain powers, empires, and civilizations is inevitably matched by the rise of others. For one thing, this overlooks the capacity of incumbent powers to adapt and prosper. Suffice here to recall the example of the Roman Empire, which appeared to be in terminal decline at the end of the fourth century, only to reinvent itself as the Eastern Roman and then Byzantine Empire, and flourish for another thousand years. And there are many other examples in history.

More important, the Kremlin's tendency to view the decline of the West and rise of the rest as interlinked phenomena oversimplifies the highly complex character of international relations. In fact, one of the notable features of recent times has been the decline, relatively speaking, of virtually *all* the major powers. It is not only the United States and the leading European nations that wield nothing like the same influence as they did a decade ago. Russia too has seen the steady erosion of its once hegemonic position in post-Soviet Eurasia.

The one major power not in relative decline has also found the road to global status and influence hard going. Despite Beijing's attempts to portray the rise of China in benign terms—"peaceful development," "harmonious world," "win-win" solutions—many countries view its expanding footprint in a negative light. Resistance is not confined to the United States and Japan, but is evident elsewhere—witness the hardening of ASEAN positions on South China Sea territoriality, the Burmese junta's decision to reach out to the West, and the disquiet being voiced by prominent figures in Africa and Latin America.[92] As a result, the Chinese have shown an understandable reluctance to supplant the United States as the "go to" power. They know that international leadership is politically and financially debilitating, and a magnet for the envy, suspicions, and anxieties of others.[93] When challenged to play a more active role in global governance, Beijing's standard response has been that China can best contribute to the international community by ensuring stability and prosperity within its own borders.[94] Although there are signs of greater ambition under Xi Jinping, this is focused on China's "core interests" in Asia. Xi's idea of a "new pattern of great power relations" with Washington should not be misread as implying a wish for China to be as globally active and committed as the United States. Rather, it is an attempt to regulate their *bilateral* interaction on terms more favorable and less intrusive to Beijing.

The issue therefore is not the decline of American leadership, as many in Russia would have it, but the demise of international leadership *in general*. The elusive nature of modern power presents serious difficulties to those countries that aspire to exert influence over others. Newton's third law of motion is apposite here: for every action, there is an equal and opposite reaction. The global preeminence of the United States provokes others to find ways of mitigating its power, while the rise of China has stimulated similar counterbalancing responses in the Asia-Pacific region. Russia too has found that attempts to reestablish something of its former influence in Eurasia have come up against the determined, and frequently successful, efforts of the ex-Soviet republics to consolidate their sovereignty. In the new world disorder, countries are much more disposed and able to resist leadership, from wherever it comes and whatever form it takes—unilateral, consultative, collective, or even "from behind."[95] Indeed, so strong is this resistance that it may be more accurate to say that the world is not witnessing the end of leadership so much as the end of "followership."[96]

Although Moscow has welcomed the swing back to the primacy of national interests and prerogatives in world politics, this has actually complicated Russian policymaking. There has been a "democratization of international relations," but not in the way the Kremlin understands it—that is, the closing of the gap between the sole superpower and the other major powers. Instead, a more comprehensive process has been at work, whereby smaller states and regional actors are no longer passive objects of great power diplomacy, but increasingly sovereign actors. Even the very weakest of them have a much wider range of options than could have been imagined a few years ago. They have not only become more adept at balancing between external powers in their individual foreign policies, but have also made skillful use of regional structures to maximize their collective weight. In August 2008, the Central Asian states exploited the framework of the Shanghai Cooperation Organization to withstand Russian pressure to recognize Abkhazia and South Ossetia. And more recently an acutely dysfunctional Ukraine has managed to gain substantial financial assistance from a divided Europe, a usually hard-nosed IMF, and a reluctant White House.

The major powers have for the most part been forced to recognize their diminished capacity to influence the behavior of smaller states. The Obama administration's consultative style in foreign policy, for example, is not born of some warm and fuzzy liberalism; it is a pragmatic response that acknowledges the need for accommodation in the absence of viable alternatives. Even when the disparities of power are huge, it is necessary to observe the proprieties of "equality" and "mutual benefit" in diplomatic dealings. Accordingly, the Kremlin has sometimes adjusted its tactical approach in post-Soviet Eurasia. Its efforts to package the Eurasian Economic Union as an equal, collective, and positive-sum enterprise acknowledge, in effect, the value of more indirect methods of projecting Russian influence. It is another matter, of course, to square such rationality with historical habits of entitlement and notions about the natural order of things—as the Ukraine crisis has highlighted.

### The de-universalization of norms and values

One of the defining features of the new world disorder is the erosion of universalism. Western-led norms and values, as enshrined in documents such as the UN Charter, the Universal Declaration of Human Rights, and the 1975 Helsinki Accords, are under serious attack. Western leaders continue to admonish (some) authoritarian regimes for human rights violations, undemocratic behavior, and the flouting of the rule of law. But both their right to criticize and their enthusiasm for the task have become decidedly tenuous.

The wars in Iraq and Afghanistan have inflicted severe damage on the West's normative reputation, which has become submerged by charges of hypocrisy and double standards. These failures have been compounded by the global financial crisis, which has opened up new opportunities for those who would challenge Western-made rules. More generally, the growing assertiveness of individual state actors and the weakness of multilateral institutions have contributed to the steady dismantling of universalist prescriptions.

All that said, the Kremlin's claims regarding a normative and civilizational multipolarity in the world are at best dubious. No coherent set of principles has emerged to challenge the Western-led consensus established after World War II. For all the publicity surrounding a putative China model, there is no "Beijing consensus."[97] The Chinese themselves regard this as a Western fiction, and, in practice, are among the biggest supporters of American-style capitalism, with its emphasis on profit, social mobility, individual aspiration, and respect for wealth. It is likewise debatable whether one can speak of a new "Putin consensus" based on traditional Russian conservatism. Although the president's personal ratings have soared following the annexation of Crimea, opinion polls have shown substantial support for "Western" notions, such as the rule of law, an independent judiciary, fair elections, and uncensored media.[98] With the crisis in Russia-West relations, there has been revived talk of an "authoritarian international" or axis between Moscow and Beijing.[99] Yet this is a hoary myth, aimed at frightening Western policymakers into being more "understanding" of (that is, compliant toward) Russian interests.

Nancy Birdsall and Francis Fukuyama have written about a "post-American consensus,"[100] but the only real consensus that exists today is a commitment to do one's own thing—a Sinatra doctrine ("my way").[101] Appealing in the name of national values and "civilization" is a legitimating device used by governments the world over to justify self-interested policies, and to stay in power. But it does not equate to the emergence of a civilizational "new world order," as suggested by the Kremlin. Instead, there is a normative fracturing, in which the erosion of Western-led norms and values has resulted in a growing ideational vacuum in international society.

This would appear to be of most concern to the United States and Europe, which have long pursued value-oriented goals in their foreign relations. However, it is no less relevant to Russia. Putin's Eurasian Union project is founded as much on civilizational bonds between the ex-USSR republics as it is on economic cooperation. But the overall trend of de-universalization in norms and values is helping to loosen these ties. Just as the West is no longer able to dominate the rest, so Moscow is discovering that its moral leadership in Eurasia is becoming more brittle. Its main partners in the Eurasian Economic

Union, Kazakhstan and Belarus, play along with the Kremlin's integrationist rhetoric. But it is clear that their attraction to the EEU is economic, not civilizational. They are strongly committed to preserving their national sovereignty, and, in the case of Kazakhstan, their cultural distinctiveness as well.[102]

### Inclusiveness and fragmentation

International relations have never been more inclusive, giving unprecedented opportunities to an expanding number of state and non-state actors. Although some countries are more globalized and powerful than others, there is no country that is completely isolated, or whose actions do not affect its neighbors. Isolation has become a relative concept; even North Korea, the eponymous "hermit kingdom," has partners. Conversely, in a globalized world no state—including the United States—is fully independent and sovereign.

In this environment countries must deal with a growing number of issues. The smallest of states has a stake in areas which once appeared to engage only the major powers. Global trade and financial flows, climate change, human development, regional conflicts, the proliferation of weapons of mass destruction, transnational crime, and energy security concern more or less everyone.

The broadening of the international agenda and its cast of players is a mixed blessing. On the plus side, many important issues that were long neglected, such as climate change, global pandemics, and water security, are belatedly receiving attention. However, the proliferation of issues and interested parties means that negotiations have become more complicated, and solutions harder to find. More countries' interests and sensitivities have to be managed, requiring more trade-offs—witness the difficulties in concluding the Doha trade round and salvaging recent climate change summits. Inevitably, too, countries disagree on what is important and what is less so. Thus Moscow and Washington differ on the gravity of the Iranian nuclear threat, and such differences of perception are replicated across many countries and issues around the world.

An inclusive and disputatious world is the polar opposite of the Kremlin's sought-after multipolar order. Small nations matter, and the major powers find it difficult to implement their agendas.[103] Although Russian policymakers are right to challenge blithe assumptions about the end of geopolitics, they underestimate the sheer ubiquity of competitive politics. It is not just the big players, such as Russia, which aim to constrain and counterbalance; the same is true of smaller states as well. This is most apparent in the latter's pursuit of "multivectored" foreign policies, whereby they exploit the competitive elements of major power relations to maximize their own independence.

Central Asian states, such as Kazakhstan, offer prime examples of such behavior, as did Ukraine under Yanukovych.[104]

There is another critical element. It is no longer appropriate to speak of globalization and regionalization as unitary phenomena. The recent rise of protectionist sentiment—in the developed as well as developing world— indicates that many countries view such trends in zero-sum terms, with clear winners and losers. Just as the Kremlin frets about the impact of globalization on Russia's manufacturing, agriculture, and information space, so elites in the ex-Soviet republics worry that a Moscow-led process of regionalization will undermine their own, much more vulnerable economies and polities. As chapter 4 explains, this has become one of the principal obstacles to post-Soviet integration. The fact that these republics are unable to compete on a level playing field has made them all the more inclined to mitigate Russian influence—not only in the economy, but also in the political, security, and cultural spheres.

## Two Worlds—and the Dysfunctionality of Russian Foreign Policy

For over a decade the Putin regime's view of the world, and Russia's place in it, has been heavily influenced by generalities, such as "the multipolar world order," "the democratization of international relations," "Europe without dividing lines," and "the primacy of the UN." More recently, there have been further additions to the lexicon, in particular "the decline of the West" and "the shift of global power to the East." The reiteration of such constructs reflects a desire to make sense of the world by establishing a conceptual framework that facilitates and legitimates a prominent role for Russia. In this, the Kremlin is hardly doing anything unusual. Regimes of all types, democratic as well as authoritarian, indulge in selective perceptions, national myths, and wishful thinking. Their foreign policies are shaped as much by their own preconceptions as by any facts on the ground.

The art, of course, is to establish an effective balance between the desire to influence the international system in one's own image and responding to the world as it actually is. This is not easy to achieve even in relatively stable and predictable times. It is all the more difficult in today's volatile international context. A world in flux presents extraordinary challenges to governments everywhere, especially to those that aspire to play a major role in global affairs. Whatever their pretensions to "strategic vision," most of the time they are confronted by trends and events that are beyond their control and often comprehension. At best they adapt after the fact—recognizing the nature and scope of change, the implications for national interests, and the opportunities that exist to maximize their countries' possibilities.

This too is Russia's task. There are few signs, however, that the Putin regime has come to terms with the "inconvenient truths" of the new world disorder. It continues to frame the landscape of contemporary politics within an artificial multipolar (polycentric) paradigm. It overestimates Russia's capacity to establish itself as a regional and global player on its own narrow terms. And it believes that the future lies not in adapting to fast-changing international realities, but in hunkering down—reaffirming time-honored principles of Russian foreign policy, such as the primacy of great power diplomacy and military strength.

The outcome of these errors of perception and commission is a dysfunctional foreign policy. In place of serious strategic thinking (let alone imagination), the Kremlin has allowed itself to be distracted by tactical "triumphs" and a large measure of self-delusion. Despite its emphasis on the "pragmatic" pursuit of national interests, its approach to international relations is skewed by a virtual world that promises much, but delivers little. In part II of the book, we examine in detail how the growing disconnect between aspiration and (non-)performance is undermining Russia's interests in key areas of its interaction with the world: global governance, the post-Soviet space, Asia, and relations with the West.

# Part II

# Performance

three

# Russia and Global Governance

We need to use the UN Security Council and believe that preserving law and order in today's complex and turbulent world is one of the few ways to keep international relations from sliding into chaos. The law is the law, and we must follow it whether we like it or not.

VLADIMIR PUTIN, SEPTEMBER 11, 2013

Russia clearly has a vocation to be a global policy leader. What is less evident is whether any other countries are inclined to follow.

DANIEL TREISMAN, JUNE 2013

In many respects Russia appears to be the very best of global citizens. It extols the United Nations as the supreme decisionmaking body in world politics. It calls for the "democratization" of international relations and the need to ensure "the rule of law in the international arena."[1] It prides itself as a stickler for correct procedure and the precise implementation of UN resolutions. It has played a leading role in establishing new multilateral structures, such as the Shanghai Cooperation Organization and the Eurasian Economic Union. And it is involved in discussions on all the big issues from economic rebalancing to conflict management to counterterrorism.

Why then, given this seemingly active engagement, has Russia acquired such a poor reputation for global governance? It is tempting to blame Western politicians and media for this. The organizations founded after World War II reflect Western interpretations of "universal" norms—a dominance accentuated by the collapse of the Soviet Union and the end of the cold war. So when Moscow resists the will of the "international community," as defined by the West, it is inevitably pilloried. And when it does cooperate, its compliance is considered the only rational and moral choice, scarcely worthy of comment, let alone praise.

But Russia's negative image is much more than the product of some Western conspiracy. For one thing, there is the stark disconnect between its formal allegiance to the "primacy of international law" and the territorial integrity of nation-states, and a highly selective approach toward implementing such principles. Fresh from criticizing American unilateralism and exceptionalism over Syria in the fall of 2013, the Kremlin revealed a "do as I say, not as I do" attitude on Ukraine only a few months later. In the process it confirmed the obvious point that the Russian national interest far outweighs quasi-theoretical standards of acceptable international behavior.

The issue is not only about hypocrisy and double standards. After all, it is difficult to imagine a more striking disregard of the United Nations and global public opinion than the 2003 U.S.-led invasion of Iraq. There is also the problem of effectiveness—or rather the lack of it. Few countries see Russia as a serious contributor to international public goods. They are not so much concerned about the morality of Moscow's actions as dismissive of its ability to make a positive difference.[2]

This is unfortunate, not least for Russia. Its willingness and capacity to play a significant role in global governance matter because it has *global* interests—in the management of the world economy, trade, resource supply, nuclear and conventional security, and the development of international norms. Notwithstanding the inclination of some in the West to belittle its importance,[3] it does not have the luxury to be a mere regional actor. In this respect, the Kremlin's conviction that Russia should be a global player is entirely appropriate.

The question is "what kind of global player?" This is where the tension between the two worlds—the perceptual and the actual—described in the previous chapter is most pronounced. Over the past 200 years, the Russian ruling elite has come to regard the status of global power as an inalienable historical right, irrespective of Russia's circumstances. In today's new world disorder, however, a "divine right of great powers" is no longer tenable. As already noted, the authority of the major powers is much weaker than before; the criteria of influence have changed; and there is the constant pressure to deliver outcomes. Simply demanding respect and talking up "indispensability" do not come close to demonstrating relevance.

This chapter analyzes the Putin regime's response to the task of reinventing or, perhaps more accurately, adapting Russia to the demands of global governance in a disorderly world. It considers the question in two parts. The first centers on matters of process, and looks at Moscow's approach to multilateral institutions. It also examines attempts to create an alternative multilateralism through other avenues, such as the BRICS and the Eurasian Economic Union. The second part of the chapter focuses on the substance of policy—how the Putin regime is addressing contemporary issues in international finance, trade, security, and normative regimes. One of the principal themes to emerge here is the Kremlin's reluctance to graduate from its preoccupation with traditional security and geopolitical priorities to tackling a new global agenda.

## Qualified Multilateralism

For much of the post-Soviet era, Russia—like the USSR before it—has observed the letter of multilateralism while often ignoring its spirit. Policymakers have adopted a formalistic approach to global governance, exploiting the cumbersome bureaucratic processes of the UN, in particular, to control rather than facilitate problem solving. They have taken particular care to ensure that any multilateral actions that are approved or tolerated do not impinge on Russia's sovereign prerogatives.

In prioritizing national interests over a larger international good, Russia behaves much like any other major power or, for that matter, the smallest UN member-state. What distinguishes it from most other countries, however, is the *degree* to which it uses multilateral mechanisms to project influence, status, and moral legitimacy. Moscow supports "the central coordinating role of the UN as the principal organization regulating international relations" precisely because this ensures "collective decisionmaking"—that is, decisionmaking by the major powers on the basis of "equality."[4] The UN, and specifically the Security Council, has mitigated the consequences of Russia's post–cold war decline by providing a significant check on American "hegemonic" power. This does not always work, as proved by Washington's decision to invade Iraq. But such exceptions do not obviate the main point, which is that the Kremlin values these institutions principally as equalizers of power and influence vis-à-vis the United States.

In a similar vein, Russia attaches greater importance to the role of multilateral institutions in reinforcing its international status than it does to their efficacy. Whereas it may—or may not—be desirable for a particular multilateral process to achieve results, participation (no matter how formalistic) is invariably essential. Influence and status are intertwined with legitimacy. International institutions are vehicles for promoting an image of Russia as a good citizen of the world. More important still, they enable Moscow to counter Western humanitarian arguments with its own reading of a higher morality. It is one thing to use its veto powers in the UN Security Council to block sanctions against the Assad regime. But it is a bonus to be able to rationalize such actions by appealing in the name of "international law."

Moscow has, however, encountered real problems with the functioning of multilateralism. One issue, raised in the previous chapter, stems from having to deal with an expanding cast of players, many of whom do not regard their modest stature as a bar to active participation in regional and global affairs. Another, more fundamental concern is that multilateral organizations challenge the sovereign prerogatives of nation-states by subjecting them to external scrutiny, criticism, and occasionally intervention. Just as Moscow exploits such mechanisms to constrain the United States, so other states call Russia to account for its support of unpleasant regimes and the failure to abide by its commitments under various normative documents, such as the Helsinki Accords. This oversight is thoroughly irksome to the Kremlin, which rejects external accountability by stressing the "inviolability" of Russian sovereignty.

The tensions are exemplified by Russia's relations with the Organization for Security and Cooperation in Europe (OSCE). During the 1990s the Yeltsin administration promoted the OSCE as the centerpiece of a Europe "without dividing lines," a more inclusive and equitable alternative to NATO. After 2000, however, Moscow became increasingly resentful of the organization's election monitoring activities in Russia and the post-Soviet space through the Office of Democratic Institutions and Human Rights (ODIHR). It reacted by obstructing ODIHR missions; accused the OSCE of losing sight of its primary security functions; and at one stage suspended budgetary contributions. To Putin the OSCE came to embody the worst shortcomings of multilateralism: lack of controllability, interference in Russia's domestic affairs, and the facilitation of Western subversion.[5]

Strangely, relations with the OSCE have improved since the annexation of Crimea and the escalating violence in eastern Ukraine.[6] The Kremlin continues to eye the organization with suspicion, and remains uncomfortable with the critical scrutiny that a substantial OSCE presence on the ground would bring. On the other hand, it seeks its imprimatur—as the representative of the wider Euro-Atlantic security community—for new power-sharing ("federalization") arrangements, and for the de facto redistribution of territory.[7] This translates into a twin-track approach: Moscow engages with Vienna at the level of high policy, while making life as difficult as possible for OSCE observer missions—either denying them entry (Crimea) or colluding in their harassment and detention by separatist groups (southeast Ukraine). The underlying message is that the OSCE is useful to Moscow only insofar as it can be exploited to serve specific national goals.

## The UN P5

For Putin the best kind of multilateralism is encapsulated by the UN Security Council, and especially proceedings involving the Permanent Five (P5) members. Along with the institutionalization of strategic parity in nuclear weapons, the P5 is the most visible symbol of Russia's formal equality with the United States and, by extension, its "permanent" status as a global power. In appearance it is a multilateral institution, but its spirit is thoroughly multipolar.

The significance of the P5 lies not in its decisionmaking capacity, which is limited, but in other factors. To the Kremlin, it represents the most effective means of limiting or counterbalancing American power, now that nuclear weapons have lost much of their utility as tools of geopolitical influence. It converts a largely abstract proposition—the multipolar order—into a substantive reality, albeit in a very particular and narrow dimension.

In this enterprise the veto plays a crucial role. Exercising the veto, or, better still, the implicit threat of its use, is seen as a key guarantee of Russia's continuing centrality in global affairs. On Syria, for example, the power of the veto has not only given Moscow a prominent voice, but also contributed to the paralysis of Western policymaking, and strengthened the position of the Assad regime. For Putin this amounts to an almost perfect set of outcomes—the West is weakened, Russia is strengthened, and the Concert of Great Powers is preserved. Compared with these dividends, the reputational damage incurred by supporting an egregious regime barely registers.

The P5 is important, too, in relation to bilateral objectives. In the lead-up to the Iraq war Moscow attempted (unsuccessfully) to parlay non-use of the veto in exchange for guarantees of the interests of Russian energy companies, such as Lukoil's concession in the west Qurna oil field.[8] The extent to which bilateral substance shapes multilateral process was also evident during the Libyan conflict. In March 2011, Russia abstained on UN Security Council Resolution (UNSCR) 1973 endorsing a NATO no-fly zone mainly because it prioritized the reset with Washington and good relations with Paris over preservation of the Gaddafi regime. But with Syria, Putin opposed sanctions because he found no compelling bilateral reasons to act differently. Here the causal relationship worked in reverse: an uncompromising approach in the P5 was seen as a way of forcing the United States to take Russia seriously.

The importance of the UN Security Council as an instrument of Russian foreign policy means that Moscow is loath to entertain significant reforms to its structure and operation. In particular, it opposes the extension of veto powers beyond the P5. The reasons for its stance are logical—and entirely self-interested. Moves to make the UNSC more representative of contemporary international society would undercut Russia's special status and the influence it derives from this. Such a concern is all the more pertinent when its substantive weight in other areas of international politics is in question. In the hypothetical event of a reformed Council, Russia would find it very difficult to pretend that it was the global equal of the United States and China.

The comparisons would instead be with India, Brazil, Germany, and Japan—unthinkable for a country that was one of only two superpowers a little over two decades ago.

That said, Moscow has adopted a judiciously ambiguous attitude in public toward UN reform. For there is an uncomfortable contradiction between adherence to a status quo that reflects the outcomes of a conflict that ended seventy years ago and its professed commitment to a new and more democratic world order. It is aware also of the need to massage the sensitivities of aspiring permanent members—and fellow BRICS countries—such as India and Brazil. It has attempted to finesse these tensions by calling for the Security Council to become "more representative," while "ensuring due efficiency of its processes" and preserving the status of the existing members of the P5.[9] But such doublespeak scarcely masks the fact that Moscow, like Washington and Beijing, has no interest at all in change.[10] Its position that "any decisions on the expansion of the Security Council should be based on a general consensus of the UN member-states" confirms as much; it knows that such a consensus is improbable.

### Multilateralism for the great and the good

The P5 is only the most conspicuous manifestation of what might be described as multilateralism for the great and the good. Moscow's ideal framework is one strong enough to restrain American power, but that limits decisionmaking to a small coterie of major powers. It is symptomatic that the Russian government's efforts in the UN have focused overwhelmingly on the Security Council. The proceedings of the General Assembly are of fleeting interest, and only when the issue is directly relevant to Russia—as with nonbinding Resolution 68/262 of March 27, 2014, on "the territorial integrity of Ukraine."[11]

It has become evident that Moscow's commitment is not to multilateralism, at least as it is commonly understood, but to multipolarity. Although the two are frequently conflated,[12] they are very different phenomena. Whereas multilateralism is inclusive, multipolarity is defined by exclusiveness. As Dmitri Trenin has observed, it is based on a "global oligarchy," whereby a few great powers collectively manage world affairs, with smaller states playing only bit parts.[13] One reason for this exclusivist bias, as articulated by a senior Russian policymaker, is the belief that the major powers speak a "common language"—only they truly understand the way things are done in the world (even while they disagree on the substance of policy).[14]

The Kremlin favors selective "multilateralism" also because in smaller forums Russia can more plausibly present itself as a significant and in some ways unique presence. Before its suspension in March 2014, it was the only non-Western member of the G-8, while in the P5 it has occasionally acted as the intermediary and balancer between East (China) and West (United States, United Kingdom, France). Russia's distinct identity within such forums encourages it to claim a standing that exceeds its actual influence—as in the negotiations over Iran's nuclear program.[15]

More inclusive frameworks such as the G-20 tend to undermine such mythologies. It is difficult to promote Russian "specialness" in conditions where there is little demand for it. The G-20, for example, focuses principally on areas where Russia is a secondary player. As one of the less advanced economies in the group, its capacity to contribute usefully to a new financial architecture or to rectify global imbalances is limited. Its chairmanship of the group in 2013 did not alter this fact. (After all, Mexico—the fourteenth ranking economy in the world—held the chairmanship in 2012.)

It is logical then that Moscow should seek to broaden the G-20's agenda to encompass political and security issues where it is a more considerable player. However, even with the potential expansion of the G-20 order of business, and retention of the Security Council in its present form, Russia's multilateral standing is weaker than it was. This is partly a function of the rise of China, India, and other emerging powers such as Brazil. But it is also a product of the more general diffusion of power across the globe and the proliferation of regional actors. In such an environment, no amount of subterfuge can mask Moscow's shrinking footprint. Russia's policymakers have therefore resorted to other methods to bolster its international position.

### The new elitism—the BRICS

The most important of these is a sustained campaign to build up the BRICS as an international body on a par with the G-8 and other Western-dominated institutions. This grouping brings together Brazil, Russia, India, China, and now South Africa on the basis of their supposed commonality as the world's leading emerging powers. Over the past few years, the Kremlin has led efforts to translate this artificial construct into something approaching a proper institutional framework, with its own organizing norms and structures. BRICS summits have become a regular feature in the calendar; in March 2013 Putin signed off on a "Concept of Participation of the Russian Federation in the BRICS";[16] and a BRICS New Development Bank (NDB) was established at the 2014 summit in Fortaleza, Brazil.[17]

Moscow's motives for promoting the BRICS, and related ideas such as the Russia-China-India foreign ministers' trilateral meeting, are fairly transparent. They boil down to the belief that "if you can't join them, beat them."

Russia is outnumbered and outweighed by the leading Western countries in the G-20 (and previously the G-8),[18] not to mention the World Bank and International Monetary Fund (IMF). In other organizations, such as the WTO, East Asia Summit (EAS), and even APEC (Asia-Pacific Economic Cooperation), which it hosted in 2012, it has negligible influence. Outside the UN Security Council there is no large international body where Russia plays a significant role. Indeed, many regional actors have more impact.

The BRICS format is an attempt to address this shortfall. It offers both exclusivity and a central role for Russia, regardless of the issues being discussed or the quality of its contributions. Ostensibly, it conforms to what Moscow calls "non-institutionalized mechanisms of global governance" and "network-based diplomacy."[19] In fact, these terms are misleading, since Putin himself has indicated that he would like to transform the BRICS from a dialogue forum into a "fully-fledged [that is, institutionalized] mechanism of strategic cooperation."[20] What is most important to the Kremlin, however, is the imagery of BRICS summitry. The public displays of bonhomie are important in reaffirming—to the leadership, the Russian public, and a wider international audience—that Russia naturally belongs to the global elite. Standing with China (in particular), India, and Brazil confers a success by association, conveying the message that Russia is part of the dynamic group of ascendant powers, in contrast to a decaying and discredited West.[21]

In a couple of respects the BRICS is an improvement on, although not a substitute for, the P5. Unlike the latter, it purports to mirror *contemporary* realities, above all the trend toward the "formation of a polycentric system," aka the multipolar order. It has become a symbol and an instrument for challenging the dominance of the West, replacing this with an alternative legitimacy—"a new model of global relations." There are calls to reform an "obsolete international financial and economic architecture" that has failed to factor in the increased economic power of the BRICS countries. There is the reaffirmation of "generally recognized principles and norms of international law," and rejection of "power politics and politics infringing on the sovereignty of other states"—in other words, Western-led moral interventionism. Despite protestations about its "non-bloc character and non-aggressive nature with regard to third parties," the BRICS for Moscow is all about countering the West in its various dimensions.

This leads to its second advantage over the P5—the absence of any Western representation. There is no risk that Russia will be overshadowed by the multidimensional power of the United States or the economic and normative influence of the Europeans. True, China has become the world's second-largest economy. But Moscow takes comfort in Sino-Russian likemindedness and Beijing's reticence in assuming international leadership. It consequently feels better able to manage proceedings. In the P5 it operates within very tight parameters. In the G-8 it was the odd one out in political and security deliberations, and excluded altogether from financial discussions. And in the G-20 it has little say in framing or implementing the agenda. But within the BRICS Russia can persuade itself that it really is a major player—setting the agenda, deciding the rules of the game, and controlling the outcomes.

The practical results of the BRICS process have, however, been unimpressive. Partly, this is because its artificiality is ill-suited to the untidy realities of international affairs. But it is also because it is a sideshow for Beijing, New Delhi, and Brasilia—a lot of pomp and circumstance, but with little substance.[22] Crucially, they do not subscribe to Moscow's principal rationale for the BRICS, namely, a consensus of the rest to counterbalance the United States. At best they see the group as a supplement to existing structures.[23] One of the few things the four original BRICS have in common is that the United States lies at the epicenter of their respective foreign policies. But while Moscow views interaction with Washington in zero-sum terms, it is a different story for the others. In the case of the Chinese, Xi Jinping's emphasis on a "new pattern of great power relations"[24] reveals an understanding that open strategic rivalry with the United States would be self-defeating, for no country has benefited more than China from U.S. leadership of the international system over the past two decades. As for India, the notion that it might make common cause with China against the United States is absurd. Whereas New Delhi's rapprochement with Washington is its most important strategic move of recent years, political and security relations with Beijing remain tense, notwithstanding their expanding economic ties.[25]

Moscow's dogged advocacy of the BRICS process highlights the disjunction between the two worlds, the perceptual and the actual, that frame its foreign policy. On the one hand, emphasizing the BRICS is consistent with the vision of a multipolar order in which the West is greatly weakened and the initiative has passed to the non-Western powers as a result of the "shift of global power to the East." On the other hand, the Kremlin's BRICS dream is stymied by all sorts of awkward realities: the disorderliness of international affairs; the lack of serious interest among other BRICS members; their reluctance to confront the United States; the thinness of political and normative likemindedness;[26] and different (and often competing) priorities. Putin's commitment to the institutional development of the BRICS is also open to question. While he would like to see a more cohesive approach vis-à-vis the United States, it is doubtful whether he would ever accept the codified rules, responsibilities, and constraints that govern bodies such as the EU. As a result of these tensions and contradictions, the story of Russia and the BRICS so far is one of aspiration over realism.

### The virtues and vices of regionalism

Where the Kremlin has shown greater pragmatism is in recognizing the importance of more effective pan-regional policies. Accordingly, it has invested considerable political and financial resources in developing the Customs Union, the Eurasian Economic Union (EEU),[27] and the Collective Security Treaty Organization (CSTO), while also maintaining a strong presence in the Shanghai Cooperation Organization (SCO). Such activism points to a heightened appreciation of the impact of regionalism and regional actors on Russian interests, as well as the sense that "global initiatives . . . no longer work in the modern world."[28]

At the same time, Moscow's approach bears the mark of Soviet pseudo-multilateralism. During the cold war, this was represented militarily by the Warsaw Pact, in trade and economic affairs by the Council for Mutual Economic Assistance (CMEA, or Comecon), and in political matters by the charade of "independent" Soviet republics acting as sovereign states in the United Nations.[29] In similar spirit the Kremlin views the Customs Union, the EEU, and the CSTO less as vehicles for solving regional problems than as instruments for promoting Russia's interests in the post-Soviet space. The Eurasian Union serves as an opposite pole of attraction to the economic and normative power of the EU and, increasingly, China,[30] while the CSTO performs much the same function vis-à-vis NATO. With both, the overarching goal is to reassert Russia's leading role in Eurasia.[31]

Although Russia does not always get its way, it dominates these organizations. Formally, decisions are reached on the basis of consensus, but in practice the consensus that matters is the one in Moscow. It is telling, for example, that in 2013 Russia sought to entice Ukraine to join the Customs Union by offering lower gas prices and other *bilateral* incentives to Kyiv. The CSTO Rapid Reaction Force (RRF) is a Russian-led and -equipped detachment, whose deployment is decided by Moscow with only minor input from other CSTO members.[32] And when the now defunct Eurasian Economic Community (EurAsEC)[33] offered Minsk a US$3 billion package to rescue the bankrupt Belarusian economy in the summer of 2011, this was a soft loan entirely "made in Moscow." The Russian government set the conditions of the loan, and reaped the benefits by forcing President Alexander Lukashenko to sell the remaining half of Belarus' national energy provider, Beltransgaz, to

Gazprom.[34] The line between the bilateral and the multilateral effectively disappeared.

Putin's approach toward regional multilateralism differs little in *intention* from that of the Communist Party of the Soviet Union. The differences are of degree and capacity. Moscow's pseudo-multilateralism is more subtle than in Soviet times, while its capacity to secure compliance from regional partners is also considerably reduced. Even under the relatively pro-Moscow regime of Viktor Yanukovych, Ukraine resisted joining the Customs Union, while weak states such as Kyrgyzstan and Tajikistan have exploited regional mechanisms to achieve a freedom of maneuver unimaginable when they were part of the USSR.[35] Such outcomes, however, are the product of circumstances on the ground, not of Moscow's conversion to multilateral ideals. On the contrary, Putin appears more committed than ever to effecting regional "integration" under Russian leadership.[36]

Consistent with this attitude, Moscow is somewhat ambivalent toward the SCO, the one truly multilateral organization in Eurasia. At various times Putin has looked to it as a counterweight to the American and NATO presence in Central Asia. This was the case at the SCO Astana summit in June 2005, when he was able to unite the other member-states in calling for a time limit on the U.S. base in Manas, Kyrgyzstan.[37] But more often than not he has been frustrated in his attempts to establish a geopolitical consensus on Russian terms.[38]

Indeed, the current is running in the opposite direction. Whereas a decade ago the SCO was dominated by a Sino-Russian tandem, today China is clearly the leading player within that organization. This reality is tacitly recognized by Moscow. It has sought to dilute Chinese influence by initiating the expansion of SCO membership to India and Pakistan,[39] and by blocking Beijing's attempts to establish an SCO Free Trade Zone.[40] More significant, it has shifted its primary focus to the Eurasian Union (in particular) and the CSTO—in other words, to organizations that are more pliant, and of which China is not a member.

## Russia and the Global Agenda

The Putin regime's approach to international institutions shapes its handling of substantive issues of regional and global governance. Under this broad rubric, there are five main areas: a new financial architecture; global trade; resource diplomacy; multilateral cooperative security; and international norms.

## A new financial architecture

The global economic downturn of 2008–12 pushed the discussion of a new financial architecture to the top of the international agenda. Although Moscow's initial reaction to the financial meltdown was that it was a Western crisis, such complacency soon gave way to the realization that Russia was more vulnerable than most to its effects. By early 2009, the leadership had started to beat the drum of financial reform, joining in calls to overhaul the Bretton Woods institutions (IMF, World Bank) and reduce dependence on the U.S. dollar as the base currency for international transactions.

Moscow's approach to global financial governance is, however, more instrumentalist than reformist. In fact, many of the changes being mooted are not necessarily to Russia's advantage—at least not in the short to medium term. For example, a general shift away from the U.S. dollar toward a basket of major currencies would devalue its still considerable holdings of U.S. treasury securities (US$86 billion in December 2014).[41] It is also questionable whether the ruble would be included in a basket of currencies if one were to be introduced. Likewise, a substantial increase in voting shares for emerging economies in the IMF and World Bank would favor China and India, not Russia. Indeed, its weight within these organizations could be diminished by institutional reform because its share of the global economy (3.3 percent in 2014) is set to decline.[42] Moscow knows, too, that Russia's fortunes depend less on financial reforms than on continuing demand for its oil, gas, and other natural resources. Like China, it has benefited greatly from international economic *imbalances* over the past decade. These have helped push commodity prices to record highs, vital to an economy that has become ever more reliant on resource exports.

If Russia has an economic interest in financial architecture, then it lies in restoring stability and predictability to the current system, not in encouraging radical change over which it would have little influence. In the global economy, Russia is predominantly a taker rather than setter of trends, and this would be especially so in a reformed system. It can pretend to be a significant player in the G-20 and in international financial institutions, but its impact in such forums is slight—and widely viewed as such.[43]

Consequently the principal drivers of Moscow's interest in "change" are geopolitical and normative: to challenge the West's post–cold war dominance of the international system and to renegotiate the terms of its engagement with the United States and Europe. Until relatively recently (2012–13), the difficulties suffered by the leading Western countries appeared to facilitate at least a partial realization of these aims. Putin lost few opportunities to contrast Russia's generally sound macroeconomic indices from 2009 with the lingering agony of the eurozone, and to draw a larger parable about Western irresponsibility and the flaws of democratic liberalism.[44]

But the pretense implicit in selling Russia as a twenty-first-century economic player has become unsustainable given the lack of structural reforms, an increasingly ugly business climate, and the onset of recession. The main themes today are import substitution and economic autarky, not Russia's transformation into a knowledge economy, or Moscow becoming an international financial center on a par with New York, London, Paris, and Hong Kong.[45] Russia's economic reputation has hit a new low, not only in the West, but also among emerging powers such as China, India, and Brazil. Few believe that it can make a worthwhile contribution to a new financial architecture and global rebalancing when its efforts at domestic modernization have been so unsuccessful.

### International trade

Nearly twenty years after first submitting its application, Russia finally entered the WTO in August 2012, the last major economy to do so. There were many reasons for the protracted delay, and Moscow was by no means entirely to blame. More than with any other applicant, Russia's path was strewn with non-trade obstacles. On several occasions, it seemed on the verge of completing negotiations when a security or political crisis would crop up to scupper the process.[46] It is also true that, as a large economy, Russia was held to higher standards than most.[47]

Nevertheless, the Russian government was primarily responsible for the slowness of the accession process. Some of its actions, such as Putin's decision in June 2009 that Russia would submit a joint Customs Union bid with Kazakhstan and Belarus instead of continuing with its individual application, were particularly unhelpful.[48] More problematic still was an equivocal attitude toward accession itself, which became a lightning rod for all sorts of anxieties about globalization, modernization, and the intrusiveness of supranational, rules-based regimes. (Unlike the P5, where it could exercise the veto, or the BRICS framework, which imposes no concrete obligations, the WTO makes rulings that its members must follow.) It did not help, either, that the Kremlin appeared to regard membership as a right rather than a privilege, and to believe that the organization needed Russia more than the other way round.[49]

Russian reservations about the WTO have only strengthened following accession. For Putin the obligations that come with membership are more than just an economic challenge. Over the past decade, he has built up his popular legitimacy by presiding over rising incomes and improved social stability in exchange for the allegiance or at least acquiescence of the population—the post-Soviet "social contract" referred to in chapter 1. Opening up the economy presents a conundrum. To achieve true competitiveness requires radical increases in labor productivity and may involve substantial layoffs in certain sectors.[50] This risks alienating core constituencies, such as blue-collar industrial workers. For many in the ruling elite, the likely political-social costs outweigh any modernizing dividend from WTO membership.[51] This is especially so given the speculative nature of World Bank estimates that membership could boost Russia's GDP by 3.3 percent over the medium term (seven to ten years).[52]

Putin, it seems, seeks the best of all worlds: dynamism without risk, growth along with social guarantees, and globalization mitigated by tight controls on competition—in other words, an economic analog of the "managed democracy" that has defined much of his presidency.[53] But in the new world disorder, such hopes are illusory. It is evident that WTO membership on its own will not bring about tangible benefits. As Clifford Gaddy has noted, the question is "whether Russia really will change in order to conform to the WTO rules, or whether it will bend or evade the rules."[54]

Almost immediately after WTO accession, the government introduced protectionist measures in a number of vulnerable sectors, including automobiles, textiles, and paper manufacturing. The 2012 decision to impose levies for recycling imported foreign cars aroused particular concern abroad for what it said about Russia's (lack of) commitment to meeting its WTO obligations.[55] More important, there is no sign of the major reforms—in corporate governance, the regulatory environment, and the rule of law—that membership is supposed to encourage.[56] On the contrary, the Ukraine crisis has strengthened autarkic tendencies. Moscow has responded to Western sanctions by suspending food imports from the EU, the United States, Australia, Canada, and Norway. While it hopes to make up some of the shortfall with imports from non-Western countries, this move also fits in with a larger intention to favor local production through import substitution policies.[57]

In lieu of an integrated approach to the WTO (and economic modernization), Moscow is pursuing a grab-bag of policies. At the rhetorical level it talks up Russia's credentials as a leading player in the international trading system. Tactically it uses the WTO as a mechanism for challenging the legality of hostile political actions, such as Western sanctions against Russian banks and energy companies.[58] And it has left the door ajar for commercial partnerships with the West in order to facilitate the transfer of advanced technology and know-how. The Kremlin hopes that if and when sanctions are relaxed or lifted, joint ventures with German, French, Japanese, and even American companies will soon pick up again.

But the most distinctive part of the Kremlin's approach to international trade is its quest to develop a distinct post-Soviet space in which Russia remains incontestably the dominant player. This amounts to an insurance policy. Should Russia's global terms of trade remain unfavorable (as a result, say, of a continuing slump in commodity prices), or its WTO obligations too onerous, it may always find refuge in its own, dedicated economic area. The Eurasian Economic Union serves this purpose. In addition to its geopolitical and normative rationale, it is a means of managing Russia's trade with post-Soviet neighbors—and achieving a level of influence and protection unattainable in larger forums, such as the WTO and APEC, where there are multiple (and stronger) actors.[59]

### Resource diplomacy

The tension between the demands of good international citizenship and the pull of national interests is nowhere more evident than in Russia's resource diplomacy. On the one hand, it is attempting to position itself as a pivotal player in regional and global energy security,[60] as well as a primary supplier of other essential resources, such as timber, non-ferrous metals, and water. This is important both for obvious economic reasons, and because the reliable supply of such commodities is the most concrete and accessible way of showcasing Russia as a major contributor to the global community. Natural resource security is, after all, a truly universal preoccupation.

On the other hand, Moscow does not want to loosen its grip on its chief instrument of influence on the Eurasian continent (and beyond). It is therefore unwilling to accept multilateral, rules-based constraints, which is the main reason why it has withdrawn from the Energy Charter Treaty.[61] For Putin Russia's vast reserves of oil and gas, and control of pipeline infrastructure, are strategic assets of the utmost importance.[62] Such advantages cannot be negotiated away or otherwise limited.

This is all the more so given the Russian economy's increasing reliance on natural resource exports. Today energy alone accounts for more than two-thirds of export revenue, half of federal budget revenue, and a quarter of GDP. Natural resources combined contribute nearly 80 percent of the value of Russian exports, a figure that rises further with Russia's two main trading partners, the EU (82 percent) and China (over 90 percent).[63] Russia's natural resources also have a crucial knock-on effect. Resource rents have become instrumental in bankrolling other, less fortunate sectors of the economy, such as manufacturing, not to mention the personal fortunes of the elite.[64]

There is a critical psychological dimension as well. As noted in chapter 1, much of the bullishness in Putin's foreign policy is the result of the boom in global oil and commodity prices from the early 2000s. The other side of the coin, however, is that this confidence is fragile—as became clear in the first year of the global financial crisis, when the price of Urals crude fell by two-thirds between July and December 2008. More recently, a further slump during the second half of 2014 has emerged as the most serious threat to the Putin regime, far more damaging than any Western sanctions. It is no surprise, then, that Moscow should view energy security through a predominantly national and competitive prism, rather than from an internationalist, global governance perspective.

This is especially apparent in Russia's gas relationships with Europe. Since the late 1960s Moscow has operated on the basis of long-term (fifteen- to twenty-year) agreements with European state energy companies on a take-or-pay basis.[65] These bilateral agreements have several important advantages for Russia: they are relatively simple to negotiate and to extend; they ensure predictability of demand; and they provide guaranteed revenue. In an uncertain world, such arrangements are more attractive than ever. Yet they are also becoming difficult to enforce. The U.S. shale revolution has created a ubiquitous market in LNG (liquefied natural gas), leading to downward pressure on global gas prices.[66] Regional gas hubs are developing, and over time a global spot market in gas may well emerge. And the Europeans have shown signs of greater unity and purpose. The EU's Third Energy Package, with its rules on the "unbundling" (separation) of gas production and distribution, has strengthened both its negotiating position *and* its confidence in dealings with Moscow.[67]

Putin feels threatened by such developments. The EU's new-found solidarity is unnerving, since it is by far Russia's largest gas market and will probably remain so for the next two decades, even if the Sino-Russian gas agreement of May 2014 (see chapter 5) is fully implemented. A united European front not only weakens Russia's bargaining position on individual supply contracts, but also its capacity to use energy as an instrument of geopolitical influence. Such considerations have become highly pertinent in light of the Ukraine crisis and the deterioration in Russia-EU relations.

To protect its geopolitical and commercial interests, Moscow has adopted various countermeasures. From time to time it has cut supply to selected post-Soviet countries, for example Ukraine and Moldova. It has actively undermined pipeline projects that seek to bypass its territory, such as the ill-starred Nabucco venture.[68] It has waged a determined campaign against the Third Energy Package, and opposed moves to achieve greater interconnectivity among EU member-states. It has tried to coopt major European customers, Germany foremost, by giving them direct access to gas through the Nordstream pipeline,[69] and by being more flexible in renegotiating take-or-pay agreements.[70] And it has taken steps to protect "strategic companies" from external investigations, such as the European Commission's anti-trust suit against Gazprom.[71] Most of all it has resurrected the specter of diverting Russian gas from Europe to Asia, encouraged by apparent breakthroughs in cooperation with China.

Such methods reveal that the Kremlin's resource diplomacy is overladen by multiple strategic, security, political, and psychological layers. Witness its reaction to the shale revolution. From the outset the Russian government has been in denial, responding with two mutually contradictory arguments. The first is that shale gas development is a speculative venture that will either not be a practical proposition for decades or is "a bubble about to burst."[72] The second argument, by contrast, emphasizes the environmental risks—the dangers posed by fracking, such as groundwater contamination and seismic disturbances.[73]

These claims have little to do with concern about global energy or environmental security, but are prompted by geopolitical and existential considerations. The shale revolution has implications not just for Russia's international influence, but also for the stability of the Putin regime. With diminishing gas and oil revenue, it would find it increasingly problematic to fund essential programs—pensions, public sector wages, housing, health, and education— and to retain the allegiance of a rent-seeking elite. It is therefore understandable that Putin should talk down the impact of shale gas on global markets, while describing it as a "very barbaric way of extracting mineral resources."[74]

Looking ahead, developments in the Arctic may suggest a possible way to reconcile Moscow's often conflicting objectives of international respectability, commercial profit, and geopolitical (and geoeconomic) advantage. Belying initial concerns, Russia has worked quite effectively with fellow Arctic countries, such as Norway. The 2010 Russian-Norwegian agreement delimiting the Barents Sea was a model of bilateral cooperation. It demonstrated that Russian policymakers are able to make pragmatic decisions that simultaneously serve national interests and abide by supranational rule-based regimes, such as the UN Convention on the Law of the Sea (UNCLOS).

But such happy outcomes are rare. The Barents Sea agreement benefited from unusually favorable conditions. Although Norway is a committed member of NATO, there were relatively few ulterior agendas or historical insecurities to exacerbate normal policy differences. (Even then, the Barents Sea agreement took more than forty years to negotiate, and has since been heavily criticized in Moscow.)[75] The situation could hardly be more different from

Russia's relations with central and eastern Europe, the United States, or the ex-Soviet republics. In these cases it has been virtually impossible to ignore the geopolitical baggage and to embrace an internationalist, positive-sum mindset—all the more so given events in Ukraine.

### Multilateral cooperative security

Much of Moscow's management of international security issues, such as strategic disarmament, missile defense, and NATO enlargement, is bound up with its relations with the United States, and will be discussed in chapter 6. Here the focus is on Russian perceptions of *multilateral* cooperative security as they relate to conflict management, counterterrorism, and WMD nonproliferation.

The Kremlin recognizes in principle that the global security agenda is evolving to take in new threats and challenges.[76] But this consciousness is nascent, and has had minimal impact on policymaking. Russia's history and strategic culture predispose it to think of security as overwhelmingly "hard" security. This bias is evident in good times and bad. At the height of the U.S.-Russia reset in 2009–10, the chief items of cooperative security were strategic disarmament, WMD nonproliferation and Iran, and the counterinsurgency in Afghanistan. Similarly, in the Sino-Russian partnership the main topics are strategic interaction vis-à-vis the United States, conflict management in the Middle East, instability in Central Asia,[77] and the threat of Islamist extremism in general. In stark contrast, human security issues such as poverty in Africa, climate change, and food and water scarcities barely feature in Russian elite (or public) discourse. There is little sense that they merit the expenditure of precious time and resources, especially when there are more pressing concerns at home and abroad.

There is a prejudice too against accepting that some of the new security issues, for example human-induced climate change, are real.[78] The Putin elite tends to regard this as a Western liberal invention, at best unproven, at worst a conspiracy to undermine growth in Russia and other emerging economies. Insofar as there is an interest, it is economic, not ecological or humanitarian. During the 1990s Russia benefited greatly from emissions trading as a result of the implosion of its industry from the late 1980s.[79] Today Moscow regards global warming in a generally positive light. Leaving aside Putin's flippant comment a few years ago that Russia could do with being a few degrees warmer, the government sees the melting of the Arctic ice pack and Siberian permafrost as opening up fresh possibilities for exploiting natural resources and developing alternative sea-lanes, such as the Northern Sea Route. There is little feeling of a downside. Even the increasing frequency of drought conditions in Russia, which in the summer of 2010 led to some of the worst fires in living memory, was considered more a quirk of nature than the result of global warming.[80] There was public anger, but this was directed at the authorities' inadequate response to a national emergency.

That said, Moscow is wary of being out of step with any international consensus that might emerge. It participates regularly in UN climate change conferences. It has made some of the right noises, such as a commitment to cut carbon dioxide emissions by 25 percent by 2020 (from 1990 levels).[81] It has adopted a generally low profile to avoid possible collateral damage in quarrels between Washington and Beijing, and between developed and developing economies. It also promotes natural gas as the most practical clean energy option—far less polluting than coal, much easier to supply on a large scale than renewables, and where Russia possesses significant comparative advantages.[82]

## The security issues that matter

While Moscow regards climate change and global poverty as nonsecurity matters of secondary importance, there are security priorities where it identifies both the need and the opportunity to cooperate with others. The common denominator is that they are all areas where Russia can advance its national interests while contributing—and being seen to contribute—to international public goods.

*Conflict management.* This is a central preoccupation of Russian policymakers for several reasons. It is high-profile, typically involving the major powers: the United States, leading Europeans, and, increasingly, non-Western countries such as China. As such, it is seen as helpful in projecting Russia's great power identity—for example, in the Middle East through the P5+1 negotiations on Iran's nuclear program and in Northeast Asia through the currently suspended Korean Six-Party talks.

Russia's leaders understand security in the first instance as the absence, or at least management, of conflict. At the most basic level, security means defending against foreign invasion and preserving the country's territorial integrity. This priority has regained prime importance following events in Ukraine and the crisis in relations between Russia and the West. Although Moscow does not yet identify the United States or NATO as direct military threats, they are viewed as dangers in the broader sense—against Russia's sovereignty, its geopolitical position, and the stability of the Putin system itself.

Conflict management is also a top priority because it is intimately linked to developments in the post-Soviet space—the so-called "frozen conflicts" in Abkhazia and South Ossetia, Nagorno-Karabakh, and Transnistria. In these cases, the combination of geographical proximity, historical antecedents, and acute geopolitical sensitivities provides an immediacy that compels the constant attention of decisionmakers. They encourage Moscow to claim a right of intervention in the affairs of its neighbors, both to protect Russian national interests and to promote itself as a responsible regional actor. Its participation in the Minsk process to mediate the conflict in Ukraine is only the latest example of its efforts to cloak self-interest with the wider legitimacy of good international citizenship.

*Combating terrorism.* Countering terrorism is important to the Kremlin, although it conceives of this somewhat differently than Western governments. During the Bush years, Moscow never subscribed to Washington's "global war on terror," whereby other players, such as Russia, performed essentially supportive and subordinate roles to U.S. policy.[83] Its perspective on terrorism was—and remains—essentially local and regional, centering on the North Caucasus and the threat posed by the Taliban to Central Asian security. It fears that the secular authoritarian regimes of the region could be destabilized, leading in turn to the radicalization of Muslims in the Russian Federation itself.[84] Consistent with this view, it is critical of American attempts to reach an accommodation with more moderate elements of the Taliban. It believes that no such moderates exist, and that a negotiated settlement based on this premise would be disastrous.[85]

The Russian government is also inclined to view the problem of terrorism instrumentally. Whenever terrorist incidents have occurred in the West, for example at the 2013 Boston Marathon, it has seized the opportunity to legitimate the harsh handling of its own insurgency in the North Caucasus. By internationalizing what is essentially an indigenous problem with a few foreign elements (such as "Wahhabi" fighters), Putin seeks Western endorsement not just of his position on terrorism, but also of his overall approach to governing Russia. In a similarly opportunistic spirit, prominent voices in Moscow used the January 2015 attack on the *Charlie Hebdo* office in Paris to inveigh against Western permissiveness, and to vindicate the conduct of Russian foreign policy.[86]

*WMD nonproliferation.* This matters to Moscow mainly because of its connection to other priorities, such as conflict management and countering missile defense. This is not to say that it cares nothing about North Korea's nuclear weapons program, or the potential for Iran to become a nuclear weapons state. But such worries are secondary to fears about American missile defense deployment in Europe, a possible Israeli strike against Tehran, and escalating tensions in Northeast Asia. The Kremlin does not view the threat of WMD proliferation as urgent, notwithstanding claims from time to time that a nuclear-weapons Iran would find it easier to hit Russian rather than American (or European) targets.[87] Moscow sees U.S. missile defense plans, by contrast, as a tangible and immediate menace, threatening to undermine one of the pillars of Russian national security: the principle of strategic parity. The cure in this case is seen as definitely worse than the disease. (It was symptomatic that Foreign Minister Sergei Lavrov should react to the reining in of Iranian nuclear activities in late 2013 by arguing that this had removed the rationale for missile defense deployment.)[88]

The thrust of Russian policy has, therefore, been to find ways of containing international tensions arising out of WMD proliferation, and to extract geopolitical capital where possible, rather than tackling the problem of proliferation itself. Putin showed little concern about a sarin attack against the Damascus suburb of Ghouta in August 2013 until it became clear that the United States and key European allies (France, the United Kingdom) might use this to justify military intervention against the Assad regime. The subsequent elimination of chemical weapons stockpiles was a desirable outcome, but it was hardly the main game. Likewise, if Tehran could be persuaded to abandon its nuclear weapons ambitions, Moscow would be relieved—but not because this would eliminate the hypothetical possibility of an Iranian missile attack on Russia. The more important point is that it would lower the security temperature in the Middle East, while enabling Russia to demonstrate (and leverage) its credentials as an indispensable player in the region.[89]

### Opposites don't attract

Moscow's concerns about conflict management, terrorism, and WMD proliferation should in theory offer plenty of scope for active cooperation between Russia and the West. But in reality this cooperation has been disappointing even in relatively good times. Western critics accuse Russia of manipulating conflicts in its neighborhood, downplay its contribution in Afghanistan, and view it as a generally obstructive presence in relation to Syria.[90] When Russian assistance is forthcoming, it is seen as narrowly self-interested, time-limited, and conditional.[91]

Much of this failure is a by-product of the chronic mistrust between Russia and the United States. But there are other causes as well, the most important being a lack of agreement over objectives, methods, and outcomes. Moscow and Western capitals speak of common threats and challenges, but beneath the surface of such platitudes they have very different things in mind. This is true not only in counterterrorism and counterproliferation, but also in their divergent readings of the sources of security (and insecurity). Most obviously, the United States and the European Union believe that democratization is the key to long-term stability in Eurasia. The Kremlin, however, looks to local authoritarian regimes as bulwarks against radical Islamism *and* Western liberal influences, which it regards as equally subversive.

Moscow also identifies an interest in sometimes manipulating conflicts. For example, far from wishing to reconcile the Abkhaz and South Ossetians with Tbilisi—admittedly, a near-impossible task—it seeks the opposite. It knows that as long as Georgia is dogged by such unresolved conflicts, it stands little chance of NATO membership, and will always be susceptible to Russian leverage. More recently, the Ukraine crisis has shown that when faced with the choice of influence or security, the Kremlin will opt for the former. Indeed, it sees this as a false choice, since it cannot conceive of true security in the neighborhood separate from a dominant Russian influence.

The cases of Georgia and Ukraine highlight a larger problem in balancing geopolitical and security interests. This is apparent even where there has been meaningful cooperation between Russia and the West, as in Central Asia. Moscow knows that the United States is the only force capable of restraining the Taliban from expanding its influence throughout the region. However, a strong American presence runs counter to every geopolitical instinct of the Russian elite. The result of this contradiction is policy confusion. Russia supports the Northern Distribution Network (NDN), but pressured Kyrgyzstan into terminating the American lease on the Manas base.[92] It has talked up cooperation with NATO in Afghanistan, and criticized the imposition of "artificial" deadlines for the withdrawal of alliance forces.[93] But almost in the same breath it claims that NATO has outstayed its welcome. It blames the Americans for the boom in heroin trafficking, yet blocks Washington's efforts to boost the counternarcotic capabilities of the Central Asian republics.[94] And in January 2013 it terminated its own counternarcotics agreement with the United States, as part of a package of retaliatory measures against the passing of the Magnitsky Act.[95]

In short, there is no consistent or coherent Russian approach toward cooperative security, but a series of unconnected actions, driven largely by instinct and opportunism. Unsurprisingly, the outcomes have been poor, not only for international security but for Russia as well. Putin aspires to position it as a leading player in setting and managing a new global security agenda. And he has shown considerable aptitude in seizing on Western policy shortcomings over Syria and Ukraine. Yet Russia's real contribution to problem solving in international security remains very modest.[96] Moreover, there is little sign of positive change. Ensconced in its perceptual world, the Kremlin believes that Russia can have it all—enhanced security, geopolitical influence, and global standing—without the need for any serious rethinking of its approach.

*International normative regimes*

One criterion of Russia's commitment to global governance is the extent to which it accepts the legitimacy of supranational or universal norms. Formally there is no quarrel with the principle of universality, as various government statements make clear. In practice it is a different story. Although Russia is a signatory to multiple international agreements and conventions, including the UN Charter, the Universal Declaration of Human Rights, and the Helsinki Accords, it has consistently resisted attempts to enforce the norms enshrined in these documents. Its approach to international normative regimes rests instead on four broad "principles": (1) opposing moral interventionism; (2) the "primacy of international law"; (3) limited sovereignty; and (4) changing the rules of global governance.

*Opposing moral interventionism.* Moscow's resistance to implementing universal norms is most apparent in this area. Importantly, its negative attitude rests on a solid consensus within the ruling elite, one that dates back to the early Yeltsin years. In 1995 the Russian government condemned the U.S. military action that prevented further massacres of the Bosnian Muslims; in 1999 it was even more vigorous in attacking the legitimacy of the NATO operation over Kosovo; and in 2003 it joined with France and Germany in opposing Washington's decision to invade Iraq. Over the same period it has emasculated various multilateral sanctions regimes—against Slobodan Milošević in Serbia, Saddam Hussein in Iraq, and Mahmoud Ahmadinejad in Iran.

It should be acknowledged that Russia has sometimes had good cause to act in this way. Along with many other countries, it was right to question the motivations, legality, and wisdom of the Iraq war. Likewise, it is hard to disagree that the application of international norms is at best uneven, and reeks of double standards. And it is true that sanctions often do not achieve their intended purposes and can cause considerable collateral damage to the innocent.

But these objections—sometimes well-founded, sometimes less so—are secondary to Moscow's main point, which is that it is up to individual governments to decide how they rule their peoples and interpret international norms within their own countries. It is not for outsiders, least of all a discredited West, to determine what is and is not moral. This standpoint originates in a long Westphalian tradition, but has been reinforced by Russia's post-Soviet experience. Conservatives and liberals alike blame Western involvement for the economic difficulties and foreign policy setbacks of the 1990s. In the eyes of many, these were not merely the unfortunate outcomes of bad advice, but were part of a larger scheme to take advantage of Russian weakness after the demise of the Soviet Union.[97] Consequently they reject the notion that outsiders may lecture Russia about good governance—and they extend this view to embrace the doctrine of noninterference in general.

Moscow has demonstrated tactical flexibility from time to time. Notwithstanding its dislike of the "responsibility to protect" (R2P), it formally accepted its doctrinal legitimacy,[98] and even tolerated its limited application. On Libya it did not veto UN Security Council Resolution 1973, while President Medvedev voiced unusually harsh criticism of the Gaddafi regime.[99] It was able to finesse this compliance because the main thrust for intervention came from the Arab League, France, and the United Kingdom, rather than the United States. The earlier decision by the Arab League to support a no-fly zone conferred a wider legitimacy that had been absent in relation to Bosnia, Kosovo, and Iraq. Arab League involvement allowed Russia to portray itself as a responsible international power on terms other than those dictated by the West—a vital face-saving consideration. By abstaining it was able simultaneously to appear cooperative, signal its reservations about military action, reinforce a distinct but constructive Russian identity in the Middle East, distance itself from a deeply unpopular regime, and sustain the reset with Washington.

Yet contrary to the hopes of some Western politicians, this flexibility did not mark a philosophical shift. The opposite has turned out to be true. Moscow has used the Libyan experience to highlight both the disingenuousness of the West and the perils of outside intervention in the name of universal values. It has accused NATO of grossly exceeding its mandate through the "illegal" pursuit of regime change.[100] It contrasts the relative stability that prevailed under Gaddafi to the anarchy of today's Libya, the spread of Islamist extremism across the Middle East, and the growing threats to regional and international security.[101] It notes that in several Arab Spring countries—Tunisia, Libya, Egypt—popular revolt that began as a predominantly liberal, middle-class phenomenon was subsequently taken over by Islamists. And it warns of a similar scenario in Syria should the Assad regime fall—an argument that has been strengthened as a result of the spectacular gains made by Islamic State (IS) forces in Iraq and eastern Syria during 2014.[102]

For the Kremlin Libya exemplified Western hypocrisy. The imbroglio over Syria offers another, starker example. The United States and the leading Europeans speak of universal values and human rights, but viewed from Moscow their policies are driven by geopolitical and commercial interests.[103] Western capitals call for the removal of Assad, yet turn a blind eye to political repression in Saudi Arabia and Bahrain, both of which happen to be key U.S. allies.[104] Russian resentment is compounded by the West's lack of squeamishness in cooperating with authoritarian regimes in the post-Soviet neighborhood, such as Kazakhstan, Azerbaijan, and Uzbekistan.

*The "primacy of international law."* Many Western commentaries have depicted Russia's conduct over Syria, and foreign policy more generally, as motivated by the worst kind of realpolitik.[105] Syria is a major arms market; Russia retains useful, if modest, naval facilities in the port of Tartus; and Damascus is its closest ally in the Middle East. These are all influential considerations, yet they tell only part of the story. Unlikely though it may seem, Moscow's position is founded on principle—that of the "primacy of international law."

Its conception of this, however, differs radically from that of most Western governments. The Kremlin interprets international law as, essentially, the body of rules and conventions that govern relations between the major powers and, through them, smaller states as well. One such rule is that of noninterference, except in cases like Mali where the host government has specifically requested outside intervention, or in the post-Soviet neighborhood, where Russia's vital interests are at stake (see below). In instances such as Syria, however, the original principle applies: foreign powers may only intervene with the endorsement of the UN Security Council, in other words, *with Russia's consent.*[106]

Moscow's frequent resort to "international law" is motivated by a mixture of self-interest, moral relativism, and basic instinct. At the most existential level it reflects opposition to the idea that grassroots democracy movements may be considered legitimate sources of regime change. The Putin elite fears that the democratic contagion of the Arab Spring and Ukraine could, if unchecked, spread to Russia and other parts of the post-Soviet space. Appealing to "international law" is therefore of a piece with the consolidation of domestic order.

As noted earlier, the Kremlin has become increasingly resistant to the perceived tyranny of a Western-imposed moral code. Emphasizing the primacy of international law has consequently become synonymous with the assertion of Russian sovereignty and independence. It does not necessarily mean abiding by the decisions of, say, the European Court on Human Rights, but sometimes entails just the opposite. For the highest law is the one that protects the inviolability of Russia's rights in the face of external "interference" and domestic subversion.

Geopolitically, international law *à la Russe* serves to restrain the exercise of American power. It is critical that the main institution for implementing its principles is not the International Criminal Court, of which Russia (along with the United States and China) is not a member, and whose decisions Moscow cannot control, but the UN Security Council, where it retains significant influence. Putin's understanding of international law is consistent with, and indispensable to, his vision of a multipolar order. The "law" here brings a measure of stability and predictability to a disorderly world.

*Limited sovereignty and the Ukrainian exception.* This raises the question of how the Kremlin is able to square the contradiction between its advocacy of national sovereignty and its annexation of Crimea and destabilization of eastern Ukraine—not to mention its interference in other ex-Soviet republics, such as Moldova and Georgia.

There is no integrated intellectual rationale to such behavior. Instead, the contradiction between theory and practice is managed through various devices. One is flat denial. The conflict in eastern Ukraine is portrayed as a civil war between the local Russian-speaking population and Kyiv, while the Kremlin rebuts Ukrainian and Western claims of Russian military involvement.

Another, more heartfelt, justification is to argue that Ukraine and Russia are not separate countries, but have been intertwined for centuries.[107] The implication is that the usual rules therefore do not apply. Since Ukraine is not a "real" country, the issue is not Russian interference, but fraternal support— a view founded in the Brezhnevian concept of limited sovereignty. This is discussed in the next chapter, but suffice it to say here that Moscow operates on the premise that international law applies only to properly independent entities. Ahistorical creations like Ukraine and other ex-Soviet republics are seen neither to merit nor to require such protection. That "obligation" falls to Russia.

This segues into the belief that instability and conflict in Ukraine affect Russia's most vital interests, including its national security. No responsible government in Moscow can afford to ignore developments in such an important neighbor—especially when the United States and European Union have conspired to overthrow its legitimately elected government. For the Kremlin their actions epitomize the depth of Western hypocrisy when it comes to observing international law.

Finally, on a narrowly legalistic level the Kremlin has given itself an out by claiming the right of humanitarian intervention on behalf of Russian expatriates, wherever they may be. To this purpose it has issued tens of thousands of passports to residents in neighboring territories and countries: Abkhazia, South Ossetia, Transnistria, Ukraine. In the 2008 Georgia war Russia claimed a right of intervention on these grounds. At the time of writing (spring 2015) it has yet to exploit this resource to justify a large-scale, official deployment of Russian troops in Ukraine. But the option remains open.

*Changing the rules of global governance.* The contrasting cases of Libya, Syria, and Ukraine highlight the particularities in Russian attitudes toward global governance. There is acceptance that this cannot simply be dismissed as an artificial Western construct. Accordingly, the Russian leadership has become more calibrated in its responses. It will almost invariably oppose external military intervention. But it also favors softer methods in defense of the sovereign rights of nation-states. These include tactical partnerships with supposedly like-minded countries, such as China, India, and Brazil; playing on the doubts of key Western players, such as Germany (over Libya and Syria);[108] using the UN and other multilateral mechanisms to mediate conflict, thereby postponing the imposition of punitive measures;[109] and reinforcing regional solidarity through organizations such as the CSTO, EEU, and SCO.

Throughout all this, however, one recurrent theme has emerged from the Kremlin: the management of international affairs can no longer be imposed on the basis of norms decided and enforced by the West. By their actions the United States and its European partners have forfeited any moral superiority they ever had. If there is to be global governance, then it must reflect the realities of a post-American century. This means, above all, a much enhanced role for the non-Western powers. Decisionmaking must be collective and equal. And it should also be somewhat exclusive, limited to the big players acting in concert.

The Putin regime's vision of global governance allows for a significant, but supporting, role for multilateral organizations. Their purpose is to provide a reliable institutional framework within which the major powers can manage the world. They are emphatically not there to democratize international politics, other than in the narrow sense of devolving decisionmaking from the United States to other centers in the "polycentric system," including Russia.

Global governance, as viewed from Moscow, entails rules that are at once more flexible *and* more binding than those of the American-led system of the past two decades. The flexibility lies in the lack of prescriptiveness regarding the domestic governance of states, which is the business of legitimate national governments. However, the norms of *international* behavior are taken as binding. Neither the United States nor any other country has the right to act solely on the basis of its national interests (let alone Western liberal values). They must abide by the rules of the central coordinating mechanism that regulates international relations—in other words the UN Security Council.

## Global Governance and the New World Disorder

How then does the Kremlin's vision of global governance tally with the realities of the new world disorder? One should start by admitting that it is not without some basis. The enormous human and financial costs of the conflicts in Iraq and Afghanistan,[110] the immorality of some of the West's actions in the conduct of these wars (Guantánamo, extraordinary rendition, Abu Ghraib), and the unsatisfactory outcomes of external intervention in Libya have severely undermined the case for supranational action, particularly when it involves military measures. These difficulties have not only discredited humanitarian intervention among a growing number of non-Western nations, but also exposed the weaknesses of American and European decisionmaking. The alacrity with which Obama seized on Putin's offer to intercede with the Syrians over chemical weapons in September 2013 suggests that Russia, rather than the West, may be on "the right side of history" in opposing moral interventionism—a position in which it is supported by China and India.

Yet moral interventionism is only one aspect of a much bigger picture. Global governance is about establishing and implementing broader principles of international conduct, and prosecuting a policy agenda that corresponds to twenty-first-century realities. It is here that the Putin concept of Russia as a global actor has shown itself to be inadequate.

The most serious weakness is that it is rooted in an idealized vision of the past, a revamped Concert of Great Powers, rather than looking to a new model of international relations that reflects the changing dynamics of power and influence in our time. The world may not be flat, as Thomas Friedman has claimed,[111] but the days of major powers running global affairs are gone. The real lesson from the fiascos in Iraq, Afghanistan, and Syria is not the decline of U.S. power, but the inability of *any* power (or powers) to direct positive change beyond its borders. Moscow is no more able to dictate to Damascus, Tehran, or Kyiv than Washington is to Jerusalem, Cairo, or Kabul. The "end of followership" is apparent everywhere. The Kremlin's construct of multipolar or polycentric governance ignores the extent to which international society has become so much more democratic and (in the Hobbesian sense) anarchic.

Another shortcoming of Putin's conception of global governance is that it is mired in a decidedly old Americacentric obsession. Moscow asserts that the era of American dominance is over, but continues to take the United States as the prime reference point not just for Russian foreign policy, but for international politics more generally. Regional and global governance has become reduced, in many instances (Central Asia, Iran, Syria, Ukraine), to an extension of the U.S.-Russia relationship. "Good" governance has come to be defined by a diminished American role and status, while "bad" governance is identified with American "unilateralism." The irony, of course, is that U.S. policy setbacks have not resulted in gains for Russia, but often just the opposite. This is especially true in central Eurasia, but it also applies to other regions, such as the Middle East and Northeast Asia.

The Kremlin's great power view of the world ensures that it continues to focus on traditional foreign policy priorities: disarmament and defense, international crisis management, geopolitical power projection, and the preservation of spheres of influence. It pays lip service to the emergence of new challenges, such as economic rebalancing, resource management, and cooperative security. But in practice Moscow treats these as subsidiary manifestations of more old-fashioned problems. Thus rebalancing is primarily a stick to challenge the economic and moral leadership of the West; resource diplomacy is oriented toward maximizing geopolitical advantages; and cooperative security is about maintaining a privileged status in the international firmament, and reinforcing the legitimacy of the Putin system.

There is no objective reason why Russia should not be a substantial contributor to global governance. Despite its troubles since the fall of the Soviet Union, it retains formidable resources: vast territorial reach, permanent membership in the UN Security Council, a pivotal position as a supplier of energy and other natural resources, a large and well-educated population, and a huge nuclear arsenal. Some of these trumps are less important than they used to be, but they are still significant.

But potential is one thing, lasting influence quite another. Under Putin, Russia has demonstrated that it retains real preventative powers. There is no doubting its capacity to make life difficult for others, whether it is the United States, the Europeans, or post-Soviet neighbors. There is also little question about its inclination to react vigorously to perceived provocations. The task, though, is to achieve something more than these negative outcomes, to move from an obsolete view of the international system and old "rights" of dubious validity and become instead a leading player in global problem solving.[112]

# four
# A Postmodern Empire

Here begins our tale. The empire, long divided, must unite; long united, must divide. Thus it has ever been.

ROMANCE OF THE THREE KINGDOMS, ATTRIBUTED TO LUO GUANZHONG, FOURTEENTH CENTURY CE

The Putin regime's handling of relations with the former Soviet republics represents the supreme test of its willingness to adapt Russian foreign policy to the circumstances of the new world disorder. It goes to the heart of one of the most critical questions of national identity, namely, Russia's evolution from empire into modern nation-state. How far is the Kremlin able to conceive of Russia in post-imperial terms, and to recognize its one-time possessions as sovereign, independent states?

There are broadly two schools of thought in this debate. The first argues that a ruling elite steeped in Soviet and Tsarist strategic culture is incapable of changing its view of the former republics. This elite might realize the difficulty of physically reconstituting the empire, but it nevertheless retains the conviction that Russia has a timeless right of ownership over the post-Soviet space[1]—a space that it has variously described as a "zone of special interests," regions of "privileged interests,"[2] and "regions that are traditionally important to us."[3] The military interventions in Georgia in 2008 and Ukraine in 2014 prove that Putin is committed to a "gathering of the Russian lands," and to reasserting Moscow's broader hegemony across Eurasia.[4]

By contrast, others claim that Russia has abandoned virtually all imperial pretensions, even while it continues to see itself as a "continental great power."[5] Not only is there no desire to rebuild the Soviet Union, but there is little interest even in exercising indirect control over the former constituent republics, except in a purely defensive sense—to protect Russian interests from diverse geopolitical, security, and normative threats. Viewed through this lens, Moscow's actions in Georgia and Ukraine were a natural and inevitable response to NATO enlargement and the overthrow of Viktor Yanukovych, respectively. But generally the ex-Soviet republics have proved far more trouble than they are worth, bleeding Russia dry, damaging its international reputation, and frequently undermining its interests. The Kremlin understands, moreover, that its prospects of pursuing a successful imperial agenda are slim to nonexistent.[6]

Neither of these explanations fully captures the tensions and contradictions in Moscow's approach to the post-Soviet space. Accordingly, this chapter puts forward a third thesis—that of Russia as a postmodern empire, in which many of the physical features of empire have disappeared, but where the imperial spirit is still present and even resurgent. It argues that Putin is not interested in reestablishing the USSR (or the Tsarist empire). Notwithstanding his claims that Ukraine and Kazakhstan are artificial creations, old-style imperial dominion remains an unattractive proposition, fraught with political risk and economically crippling. But there is also an enduring reluctance to recognize the erstwhile Soviet republics as genuinely sovereign, or to regard Western political and security involvement in the post-Soviet space as legitimate. The Russian government uses different terminology and methods these days, but its overarching objectives have scarcely changed. They are strategic, economic, and normative leadership in post-Soviet Eurasia; preserving a power relationship over the ex-Soviet republics; and the marginalization of outside—especially Western—interests and influence.

## Understandings of Empire

It is important to establish what is meant by "empire" or "imperial mindset." Empire can signify many things. We are accustomed to thinking of it as something physical, characterized by the projection of hard power, and expansionist in spirit. Yet there are other conceptions of empire that are no less valid. For example, the Australian Sinologist Ross Terrill describes the "New Chinese Empire" of the early twenty-first century as an introspective entity, uninterested in territorial expansion. To Terrill China's imperial mindset is defined above all by an innate sense of empire, a historical-civilizational phenomenon that has an identity beyond that of a nation-state and that is equipped with a whole edifice of supporting mechanisms and myths.[7]

The classical, predominantly Western genre of empire has become extinct. Not only has the USSR disintegrated, but so have the British, French, German, and other European empires, while there has been no Asian exemplar since Japan's crushing defeat in World War II. Even the United States, the dominant power of the last two decades, bears little resemblance to the empires of the nineteenth or mid-twentieth centuries. For all its preponderant military and economic power, it has rarely set out to conquer territories, and those that it has annexed have, with few exceptions, been quickly decolonized.

But if the traditional empire has disappeared, the same cannot be said of its postmodern successor. This type is characterized by indirect control rather than direct rule, and prefers to employ economic and cultural means instead of blunter military or political instruments. It is a version of empire tailored to a post-imperial era in international politics, when it is rarely acceptable to speak of such things except in a pejorative sense. It aims for the best of all worlds: enduring influence and power, but with a minimum of responsibility.

Such thinking underpins contemporary Russian understandings. It is obvious to most of the political elite that the Soviet Union cannot be put back together, at least not in the form in which it once existed. However, if the empire in its physical manifestation has ended, then the *idea of empire* remains very much alive.

It is characterized, first, by a sense of entitlement toward the former Soviet republics, arising from perceptions of a shared history, civilization, and language, as well as of Russia's strategic imperatives in an unstable regional and global environment. This attitude is more muted and less transparent than in the past; Moscow accepts that it cannot simply command. It is also more variegated. There is a far greater sense of entitlement vis-à-vis Ukraine than, say, the Baltic states. Indeed, Russian policymakers have found it relatively easy to view the latter through a post-imperial prism, largely because they were late annexations to the Soviet Union, had previously been part of the European mainstream since the Middle Ages, and are members of NATO and the EU.

Elsewhere in the post-Soviet space, however, Russia's imperial spirit survives in the belief that it is more than just another external player—or ex-empire. The USSR may have broken up more than twenty years ago, but many Russians still struggle to accept its former republics as independent countries. They see instead a bunch of quasi-states—politically primitive, economically feeble, and vulnerable to foreign intrigues, and whose only common denominator is their close relationship with, and dependence on, Russia. There is consequently an implicit (and often explicit) expectation that they will be sensitive to its interests, and that Moscow will remain involved in their affairs.

A second important indication of a continuing imperial spirit is the view that other countries—especially major powers—cannot treat the post-Soviet space as a part of the world like any other. Just as the Kremlin expects the former Soviet republics to factor Russian interests into their decisionmaking, so it demands the same of external actors. In this connection, the use of the term "space" (*prostrantsvo*) in Russian discourse is revealing. Moscow's primary goal is not so much the development of close ties with the republics, but control of the strategic space in which they are situated. While outsiders may engage in the region—something that cannot be prevented anyway—they should respect that this is *Russia's space*, and tailor their economic and especially security involvement accordingly.[8] The tensions that have arisen as a result of the EU's Eastern Partnership (EaP) program underline this point. Brussels speaks of a Common Neighborhood to its east and Russia's west, whereas for Moscow the neighborhood is anything but common; the Europeans (and others) are there on sufferance.

Third, a feeling for empire is apparent in the related idea of the post-Soviet space as a buffer zone. There is a security complex here that goes beyond the usual proprietorial instincts. At the most emotional level, it takes the form of a protracted hangover in response to the collapse of the USSR and the end of superpower status. More concretely, it is a reaction to the loss of empire and geopolitical influence in central and eastern Europe. And in its most immediate guise it is a reflex against NATO and EU eastward enlargement and other Western actions, such as missile defense, that are seen to target Russia.

These considerations coalesce to ensure that Moscow remains allergic to the possibility that the ex-Soviet republics may align themselves with another power against Russia. This emerged most clearly in its determined efforts to derail Ukraine's Association Agreement negotiations with the EU in 2013, and its military response to the Maidan revolution. But it has been a recurring theme throughout Putin's presidency, and particularly since the 2004 Orange Revolution. In 2008, for example, the (remote) prospect of NATO membership for Georgia and Ukraine was used as an excuse for the escalation of tensions with Tbilisi, and the onset of war. At a minimum Moscow aspires to a "Finlandization-plus" arrangement, in which the former Soviet republics have closer political and military ties to Russia than to any other country or group. (The three Baltic states are a partial exception to the rule: as members of NATO and the EU they have already gone over to the other side, although their continuing vulnerability makes them an attractive target for Kremlin pressure.)[9]

The notion of a buffer has also acquired a normative dimension—that of a *cordon sanitaire*. Since the color revolutions in Georgia and Ukraine in 2003–04, the Kremlin has committed itself to opposing the influx of Western liberal ideas. It regards the post-Soviet space as a forward defense area for authoritarian values, whose consolidation enhances Russia's political and social stability. Such thinking has been reinforced as a result of the anti-Putin protests in 2011–12 and the Ukrainian revolution. The emphasis on the civilizational and normative dimension of the Eurasian Union not only reflects the belief in a common culture and history (see below), but also stems from political calculation.

Fourth, the notion of empire carries powerful connotations of cultural identification. There are parallels here with Chinese concepts of a wider nation, in that "Russian-ness" is not limited to citizens living in the Russian Federation. Moscow has stepped up its efforts to engage with expatriates living in Europe, America, and especially the former Soviet Union. In the last case, there is a strong practical motivation. By granting dual nationality and Russian passports to residents in Abkhazia, South Ossetia, Transnistria, and now parts of Ukraine, Moscow arrogates to itself the right of direct intervention whenever it chooses.

But there is more to cultural identification than such maneuvers would suggest. When Foreign Minister Sergei Lavrov speaks of "civilizational commonality,"[10] he is articulating the popular view that post-Soviet Eurasia represents a single cultural space, with shared traditions, values, and understandings. Putin's famous description of the collapse of the USSR as the greatest geopolitical catastrophe of the twentieth century revealed not only regret at its strategic and security consequences, but also the conviction that it was a wholly unnatural event.[11] Moscow therefore seeks to realize a *mission civilisatrice*. Russian TV and radio broadcasts to the ex-Soviet republics have increased dramatically since the 1990s, and organizations such as RT and Russkii Mir actively promote Russia as the cultural and normative hub of Eurasia.[12]

Finally, the idea of empire is evident in its economic dimension. In 2003 Anatoly Chubais, one of the architects of Russia's transition to market in the 1990s, put forward the notion of a "liberal empire." This empire would be different from previous incarnations in Russian and world history in that it was defined not by territorial extent or traditional power projection, but by economic influence.[13] Two things are striking about Chubais's concept. It originated from a man of strong liberal credentials, in other words, an unlikely candidate to articulate an imperial vision *of any kind*.[14] Equally noteworthy is that Chubais's emphasis on economic leadership has, somewhat accidentally, become part of the new conservative orthodoxy.

Notwithstanding recent actions, Putin has not demonstrated any particular commitment to restoring a physical empire, even one limited to a Slavic core of Russia, Ukraine, and Belarus. Instead, he has prioritized the tightening of trade links with individual republics and regional economic cooperation through bodies such as the Eurasian Economic Union (EEU) and previously the Customs Union. This reflects a broader, if still nascent, shift from a purely entitlement-driven view of the post-Soviet space to one that recognizes the value of appealing to the concrete interests of the ex-Soviet republics, or rather their elites.

Ultimately, the Kremlin hopes for an empire in which Russia would continue to exercise a dominant influence, but no longer bear a costly imperial burden.[15] It would not have to assert its authority, but would find that others chose to maintain close ties with it out of self-interest (and self-preservation). These states would become more functional and stable, and be less needy toward Moscow or susceptible to external influences, whether of the Western liberal or radical Islamist persuasion. But they would not get so comfortable as to develop into genuinely independent entities. They would remain reliant on Moscow, and be subject to its leverage whenever required. In this way, today's "arc of instability" around Russia's borders[16] would evolve gradually into a zone of Russian-led stability. And outside actors would engage with the region only in conjunction with Russia or in ways that did not threaten its interests.

Hope is one thing, of course; events are quite another. The Ukrainian revolution has proved just how difficult it is to implement this idealized vision in the face of fluid circumstances on the ground—a *regional disorder*, if you will. And there are plenty of other instances where practical problems have conspired to wreck or obstruct Kremlin aims in the post-Soviet space. As a result, Putin has frequently been forced to improvise, making policy on the hoof in response to developments whose impact he has either failed to foresee or has underestimated. (It is richly ironic that he has developed a reputation in the West as a clever chess player, for his lack of strategic insight or sense of danger points to just the opposite—as no less an authority than former world chess champion Garry Kasparov has observed.)[17]

## Disaggregating the Post-Soviet Space

Despite the commonalities in Russian conceptions of empire and the post-Soviet space, Moscow interacts with individual republics in very different ways. It is tempting to see this as evidence of an emerging post-imperialist mentality, as some commentators have argued.[18] But in fact such differentiation existed in the 1990s; the interest levels of the Yeltsin administration varied enormously, from close involvement in Ukraine[19] to an almost total indifference toward Central Asia.[20] What has changed under Putin is the geographical distribution of Moscow's interest. Ukraine remains a priority of the very first importance, as events have shown, but there have been significant shifts elsewhere. Central Asia, in particular, has assumed a much higher profile, partly as a result of U.S. and NATO involvement in the war in Afghanistan, but also because of China's growing influence in the region. (Even within Central Asia, there has been movement, notably the rise of Kazakhstan as a regional power.)

In practice, Putin's approach to the post-Soviet space is shaped not by an integrated conception, but by a patchwork of individual bilateral relationships. It makes sense, therefore, to categorize these not in the usual geographical way—that is, within the subregional clusters of the western CIS (Commonwealth of Independent States), the Transcaucasus, and Central Asia—but according to their priority in Russian policymaking.

There are three categories. The first comprises the countries of primary strategic significance to Moscow: Ukraine, Kazakhstan, and Belarus. These relationships are the focus of intense policy attention and considerable financial investment. They are vital not only in regional terms, but also in the larger picture of Russian foreign policy.

The second category brings together states that Moscow regards as important, but not to the same existential degree as those in the first group. The nature of their importance also differs from case to case; it may be predominantly security-based, or determined principally by economic factors. This somewhat disparate group includes Georgia, Azerbaijan, Uzbekistan, and Turkmenistan.

The third category covers the rest: Moldova, Kyrgyzstan, Tajikistan, and Armenia. They retain some importance for Moscow, but considerably less than the countries in the first two categories. Typically, their significance is largely instrumental or prophylactic, and fluctuates according to the extent of outside (U.S., European, Chinese) interest in their affairs.

Two caveats should be mentioned. First, the priority Moscow attaches to individual ex-Soviet republics varies according to time and circumstance. The current classifications (and ranking within them) are neither fixed nor necessarily long term. During the 1990s Belarus was a higher priority than Kazakhstan, whereas today the opposite is true. Similarly, Georgia's profile in Russian foreign policy has fallen since the defeat of Mikheil Saakashvili's United National Movement (UNM) in the parliamentary elections of October 2012. But it would rise again if Georgian ambitions to join NATO were to gain traction. Second, the importance of a relationship depends on the perspective and objectives of the beholder. Kazakhstan matters especially to Putin because it is central, along with Ukraine, to the viability of his Eurasian Union project. But to a different, more Western-leaning leadership in Moscow, it might lose some of its salience.

## The Primary Priorities

### Ukraine

There is no single relationship more important to Moscow than its intimate, but often fractious, interaction with Kyiv. Ukraine is more than just a foreign policy preoccupation. It occupies a central place in Russian conceptions of identity, culture, and history. For Putin—and arguably most Russians—the notion of an independent and separate Ukraine has no meaning, given their shared history since the founding of the Kievan Rus in the tenth century, and particularly since the union of 1654.[21] As he has put it, Ukraine "is part of our greater Russian, or Russian-Ukrainian, world."[22] And while he has denied any intention to establish a new unitary state, he clearly sees a sovereign Ukraine as an unfortunate historical accident.

But Ukraine's prominence in Russian elite and public consciousness is no mere relic of history. Just as critical is its pivotal strategic location. Viewed from Moscow, whoever controls Ukraine dominates eastern Europe, and exerts a larger influence across Europe and Eurasia. Here, the contest for influence extends beyond static notions of geopolitical space to mastery over the vital pipeline and transport routes between Europe and Asia. In the same vein, control over Ukraine is integral to Russian understandings of national security. To "lose" Ukraine is to compromise the safety of the Rus-sian Federation itself. Economically, too, Ukraine is of major importance. It is Russia's third-largest trading partner after the EU and China. Despite a sharp fall in direct imports, it remains a significant Gazprom client.[23] The Russian and Ukrainian military-industrial complexes have been intertwined since Soviet times. And Russia was, until recently, by far the largest recipient of Ukrainian agricultural exports.

Such considerations have acquired an added edge as a result of domestic developments in both countries. As early as 2004, Putin was sufficiently concerned about the wider impact of the Orange Revolution to take steps to consolidate his authority, even though his political fortunes were in the ascendancy on the back of rising oil prices and 6–7 percent annual growth.[24] A decade later, his anxiety levels are notably higher. The anti-Putin protests of 2011–12 shook the regime's complacency, while the stagnation of the Russian economy since 2013 threatens the basis of the Putin social contract: material well-being in return for political compliance. In these circumstances, the danger posed by the Ukrainian revolution feels much more existential.

Putin has invested so much of himself over Ukraine that any triumph or reverse is instantly personalized. The fall of Viktor Yanukovych in February 2014 was not only one of the worst setbacks of Russian foreign policy in the post-Soviet era. It was a deep personal humiliation, which Putin could not let pass.[25] Conversely, the subsequent annexation of Crimea mattered to him primarily not as a righting of perceived historical wrongs, a moral act on behalf of a downtrodden minority, or a victory over Ukrainian "fascists" and the Western powers. It was significant above all because it was Putin's individual triumph—a reality confirmed by the unprecedented boost in his approval ratings.[26]

It is difficult to identify a cohesive Russian strategy toward Ukraine. Instead, there is an odd mélange of mystical vision, historical and geopolitical anxieties, feelings of strategic entitlement, gut instincts, and tactical dexterity. Putin's approach reflects the contradictory influences of the two worlds that shape his foreign policy more generally. On the one hand, the Kremlin conceives of Ukraine, and Russia's relationship with it, in terms of historical inevitabilities. On the other hand, developments in the real world act as a constant reminder of the artificiality of such hopes.

Contrary to the view of some Western commentators, there is little evidence of a grand plan to absorb Ukraine into the Russian Federation. It is pertinent that Putin consistently rejected calls to reincorporate Crimea right until the moment of Yanukovych's fall—a position at odds with much of the Russian political establishment since the early 1990s. This relative restraint was partly born of his legalistic mindset, which makes a point of observing the letter, if not the spirit, of the law. In much the same way as he used the expedient of the Medvedev presidency to get around the prohibition on serving three consecutive presidential terms, so he is keen to mask Russian policy toward Ukraine with a veneer of due process. Thus the annexation of Crimea was executed through the device of a referendum as the formal expression of its population's right to self-determination. (It mattered little to the Kremlin that the referendum was a charade; the point was that it took place.)

But it is not primarily legalism that discourages Putin from attempting to reacquire Ukraine; it is the impracticality of this course. The deterrent here is not the impact of Western sanctions, which is a relatively minor consideration. The real issue is that taking on Ukraine as a constituent part of the Russian Federation would impose a crippling burden on Moscow, all the more so when it faces mounting economic pressures (already evident pre-sanctions). As Clifford Gaddy and Barry Ickes have observed, Russia "could not afford . . . to win Ukraine, that is, be saddled with not only its current costs of up to $10 billion a year for eastern Ukraine, but the much larger amounts that would be needed to support the rest of the country if they were cut off from Western markets."[27] There is also the obvious danger that the more directly involved Russia is in Ukraine, the greater the popular resistance to its goals. Already, pro-European and pro-NATO sentiment has risen dramatically as a result of Moscow's actions in Crimea and southeast Ukraine.[28]

From the Kremlin's perspective the best-case scenario is for Ukraine to be a dysfunctional but more or less stable polity, with intimate political, strategic, and economic ties to Russia. Such a condition would enable Moscow to steer a middle course between having to hold up a crisis-ridden and chronically dependent neighbor, constantly on the verge of state failure, and wrestling with a confident Ukraine, committed to pursuing an independent, Europe-oriented foreign policy. Such a middling—and muddling—Ukraine would be more inclined to comply with Russian priorities, while remaining an unattractive subject for Western engagement.

*The best laid plans . . .* However, as Yeltsin's former prime minister, Viktor Chernomyrdin, once famously remarked, "We wanted the best, but it turned out [badly] like it always does."[29] Over the years Putin has found Kyiv to be an enormously frustrating partner. He has not only suffered two huge setbacks—the 2004 Orange Revolution and 2014 Maidan revolution—but even when there has been a more congenial figure in Kyiv, getting the Ukrainians to do his bidding has been very difficult. He had hoped, for example, that Yanukovych's victory in the 2010 presidential elections would see the normalization of relations, which had deteriorated badly under his predecessor Viktor Yushchenko. And to some extent this did occur. The bilateral atmosphere improved markedly; already close personal ties between the respective political, security, and military establishments were strengthened;[30] and Kyiv quickly agreed to extend the lease of the Russian Black Sea Fleet at Sevastopol by another twenty-five years until 2042. Yanukovych also let up on sensitive historical issues, such as the famine of 1932–33 (*Holodomor*), in which at least three million Ukrainians died.[31]

But the subsequent course of relations proved a severe disappointment to the Kremlin. Notwithstanding the closeness of inter-elite ties, the Yanukovych regime sought to widen its options by looking elsewhere for military support, technology, and trade. Ukraine participated regularly in activities within NATO's Partnership for Peace program,[32] and although membership in the alliance was put on the back burner, cooperation grew in areas such as force training.[33] Nor were Ukraine's horizons limited to Europe. It expanded military-technical cooperation with China, a development boosted by the visit in June 2011 of President Hu Jintao.[34] In December 2013 when the Maidan protests were intensifying, Yanukovych still took time to travel to Beijing to sign agreements worth an estimated US$30 billion.[35]

Ukrainian resistance to Russian pressure and blandishments was most evident in the economic sphere. Local oligarchs such as Rinat Akhmetov,

Dmytro Firtash, and Viktor Pinchuk defended their business empires against predatory Russian interests.[36] Yanukovych stood firm in opposing a Gazprom takeover of Naftohaz and Ukraine's pipeline system. He also sought to renegotiate a 2009 gas deal concluded between then prime minister Yulia Tymoshenko and Putin, under which Ukraine ended up paying a price far higher than some European customers such as Germany and Italy. Direct imports from Russia fell by nearly half, with the shortfall being met by cheaper Russian gas bought from Germany.[37] Kyiv even concluded two US$10 billion contracts with Royal Dutch Shell and Chevron for shale gas exploration and extraction. (These have since been suspended as a result of the current conflict, the fall in global oil prices, and the collapse of the Ukrainian economy.)

Most emblematical, Yanukovych rebuffed Russian pressure to join the Customs Union. Although he pulled back at the last moment from signing an Association Agreement with the EU in November 2013, he played Brussels and Moscow off against each other right until the end. He not only attempted to extract a US$20 billion subsidy from the EU, but also sought the (nonexistent) status of associate membership in the Customs Union—hoping to gain the benefits of membership without being held to any of its commitments. The Kremlin resented Kyiv's tactics, but saw no alternative to working with Yanukovych as long as he dominated Ukrainian politics.[38]

It is easy to forget, in the wake of the Ukrainian revolution, just how differently Putin and Yanukovych viewed the bilateral relationship and Ukraine's place in the international system. Faced with a direct threat to his personal business interests, Yanukovych was forced to accept the Kremlin's deal of a US$15 billion state bailout package and one-third discount for Russian gas imports, in exchange for withdrawing from the Association Agreement negotiations with Brussels. Nevertheless, he hoped to keep the European option open. In striving to preserve strategic flexibility, Ukrainian independence, and economic integration with Europe, he had much more in common with his political opponents than is generally recognized.

*Same goals, different circumstances.* The demise of Yanukovych has sharpened Moscow's focus and actions in Ukraine. Against the background of worsening relations with Europe and (especially) the United States, the Kremlin's zero-sum calculus has emerged in all its starkness. Yet its underlying assumptions and objectives remain essentially unaltered. The primary goal, as before, is *control, not conquest*—or, to put it another way, power projection with limited responsibility. Putin continues to act on the basis that Russia has a primary interest in the governance of Ukraine, particularly (but not only) in the areas of foreign and security policy. This resembles Leonid

Brezhnev's concept of "limited sovereignty," as applied to the Soviet Union's relations with the Warsaw Pact countries. Ukraine would be formally independent, but not fully sovereign. Russia would not involve itself in its day-to-day decisionmaking, but retain a de facto power of veto.

What have changed, of course, are the circumstances in which Moscow pursues its objectives. Most obviously, the chief instrument for mediating Russian influence—unsatisfactory to be sure, but once the best available—has been written out of the equation. With no Yanukovych (or acceptable alternative) in Kyiv, Moscow is looking for other ways to promote Russian interests.

This is why it has been beating the "federalization" drum for eastern Ukraine.[39] Its capacity to bend the administration of President Petro Poroshenko to its will is considerably reduced, so it has focused its efforts instead on the regions—Luhansk and Donetsk—that are geographically, ethnically, and culturally closest to Russia. But even here it has found that most local inhabitants are almost as opposed to the idea of secession or incorporation into Russia as they are to the new government in Kyiv.[40] Consequently Russian policy has become increasingly ad hoc and contradictory. It acts on the premise that a divided and dysfunctional Ukraine is desirable in that it is more susceptible to pressure. Yet it is concerned that a prolonged conflict could be a lasting drain on Russia's resources, destabilize its own western regions, and consign relations with Europe to the deep-freezer.

The Kremlin is looking to the West to help resolve this conundrum. Although it does not generally welcome the participation of Western governments and organizations, it knows there is little it can do to prevent this for the time being. The potential upside is that European leaders, keen to extricate themselves from burdensome obligations, may pressure Poroshenko to agree to concessions on Russian terms, most notably on federalization. The devolution of significant constitutional powers to Ukraine's eastern regions would entrench Russian influence there; allow Moscow to leverage the threat of their possible secession in future dealings with Kyiv; and rule out Ukrainian membership in NATO or the EU for decades. From the Kremlin's perspective, it would be a huge bonus if such arrangements could be legitimized whether through the Minsk accords involving Angela Merkel and François Hollande, or more formally with the imprimatur of the OSCE.[41]

It is unclear how Russian policy in Ukraine will play out over the next few years. In the immediate term, Moscow is creating new facts on the ground in order to force the West—and Kyiv—to come to terms. The takeover of Donetsk airport in January 2015, and of the strategically important town of Debaltseve a month later, was consistent with this purpose.[42] How far Putin goes will depend on many factors: the strength or weakness of Western, especially European, policy responses; the degree to which Poroshenko is able to restore functional governance to Ukraine, including building bridges with the east and arresting the catastrophic decline of the economy; and the Kremlin's own level of confidence, which in turn will be influenced by political and economic conditions in Russia.

As of spring 2015, the likelihood is that there will be no full-scale Russian invasion of eastern Ukraine. But such a (non-)outcome is hostage to multiple unstable elements. Putin may well be averse to a substantial Russian military deployment, and have no intention of fulfilling the historical vision of Novorossiya ("New Russia"). However, there is a substantial risk that if he is unable to extract a favorable political accommodation, levels of violence will escalate to the point where a Russian occupation of large parts of Ukraine becomes possible. Moscow has already laid some of the groundwork for just such a contingency, describing Kyiv's "anti-terrorist" operation against the separatists of the so-called Donetsk People's Republic during the summer of 2014 as "developing into genocide."[43] In a febrile climate where short-termism trumps rationality, no scenario can be safely ruled out.[44]

In *The Grand Chessboard* (1996), Zbigniew Brzezinski wrote that Ukraine's "very existence as an independent country helps to transform Russia. Without Ukraine, Russia ceases to be a Eurasian Empire."[45] Brzezinski's comment still holds true; Ukraine remains the supreme litmus test. A Russia able to accept a decision in Kyiv to move closer to the EU or expand cooperation with NATO would show signs of shedding its imperial past. But this is a remote prospect as long as Moscow continues to regard such outcomes as extraordinary events, requiring vigorous "defensive measures."[46] Developments since 2013 confirm that Putin—and the political elite more generally—is unable to re-imagine Russia as just another influential neighbor and major power. The antiquity of historical-civilizational ties and the recentness of their imperial relationship represent truly daunting obstacles to the attitudinal shift Brzezinski was hoping for.

### Kazakhstan

Kazakhstan has been the most successful of the ex-Soviet republics, judged by the criteria of political stability, economic growth, and foreign policy management. While it has benefited from a resources bonanza and high global oil prices, it has also made the most of its luck. It has established an attractive business environment despite problems with corruption and the rule of law. It has pursued a tri-vectored foreign policy with Russia, China, and the West that has maximized its strategic independence. It has managed relations with potentially awkward neighbors, for example Uzbekistan.[47] It is an important player in regional bodies such as the EEU (and previously the Customs Union), the Shanghai Cooperation Organization (SCO), and the CSTO. And it has positioned itself as a constructive international citizen through such mechanisms as the OSCE presidency (in 2010).

Furthermore, Kazakhstan has achieved all this without, for the most part, upsetting Russian sensitivities or provoking imperial envy in Moscow. A good relationship with Astana has been one of the constants in Putin's foreign policy and appears to offer a potential model of post-imperial accommodation. Although Kazakhstan has emerged as the leading regional power in Central Asia, it is also Russia's most reliable and useful partner among the ex-Soviet republics. President Nursultan Nazarbaev is respected by the Kremlin as a figure of substance. His skillful conduct of foreign policy has not only stymied neoimperial ambitions in Moscow, but also made them unnecessary.[48] The EU has become Kazakhstan's number one trading partner,[49] but Russia's multidimensional influence ensures that it remains the leading external player. As one local commentator has observed, "Kazakhstan can be seen as a vast area for actions aimed at preserving Russia's influence and protecting its interests in central Eurasia."[50] It is telling that Nazarbaev has largely sided with Putin over Ukraine, despite concerns about the implications of Russian behavior for Kazakhstan's territorial integrity.

However, the very centrality of Nazarbaev to the good order of Russia-Kazakhstan relations represents a source of vulnerability. Much of the current equilibrium depends directly on him, raising the question of what happens when he dies, becomes incapacitated, or retires from political life.[51] There are several potential areas of concern. One is that Kazakhstan, in common with all the ex-Soviet republics, has feeble institutions and opaque rules of succession. When Nazarbaev eventually departs, there may be considerable political uncertainty, leading in a worst-case scenario to serious conflicts within the ruling elite. In a system marked by personalized rule, his successor may not have the experience, savvy, or luck to ensure continued stability and prosperity. The riots of December 2011 in the western town of Zhanaozen revealed cracks in the system, and pointed to what could eventuate in a post-Nazarbaev Kazakhstan.

The second variable is that a resource-rich Central Asia is likely to be subject to increased security and economic attention in coming decades. Even allowing for a smooth succession, Kazakhstan will find it more difficult to balance the competing interests not just of Russia, China, and the West, but also of emerging players such as India, Iran, and Turkey. Central Asia, like many other parts of the world, is becoming more geopolitically diverse and disorderly. This will place growing strain on the relationship between Moscow and Astana, requiring skillful management from both sides.

A taster of incipient problems came in early 2012, with reports that Nazarbaev was beginning to resent Russian pressure to buy into a more ambitious vision of the Eurasian Union, and to become worried about the implications for Kazakhstan's sovereignty. These reservations have since become more public and insistent. Nazarbaev has criticized the "politicization" of the Union, which diverges significantly from his original vision of Eurasian *economic* integration.[52] He has excluded a whole raft of areas from its purview, including border security, immigration, and defense and security,[53] and refused to devolve trade policy powers to the EEU's Economic Commission. No less significant, in October 2014 Kazakhstan concluded an enhanced Partnership and Cooperation Agreement (PCA) with the EU.[54]

For the time being differences with Moscow have been papered over by the time-honored expedient of a grand framework agreement—the Eurasian Economic Union Treaty signed by Putin, Nazarbaev, and Lukashenko on May 29, 2014. But as Putin's Eurasian project unfolds, its practical implications become clearer, and Nazarbaev gets older, the contradictions between Moscow and Astana could become more serious. And they would acquire real intensity should a new generation of leaders commit Kazakhstan to a more pro-Western or (less probable) pro-Chinese strategic choice. Ominously, in August 2014 Putin reacted to Nazarbaev's suggestion that Kazakhstan could leave the Eurasian Union if it felt its independence to be threatened, by claiming that the president had "created a state in a territory that had never had a state before."[55] This emphasis on the artificiality of an independent Kazakhstan was reminiscent of his remarks to George W. Bush at the 2008 Bucharest NATO summit that Ukraine was "not even a state."[56]

The third cloud on the (near) horizon is the rise of radical Islamism in Central Asia, particularly if Pakistan becomes a failed state and the security situation in Afghanistan deteriorates following the withdrawal of American combat troops. Kazakhstan could then end up facing a perfect storm of domestic instability, escalating geopolitical rivalries, and Islamist extremism and terrorism. Although it is better equipped than other Central Asian republics to deal with these challenges, the extent of the disorder could be beyond its capacity to manage.

In a scenario where Kazakhstan "goes wrong," it is not hard to imagine Russia attempting to reassert its former, Soviet-era influence. Today its relative restraint and lack of obvious imperial ambition are the result of satisfaction with the state of bilateral relations, and also the knowledge that it is hardly in a position to adopt a more active posture. But intentions—and capabilities—do change. Given Kazakhstan's geopolitical and geoeconomic significance to Moscow, it is a prime candidate for a more interventionist approach in the future. This will not necessarily assume military form, given the huge logistical challenges involved in mounting such operations. But the Kremlin could attempt to exploit Kazakhstan's continuing economic dependence on Russia, for example by placing restrictions on goods transiting its territory,[57] or ratcheting up the pressure to expand the remit of the Eurasian Union. It may also reach out to the large ethnic Russian minority, most of which lives in the northern provinces adjoining Russia. This issue has been largely dormant under Nazarbaev, but there is potential for it to reemerge. According to the latest (2009) national census, ethnic Russians comprise 23.7 percent of Kazakhstan's total population, a substantially higher proportion than in Ukraine (17 percent).[58]

### Belarus

Belarus under the regime of Alexander Lukashenko exemplifies the costs and inconveniences of pursuing a patrimonial foreign policy. Acute political dysfunctionality, a moribund economy,[59] and an exceptionally poor international image[60] have made it an unattractive prize. Far from exerting the prerogatives of an imperial master, Moscow has found it very difficult to influence Lukashenko's behavior. Attempts to rein in his excesses, prevent the on-sale of subsidized Russian oil, and protect Russian journalists from harassment have sometimes rebounded. During 2009–10 Lukashenko leveraged Belarus's membership in the Eastern Partnership program in a transparent attempt to blackmail Moscow into a more accommodating stance. This led to the surreal spectacle of Belarus posing as the plucky underdog against a bullying Russia— and, more bizarrely still, convincing some gullible Europeans of the charade.[61]

The unsatisfactory nature of the Russia-Belarus relationship raises the question of why Moscow continues to support Lukashenko. There are several reasons. At the broad conceptual level, Belarus has long occupied a central position in post-Soviet integration projects—from the founding of the CIS in 1991 to today's more tangible institutions, such as the Customs Union, EEU, and CSTO. Its presence is key to sustaining the mythology of a distinct post-Soviet space. As part of the Slavic core, Belarus is almost as important as Ukraine in this respect.

Belarus has also been one of Russia's few supporters over the past two decades. More often than not, Moscow has been able to rely on Minsk to stand by it in the face of Western criticisms. Naturally, such solidarity is a dubious blessing. Not only has Belarus been the most parasitic of friends, but its close association has inflicted significant reputational damage on Russia.

Nevertheless, its geographical location—on the historical invasion route followed by Napoleon, Hitler, and many others—means that it is central to Russia's strategic and security calculus. Indeed, given developments in Ukraine, Belarus's importance to Moscow has grown. Military and intelligence cooperation is expanding from already high levels, and there are plans for a new Russian air force base in Babruysk in the east of the country.[62] In effect Belarus has become a military outpost of the Russian Federation, despite continuing political and commercial tensions.

But perhaps the most compelling reason for supporting Lukashenko is that Moscow sees no plausible alternative. There are some parallels here with Ukraine under Yanukovych. The Kremlin has few illusions about Lukashenko's (lack of) loyalty to Russian interests, and has observed his periodic flirtations with Brussels. But bad though he is, who could possibly replace him? The leading Belarusian opposition figures support closer engagement with Europe, and are committed to democratic reforms. A post-Lukashenko regime might therefore resemble the one that has emerged in Kyiv. It would develop close ties with the EU and NATO. It would open up the Belarusian economy to Western companies, thereby disadvantaging Russian interests that have thrived in a closed business environment. And it would offer a model for domestic transformation in Russia itself—a prospect all the more uncomfortable in light of the Ukrainian revolution.

The Kremlin operates on the assumption that as long as Lukashenko stays in power, Russia will remain the dominant external actor in Belarus. Lukashenko would continue to be awkward and ungrateful, but possess the supreme virtue of being better disposed toward Russia than toward the West. Close military and security cooperation would be sustained; the systemic insolvency of the Belarusian economy would enable Russian enterprises to control strategic sectors, such as energy;[63] and Minsk would remain a valuable ally in containing any democratic "contagion."

That said, Moscow faces a conundrum. The longer Lukashenko stays in power, the more independently he will behave,[64] and the harder it may be to build a cooperative relationship with an eventual post-Lukashenko Belarus. Ideally from Moscow's perspective, a palatable successor would emerge from within the ruling clique: someone less mercurial, but still maintaining tight political control, who would continue to favor Russian security and economic interests while minimizing the financial burden on Moscow. Such a person might be a Belarusian equivalent of Putin, with a pragmatic appreciation of the benefits of close cooperation with Russia.

For now, though, the Kremlin is committed to supporting Lukashenko against any domestic opposition, and reinforcing Belarus as Russia's geopolitical bastion. With the ouster of Yanukovych, Lukashenko has become Putin's last remaining ally on the "western front." The longer-term consequences of this are unclear. Lukashenko enjoys leverage by virtue of being invaluable to Moscow and through his mediatory role in the Minsk Accords. However, the Kremlin's tolerance of his erratic behavior is likely to be reduced, given the stakes involved: the perpetuation of a dominant Russian influence in the neighborhood; the maintenance of key forward defense capabilities; powerful commercial interests; and the possible eventual threat of democratization. As with Ukraine, Putin will continue to work through proxies rather than attempt direct rule, with all its attendant risks and costs. But should this "indirect imperialism" fail, it would be no great surprise if he resorted to more forcible methods. In the current climate, even a modest rapprochement between Brussels and Minsk could elicit a vigorous Russian reaction.[65]

## Important (but Less Vital) Priorities

### Georgia

Georgia is sometimes presented as Exhibit A in the case for the prosecution against Russian imperialism. Many Western commentators saw the 2008 war as heralding a new age of aggressive expansionism, the first step in a systematic campaign of territorial annexation that aimed to swallow up Georgia, Crimea, and eventually the whole of Ukraine.[66] There seemed good reason for imagining the worst. The rhetoric coming out of Moscow that summer exuded triumphalism and strident nationalism, and there appeared to be little to prevent Russia from taking larger advantage of its military success.

Yet the Georgia war did not mark a new period of Russian imperialism. Indeed, the conflict highlighted the difficulties of such a course by exposing the limitations of the Russian military[67] and the fragility of Moscow's influence in its so-called Near Abroad. The refusal of formerly compliant neighbors to follow the Kremlin's lead in recognizing Abkhazia and South Ossetia transformed a military victory into something of a diplomatic setback. The war may have killed off the prospect of Georgian membership in NATO—not that there was any likelihood of this after the alliance's Bucharest summit[68]— but it did little to further any hegemonic ambitions Moscow might have had in the post-Soviet space. Fearful that Russia could seek to reimpose an imperial diktat, regional elites stepped up their efforts to expand security and economic cooperation with the United States, Europe, China, and other outside players, while being wary in their own engagement with Moscow.

Moreover, despite compelling evidence that Putin deliberately drew Saakashvili into a conflict,[69] it is doubtful that he wanted to annex or otherwise subjugate all of Georgia. In many respects, the status quo before August 2008 suited Moscow just fine. The breakaway regions were a constant irritation and distraction to the Saakashvili regime; Russia maintained a significant military presence there under the legal umbrella of a UN peacekeeping operation; and Russian businesspeople and tourists could come and go as they pleased. Moscow and Tbilisi preserved more or less normal trade relations, and there were large numbers of Georgian migrant workers in Russia.[70] The war disrupted these cozy arrangements. It raised the specter of imperial revanchism, and outraged normally well-disposed Western governments, such as Germany and France. Even the Chinese were discomfited by Moscow's decision to recognize Abkhazia and South Ossetia as independent states.[71]

Russia-Georgia relations have yet to recover from the war. Although the defeat of Saakashvili's UNM in the 2012 parliamentary elections led to a partial thaw, bilateral interaction remains difficult. Moscow has lifted a ban on imports of Georgian wine and mineral water, while the Georgian Dream government that succeeded Saakashvili has committed itself to improving ties with Russia.[72] But there is no getting around the problem of the status of Abkhazia and South Ossetia. It would be political suicide for any Georgian administration to accept their formal secession. Meanwhile, the Russian military and economic presence in the territories continues to grow, and Moscow may even choose to incorporate them into the Russian Federation.[73] In November 2014, Putin signed a new partnership agreement with Abkhaz President Raul Khajimba (like him, a former KGB officer), establishing a joint military force and providing for substantial direct subsidies to Sukhumi.[74] Subsequently, in March 2015 a similar agreement was concluded with South Ossetia.[75] The real question for Putin is whether he would be better off reserving the threat of annexation as leverage against Tbilisi.

All this comes down to the issue of Georgia's European orientation. Although NATO and EU membership are improbable in the near future, Tbilisi remains committed to the EU's Eastern Partnership and military cooperation with NATO. If anything, the pace of European integration has picked up. In July 2013, Brussels and Tbilisi finalized negotiations on a Deep and Comprehensive Free Trade Area (DCFTA), which was initialed at the Vilnius Eastern Partnership summit in November.[76] And on June 27, 2014, Georgia, along with Moldova and Ukraine, signed the Association Agreement with the EU.[77] Predictably, it has shown zero interest in the Kremlin's attempts to involve it in post-Soviet integration projects, such as the Customs Union.

The current state of Russia-Georgia relations highlights the weaknesses of Moscow's heavy-handed approach. It has threatened Tbilisi with various punitive measures, including export bans and tighter immigration restrictions. However, sanctions have only encouraged the Georgians to hug the EU more tightly, and to press their case for NATO membership. The annexation of Crimea and ongoing destabilization of eastern Ukraine have accentuated a stark dichotomy between a benign and still prosperous Europe and a politically tyrannical and economically dysfunctional Russia.[78]

Over the next few years, relations are likely to remain volatile, and there is ample scope for a serious escalation of tensions. Many of the underlying problems are unresolved, and may worsen as Georgia becomes more institutionally tied to Europe and Moscow raises the stakes. Russian aims will be broadly constant: to consolidate its military presence in Abkhazia and South Ossetia; counter Georgian efforts to achieve integration with Europe, in particular, to kill off ambitions for NATO membership; stymie pipeline projects going through the "Southern Corridor";[79] promote Russian business and security activities; and support pro-Russian constituencies in Georgia, such as the Orthodox Church.[80]

Although much of this behavior suggests imperial ambition, Moscow will be motivated primarily by a defensive geopolitical calculus, rather than the desire to project active power. For the end-goal is not to govern Georgia, but to preserve it as a weak and relatively isolated state, and prevent it from becoming a base for Western influence in Eurasia. If the Kremlin manages to "sanitize" Georgia in this way, the latter's profile in Russian foreign policy will fall steadily. But if it fails Georgia could once again be in the front line in a further confrontation between Russia and the West. In that event its status as an independent state could be in jeopardy.

### Azerbaijan

Russian attitudes toward Azerbaijan are highly ambivalent. In several respects, it is seen as a problematic partner. It is a nonaligned and increasingly independent player in the region; it is more resistant than most to Russian pressure; and it is engaged in significant security and economic cooperation with the West. As a major oil and gas producer, its interests sometimes clash with Russia's. In the 1990s, Baku defied Moscow by concluding the "Contract of the Century" under which BP developed Azerbaijan's oil fields in the Caspian, and it was again a key participant in the American-inspired Baku-

Tbilisi-Ceyhan (BTC) gas pipeline project. More recently the two sides have been involved in a lengthy dispute over the legality of a prospective Trans-Caspian gas pipeline, linking the port of Turkmenbashi (in Turkmenistan) to Baku and bypassing Russia. This has highlighted significant differences between the two countries on the delimitation of the Caspian Sea and its resources.[81]

Most critically, the "frozen conflict" over the enclave of Nagorno-Karabakh has been a sore in their relationship for more than two decades. Although Moscow is not a direct party to the dispute between Azerbaijan and Armenia, its alliance with the latter (see below) has soured relations with Baku. The Azerbaijanis regard Russia as a self-serving party that exploits the dispute to exercise leverage on other issues, such as the Trans-Caspian pipeline, and to constrain Azerbaijan's independence more generally.[82] Moscow, for its part, is concerned that the frozen status of the conflict may not last, given Baku's bellicose declarations and military buildup.[83] If a major conflict were to erupt, Moscow would be formally obliged to intervene on Armenia's behalf under Article 4 of the Collective Security Treaty.[84]

That said, there are positive aspects to the Russia-Azerbaijan relationship. It benefits, in particular, from a normative likemindedness. Russian decisionmakers empathize with the secular authoritarianism of the Aliyev regime, which they view as one of the more stable governments in the post-Soviet space.[85] They also recognize that Azerbaijan is pursuing a multi-vectored rather than pro-Western foreign policy; while Baku is expanding cooperation with the United States and Europe, it retains close ties with Russian security and energy interests. One of the singularities of their relationship is that Moscow sells Baku high-grade weaponry, such as T-90 tanks, while acting as the guarantor of Armenia's security—against Azerbaijan's growing force capabilities![86]

The last few years have seen some improvement in the substance and atmosphere of the relationship. Russia is Azerbaijan's third-largest trading partner after the EU and Turkey;[87] there is little sense in Moscow of an imminent geopolitical threat emanating from Baku;[88] and evidence of a Russian imperial agenda vis-à-vis Azerbaijan is notably lacking. But as with Kazakhstan, the status quo is fragile, all the more so given recent developments. The range and gravity of unresolved issues offer plenty of potential for trouble down the road. In addition to the lasting sore of Nagorno-Karabakh, Baku may become increasingly inclined to gravitate toward the West—either from fear or resentment of Moscow, or out of economic self-interest (in 2013 trade with the EU was already seven times greater than trade with Russia). Whatever the motivation, such a shift could prompt an aggressive response. Moscow could adopt an overtly pro-Yerevan position on Nagorno-Karabakh;

accelerate the buildup of its Caspian Sea flotilla;[89] crack down on the estimated two million Azerbaijani migrant workers in Russia; and disrupt Azerbaijani gas exports to Europe.

Looking ahead, the opening of the Trans-Adriatic Pipeline (TAP) in the
next five to ten years will provide an interesting test of their interaction—and
of the Kremlin's pragmatism. The TAP will result in greater competition for
Gazprom in Europe. However, it will not challenge Russia's market dominance in central and eastern Europe (Bulgaria, Romania, and Hungary), but
target less sensitive markets further to the south and west.[90] Moscow may
therefore take the view that this is something it can live with. Yet, it would be
unwise to assume that cool rationality will necessarily prevail.

## Uzbekistan

To Moscow, Uzbekistan bears uncomfortable parallels with Belarus in that it
is a highly personalized authoritarian regime, and a prickly partner.[91] Relations between Moscow and Tashkent have gone through many ups and
downs, and remain difficult. Like Kazakhstan, Uzbekistan has pursued a
multi-vectored foreign policy, engaging with the United States and China, as
well as Russia. But unlike Kazakhstan, it has managed to alienate Moscow
and Washington at different times, partly because of the crudeness of its balancing, and partly because President Islam Karimov has proved a capricious
"ally" even when nominally onside.[92] Uzbekistan is formally a member of the
SCO, yet has abstained from active involvement in military exercises. It with-
drew from the Eurasian Economic Community (EurAsEC) in November
2008, and in August 2012 it pulled out of the CSTO for the second time.[93]

Moscow would like to ignore Uzbekistan but cannot afford to do so given
its geopolitical and security importance. Uzbekistan is located in the heart of
Eurasia; its population of 37 million is larger than that of the other Central
Asian republics combined; and it shares a short, but porous border with
Afghanistan. With a history of religious and ethnic unrest in its eastern
regions (in particular the Fergana Valley), it is also a receptive environment
for Islamist extremism. It has tense and sometimes hostile relations with its
neighbors, such as Kyrgyzstan and Tajikistan, and is seemingly ready at any
moment to jump into bed with the United States or China.[94]

Following the Andijon massacre in May 2005, and Karimov's angry reaction to Western criticisms,[95] the Kremlin had hoped that Tashkent would
become an important ally, against both Islamist terrorism emanating out of
Afghanistan and the West's geopolitical presence in Central Asia. That optimism has long since evaporated. Moscow recognizes that its influence in Uzbekistan is waning, as Tashkent becomes bolder in asserting its independence.

Karimov has developed closer political and security ties with the United States; a NATO Liaison Office was established in May 2014; and, perhaps most significant, the visit of Chinese President Xi Jinping in September 2013 saw the signing of US$15 billion worth of oil, gas, and gold agreements.[96] Relations between Tashkent and Beijing have been further boosted by Karimov's state visit to China in August 2014 and the signing of a strategic development program for 2014–18.

Russian policy toward Uzbekistan is largely passive. Moscow has learned to moderate its expectations during (relatively) good times, while ignoring Karimov's periodic claims about Russian imperial ambitions.[97] It has taken the pragmatic view that Uzbekistan's non-involvement in Russia-led regional bodies such as the CSTO is no bad thing, since it facilitates institutional consensus.[98] And it has refrained from leveraging the estimated 2.5 million Uzbekistani migrant workers in Russia—conscious that the Russian economy suffers from labor shortages, and that attempts to pressure Karimov would be counterproductive. As with Lukashenko, Putin's dislike of him is outweighed by the fear that he could be replaced by someone worse.[99]

The future, however, is uncertain and troubling. The Kremlin hopes that Uzbekistan will remain politically stable; that Karimov manages to keep a lid on ethnic tensions and Islamist extremism; that Uzbekistan's quarrels with its neighbors do not escalate into open conflict; that the American military does not become entrenched; that the Chinese do not translate their growing economic influence into a substantial strategic presence; and that when there is eventually a change of leadership in Tashkent (Karimov celebrated his seventy-seventh birthday on January 30, 2015), it will result in a more predictable and amenable regime. But there is no great confidence that all—or indeed any—of this will be realized.

### Turkmenistan

For most of the post-Soviet period, Turkmenistan has been *sui generis*, remarkable for its poor governance, backwardness, and isolation.[100] This suited Moscow. The Turkmenistani economy was dependent on gas exports to Russia, which also supplied the vast majority of the country's imports. Gazprom's privileged position enabled it to pay Ashgabat very little for its gas, which it then re-exported for a much higher price to European customers.

In recent years, however, the situation has changed to Moscow's disadvantage. The death of long-time leader Saparmurad Niyazov in 2006 and his succession by Gurbanguly Berdymukhammedov has led to a more outward-looking and independent foreign policy. The new president drove a much tougher bargain with Gazprom, obtaining significantly higher prices for his country's gas; presided over the construction of the Central Asia–China gas pipeline (CAGP); and openly courted the United States and the European Union.

The global economic downturn and the eurozone crisis further undermined what had been a stable, if undynamic relationship. Slumping European gas demand during 2008–09 led to a drastic fall-off in Gazprom's requirements for imports from Turkmenistan, leading it to look for a way out of arrangements that had ceased to be profitable. In April 2009, Moscow used the excuse of an unexplained explosion in the main Russia-Turkmenistan pipeline to cut its annual intake of gas from around 50 billion cubic meters (bcm) to 10–13 bcm.[101] The issue cast a pall over relations with Ashgabat, whose trust in Russia has yet to recover.[102] In the meantime the CAGP, which runs from Turkmenistan to western China, via Uzbekistan and Kazakhstan, has enabled China to become Turkmenistan's number one energy customer and trading partner.

With its vast gas reserves, and pivotal location between Central Asia and the Caspian Sea, Turkmenistan is of long-term strategic significance to Russia. Thus far, however, Moscow's approach has been mostly opportunistic— as exemplified by the short-sighted decision to reduce gas imports after the pipeline explosion. If there is a common thread running through Russian policy, it is one of geopolitical defense: no longer able to maintain a dominant position in Turkmenistan, it strives to prevent the West from filling the vacuum. This means, specifically, blocking the export of gas to Europe via routes that bypass Russia, such as the Trans-Caspian pipeline. Although Moscow is not happy that the Chinese have made major inroads into Caspian Sea/Central Asian energy development, it regards this as the least bad outcome.[103]

As with so many of the ex-Soviet republics, the future of Russia's relations with Turkmenistan is unstable. Ashgabat's growing confidence in dealings with outside players increases the risk of misunderstandings with Moscow, and there are several potential flashpoints. One is the mistreatment of the Russian minority in Turkmenistan (6.7 percent of the total population, according to the last, 1995 census). During the Niyazov era the Kremlin turned a blind eye—in contrast to its vociferous complaints about the (far more fortunate) condition of Russian minorities in the Baltic states. This tolerance was a payoff to preserve Russia's economic and geopolitical dominance in Turkmenistan.[104] However, a Turkmenistan that is more assertive and less cooperative toward Russian interests could well revive neoimperial impulses in Moscow.

## Secondary Priorities

### Moldova

Over the past few years, Moldova has been caught up in a larger contest for influence between Russia and the EU. Although Moscow has no wish to take responsibility for a small, resource-poor country in the southeastern corner of Europe, it is implacably opposed to its integration into an EU-centered economic and political space. In this respect, Moldova has come to epitomize the preventative dimension of Russian policy toward the ex-Soviet republics.

During 2012–13 Moscow exerted considerable pressure on Chisinau to join the Customs Union. In fact, the real objective was to prevent it from finalizing a DCFTA and Association Agreement with the EU. The Kremlin knows that Chisinau's orientation toward Brussels poses no material threat to Russian interests.[105] But psychologically it is a different story. Moldova has become hostage to a zero-sum mindset, whereby any step toward European integration equates to a win for the EU and a loss for Russia. Viewed through this prism, the signing by Prime Minister Iurie Leanca of the Association Agreement in June 2014 represented a significant setback.

The Kremlin will continue to work toward the goal of a federalized and (at worst) neutral Moldovan state. It may not be able to force it into a Russian sphere of influence, but it aims at the very least to maintain significant leverage.[106] In the past it has tightened customs procedures, imposed trade bans on major Moldovan exports (such as wine), and threatened to interrupt gas supply unless Chisinau covers Russian energy subsidies to the breakaway region of Transnistria.[107] And these options remain open.

Above all, Moscow is reinforcing its special relationship with the authorities in Tiraspol, the Transnistrian capital. For over two decades it has supported Transnistria as a de facto independent entity in the face of opposition from the Moldovan government, the EU, and the OSCE.[108] On top of subsidizing the local economy, it has stationed troops from the 14th army. In the process, Transnistria has turned into a criminalized micro-state—a matter of some indifference to Moscow, which is more concerned to exploit the region's autonomy to lean on Chisinau.[109]

A resolution of the Transnistrian problem is more distant than ever. Any progress will be contingent on a major improvement in Russia-West relations—something that is very hard to picture today. Indeed, the Kremlin may raise the stakes. It could formally recognize the "independence" of Transnistria, as it has done with Abkhazia and South Ossetia. It could annex the region through the procedure of a local referendum, as in the case of Crimea. The newly incorporated Transnistria might then form part of a revived Novorossiya, stretching the length of the Black Sea coast from Donetsk in the east. Or Moscow could leave things in a state of suspended animation, in order to extract more cooperative behavior from Chisinau.[110]

## Kyrgyzstan

To some observers the crisis in Kyrgyzstan in the spring and early summer of 2010 proved that Russian foreign policy had become post-imperial.[111] Instead of intervening either directly or through the mechanism of the CSTO, Moscow appeared keen to avoid any involvement at all. And when it did finally engage, it enlisted the United States, the EU, and the OSCE to help broker a solution.

Such behavior was all the more surprising given Moscow's attitude over the previous decade.[112] Although Putin had endorsed the deployment of U.S. troops in Afghanistan after 9/11 and their use of military bases in Kyrgyzstan (Manas) and Uzbekistan (Karshi-Khanabad), it was not long before the Russian government began to agitate for the leases to be terminated and the Americans to leave. The deterioration in relations with the regime of then president Kurmanbek Bakiyev during 2009–10 was largely due to the latter's refusal to follow through on an earlier commitment to close down Manas.[113]

Moscow's outbreak of post-imperial spirit in 2010 appeared to be one of the dividends of the U.S.-Russia reset. However, hopes of a new quality of security relationship soon dissipated. Although the Kremlin still wanted Washington to take primary responsibility for containing the Taliban, it persuaded the new administration of President Almazbek Atambaev to close the Manas base, and blocked a U.S. government project to establish joint counternarcotics centers in each of the Central Asian republics.[114] Such moves demonstrated that the geopolitical considerations that had earlier shaped Russia's negative attitude toward a long-term American presence in Central Asia were again predominant. With the worst of the Kyrgyzstan crisis over, Moscow was anxious to limit the influence of other external actors.

The case of Kyrgyzstan encapsulates the ambiguities in Moscow's approach to the ex-Soviet republics. It wants local states and outside powers alike to recognize Russia's regional primacy as a matter of right. However, it also seeks to minimize the responsibilities and risks of direct engagement. Accordingly, it favors economic and political incentives as the best way to promote Russian interests. Russian companies are engaged in major infrastructural projects, such as the controversial Naryn dam;[115] the Russian military is providing significant financial and material assistance; and Russia is host to more than 700,000 Kyrgyzstani migrant workers, sending home an estimated US$2 billion per annum.[116]

Nevertheless, Moscow has found it hard to shed old proprietorial instincts. It has become noticeably anxious about China's expanding footprint, which has graduated quickly from domination of the local retail trade to large-scale investment in energy and infrastructural projects.[117] It has therefore expedited Kyrgyzstan's accession to the EEU—a move it hopes will crimp Chinese interests and reassert Russia's leading influence. Although this does not come cheap, the anticipated strategic dividends and psychological comfort make the expense worthwhile for the Kremlin.[118]

## Tajikistan

Tajikistan is the poorest of the ex-Soviet republics, and arguably the worst governed. President Emomali Rakhmon has done little to check the growth of Islamist extremism and drug-trafficking, while the country's geographical location next to Afghanistan makes it especially vulnerable to external threats. There are significant ethnic tensions involving the Uzbek minority, as well as an increasingly disenchanted younger generation. All these factors add up to a state that is fundamentally unstable.

Russia has maintained a substantial military presence in Tajikistan since independence, and its troops played a crucial role in the civil war of the 1990s that cost an estimated 50,000 lives. More recently, this presence has become somewhat contentious, with Dushanbe demanding an annual rent of US$300 million for the continued lease of the military airport at Ayni. To strengthen their bargaining position, the Tajikistanis hawked the use of the airport to the United States and India, although without success. The Rakhmon regime's near-total dependence on Russian support undercut its leverage, and in October 2012 Moscow secured agreement to a thirty-year lease extension.[119]

Although Moscow was eventually able to resolve the Ayni dispute on its terms, the episode highlighted the difficulties that large powers have in dealing with weak states in their vicinity. Tajikistan is almost entirely reliant on Russian support—not only for security, but also for economic survival. Remittances from migrant workers in Russia comprise around 45 percent of GDP, and are crucial to the stability of the regime.[120] However, Tajikistan's vulnerabilities also enable it to "threaten" Russia with weakness, playing on fears about regime collapse and regional destabilization, and of other powers moving in to fill the security vacuum.[121] In these circumstances, Moscow believes that it has no choice but to maintain substantial assistance to Tajikistan.

## Armenia

Of all the ex-Soviet republics, Armenia has been the most consistently supportive of Russia. The closeness of their ties is apparent in many areas. Moscow acts as guarantor of the status quo in Nagorno-Karabakh, while Russian business interests dominate the Armenian economy.[122] President Serzh Sargisyan is a frequent visitor to Moscow, and there are tight links between the respective security and military establishments. In July 2011, Yerevan agreed to extend until 2044 the lease for the Russian military base in Gyumri. And on January 2, 2015, Armenia joined the EEU.

The Russia-Armenia relationship could hardly be more unequal. Yet it would be wrong to view Armenia merely as a Russian satrapy, given its large and influential diaspora, particularly in the United States and France. Despite pulling out of Association Agreement negotiations in 2013, Armenia's major trading partner in recent years has been the EU (although this may change as a result of European sanctions and Russian counter-sanctions over Ukraine).[123]

There is little indication that Moscow views Armenia as a strategic ally to assist the *active* projection of power. Its main value is defensive—as a check on Azerbaijan's freedom of maneuver should Baku get too close to the West—and psychological. Even then its utility is limited. Armenia is poor and isolated; it has few assets; and it is engaged in a seemingly interminable frozen conflict that demands Russia's constant vigilance. Moscow would like to concentrate on more important priorities elsewhere, yet is disinclined to "surrender" Armenia to the West.

## Post-Imperialism . . . or Postmodern Imperialism?

In surveying Russia's relations with the ex-Soviet republics, it is apparent that there is no empire—or imperial mentality—in the way there was once a Soviet empire. All the republics have been independent for more than two decades, and are able in varying degrees to exercise sovereign choices. It is equally evident, though, that Moscow does not regard them as *fully* sovereign. It acts on the premise that it has a *prima facie* right to influence their decisionmaking, particularly in foreign and security policy. These countries were not only part of the Soviet and Tsarist empires, but they are also neighbors whose actions and frailties affect Russia's vital interests.

However one describes it—imperialist, neoimperialist, post-imperialist, or even "trans-imperialist"[124]—the Kremlin's approach reveals several truths.

The first is that different countries matter differently. Moscow attaches by far the greatest importance to Ukraine because of its critical strategic location, the intimacy of their shared history, and Putin's political and personal stake. By contrast, its interest in Moldova is almost exclusively prophylactic—to prevent its integration into mainstream Europe—while it resents the costs of supporting erratic regimes in Belarus and Tajikistan. There are some countries, again Ukraine, which it believes have a duty to closely coordinate their policies with Russia. And then there are others—Kazakhstan, Azerbaijan, and Uzbekistan—that it has effectively let go, at least for the time being. If Russia is still an empire, then it is a very uneven empire.

Second, Moscow's attitude remains more calculating than messianic. Notwithstanding Putin's vision of a multidimensional Eurasian Union and the resurrection of pseudo-historical constructs such as Novorossiya, Russian policy is not driven primarily by an evangelical sense of purpose. It is based on a more prosaic evaluation of the costs and benefits of regional leadership, and of what seems achievable. It is, in some degree, an imperialism devised and implemented by bureaucrats. The Kremlin has become more discriminating in subsidizing the ex-Soviet republics. It will continue to do so where circumstances require, for example, with Belarus. But it will not be blackmailed or hustled into offering disproportionate concessions—witness the facing down of Dushanbe over the Ayni air base. Even in its engagement with Minsk, Moscow has extracted a significant quid pro quo by taking over strategic sectors of the Belarusian economy.

Third, Russia's mindset is essentially inward-looking and defensive, encapsulated by the principle of "what we (still) have, we hold." Its priority is less to rule or actively project power, though the latter is of course desirable, than to ensure that other outside parties are unable to do so. Thus Moscow's main interest in Georgia is to prevent it from becoming the launchpad for Western interests and influence in Eurasia. Russian activity in the post-Soviet space is often proportional to the extent of external interest in a given country. For example, Turkmenistan is important not because of its gas exports to Russia (which have plummeted), but because it has been courted by Europe and China, which see it as a key player in the geoeconomics of the Caspian Sea region. Similarly, it is debatable whether Moscow would pay much heed to Kyrgyzstan were it not for the American-led operation in Afghanistan and growing Chinese activity in the region.

Fourth, Moscow has limited capacity to enforce its writ in the former Soviet republics. This may seem an implausible claim, given Russian military successes in Crimea and eastern Ukraine. Nevertheless, there is a world of difference between a capacity to destabilize neighboring states and the establishment of a *pax Rossica* that ensures its political, security, and economic interests in the long term. It is striking that Georgia today is as firmly set on the path of European integration as it ever was under Saakashvili. As for Ukraine, the Kremlin's pressure on Yanukovych had the unintended consequence of initiating his political demise, while the annexation of Crimea accelerated Kyiv's drift away from Moscow.

There has also been a wider deterrent effect, as noted by the former British ambassador to Moscow, Andrew Wood: "Attempts to enforce . . . fraternal unity across the former Soviet space are futile. The effect of trying has already been to inject a lasting poison into Russia's relationship with all other countries sharing that Soviet background."[125] Tellingly, the Georgian and Moldovan governments reacted to events in Ukraine by hurrying to sign their Association Agreements with the EU, while Kazakhstan, Uzbekistan, and Belarus have become noticeably more vocal about safeguarding their national sovereignty. Even milder forms of hard power, such as the use of pipeline dominance to extract concessions, have become counterproductive. Gazprom's decision to cut imports from Turkmenistan following the 2009 "accident" to the Davletbat-Dariyalyk pipeline encouraged Ashgabat to gravitate further toward China, while Moscow's threats to cut gas supplies to Ukraine have reinforced the latter's European orientation and efforts to reduce energy dependence on Russia.

All this raises the question of whether recent Russian actions signal a regression to the imperial mean or whether they should be viewed as part of a prolonged agony of post-imperial adjustment. The military operations in Crimea and eastern Ukraine, and previously Georgia, could turn out to be the last throes of the imperial spirit, akin to the Anglo-French Suez intervention of 1956, and the Algerian war of independence (1954–62). To date, however, there has been little evidence of a transformation in aims and mentality. If there has been change, then it has mainly been in the means Moscow has employed to support its objectives. A more differentiated and calculating approach toward preserving its influence in the post-Soviet space signals an appreciation that the old ways are not always the best ways. But it does not equate to a qualitatively new understanding of relations with its former subjects.

This is hardly surprising. It is unrealistic to expect Russia to be the exception to the rule that empires, modern and ancient, do not go quietly. They either collapse as a result of crushing defeat (Germany, Japan) or domestic implosion (China), or they strive for decades to cling on to the scraps of their imperial past (Great Britain, France). Less than twenty-five years ago, Russia was the largest land empire in history. The current political generation was born and raised in imperial times. And developments in its former possessions still have a significant impact on Russian interests (more so than with far-flung sea empires, such as the British and the French). It would be miraculous indeed if Russia's ruling elite were able to transcend history so soon after the demise of the USSR. And of course they haven't.[126]

A genuinely post-imperial mindset may eventually emerge. Ordinary logic suggests that the longer the ex-USSR republics are independent, the more confident they will become in exercising their sovereign prerogatives, and the less likely Moscow will be to intervene even when Russian interests are at stake. Thus as unthinkable as NATO membership for Ukraine appears today, it may one day become an acceptable and then an unstoppable reality—or the issue becomes moot, either because Russia is fully integrated into Euro-Atlantic security structures or because NATO ceases to exist.

In the meantime the potential for resurgent imperial behavior should not be underestimated—and not only in relation to the "usual suspects," such as Ukraine and Georgia. Domestic instability in a post-Nazarbaev Kazakhstan or post-Karimov Uzbekistan; the conversion of Chinese economic influence into an enhanced strategic presence in Central Asia; renewed conflict between Azerbaijan and Armenia over Nagorno-Karabakh—these are just some of the scenarios that may fuel more assertive and interventionist instincts in Moscow. Military action cannot be excluded, as has been demonstrated in Ukraine. But the use of economic and political leverage seems more likely, making plain to the ex-Soviet republics the consequences of not pursuing Russia-first policies, yet avoiding the perils of imperial overstretch.

Much will depend on what happens in Russia itself. A stable and confident leadership, a return to growth, and real progress on modernization would engender a more relaxed attitude toward the neighborhood. Conversely, political uncertainty, economic recession, social discontent, and the rise of hyper-nationalism are liable to trigger more allergic responses.

Moscow's approach will also be affected by the larger context of Russian foreign policy and, especially, relations with the United States and China. It is revealing that during the heyday of the reset in 2009–10 the topicality and sensitivity of neighborhood issues diminished considerably. The main priorities then were the normalization of relations with Washington; promoting Russia as a good international citizen; and enlisting external assistance in support of economic modernization. Imperial-type behavior was deemed neither necessary nor productive.

But the subsequent deterioration of relations with the West saw a reversion to the status quo ante. Hillary Clinton's description in December 2012 of the Eurasian Union project as "a move to re-Sovietize the region" did not come out of the blue, but against the background of rising tensions between

Moscow and Washington on a whole raft of issues, from the Syrian conflict to Putin's domestic crackdown.[127] Likewise, frustrations between Brussels and Moscow in other areas of their relationship have added a real edge to their disagreement over the (anything but) common neighborhood.

Moscow retains many instruments of influence in post-Soviet Eurasia. Inter-elite ties are still close, reinforced by a substantial authoritarian like-mindedness. Russia controls the infrastructure through which many of the region's oil and gas exports pass. It remains a vital trading partner and source of foreign investment. It provides employment to more than ten million expatriate workers from the ex-USSR. Its military capacities are sometimes helpful in reinforcing the stability of various regimes.[128] And Russian continues to be widely spoken, while Russian TV, radio, and culture remain very popular.

Used judiciously, these trumps will ensure a strong position in Eurasia for decades, notwithstanding the rise of China and growing involvement of other regional players, such as Iran and Turkey. But Russia's long-term fortunes will depend on whether it is able to embrace a post-imperial mindset, whereby the former republics are treated as sovereign equals rather than as subjects. It will need to recognize that they have a greater range of options than before, and that they will stay close only if cooperation brings real benefits. Moscow therefore faces a stark choice: either it recalibrates its approach toward post-Soviet Eurasia, with excellent prospects of success; or it stands on its imperial dignity, and sees its influence ebb away.[129]

# five
# A Turn to the East

If you want to go east, don't go west.

RAMAKRISHNA, NINETEENTH-CENTURY MYSTIC

I do not agree with the term "pivot to Asia" . . . nothing spectacular is taking place and nothing major has been achieved in Russia's foreign policy strategy.

AMBASSADOR DU QIWEN, SEPTEMBER 2014

The need for Russia to embrace cooperation with Asia should scarcely be a matter for debate. Even during the 1990s, when Europe was enjoying unprecedented prosperity, the Asia-Pacific region was beginning to emerge as the principal arena of global political and economic activity. Any self-respecting major power would surely seek to play a significant role in its affairs, all the more so if three-fourths of its territory and most of its natural resources lay in Asia.

And yet this is precisely what Russia has failed to do for much of the post-Soviet period. Despite repeatedly proclaiming its commitment to a "multi-vectored" foreign policy,[1] Moscow's interest in Asian affairs has been uneven at best, often nonexistent, and its focus overwhelmingly instrumental. If Asia has mattered, then it has largely been because of its relevance to Russia's interaction with the West, and, by extension, its position in the world.

There are good reasons for this neglect. Only 20 percent of Russia's population lives east of the Ural Mountains, the traditional divide between Europe and Asia. The main centers of Russian political, economic, and cultural activity are located in the European part of the country. Add to this the traumatic impact of the Mongol invasion in the thirteenth century, and subsequent three centuries of Mongol occupation (the so-called Mongol yoke—*mongolskoe igo*),[2] and one can understand why successive regimes—Tsarist, Communist, and post-Soviet—have found it difficult to engage with Asia. To most Russians it is the very embodiment of the "other": at times threatening, at other times an object of contempt or puzzlement, but always alien.

Given this mindset, the rise of Asia presents especially difficult challenges to a Russia seeking to reassert its international influence. Decisionmakers in Moscow call for the end of the American-led political order and Western-dominated global economy. But the arrival of a "post-American world" requires them to make counterintuitive choices, including overcoming the prejudices and ignorance that have historically constrained Russia's approach toward Asia.

The ongoing discussion about Moscow's "turn to the East" (*povorot na vostok*)[3] exemplifies this conundrum. There is intellectual acceptance that Russian foreign policy must adapt to a world in which "global power . . . is shifting to the East, primarily to the Asia-Pacific region." There is also optimism regarding Russia's place as "an integral part of this fastest-developing geopolitical zone."[4] However, many observers are apprehensive that it may struggle to prosper in a world of rapid transition and new realities.[5] Regime pronouncements highlight the opportunities,[6] but the challenges and potential threats to Russian interests posed by the rise of Asia are formidable—not least the issue of relative weakness vis-à-vis China.[7] Far from being one of the winners in the emerging international system, Russia could find itself cast adrift by the dynamism of contemporary politics.

The issue, then, is not whether Moscow needs to engage more seriously with Asia, but how. What should it be trying to achieve, and by what means? The natural inclination is to resort to the familiar: emphasizing Russia's traditional persona as a geopolitical great power. Even if it cannot match the United States and China, so the argument goes, it can play the part of "swing state."[8] But such ambitions are scarcely pertinent to the new world disorder—and Asian regional disorder—in which Russia must operate. They reveal an outdated and self-defeating view of Asia as a theater of global grand strategy. They misunderstand the dynamics of regional political and economic processes. And they threaten to reduce Russia's "turn to the East" to an empty slogan.

## Defining Asia and "Asian-ness"

Physically, Asia extends west-east from the Ural Mountains to the Pacific Ocean, and north-south from the Arctic to the Indian Ocean and Southeast Asia. Russians, however, tend to understand Asia in narrower terms—as the Asia-Pacific region plus India.[9] Iran and the Arab world are regarded as part of the Near East (*blizhnii vostok*), while Central Asia belongs to the post-Soviet space (*post-sovetskoe prostrantsvo*), Near Abroad (*blizhnii zarubezh*), or Eurasia (*Evraziya*). There are a few exceptions that do not fit within these parameters, such as Afghanistan, Pakistan, and Mongolia, but overall the Russian elite retains a strongly East Asia–centric view of the Asian continent.

The phrase "a turn to the East" reflects this geographical bias. Whereas the Middle East and Central Asia are routinely described as part of the "south" (*yug*), China, India, Japan, the Koreas, and Southeast Asia fall within the larger "East" (*vostok*). As for the United States, it is seen as an interloper. In the mainstream Russian narrative it is a Euro-Atlantic power and Western civilization, which is active in Asia not because it belongs there, but by virtue of being the sole superpower.

This leads to the question of how Asian Russia feels. It has long been axiomatic to describe it as a European civilization, but a Eurasian empire.[10] But in recent years descriptions such as "Euro-Pacific power" have become fashionable, adding to an already confusing lexicon (Asian, Eurasian, Asia-Pacific, and so forth).

It is important to distinguish between Eurasian and Euro-Pacific. At first sight, they appear near-synonyms, but culturally and historically they are very different. To describe Russia as Eurasian is to emphasize both its distinctiveness and its geopolitical position as the heartland power.[11] Eurasian denotes that unique blend of Western civilization and eastern influences that has marked Russian identity since the Mongol invasion. It also refers to the vast space between Europe and (East) Asia, which Russia has occupied since the conquest of Siberia in the early seventeenth century. Crucially, Eurasian does not imply that Russia is Asian as such, but rather an in-between—and independent—civilization. This self-identification is at the root of the popular notions of Russia as a bridge between civilizations, and geopolitical balancer between the United States and China (see chapter 2).

Euro-Pacific, by contrast, is a modern concept that highlights changing international trends as seen from Moscow: the decline of the West, the rise of the rest, and the shift of global power to the East. It is a loaded term that rejects the dominance of the West, and advocates instead an enhanced commitment to engagement with the Asia-Pacific region. Unlike Eurasianism it reflects a forward-looking agenda; whereas Russia has been a Eurasian power for several centuries, it has yet to become a Euro-Pacific—and properly Asian—power. The Euro-Pacific vision is more ambitious than Eurasianism. It does not only seek to preserve Russia's national and trans-continental identity, but to build on it in light of contemporary realities.[12] A Russia that has arrived as a Euro-Pacific power would combine the dynamism of East Asia with the still powerful trumps of Western culture and technology, and, of course, Russian tradition.

## Betwixt Aspiration and Achievement

But to realize such an ambitious vision will be impossible unless Moscow is able to address three long-standing problems of Russian policy in Asia: (1) an instrumentalism that has distorted its engagement with Asian countries and organizations; (2) an excessive Sinocentrism that has caused it to neglect key Asian relationships; and (3) the disconnect between grandiose rhetoric and underwhelming achievement. For much of the post-Soviet era these deficiencies have conspired to relegate Russia to the periphery of Asia.

### Instrumentalism

The most serious weakness has been an inability to value engagement on its own merits. For much of the past century, Asia's chief importance to Moscow has stemmed from its place within a larger Russian and Soviet global design. It was a theater of superpower rivalry with the United States, and the front line in a separate, mostly "cold" confrontation with China.[13] But Moscow's interest in Asian affairs as such was minimal, despite occasional attempts to articulate a policy.[14] Instead, Soviet attention was focused on triangular diplomacy with the United States and China. During the period of "unbreakable friendship" with Beijing in the 1950s,[15] the Kremlin hoped to enlist Mao Zedong as an ally against the United States (and its Asian allies). After U.S. President Richard Nixon's 1972 visit to China, this gave way to a siege mentality in the face of the new Sino-American concordat.[16]

As chapter 2 showed, such triangularism continued even after the fall of the Soviet Union and the collapse in Russia's strategic and economic fortunes. The Yeltsin administration invested heavily in instrumentalist notions, such as the "multipolar world order."[17] Multipolarity became shorthand for a revised or pseudo bipolarity.[18] If Russia could no longer match the United States on its own, it would seek likeminded partners to counterbalance American "unipolar" power. China, by virtue of its size and potential, was the natural candidate to fulfill this role.

Except that Beijing had its own agenda—to relaunch Chinese foreign policy and break out of the isolation caused by the Tiananmen crackdown in June 1989. The Communist Party leadership's emphasis on domestic modernization and engagement with the West, embodied in the idea of "peaceful rise,"[19] and its corresponding lack of interest in geopolitical balancing, meant that Russia became increasingly marginalized in both East and West. Chinese lip service to multipolarity belied a generally dismissive attitude toward a concept rooted in cold war thinking.

During the 1990s Moscow's stubborn attachment to competitive multipolarity limited its capacity to develop effective strategies toward Asia. It conveyed the unfortunate message that Asia was of interest only as a subset of Russia's relations with the West: a counterweight to American power and a means of extracting greater consideration for Russian interests in areas that had little to do with Asia, such as NATO enlargement and the post-Soviet space.

The effects of the Kremlin's instrumentalism were exacerbated by an all too obvious tokenism in relation to regional multilateral mechanisms. At the same time as Russia was beginning to engage with pan-European institutions—NATO, the Council of Europe, the OSCE—there was no corresponding effort in Asia. Although Russia was a member of the ARF (ASEAN Regional Forum), and entered APEC (Asia-Pacific Economic Cooperation) in 1998, it remained an uninterested bystander in larger processes of Asian security-building and economic cooperation.[20]

This instrumentalism established a pattern whereby Russia's engagement with Asia would inevitably be affected by the vagaries of its relations with the United States and Europe. Typically, policymakers would talk up the importance of Asia, and Sino-Russian partnership in particular, during difficult times—in the second half of the 1990s, in the wake of the 1999 Kosovo crisis, and following the U.S.-led intervention in Iraq and the Orange Revolution in Ukraine. But Asia's profile in Russian foreign policy would fall markedly whenever there was a rapprochement with the West—immediately after the collapse of the Soviet Union, in the aftermath of 9/11, and at the height of the U.S.-Russia reset (2009–10).

The zero-sum mentality that afflicted other areas of Russian foreign policy was especially apparent in relation to Asia. Cooperation was frequently cast in revanchist terms, as a reaction to the slights Russia had suffered at the hands of the West, rather than as the rational rebalancing of a foreign policy that was overly centered on the United States and (to a lesser extent) Europe.[21] In other words, the accent was less on engaging with the East than withdrawing from the West (or teaching it a lesson). Unsurprisingly, Asian elites took the view that Russia was rarely serious about cooperation for its own sake, but harbored ulterior motives born of an irredeemably Westerncentric outlook.[22]

After Putin came to power in January 2000, bilateral issues began to assume a higher profile in Russia's major relationships in Asia. The most impressive progress was in the strengthening and expansion of ties with China. The border was finalized in 2005; trade increased eightfold between 1998 and 2007, from US$5.7 billion to US$48 billion; and there was a spectacular increase in human contacts. (In 2006, for example, there were some two million Russian visits to China, and 900,000 Chinese visits to Russia.)[23] Trade with Japan also grew substantially,[24] and there were signs that the Russian elite was beginning to appreciate the intrinsic importance of engaging with Asia, even if Asia still meant the major Asian powers—China, Japan, and India.

Nevertheless, during Putin's first two presidential terms Moscow still viewed Asia's importance primarily in terms of promoting Russia as a center of global power in the multipolar world. Its policy priorities were focused almost entirely on the West. These encompassed not only "Western" issues, such as missile defense, NATO enlargement, and the future of Euro-Atlantic security, but also matters of wider international remit—the war in Afghanistan, sanctions against Iran, international terrorism, and WMD proliferation. In these discussions Asian countries were either ignored or, in the case of China and to a much lesser extent India, enlisted as makeweights to counter the preponderance of Western power. Meanwhile, Moscow showed little interest in areas where Asian countries were the principal actors. Its involvement on the Korean peninsula was marginal, and its participation in Asian security and economic matters nominal.

### Sinocentrism

One of the more consistent features of Russian engagement with Asia is the extent to which it has been dominated by the relationship with China. There have been brief periods when other Asian countries have assumed a high profile: Japan during World War II and the Russo-Japanese war of 1904–05, and India in the 1970s when Indira Gandhi was prime minister and Leonid Brezhnev was leader of the Soviet Union. But more often than not China has been synonymous with Asia. Even today, many Russians understand the "shift of global power to the East" as signifying above all the rise of China.

In many respects the case for a China-first approach is incontrovertible. China is Russia's largest neighbor, with the two countries sharing a border of more than 4,000 kilometers (7,000 km in Soviet times). It is the biggest economy in Asia, and will overtake the United States in size of GDP sometime in the next few years. Its regional influence is growing rapidly, with direct implications for the Russian Far East (RFE) and Central Asia. It represents an enormous and fast expanding energy market. And it is on track to become the next superpower—a position from which it will affect the full range of Russian interests. It is logical, therefore, that Moscow should prioritize partnership with Beijing.

The problem is one of degree. Such has been the focus on China, under Yeltsin and then Putin, that it is no exaggeration to say that for much of the past two decades Russia has not had an Asia policy so much as a "China-plus" policy in Asia. At different times it has attempted a more diversified approach, but with no great perseverance. In the 1990s, the Yeltsin administration flirted with Tokyo in an attempt to counterbalance China in Northeast Asia, while later Putin played the Japan card in order to negotiate a better deal on the East Siberian–Pacific Ocean (ESPO) oil pipeline.[25] But these efforts met with little success, largely because of irreconcilable differences with Tokyo over the sovereignty of the South Kuriles/Northern Territories (see below). Likewise, Russian policymakers have occasionally been moved to build closer ties with India—in the late 1990s with a Moscow–Beijing–New Delhi axis,[26] and again from the mid-2000s—but with unimpressive results.

Consequently, although ideas of strategic diversity featured quite prominently during Putin's first presidential term, after 2004–05 they gave way to an emphasis on Sino-Russian convergence. This shift was partly a reaction to the deterioration in Russia-U.S. relations. But there were other reasons too. The Kremlin saw a close relationship with Beijing not only as a security imperative—reinforcing the RFE—but as critical to Russia's standing in the world. In light of China's growing self-confidence and capabilities, there was a strong desire to associate with it in preference to a weakened Japan and an India yet to make its mark internationally.

Sinocentrism is by its very nature self-reinforcing and self-excluding. The more Moscow stakes on China, the closer it ties itself to Beijing's interests and priorities, and the harder it is to develop more fruitful relations with other Asian countries. Excessive Sinocentrism is the antithesis of a flexible and comprehensive Asian strategy. Moscow's ability to wean itself from its China addiction is, however, contingent on larger changes in its foreign policy thinking. Chief among these is the dilution of a strategic culture that assumes that great powers and geopolitics will dominate the international system for the foreseeable future. As long as the Russian political elite holds such views, Beijing will remain pivotal in any Asia policy coming out of Moscow. Indeed, given the perception that China is catching up with the United States, there is a growing temptation to see partnership with Beijing as the centerpiece of Russia's *overall* foreign policy.

### Rhetoric versus substance

The third historical failing of Russian engagement in Asia is the disconnect between rhetoric and substance. At the most general level, this is apparent in the fiction that Moscow attaches as much importance to Asia as it does to the West. The theme of geographical balance has been a staple of successive foreign policy and national security concepts, military doctrines, and summit communiqués. However, the *practice* of Russian foreign policy has remained overwhelmingly centered on the West.

The myth of evenhandedness is also contradicted by economic realities. Moscow has been proclaiming its commitment to developing trade and investment with the Asia-Pacific region since the early 1990s. However, in 2012 Russia accounted for only 1 percent of total trade in the region.[27] Even the relative success story of Sino-Russian trade needs to be placed in proper context. Moscow identifies China as its most important economic partner, and this is true inasmuch as trade with China is greater than with any *single* EU member-state—a function largely of the boom in global energy and commodity prices.[28] Yet this glosses over the fact that in 2013 the EU accounted for nearly 50 percent of Russia's total trade, compared with China's 11 percent,[29] while Europe and North America provided over 90 percent of foreign direct investment into Russia.[30] It is easy to forget, in all the excitement about the Sino-Russian oil and gas deals of 2013–14, that more than 90 percent of Russian energy exports went to Europe.[31] While this share is set to decline post-Crimea, it will take two decades (at least) for Asia to become the primary destination of Russian oil and gas.

There are objective reasons why Russia's trade and investment ties with Asia should be underdeveloped, such as a long-time political and civilizational orientation toward Europe and the evident constraints of distance and demography. But human failings have also had a corrosive effect on cooperation. The fear that Asian countries, China in particular, may outwit a "too trusting" Russia is less overt than with the United States and Europe, but still powerful. Such apprehension has delayed progress in gas negotiations, deterred significant investment into Russia, limited military cooperation, and reinforced the isolation of the RFE. In the process it has highlighted the contradiction between official rhetoric about "win-win outcomes" and a defensive mentality in which the fear of losing control outweighs the sense of opportunity.

Another set of myths relates to the alleged normative convergence between Moscow and Beijing, including on so-called state capitalism. Russian politicians and commentators have regularly claimed that the Soviet Union would have prospered had Gorbachev pursued the "Chinese path" to reform, based on top-down economic modernization.[32] In recent years, this has shifted to the narrative of a China model (or Beijing consensus) as an alternative to Western democratic capitalism. Yet the truth is that Russians have never subscribed to, or even understood, any such "model." They have envied China's success, but have shown no desire to undertake the radical changes—most of which were bottom-up—that have underpinned its modernization.[33]

Partly, this reflects a risk-averse mentality, but it also highlights a lasting conviction that the West remains the benchmark in many respects. Members of the Russian elite send their children to study in Europe and the United States;[34] Russian scientists work in Western universities and research institutes; IT specialists and programmers go to Silicon Valley; Russian companies have sought Western technology and know-how; and middle-class Russians see themselves as part of a superior European civilization. Even proponents of Eurasianism advertise the distinctiveness of Russian national values, rather than any similarities to Asian culture. With the steady growth of disposable income during the Putin years, many more Russians have been traveling to Asia. But this hardly signifies empathy, let alone identification. Asia represents exotica and difference—more accessible than before, but still a world apart.

Much of this mythmaking is relatively harmless. It should not matter that Russia is "in Asia, but not *of* Asia";[35] a lack of "Asian-ness" has hardly stopped countries as different as Germany and Brazil from operating effectively there. The problem is the gulf between Russian self-perceptions—as a great power with accompanying sense of entitlement—and the generally dismissive view of Asian elites regarding its contribution to regional and global affairs.[36]

## Learning New Lessons—or Repeating Old Mistakes?

Russia's prospects of becoming a serious player in Asia depend on how far it is able to address the weaknesses of instrumentalism, excessive Sinocentrism, and the disjunction between rhetoric and achievement. These are deep-seated problems, and it is unrealistic to expect an early transformation in Russian thinking and policy. What is reasonable, though, is to look for signs of evolving attitudes, even if these take time to translate into tangible outcomes. Has Moscow learned from past mistakes and failures, or does it believe that it is on the right track, with only a little tweaking required here and there?

It should be recognized at the outset that there has been some progress. Moscow's turn to the East represents in itself acknowledgment that Russian policy toward Asia has been flawed for much of the post-Soviet era. In late 2010 the National Committee of the Council for Security Cooperation in the Asia-Pacific (CSCAP-Russia) remarked on the political and economic elite's "disdainful attitude toward Asia as a secondary region of the world"; admitted that "other countries of the region do not regard Russia as an Asia-Pacific country"; and described its role in Asia-Pacific affairs as "marginal."[37]

The government knows it must do better. Accordingly, since 2011 it has begun to address some of the underlying problems. There is now a general acceptance that Asia matters in and of itself, and not merely as a theater of global geopolitics and adjunct (and instrument) of Russian foreign policy. The Kremlin has invested greater efforts into diversifying Russia's ties in Asia, looking beyond China to countries such as Japan, Vietnam, and India. And it is less complacent about Russia's place or destiny in Asia. There is an improved commitment to substantive cooperation, for example, involving Russian big business in major commercial ventures.

The Kremlin hopes that this push ("turn," "pivot") to the East will be a game changer, both for Russia's relationships with individual Asian countries and in terms of its broader influence in the Asia-Pacific region. Russia would retain its traditional strengths—as the natural geopolitical balancer between the United States and China and civilizational bridge between East and West—but also exploit more modern advantages. It would become the leading supplier of Asia's energy requirements; a key source of arms and civilian nuclear technology; and, in the longer term, the answer to the food and water needs of the whole Eurasian continent.

But, as in other areas of foreign policy, Putin's idealized vision is constantly confronted by forces beyond his control: systemic trends within and beyond Asia; unforeseen events; and ingrained instincts. It is no small achievement for the Russian elite to have moved toward a sharper, more sophisticated consciousness of Asia. But to convert this into effective decisionmaking presents more difficult challenges still. This emerges clearly when we examine Russia's major relationships in Asia, starting with China.

## China

*Instrumentalism and post-instrumentalism.* The Sino-Russian partnership is central to the whole iconography about a turn to the East and Russia as a Euro-Pacific power. It also raises a critical ambiguity. Does Putin's emphasis on close ties with Beijing point to a new interest in Asia or instead reaffirm old geopolitical thinking based on the continuing dominance of the great powers? The China relationship is the litmus test of whether Russian policymakers have graduated from an instrumentalist mindset to a more businesslike engagement with Asia.

As noted earlier, during Putin's first two terms Moscow was already exhibiting greater interest in bilateral issues than under Yeltsin. The global financial crisis accelerated this trend. China's resilience to its effects appeared to show that it had emerged as a bona fide global power, reinforcing an already compelling case for expanded cooperation. Simultaneously Russian concerns about overreliance on the leading Western economies intensified the search for new energy markets and sources of foreign investment.[38] In the wake of the great crash, China represented a highly attractive proposition: its demand for energy and other natural resources was rising rapidly; it had money to burn; and the growth of interregional ties offered a potential solution to the perennial problem of under-development in the RFE.

But if bilateral cooperation has acquired greater intrinsic importance, Russian policy toward China has yet to move into a post-instrumentalist phase. At the height of the reset with Washington there were hopes that Russia could have it all: productive relations with the United States and Europe, and strategic partnership with China. But once the reset began to lose momentum from 2011, old habits of geopolitical balancing returned. The traditional nexus of difficulties with Washington equating to enhanced engagement with Beijing reemerged, as differences over missile defense, Syria, and Russian domestic politics widened. Today, more than ever, Sino-Russian statements give pride of place to the two countries' "identical" positions on world affairs, and their common opposition to American "unilateralism" and Western moral interventionism.[39] Moscow courts Beijing in promoting the BRICS as a global institution to challenge the primacy of the West, and seeks its political support on core Russian interests.[40]

China's instrumental importance has been starkly evident during the Ukraine crisis. There has been copious commentary about a new Sino-Russian strategic convergence in opposition to the West.[41] This misunderstands the nature of the relationship, as we shall see later. Nevertheless, it is a story that underpins a number of Kremlin narratives: that of Russia as an independent center of global power, no longer beholden to the West; Russia and China as part of the dynamic new world order in contrast to an arrogant United States and decaying Europe; and Russia as the wronged party, forced to turn East as a result of Western hostility.[42] In the process, partnership with China has become the principal source of geopolitical succor to the Putin regime, and its main hope of leveraging Western governments.

Even substantive bilateral achievements, such as the Sino-Russian gas deal of May 2014, have a significance that extends well beyond their commercial value. Although there were sound economic reasons to conclude the agreement, until recently these were insufficient to resolve a decade-long impasse. The Ukraine crisis, and subsequent Western sanctions against Moscow, turned out to be the catalyst for a breakthrough. The primary issue was no longer price, energy security, or development of new markets. What mattered most to Putin was signaling to the United States and Europe that Russia was strategically independent, would not be intimidated by the imposition of sanctions, and possessed powerful friends. In other words, political—and instrumental—considerations proved decisive.

*Sinocentrism versus diversification.* The Kremlin is sensitive to the risks of a China-dependent approach within Asia. At the most instinctive level it is concerned that this could result in Russia becoming the junior partner in the relationship, in thrall to Chinese interests and priorities. There is a significant psychological dimension as well. For the last 300 years Russians have been accustomed to seeing China as weak, backward, and inferior in virtually every respect. While this view has become obsolete as a result of the latter's transformation post-Mao, Moscow is far from ready to accept China as the senior partner and more influential power. To admit this would be at odds with the message of a resurgent Russia second to none. Moscow is therefore keen to downplay any impression of neediness, and to show Beijing that it has other friends and options in Asia.

Putin also understands that China is not Asia, or at least not the whole of Asia. If Russia is to turn East in earnest, it must look beyond Beijing. This realization has been reinforced by developments since the onset of the global financial crisis. The growing assertiveness of Chinese foreign policy, and the apprehensions this has elicited among its neighbors, has demonstrated that a China-first approach and an Asian strategy are not synonymous and may sometimes be incompatible. There has consequently been a revival of Russian interest in pursuing strategic diversity at the regional as well as global level—developing ties with Tokyo, New Delhi, and Hanoi as counterpoints to the partnership with Beijing. Such moves contain a large element of opportunism. A tense Asia-Pacific environment appears to allow Russia to play the part of regional balancer, as other major actors seek its cooperation in hedging against China, or, in China's case, against the United States and Japan.[43]

Moscow has moved from declaratory intent to practical steps. In 2013 it responded to Japanese overtures for a political rapprochement (see below). It has proceeded with major arms sales and nuclear cooperation with India. It has sold advanced weaponry to Vietnam, and is exploring gas options in the South China Sea.[44] And it used the opportunity of hosting the 2012 APEC summit to tout its Asian credentials to a wide regional audience, including South Korea and the ASEAN countries.[45]

It is an odd paradox, then, that despite these efforts Russian policy in Asia has become more, not less, Sinocentric. And this was true even before the Ukraine crisis pushed the Kremlin further toward Beijing. Between 2010 and 2013 the importance of Sino-Russian partnership increased relative to Russia's ties with other Asian countries in just about every respect. Political coordination in the UN Security Council became closer, especially but not only on Syria. The leitmotif of identical views on international issues became more insistent. Energy cooperation received a major boost as a result of the global financial crisis. Chinese banks provided the critical loans (US$25 billion) to Rosneft and Transneft that Western—and Japanese—institutions had refused, in return for which the Russians finally completed the Daqing spur of the ESPO oil pipeline in September 2010. Military-to-military cooperation reached new levels, with several large joint exercises, while for the first time since 2006 there was progress toward high-end arms sales.[46] China's share of Russian trade in Asia also increased substantially. In 2008 this was worth US$57 billion, compared with US$29 billion for Japan, and US$18 billion for the Republic of Korea (ROK). In 2013 the corresponding figures were US$89 billion, US$33 billion, and US$25 billion.[47]

Moscow has become more pro-Chinese on important regional issues as well. Whereas it was once content to do the bare minimum—subscribing to the "one China" policy vis-à-vis Taiwan and Tibet—it now leans toward Beijing in areas where it was previously neutral, such as maritime sovereignty in the South China Sea. Thus it advocates bilateral negotiations between the disputants instead of a multilateral process (as favored by Vietnam and the Philippines), and condemns U.S. mediation efforts as unwarranted interference in the affairs of the region.[48] On the Korean question it has closely followed Beijing's lead in pressing for the resumption of the Six-Party talks, and similarly indulged Pyongyang's excesses.[49] Even its neutral stance on the Senkaku/Diaoyu islands dispute has worked out well for Beijing. By staying out of the dispute, Moscow has fallen in with the Chinese desire to keep this a purely bilateral affair with Japan.[50]

Sometimes Moscow's amenability to Chinese objectives reflects a genuine likemindedness, for example in opposing Western military intervention in Syria. On other occasions Russian policy is influenced by an eye for the tactical chance—as when it exploited U.S.-China divisions at the 2009 Copenhagen climate change summit to oppose mandatory targets for carbon dioxide emissions, thereby limiting its own obligations. But the main reason why Moscow is so compliant toward Beijing is that it wishes to avoid unnecessary tensions over secondary priorities. In this, it is heavily influenced by classical understandings of power. While Putin recognizes the merits of a diversified approach in Asia, he believes that the road to a more secure and influential Russia ultimately runs through Beijing; no amount of improvement in ties with other Asian countries can compensate for a deterioration in relations with China. Such a course becomes all the more palatable when Chinese leaders and media flatter Russian sensibilities—extolling Sino-Russian partnership, inflating Russia's importance in the world, and praising the personal achievements of President Putin.[51]

This has emerged very clearly in the course of the Ukraine crisis. The crisis was not a game changer in the sense of introducing a new set of assumptions to Russia's relations with China and Asia. What it did was to reinforce long-established truths. It highlighted the obvious point that China is the closest thing to a friend that Russia has in the Asia-Pacific region. Well might the Kremlin hope to balance Beijing's growing influence through political rapprochement with Tokyo or improved economic cooperation with New Delhi. But this goal pales into insignificance compared with the *global* imperative of balancing the United States (and Europe). For all the fabled independence of Russian foreign policy, Moscow looks more than ever to Beijing for geopolitical support, new energy markets, investment in infrastructure, and normative solidarity. The Ukraine crisis has exposed the flimsiness of its attempts at diversification, the extent of Russia's strategic dependence on China, and the narrowness of the "turn to the East."

*Cooperation in theory and practice.* If the Sino-Russian partnership dwarfs Moscow's other relationships in Asia, then their bilateral cooperation remains modest nonetheless. Although trade has expanded considerably over the past decade—from less than US$16 billion in 2003 to US$89 billion in 2013—it scarcely reflects the size and proximity of the two economies, as Russian and Chinese leaders themselves have acknowledged.[52] In 2013 Russia ranked ninth among China's trading partners, accounting for a share of 2.2 percent—not only well behind the EU (13.4 percent share), the United States (12.4 percent), and Japan (7.5 percent), but also South Korea, Australia, Malaysia, and Brazil.[53] Moscow is also unhappy about the "unbalanced" nature of trade, which resembles that of developing countries in Africa and Latin America with Beijing—natural resource exports in return for manufacturing imports.[54] Although such asymmetry reflects their comparative advantages, many Russians find it hard to swallow the idea of being a "raw materials appendage" or resource-cow for Chinese modernization.[55]

For a long time the investment picture was especially unimpressive; in 2011 China invested a measly US$300 million into the Russian economy—0.5 percent of its total overseas amount that year.[56] The situation is changing, but only because of the drastic shortfall in Western investment and credit finance following the imposition of sanctions. The Kremlin simply has nowhere else to go to access significant external funding. Even so, Chinese investment is focused mainly on natural resources extraction rather than value-added industries.[57]

*Energy cooperation—a game changer?* It is symptomatic of the difficulties in Sino-Russian cooperation that the natural complementarity between the world's largest energy exporter and its biggest importer has taken so long to be realized, and then thanks largely to extraneous factors. Without the global financial crisis and refusal of Western banks to lend to Rosneft and Transneft, there would have been no oil-for-loan arrangement in 2009 and little likelihood of the Daqing spur to the ESPO pipeline being completed anytime soon.[58] Similarly, the June 2013 deal between Rosneft and CNPC to export 360 million tonnes of oil over 25 years, worth an estimated US$270 billion,[59] benefited from the deterioration of Russia-West relations, and more specific disagreements on energy policy between Moscow and Brussels. The most recent illustration of the power of external influences is the May 2014 gas agreement, which was motivated principally by Putin's determination to assert Russian "independence" in the face of Western sanctions.

One could argue that it does not matter how the deals are done; what counts is the end result. However, the experience of Sino-Russian energy cooperation demonstrates that signing the contract is only the first stage in an often protracted and difficult process. The 2009 oil-for-loan agreement, for example, suffered serious teething problems, with Moscow accusing the Chinese of failing to keep up with payments. With the 2013 oil agreement, there are bound to be significant fluctuations in price over such a long time frame, not to mention other changes in circumstances. An earlier arrangement between Rosneft and CNPC almost unraveled as a result of the boom in global prices after 2004, and had to be renegotiated amid much ill-feeling on both sides.[60] And even if the latest oil agreement is fully implemented, Russia will be only one of a growing number of suppliers to China. In 2013 its market share was 9 percent, well behind Saudi Arabia (19 percent) and Angola (14 percent), and roughly the same as Oman, Iran, and Iraq.[61] Although this percentage is set to rise, Beijing's breadth of options may tempt it to renegotiate or renege on the deal at some stage.[62]

The prospect of Russian gas deliveries to China is more uncertain still. It may be that the May 2014 agreement "will have serious impacts on both regional and global patterns of gas trade and energy security,"[63] but there are many complex challenges that need to be overcome first: lack of clarity over price; outstanding issues regarding the construction and routing of pipelines; and securing the vast amounts of funding required to make cooperation a reality.[64] The track record with other projects suggests that the anticipated start time of 2018 for gas deliveries is highly optimistic; an otherwise bullish Sberbank report from 2014 estimates that the anticipated annual volume of 38 bcm will probably not be reached until the late 2020s.[65] More worryingly, in March 2015 there were reports that the project had been suspended because slumping energy prices had made it economically unviable. The environment is not likely to get any easier. The development of regional gas hubs and possibly a global gas market over the next decade will lead to greater price volatility. (This was an issue earlier in the negotiations, when Gazprom flatly rejected CNPC's suggestion of indexing the price to the very low U.S. Henry Hub benchmark.)[66]

But perhaps the most serious risk to Sino-Russian gas cooperation comes from Chinese energy policy. As with oil imports, Beijing has worked assiduously to broaden its options in gas, coal, and renewables. China is now the leading energy player in Central Asia. In 2013 gas imports from Turkmenistan exceeded 24 bcm, and this volume is expected to reach 40 bcm in 2014 and 65 bcm by 2020.[67] Unlike the Power of Siberia pipeline envisaged by the Sino-Russian agreement, the Central Asia–China Gas Pipeline (CAGP) system is not only in existence but expanding rapidly.[68] The Chinese are also building scores of new LNG terminals, with the intention of significantly increasing imports from Australia, Qatar, Indonesia, and Malaysia. They are developing potentially the world's largest reserves of shale gas.[69] And Beijing has committed itself to increasing the share of renewables in Chinese energy consumption to 15 percent by 2020.

These considerations raise doubts about the sustainability of the May 2014 agreement and future cooperation. While China's escalating requirements mean that it will look to import significant volumes of Russian gas, it will hardly fail to exploit its growing energy diversification as leverage. Unlike many EU member-states, it can turn elsewhere if need be, to Central Asia in the first instance. Moreover, Moscow and Beijing have different goals. The Chinese have no interest in assisting Russia to become a primary supplier across the Asia-Pacific; they do not just want the gas but also to control the regional gas market. Such differences are likely to become growing sources of friction. Instead of being the swing energy power between Europe and Asia, as the Kremlin hopes, Russia may end up as a victim of increased regional competition, a global glut, and falling prices—with negative consequences for the wider bilateral relationship.

For a long time Moscow pursued a de facto policy of "anyone but the Chinese" in energy exploration and development. It routinely barred Chinese companies from acquiring equity in major projects, while encouraging other foreign partners—Americans, Europeans, Japanese, and Indians—to become more actively involved. Against this background, 2013 was something of a breakthrough year. Rosneft allowed CNPC into joint exploration projects in the Arctic and the RFE, while Russia's largest private gas company, Novatek, sold a 20 percent stake in its Yamal venture to CNPC.[70]

This new-found flexibility reflects the evolution of a less defensive mindset. But it would be naïve to imagine that long-standing problems of mistrust have miraculously disappeared with a few strokes of the pen. The Rosneft-CNPC joint ventures are necessarily speculative, and dwarfed by the much more substantial partnerships Rosneft concluded previously with ExxonMobil.[71] When it comes to the business of large-scale energy development, the Kremlin looks to Western international oil companies (IOCs) first. This is mainly because they alone can provide the advanced technology Russia needs. But it also owes something to the perception that they are independent entities and not agencies of a foreign state, as is the case with CNPC. Western sanctions over Ukraine have challenged, but not nullified, these assumptions. It is telling that, as of spring 2015, ExxonMobil remains the biggest outside investor in the Russian Far East, despite the deepening crisis in Russia-U.S. relations.

*The myth of identical views.* The gap between rhetoric and reality is also evident in the political relationship. Over the past twenty years, this has gone steadily through the gears—from normalization to "strategic partnership relations" to today's "comprehensive strategic partnership of coordination."[72] In the process a virtual reality has emerged to the effect that Russia and China are of one mind in their view of the world and its challenges. This pretense has managed to fool at least some of the people some of the time, with a number of Western commentators subscribing to the myth of an authoritarian alliance directed against Western interests and values.[73]

While Moscow and Beijing agree on much—such as the unacceptability of moral interventionism, the threat posed by Islamist extremism, and the undesirability of an overly powerful United States—there are many areas where their interests and priorities diverge. Ironically, the most important difference is where they are often said to be in complete agreement, namely, attitudes toward the United States. For Beijing, America is the one truly indispensable partner, of immeasurably greater importance than Russia. The China-U.S. relationship is dogged by considerable tensions, but is also characterized by a high degree of interdependence and cooperation.[74] China's leadership recognizes, moreover, that the post-Mao transformation would not have happened without the support of the U.S.-led political and economic order. While it seeks changes that would allow it greater influence within the existing global system, it has little interest in pursuing the ambition of a new order with all its attendant risks and responsibilities.

Moscow counts on tapping into Chinese unhappiness about the Obama administration's "rebalancing" toward Asia.[75] But Beijing has few illusions that Russia is a capable or even willing counterweight to the United States.[76] And it scarcely believes in a tripolar world; Xi's "new pattern of great power relations" is an openly bipolar concept. Conversely, while the Kremlin retains a generally optimistic view of Russia's international prospects, it is wary about China's long-term intentions and fast-improving military capabilities. It has no more liking for a potentially hegemonic China than for a domineering America; it is just that the latter is a far more pressing concern.[77] This caution is one reason why Moscow will not agree to further cuts in Russia's nuclear arsenal unless future disarmament negotiations are "multilateralized" and the Chinese brought into the process.[78] Underlying all this is the theme of strategic independence. The long-term rationale behind Russia's turn to the East is not to side with China against the United States, but to position itself as the indispensable power—needed by both and taken for granted by neither. A formal alliance with Beijing would undermine this purpose.

*Changing threat perceptions.* Although the narrative of Chinese irredentism in the Russian Far East has subsided since its heyday in the 1990s, it is not extinct. The historical bogey of "millions of Chinese" flooding across the border may have given way to the image of "illegal" Central Asian migrants. But the threat of the great Chinese takeaway remains, albeit in softer form. Moscow hawks the RFE's potential as an Asia-Pacific economic hub, yet is guarded about increased commercial participation by China.[79]

The discrepancies between public face and policy reality are likewise evident in relation to Central Asia. During the Putin era, Moscow and Beijing have maintained a pragmatic arrangement. The latter has expanded its economic influence, but not attempted to establish a significant political or security presence. It has also talked up Russia's credentials as the regional leader. For its part Moscow has made only half-hearted attempts to contain Chinese commercial interests and been publicly supportive of institutions such as the SCO. This mutual accommodation has been eased by the fact that the region has been a secondary priority in their respective foreign policies. Neither side has an interest in confrontation, especially given more important concerns elsewhere.

Lately, however, this arrangement has come under some strain. Putin's pursuit of a Eurasian Union is generally portrayed as a response to the EU's Eastern Partnership program.[80] Yet it is also targeted at China. Pressuring Kyrgyzstan (and, in time, Tajikistan) to join the EEU is intended to shore up Russian influence against the one country that poses a long-term threat to its primacy in Central Asia. At the same time, the Chinese are moving beyond an economics-only approach. Xi's tour of four Central Asian countries (Turkmenistan, Kazakhstan, Uzbekistan, and Kyrgyzstan) in September 2013 was notable not only for several huge commercial deals, but also for agreements on political cooperation.[81] Although Moscow and Beijing are committed to managing any differences, the drawdown of U.S. combat troops from Afghanistan will test the strength of their security cooperation and geopolitical accommodation.[82]

Looking further ahead, Xi's vision of a "Silk Road economic belt" could, if realized, have far-reaching consequences both for the regional balance of influence and for the way Russia and China view each other.

To sum up the Putin regime's approach toward China, the principal theme is one of broad continuity. There have been some adjustments and changes of emphasis—such as a greater appreciation of the intrinsic importance of the relationship and a determined effort to inject substance into economic ties. But the fundamentals have remained largely the same. In important respects, the relationship is better and more substantial than it has ever been, and China will be Russia's most important partner in Asia for at least the next decade and probably beyond. Yet their interaction continues to be hampered by ambivalence, lack of trust, and often conflicting priorities. Not only is there no Sino-Russian alliance, but even the official claim that they are strategic partners is open to question. For this implies that they have a common view of the international system, of their respective places in it, and of the bilateral relationship. In fact, what Moscow and Beijing have is a fairly cynical partnership of convenience, whereby each pursues its particular interests and is not afraid to let the other side down should the need arise.[83]

### Japan

*Early promise.* Japan was the great hope of Russian policy in Asia during the 1990s. Although Moscow and Tokyo remained far apart on the question of sovereignty over the South Kuriles/Northern Territories,[84] there was nevertheless a conviction in parts of the Yeltsin administration that a solution could eventually be negotiated.[85] The personal chemistry between Yeltsin and Japanese Prime Minister Ryutaro Hashimoto led to two reasonably successful "no neckties" (*bez galstukov*) summits in Krasnoyarsk in November 1997 and Kawana in April 1998, and the prospects for progress under the so-called Yeltsin-Hashimoto plan looked promising.[86] The notion of "parallel wheels," whereby the territorial question and economic cooperation would be discussed simultaneously but separately, appeared to offer a way forward.[87]

Despite concerns in Tokyo that the Putin succession would see the return to a hardline Russian position, initially these fears were not realized. During his first term Putin worked hard to reach a compromise over the disputed islands on the basis of the 1956 Khrushchev formula,[88] while exploring ways of furthering bilateral cooperation. Moscow sometimes favored Japanese over Chinese interests—notably on the ESPO pipeline—and as late as 2004–05 an important strand within the Russian elite continued to believe that Japan was Russia's most natural partner in Asia.[89] It was more technologically advanced than China, and posed no threat to Russian security and economic interests.

*Conflicting perceptions.* This apparent promise, however, did not translate into a lasting rapprochement. By 2006 any positive momentum had dissipated. The Kremlin gravitated steadily toward a view of Japan as, at best, a secondary economic partner, while the political relationship slipped to a post–cold war low. With hindsight, Moscow and Tokyo were both culpable of a failure of understanding. The Russian side believed that it could insulate economic cooperation from the contaminating effect of the territorial issue; time, it hoped, would either heal historical wounds or encourage forgetfulness.[90] For their part the Japanese thought that concerns over the rise of China would make Moscow "see sense" and agree to the return of the islands under certain conditions: for example, de facto Russian administration for a number of years (the "Hong Kong option"); and joint development of the islands and common access to fisheries resources in the surrounding waters.[91]

In reality, for Putin and Japanese Prime Minister Junichiro Koizumi (2001–06), giving up sovereignty over the islands was extremely difficult not only for all the usual reasons, but also because they had staked their political credibility on being strong leaders. There was little room for maneuver, and ample scope for misunderstandings and recriminations. When Putin's attempts to finesse a solution via the Khrushchev formula were rebuffed, he accused the Japanese of negotiating in bad faith.[92]

The damage caused by the gulf between unrealistic expectations and disappointing outcomes has been aggravated by Japan's domestic difficulties over the past decade. Strangely, it is the political rather than economic dimension that has been most problematic. Notwithstanding the slowdown in Japanese growth from the 1980s, Russian politicians and businesspeople have retained a high regard for Japanese companies. What shocked them, however, was the unraveling of the Japanese political system post-Koizumi, signposted by a succession of weak prime ministers.[93] During this time the contrast between a dysfunctional Japan and buoyant China had never seemed more vivid, and the idea that Moscow might favor Tokyo over Beijing, or regard them as equivalent partners, became thoroughly implausible.

Russian favoritism toward China was reinforced by the continuing strength of the U.S.-Japan alliance. When the Liberal Democratic Party (LDP) lost control of the lower house of the Diet (parliament) to the Democratic Party of Japan in 2009, Moscow hoped that the change might loosen ties between Washington and Tokyo—hopes that were boosted by a bitter dispute over the future of the U.S. Marine Corps base at Futenma. These illusions were soon shattered. Instead of weakening, the alliance was strengthened by a series of developments: growing Chinese assertiveness in East Asia and the South China Sea; trade tensions between Washington and Beijing;

Obama's "rebalancing" toward Asia; shared anxieties about North Korea;[94] and the LDP's return to power in December 2012.

*A new thaw?* That said, the new LDP prime minister Shinzo Abe lost no time in reaching out to Putin, who had earlier been one of the first foreign leaders to offer assistance to Japan after the 2011 Tohoku earthquake and tsunami and Fukushima nuclear disaster. Abe's subsequent visit to Moscow in April 2013—the first by a Japanese prime minister to Russia in ten years— encouraged hopes of a major thaw.[95] Moscow and Tokyo established a 2+2 framework for regular consultations between their respective foreign and defense ministers, and the economic relationship enjoyed a significant upturn. Nissan and Toyota expanded their presence in the Russian car market;[96] Japan imported record volumes of Russian oil and LNG;[97] and the two countries moved to develop a US$7 billion LNG plant near Vladivostok. Some Japanese commentators attributed the rapprochement to mutual concerns about Chinese foreign policy behavior, and speculated that Moscow might offer compromises to resolve the territorial dispute.[98]

This optimism was misplaced, and repeated some of the misperceptions of the late 1990s and early 2000s. Even before the Ukraine crisis, it was improbable that Putin would give up the islands in return for the somewhat nebulous gain of enhanced political and economic partnership with Tokyo.[99] Such a (mis)calculation overestimated the value he placed on this; disregarded his assessment of the United States (Japan's closest ally) as Russia's number one geopolitical foe; and underestimated his commitment to Sino-Russian partnership.[100] His receptiveness to Abe's overtures indicated interest in pursuing a Japan option in Asian regional geopolitics. But, as noted earlier, Putin attached much greater priority to working with Xi Jinping to challenge U.S. global leadership.

In general the Kremlin operates on the premise that it holds all the high cards in its dealings with Tokyo. It was Abe, after all, who initiated the political rapprochement in late 2012. Moscow's concerns about the long-term implications of China's rise are insignificant compared with Japan's present and existential fears. And Russia feels under no particular pressure to surrender the disputed islands. On the contrary, it has the option of raising the stakes—as it did in 2010–12, when then president Medvedev, Deputy Prime Minister Igor Shuvalov, and Defense Minister Anatolii Serdyukov visited the islands, and the Russian government announced a military buildup to defend them against "foreign attack."[101]

*The Ukraine factor.* Events in Ukraine, the crisis in Russia-U.S. relations, and the Kremlin's renewed emphasis on strategic convergence with China have stalled the latest rapprochement. Although Tokyo's support for G-7 sanctions against Russia was lukewarm, it was enough to confirm the self-evident truth that Japan is politically, militarily, and economically aligned with the West. While Abe seeks better relations with Moscow, he will always be constrained in this by Japan's dependence on the United States' security umbrella and fear of China.

In these circumstances Russian ambitions of strategic diversity in Asia through a political rapprochement with Tokyo have been frozen, and even commercial cooperation is suffering. There is not only the obstacle of the territorial dispute, but also Moscow's overall leaning toward Beijing. Thus while it hopes to export oil and gas to the wider Asia-Pacific region, including Japan and South Korea, it is increasingly committed to the Chinese energy market—as the Rosneft and Gazprom deals of 2013–14 indicate. These agreements, along with low global oil prices, have scuppered the Vladivostok LNG project for the time being.

A resumption of the thaw between Moscow and Tokyo cannot be excluded, particularly if Russia's relations with the United States and Europe emerge from the current crisis. But there is a larger problem: in a disorderly regional environment, marked by serious Sino-Japanese tensions, Moscow's options are very restricted. Far from being able to play the part of a geopolitical swing power, it faces the prospect of having to pick sides on a growing number of highly sensitive issues. It has already discovered that close partnership with China means keeping Japan at arm's length, substantially reducing Russian chances of implementing a diversified Asia strategy over the next few years.

## India

India presents tricky challenges for a Russia struggling to develop an effective policy in Asia. In the first place, there can be little question of normative like-mindedness between an authoritarian regime in Moscow and a country where there is real political pluralism, rule of law, and a vibrant civil society. Although New Delhi shares Moscow's opposition to moral interventionism, and has maintained a neutral stance during the Ukraine crisis, it does not buy into relativistic ideas about democracy and human rights. Accordingly, myth-making of the sort that characterizes the Sino-Russian partnership has less purchase, which means there is more pressure to deliver on the substance of cooperation.

Second, the historical mistrust between Beijing and New Delhi tests Moscow's capacity to pursue a diversified strategy in Asia without prejudice to individual relationships. It is a challenging task to steer through the complications of continuing Sino-Indian tensions over Arunachal Pradesh, their disagreements over Pakistan and Kashmir, and Chinese suspicions that India is complicit in U.S. rebalancing toward Asia. Moreover, Moscow must not only reconcile cooperation with both China and India, but also accept that New Delhi, like Beijing, attaches primary importance to its relationship with Washington.

Third, India's aversion to geopolitical games poses the question of whether the Putin regime is capable of developing relations with New Delhi on a qualitatively different basis—that of bilateral economic interest rather than great power collusion. The task of establishing a new paradigm of relations is all the more difficult given the modest level of bilateral trade—around US$10 billion in 2013.[102]

The last few years have seen a number of positive developments in the relationship, notably cooperation in civilian nuclear energy and arms transfers. The Kudankulam nuclear power project in Tamil Nadu has made real progress, although its future has been complicated as a result of the antinuclear backlash after the Fukushima accident.[103] India has also replaced China as Russia's most important arms customer, in terms of both value and quality of weaponry.[104] There are no contentious bilateral issues, and so far Moscow has managed to stay clear of trouble over Arunachal Pradesh, Kashmir, and other sensitive questions.

However, the weaknesses that have hitherto constrained the relationship remain unresolved. The most cardinal of these is a bilateral agenda lacking in substance. There is no meaningful interaction on security issues, since the two countries do not share a common border, while India's remoteness from Central Asia makes it a secondary player in that region. Economic cooperation faces serious hurdles too. The development of major energy and infrastructural projects, such as the TAPI (Turkmenistan-Afghanistan-Pakistan-India) gas pipeline, is constrained by physical distance, an intimidating topography, and seemingly intractable political and security problems.[105] And several projects that have gone ahead have encountered serious difficulties. For example, the reconditioned aircraft carrier *Vikramaditya* (formerly *Admiral Gorshkov*) did not enter into service until 2013, nearly a decade after the initial deal was signed.[106] Most recently the onset of recession in Russia has hosed down earlier optimism about trade prospects.[107]

The upshot of these difficulties is that Russian policymakers still view India primarily through a globalist lens—as an instrument of geopolitical grand strategy and ally in a putative post-American order. Such an approach, however, is at odds with India's priorities, which remain centered on bilateral economic cooperation (arms, civilian nuclear energy, oil and gas ventures) and securing Russian support for its claims to a permanent seat in the UN Security Council.

This disjunction was already apparent in the 1990s, when the Indian government turned down Yevgeny Primakov's proposal for a Moscow–Beijing–New Delhi axis to counterbalance the United States.[108] Today India's aversion to an anti-American coalition (however dressed up) is even more palpable, and explains why it is the least committed member of the BRICS, and the keenest to ensure that it does not become a forum for beating up on the United States.

Moscow's hope that New Delhi might make common cause with Beijing against Washington is especially ill-founded given the U.S.-India strategic rapprochement initiated by George W. Bush in 2005, and revived by Obama in 2010.[109] It ignores concern in New Delhi about China's foreign policy assertiveness and military ties with India's neighbors, such as Pakistan and Sri Lanka.[110] Against this background the annual trilateral meeting between the foreign ministers of Russia, China, and India has become little more than a forum for exchanging polite views about the international situation. UN Security Council reform, in the meantime, is going nowhere. Although Moscow has expressed public support for New Delhi's claims to a permanent seat, in practice it has been the strongest advocate, along with Beijing, of the status quo.[111]

Russian policymakers have occasionally flirted with the idea of enlisting India as a counterweight to China in Central Asia. Their efforts have opened the way for Indian membership in the SCO, ostensibly to strengthen the regional consensus against the "three evils" of terrorism, separatism, and extremism, but really to mitigate China's dominant influence within the organization. However, for the most part Moscow has been careful not to be seen to pursue a containment policy against China, no matter how soft. In fact, it has taken steps in the other direction by drawing closer to Pakistan.[112] This reflects a perception that Islamabad may turn out to be the more useful security partner in central Eurasia following the withdrawal of NATO combat troops from Afghanistan.[113]

Judging by present trends, Russia-India relations will remain relatively stable and trouble-free, but undynamic. Despite continuing cooperation in the civilian nuclear sector and weapons sales, Moscow's influence in New Delhi is set to decline in the longer term, as Russian commercial interests are gradually squeezed out by American, European, and Chinese competition. This is already starting to happen in the arms trade.[114] Equally, the Indian vector in Russian foreign policy is likely to become less important, as its utility to

Moscow's geopolitical objectives in the Asia-Pacific region, Central Asia, and global politics becomes harder to demonstrate.

### The Koreas

Moscow's approach to the Korean peninsula has undergone many vicissitudes over the past two decades. During the 1990s the Yeltsin administration dismissed the idea of cooperation with North Korea, instead looking to South Korea as a promising source of foreign investment in the RFE and key customer for Russian gas. Although a close ally of the United States, Seoul was by no means servile to Washington, and might therefore serve as a partial regional alternative to Beijing and Tokyo.

By the end of the decade, these hopes had faded. Anticipated levels of South Korean trade and investment failed to materialize, and Seoul seemed fixated on the narrow priority of enlisting Moscow to help restrain North Korea. The mainstream Russian narrative on the Koreas became one of strategic regret—that Gorbachev had not obtained a better price for Moscow's "too cheap" diplomatic recognition of the Republic of Korea, and that Yeltsin had focused too much on engagement with the South while neglecting the North.[115]

This sense of regret—and determination to do better—has shaped Putin's policies toward the Korean peninsula. In 2000, his first year as president, he invited Kim Jong-il to Russia and renewed the Treaty of Friendship, Good-Neighborly Relations and Cooperation that had been in abeyance for several years.[116] Although Kim misled Putin by pretending to end North Korea's nuclear weapons program, this setback had no lasting effect. Much more influential was the conviction in Moscow that Russian influence in Northeast Asia, and on the Korean peninsula specifically, could only be preserved by maintaining an even-handed approach that made little political or moral distinction between North and South.[117] Accordingly, for the past fifteen years Moscow has balanced growing economic cooperation with South Korea (bilateral trade of US$25 billion in 2013) with closer political and security ties with North Korea.

Developments since the global financial crash have reinforced this dualist approach. Russia's growing dependence on China has ensured that much of its Korean policy is an extension of its partnership with Beijing. Moscow understands that the fate of North Korea is as important to China as Ukraine's is to Russia. It has therefore supported Beijing in its determination to maintain the Pyongyang regime at almost any cost. This includes de facto acquiescence in the North Korean nuclear program, even though it goes through the motions—like Beijing—of condemning nuclear testing.[118] Such compliant behavior reflects tacit acknowledgment that Russia has little independent standing on the Korean peninsula. While it might dream of one day restoring some of its Soviet-era influence in Pyongyang, this is improbable given the latter's economic dependence on Beijing, the shallowness of Russia's footprint in Northeast Asia, and the vast financial burden involved in sustaining North Korea.[119]

The outlook is somewhat more promising vis-à-vis South Korea. Although there is little prospect of genuine political convergence, the trend in economic relations is positive, with the ROK closing on Japan as Russia's second-largest trading partner in Asia after China.[120] President Park Geun-Hye has made encouraging noises about investing in trans-Eurasian infrastructural projects,[121] while consideration is being given to an undersea gas pipeline from China to Russia via Seoul (the so-called Weihai option).[122] Public attitudes toward Russia are also comparatively positive.[123] However, these modest achievements hardly amount to game changers, and it is doubtful whether they will greatly expand Russia's options in Northeast Asia. The proposed gas pipeline, for example, would bring it further into China's economic orbit, and the same is true for any projects involving North Korea.

### Southeast Asia

Southeast Asia has long been a backwater of Russian foreign policy. Following the collapse of the Soviet Union and the massive downsizing of the Soviet military, Russia's presence in the region became negligible.[124] Efforts in the 1990s to sell arms to Malaysia and floating nuclear reactors to Indonesia were undermined by the 1997 Asian financial crisis, and Russian interaction with the ASEAN member-states did not extend much beyond pro forma participation in various multilateral forums. Bilateral trade was minimal, and cultural and human contacts were limited to Russian package tourism to Southeast Asian resorts. This lack of attention was unsurprising, given Moscow's Westerncentrism, great power strategic culture, and dislike of multilateralism.

Lately there has been a partial revival of Russia's fortunes in Southeast Asia, mainly on the back of various arms deals. Moscow has concluded agreements with Vietnam, Malaysia, Myanmar, and Indonesia. Vietnam, in particular, has become a major customer, having purchased in 2009 six Kilo-class submarines and an additional twelve Su-30MK2 multipurpose fighters.[125] Russian policymakers have also started to engage a little more actively with ASEAN member-states within the framework of the ASEAN-plus dialogue.

Nevertheless, the significance of these developments should not be exaggerated. Southeast Asia still ranks very low among Russian priorities in Asia, and Vietnam, despite the arms deals and nascent energy cooperation, is hardly seen as a strategic alternative or counterweight to China.[126] Putin's de facto foreign policy statement of February 2012, "Russia and the changing world," referred to "the growing weight of the entire Asia-Pacific region," but did not mention the ASEAN member-states at all, either singly or collectively. And in the 2013 Foreign Policy Concept, Southeast Asia was accorded one anodyne sentence: "Russia seeks to consistently deepen its strategic partnership with Vietnam, and increase its cooperation with other ASEAN member-states."[127]

The slight increase in Russian interest does not therefore point to a more diversified approach toward the Asia-Pacific. Although Moscow is always on the lookout for new commercial opportunities, especially in the arms trade[128] and the energy sector, its Sinocentrism is as evident in Southeast Asia as it is elsewhere. This is exemplified, among other things, by its tacitly pro-Beijing stance on the disputed Spratley and Paracel Islands in the South China Sea.[129] While there is discomfort about some aspects of Chinese behavior, Moscow acts according to the principle that it is more important to keep Beijing onside than to strive, with few prospects of success, to be a major player in Southeast Asia.

### The United States

Although the United States has been the leading player in the Asia-Pacific for the past six decades, the Putin regime views it as an alien and not entirely legitimate presence in the region. Moscow periodically criticizes the U.S.-Japan and U.S.-ROK military alliances as cold war anachronisms, although admits—grudgingly—that they sometimes serve a useful purpose.[130] There is appreciation, for example, that the United States' umbrella has dissuaded Japan from going down the nuclear weapons route, and moderated South Korean responses to Pyongyang's provocations. Nevertheless, Moscow believes that the United States should play a reduced role in Asian affairs, and it takes a jaundiced view of the Obama administration's "pivot."[131] The fact that the latter has been oversold is irrelevant; Moscow dislikes the very *idea* of an enhanced American strategic presence in the region. And such sentiments have only strengthened as a result of the Ukraine crisis and general deterioration in Russia-U.S. relations.

Pivot or no pivot, Moscow believes that the United States is steadily losing ground to China.[132] Yet, it also recognizes that Washington continues to exert a critical influence in Asia by virtue of American military and economic power, and indirectly through its alliances with Japan, the ROK, Indonesia, Thailand, and Singapore. Russian policymakers are conscious that many Asian countries see the United States as a hedge against an overly assertive

China. In this climate strident anti-Americanism would only undermine such influence as Russia does possess.

The result of these contradictions is a position of minimalist engagement. Although Russia clearly favors China over the United States in the Asia-Pacific, its priority is to avoid collateral damage from regional tensions between the two. Looking to the longer term, it does not want to see one dominate the other (as noted earlier). A rough equilibrium would allow it still to dream of playing the part of geopolitical swing state within Asia and globally.[133] The irony, of course, is that this cannot happen unless the United States remains heavily engaged in the region.

### Asian multilateralism

Moscow has begun to grasp that nominal participation in institutions such as APEC, the ARF, and the ASEAN-plus dialogue is not merely insufficient to promote Russia as a credible player, but actually counterproductive. Accordingly, it has raised the level of its involvement. Putin has participated regularly in APEC summits (unlike Obama); Russia hosted the 2012 APEC summit in Vladivostok; and it has become more active in second-track diplomacy, through mechanisms such as the Shangri-La Forum in Singapore. In 2011 then deputy prime minister Sergei Ivanov became the most senior Russian ever to attend this important regional gathering.[134]

Such activity reflects a realization that multilateralism is the "Asian way"— or at least the way of many Asian countries. The growth of multilateralism is evident not only in the functioning of well-established bodies such as ASEAN and APEC, but also in emerging frameworks such as the East Asia Summit (EAS) and, most recently, the Asian Infrastructure Investment Bank (AIIB). If Russia is to cut any sort of figure in Asia, it has no choice but to go along with this trend.

Heightened awareness, however, has yet to translate into consistent performance. Putin turns up at APEC summits, but he has still not attended an EAS forum despite several opportunities to do so. More important, he has made little secret of his preference for managed forms of multilateralism: either subregional structures along the lines of the EEU and CSTO, or more exclusive arrangements, such as the Korean Six-Party talks. The Russian distaste for more inclusive and democratic forums is as visible in East Asia as it is elsewhere.

Moscow's great power bias means also that it values large multilateral gatherings primarily as opportunities for bilateral meetings with key players, such as the Americans and the Chinese, or in touting for foreign investment. It struggles to muster more than superficial interest in pan-regional affairs. As a result, its contributions at APEC, the ARF, and the EAS lack substance. It was revealing that Putin should have used the 2013 APEC summit in Bali not to detail what Russia could do for the Asia-Pacific region, but as a fishing expedition for outside investment in the Russian Far East.[135] Such a narrowly self-interested approach does little for Russia's regional standing.[136]

### The Russian Far East

The proof of Russia's Asian credentials lies not in the number of high-level bilateral and multilateral meetings its leaders attend, but in its practical commitment to integration with the wider Asia-Pacific region. In this context the most important relationship is with itself—that is, with the Russian Far East.[137]

The RFE is at once Russia's shop-window in Asia, and a barometer of its turn to the East. If Putin is able to make good on his promise to transform it into a hub of intra-regional cooperation, Russia will have taken a huge step to becoming a serious player in the Asia-Pacific. But as long as the RFE remains one of the most backward regions in Northeast Asia, exceeded in this respect only by North Korea,[138] Russia will be regarded as little more than a purveyor of natural resources and weapons. The RFE itself would become increasingly vulnerable to a cascade of domestic and external risks: further deindustrialization (and criminalization) of the local economy; social demoralization and unrest; and the steady erosion of Russian sovereignty.[139]

The RFE's course over the next ten to fifteen years will indicate how successfully—or otherwise—Moscow is addressing some of the critical weaknesses in its approach toward Asia, such as instrumentalism. Historically, the RFE has mattered to it primarily as a springboard for asserting Russia as a Eurasian empire and Pacific power.[140] This is still broadly true today. Putin's main purpose in building up the RFE is geopolitical, in particular to retain control over the vast strategic space east of Lake Baikal. In effect this ties the fate of a twenty-first-century objective—establishing decent economic and social conditions in the RFE (and Eastern Siberia)—to a distinctly nineteenth-century mission, that of asserting Russia's "great power-ness" in Asia. Regional development for its own sake holds little attraction for the Kremlin.

Similarly, the RFE is a test-case of Moscow's capacity to dilute its Sinocentrism and implement a more diversified approach to regional development. The signs are not especially promising. In 2013 China already accounted for 87 percent of the external trade in Amur territory, 82 percent in the Jewish Autonomous Region, 52 percent in Primorye (Vladivostok), and 46 percent in Khabarovsk[141]—numbers that will surely increase as a result of the fallout from Ukraine. Meanwhile, the lopsided character of Sino-Russian trade will become accentuated, since the Chinese priority is to access the RFE's natural resources (energy, metals, timber) rather than assist in its economic and social development.[142] The paradoxical consequence of this is that one of Moscow's atavistic anxieties—Chinese domination of the RFE and Eastern Siberia—is closer to being realized. Although Putin touts for investment from other Asian countries,[143] in the current environment China is not just the partner of choice, but sometimes the *only* partner.

The general problem of matching substance to rhetoric is reflected in the disjunction between the formulation of ambitious regional development programs and their poor implementation—a bugbear since Soviet times. The present situation highlights three major problems. The first is the Kremlin's propensity for administrative fiat, such as the creation in May 2012 of a Ministry for Far Eastern Development. This has been a fiasco, as Putin himself has admitted.[144] The belief that Moscow could micromanage things from 6,000 kilometers away has been amply disproved. (Prime Minister Medvedev's announcement in January 2014 that he would be "personally engaged" in improving the business climate in Siberia and the RFE testifies to the government's desperation to salvage something from the wreckage.)[145]

The second failing is Moscow's penchant for colossally expensive prestige projects, such as the 2012 APEC summit in Vladivostok. The issue is less the hosting of such events than the massive cost overruns, in turn the result of systemic corruption.[146] The summit cost an estimated US$22 billion, 50 percent more than the London Summer Olympics a month earlier.[147] Preparations were dogged by lengthy delays, considerable embezzlement, and the noncompletion of projects.[148] Vladivostok was intended to show off Russia's Asian credentials. Instead, it exposed some of the most negative aspects of life in the RFE (and Russia in general). And rather than stimulating a new quality of engagement with the Asia-Pacific region, the summit became a monument to the inadequacies of Russia's "Eastern direction."[149]

Finally, the Kremlin has rarely sustained its interest in the RFE long enough to follow through on regional development programs. This was the fate of the "Program for the Economic and Social Development of the Far East and Baikal Region [from 2008] up to 2013." As of December 2013, only a third of the program's objectives had been met,[150] and there are justified fears that eastern Russia's moment in the Kremlin sun may have passed, with federal funding being directed to other national projects—the 2014 Sochi Winter Olympics, the 2018 soccer World Cup, and the subsidization of the newly acquired territory of Crimea.[151] At a time of recession and tight budgetary constraints, the prospects for the RFE look very bleak without massive foreign investment.

## Aspiration over Substance

Russia faces huge obstacles in advancing its interests in Asia. The most obvious is distance—the many thousands of kilometers separating its major population centers from the Asia-Pacific region. Until now, it has hardly helped that the Russian Far East is physically located in Northeast Asia: to all intents and purposes it has been an outpost of European Russia—more a barrier against than gateway to Asia.

Another major hurdle to integration is the view among Asian elites that Russia will never be Asian except in the most literal sense of possessing (very sparsely populated) territory in Asia. They believe that it is incorrigibly Westerncentric, and that it looks at Asia from the distorted perspective of an outside power. To overturn or modify these perceptions will be extraordinarily difficult, and is the work of generations.

This is all the more so since Russia generally is viewed in a negative light—as a country with a stagnant political system, non-modernizing economy, and complacent elite. Many Asians doubt its capacity and commitment to contribute meaningfully, except as an exporter of natural resources and weapons. Russia's attempts to associate itself with the "rise of the rest" are not taken seriously. Instead, it has become the antithesis of a modern state, afflicted by a sclerosis worse than anything seen in the West.[152]

Meanwhile, the Asia-Pacific region has become a ferociously competitive environment. It is home to the sole superpower (the United States); the world's next superpower (China); the third-largest economy on the planet (Japan); and a country that is widely expected to emerge as a global force by the middle of the century (India). In addition, there are a number of influential regional actors, such as Indonesia, South Korea, Australia, and Vietnam. The Asian continent is becoming a very crowded place, with diminishing scope for outsiders to make their mark. Moscow speaks of turning to the East, but much of this "East" sees little interest in the involvement of another outsized power with accompanying sense of entitlement. Crucially, the United States and China have no desire for Russia to play an influential role.[153] In short, its possibilities are circumscribed as much by objective realities and the prejudices of others as by its own shortcomings. Even in the best-case scenario, Russia will struggle to make its presence felt and gain acceptance as a legitimate and useful player in Asia.[154]

All that said, Moscow's turn to the East has underachieved—or to put it more charitably, it is in its very early stages. The political class is beginning to comprehend that engagement with Asia is of vital importance to Russia's prospects. But beyond that limited achievement there have been few changes in policy, much less mentality. The principal deficiencies identified earlier have yet to be properly addressed. Instrumental considerations still predominate, especially in relations with Beijing and New Delhi. Attitudes toward Asia remain colored by an enduring Sinocentrism. And the rhetoric of Russia as a Euro-Pacific power is contradicted by its very modest footprint and the debilitating backwardness of the RFE. It will take more than a couple of energy agreements to reverse the neglect and bad habits of centuries.

Developments in the wake of the Ukraine crisis have only confirmed that what passes for an Asian strategy is often directed at fulfilling "greater" goals: countering the United States in global geopolitics; establishing an alternative legitimacy to Western-led governance; reinforcing Russia as an independent center of power; and reaffirming its uniqueness and indispensability. There has been little dilution in Moscow's Westerncentrism, and its relationships in Asia, with the exception of the Sino-Russian partnership, are weak and underdeveloped. In this connection, China's growing importance to Moscow does not point to a *new* Asian direction so much as an *old* reliance on geopolitical balancing. China matters above all because it is the next global power, not because it is Asian.

Much of the discussion in Russia about the turn to the East misses the point. It is not that Moscow should move from engaging primarily with the West to putting Asia first; what matters is that it develops relations with *both* on a more stable and less reflexive basis. This requires a better appreciation of regional dynamics in Asia, including that the major powers do not run the show there, any more than they do in other parts of the world. It means forsaking dreams of geopolitical balancing between Washington and Beijing, and of Russia's miraculous transfiguration into a Euro-Pacific power or bridge between Europe and Asia. Most of all, it entails practical steps to improve the quality and diversity of cooperation—whether in relatively established sectors such as energy and natural resources or in potential new areas of development, for example food and water security.

For this to happen, however, requires a domestic as well as foreign policy transformation. Unless the Kremlin tackles the key challenges of economic modernization and the rule of law at home, Russia will be unable to exert any kind of meaningful influence in the Asia-Pacific region. Economically it would continue to be viewed in a similar way as resource-rich but developing countries in Africa and Latin America. Politically it would be largely ignored. And in the domain of international security, others would look to marginalize it.

To alter this fate Moscow will need to recognize that tired strategic habits and an indigenous neoconservatism offer Russia nothing. But such a message is not easily absorbed. Today the Kremlin's self-satisfaction appears stronger than ever, driven by the anticipation of a new multipolar order in which Russia stands as an equal with the United States and China.[155] As long as this illusion persists, the likelihood of a productive approach toward Asia will be slim, and the "turn to the East" will remain a fantasy.

# six
# Engaging with the West

Basically, the antagonism remains. . . . And from it flow many of the phenomena which we find disturbing in the Kremlin's conduct of foreign policy: the secretiveness, the lack of frankness, the duplicity, the wary suspiciousness, and the basic unfriendliness of purpose. These phenomena are there to stay, for the foreseeable future. There can be variations of degree and of emphasis. When there is something the Russians want from us, one or the other of these features of their policy may be thrust temporarily into the background. . . . But we should not be misled by tactical maneuvers.

GEORGE KENNAN, 1947

In the twenty-three years since the end of the Soviet Union, there have been three brief periods of relatively smooth engagement between Russia and the West. The first was right at the beginning of the post-Soviet era, when Boris Yeltsin's desire for a full-fledged partnership with the United States led to the most pro-Western foreign policy Russia has ever had. The second came after the events of 9/11, when Vladimir Putin made his "strategic choice" in favor of Washington.[1] And the third was initiated by Barack Obama's reset policy in early 2009, which looked to reengage with Moscow after the hiatus of the Russia-Georgia war.

These moments have provided only temporary respite from what has been a consistently difficult and often acrimonious interaction. Russia-West relations have been rocked by a succession of crises, each seemingly graver than the last: the protracted controversy over the first wave of NATO enlargement; the rupture following the alliance's intervention over Kosovo in 1999; the row over the 2004 Orange Revolution; the Georgia war; and, most recently, events in Ukraine.

Most strikingly, the "normal" (that is, non-crisis) mode of Russia-West relations has been thoroughly abnormal. From the outset, there have been excessive expectations, major disappointments, and severe recriminations. The successes have not only been short-lived, but in some ways have made things worse. Thus the initial optimism in 1992 surrounding the "new Russia" ensured that the subsequent sense of disillusionment and betrayal would be all the more acute. It was a similar story post-9/11, when hopes of a constructive partnership in the face of "common threats and challenges" were sharply disabused. And finally, the positivity of the reset has given way to a geopolitical and normative chasm, and deep pessimism about the prospects for any improvement in the foreseeable future.

The Ukraine crisis has brought matters to a head. Whether one views it as a game changer or as confirmation of long-term trends in Russian foreign policy, there is little doubt that Moscow's relations with the West stand at a critical juncture. Some policymakers and commentators believe that a level of cooperative engagement may still be achievable, although not without considerable difficulty. Their relative optimism rests on two pillars: close economic interdependence between Russia and Europe; and a common imperative to meet existential threats, notably the rise of Islamist extremism.[2]

In stark contrast there is the resurgent theory of a new cold war. According to this, Ukraine is merely one front in a systemic and multidimensional confrontation between two opposing camps: on one side an authoritarian Russia (allied to or at least converging with China); on the other a liberal democratic West.[3] Even if this latest crisis is defused, others will surely follow. In fact, the overall situation may be worse than during the original cold war, in that it is more unpredictable and there are fewer checks against an escalation into open conflict.

This chapter sets out a somewhat different, although barely more optimistic, view. Russia-West relations are set on a path of negative continuity: an overall downward trend, punctuated by periodic crises and, more rarely, brief upturns. There is little appetite for a resumption of confrontation along the lines of the cold war. Equally, however, the belief necessary to reverse or arrest the current negative trend is almost entirely absent. Growing policy differences, clashing values, and the perception of shrinking common interests have sapped the desire and capacity of Russia and the West to work together. The defining themes today are not the obvious ones of crisis and conflict, but rather fatigue and alienation.

In thinking about how we arrived at this point, it is helpful to look at Moscow's engagement with the West in terms of four key questions. The first centers on the Russia-U.S. relationship, and how far—or little—this has evolved since Soviet times. Inevitably, much of the discussion has revolved around the reset—whether it was justified in the first place, and whether it achieved anything worthwhile during its short life. But more important is what the rise and fall of the reset tell us about the character and underlying assumptions of the relationship. Why has this been so dysfunctional? It is not just that Moscow and Washington are unable to cooperate on a long list of regional and international issues, including in areas where their interests broadly coincide. Neither seems able to read the other's intentions, with the result that rational expectations have given way to tendentious suppositions and erratic decisionmaking.[4]

The second question considers Russia's disaggregated engagement with Europe. It is often stated as incontrovertible fact that Russia is a European civilization.[5] But the meaning of this has become obscured. How does Moscow see its place in Europe against the backdrop of the "shift of global power to the East"? Some of the political elite are openly challenging the validity and utility of Russia's European-ness in light of recent developments—the global financial crisis, the anti-Putin protests of 2011–12, and the Maidan revolution. Other, less reactionary voices call for a greater Europe that would no longer be dominated by the EU, but reflect a more equitable convergence on the continent. Such debates highlight the unstable—and generally negative—character of Moscow's relations with European countries and institutions.

Third, what is the place and purpose of the West in contemporary Russian foreign policy—useful enemy, essential partner and resource, geopolitical menace, normative threat, or all of the above? Putin's emphasis on native Russian values and traditions, not to mention the "turn to the East," suggests that the Kremlin is moving away from its historical Westerncentrism. But the picture is not at all clear. The phenomenon of "the West" is ubiquitous. Although respect for Western power, institutions, and norms is at a post-Soviet low, old perceptions and habits die hard. The most significant change may turn out to be the Kremlin's shift to selective engagement—cherry-picking those aspects of the West it likes or feels able to use and discarding those that it finds threatening or unpalatable.

Fourth, how is Moscow's interaction with the West influencing its overall conduct of foreign policy? Western actions have been blamed for the renewed emphasis on geopolitics in Moscow. But one can equally argue that, for the Kremlin, they have merely confirmed timeless truths: the inevitability of great power competition, the West's innate hostility to a "strong Russia," and the importance of advancing national interests even in the face of powerful opposition.

Of course, we may be asking the question the wrong way round. In a world preoccupied by the rise of China, and characterized by the diffusion of power, perhaps the real issue is how this external environment—the new world disorder—is shaping Moscow's dealings with the United States and Europe. Conventional wisdom says that Russian attitudes and policies toward the West are an extension of Russian domestic politics. However, the chief determinants may turn out to be the fraying of international structures and de-universalization of norms; the continuing global reach of a weakened but still preeminent America; and an Asia in which many countries are exhibiting new levels of capacity and ambition. Such conditions could yet encourage a new rapprochement between Russia and the West, or lead to further and increasingly serious rifts.

## The Russia-U.S. Relationship

It has become commonplace to dismiss the reset not only as a failure, but as a policy whose rationale was flawed from its inception. The term itself has become a byword for the naivité and haplessness of the Obama administration in foreign affairs. But it was not always thus. While there were some early critics of the initiative, particularly in the former Warsaw Pact countries and the Baltic states,[6] the principle of reestablishing a functional relationship with Moscow found considerable support in the United States and Europe. Matters had deteriorated dangerously under the previous Bush administration, as highlighted by the Georgia war, and there was a strong feeling that something had to be done to arrest the downward spiral.[7] The attraction of a new course was accentuated by other factors, too: the need for Washington to concentrate on economic recovery at a time of recession; public pressure to get the troops home from Afghanistan, for which Moscow's assistance was important; and the natural inclination of all incoming administrations to put their individual stamp on policy, and, specifically, to "fix Russia."

It is easy to be critical about the outcomes of the reset in hindsight. Today Russia-U.S. relations are worse than any time during the Bush presidency. Although tensions ran very high during the Georgia war,[8] the impact of Moscow's annexation of Crimea (and subsequent actions in eastern Ukraine) is already far greater, and shows every sign of being longer-lasting. Tellingly, mutual hostility is not restricted to political elites, but is evident at the societal level. A Levada poll from December 2014 found that 74 percent of Russians had a generally negative or very negative view of the United States.[9] American public attitudes toward Russia have mirrored these results, with a Pew Global Attitudes survey from July 2014 showing a 72 percent "unfavorable" rating.[10] In both countries these represented record low approval ratings.

## Giving the reset its due

And yet the reset did achieve some real successes during its short and rather brutish existence. In early 2009 few outside the Obama administration believed that it would amount to much. After all, worthy sentiments about common interests and the need to improve cooperation had been uttered many times before, with little effect. And expectations remained modest even after the reset had been under way for some time. There was hope of progress toward a new START (Strategic Arms Reduction Treaty) agreement, of Russian assistance over Afghanistan, increased pressure on Iran, and stabilization of the bilateral relationship. But that was the outer limit of expectations; it was not anticipated that Moscow would respond as positively as it did, or that the two sides would quickly engage in an active process of normalization.[11]

As it happened Russia and the United States made significant progress on several issues that had previously been deadlocked. The most publicized achievement was the 2010 START agreement. Although this represented unfinished business from the 1990s, the deterioration of bilateral relations after 2003 had blocked progress. The one agreement that had been concluded during the Bush presidency, the Strategic Offensive Reductions Treaty (SORT) in May 2002, was a minimalist document, resented by the Russians as a meager consolation prize.[12] The new START agreement, by contrast, provided for significant, binding, and verifiable reductions in both missiles and missile launchers.[13] Although Obama subsequently oversold the agreement as a major step in the evolution of a "global-zero" world, it nevertheless remains the most significant disarmament achievement since START-2 in 1993.

No less important was the development of the Northern Distribution Network (NDN). During 2009–12 more than 400,000 American troops, as well as large consignments of lethal and nonlethal goods, entered and exited Afghanistan through the NDN.[14] It played an especially vital role in 2012 when Islamabad temporarily closed the supply routes going through Pakistan.[15] The operation of the NDN demonstrated that Moscow could work with Washington on matters of primary importance to U.S. interests, rather than simply be contrary. Moreover, this cooperation continued despite the souring of the wider relationship from 2011.

Naturally, Russian assistance was motivated by self-interest, in particular the fear of Islamist extremism spreading throughout Central Asia and into Russia itself. However, such anxieties had existed prior to the reset, and yet had failed to generate meaningful cooperation. The spirit of pragmatic engagement was not limited to Afghanistan alone. During the April–May

2010 crisis in Kyrgyzstan, Moscow invited the United States to help stabilize the country after the fall of the Bakiyev regime. In the past, Moscow had resisted on principle any U.S. participation in post-Soviet conflict management.

There was tangible progress too on Iran, where Russia and the rest of the P5+1 (Germany) agreed on measures to check its nuclear weapons potential. In June 2010, Moscow not only supported tougher sanctions against Tehran under UN Security Council Resolution (UNSCR) 1929, but also brought the Chinese on board—an impressive feat given the closeness of Sino-Iranian commercial ties and Beijing's adherence to the principle of noninterference. At the bilateral level the Russian government first suspended and then terminated the sale of S-300 antiaircraft missile systems to Tehran.[16] None of this would have happened without the reset.

The reset was the catalyst for Russia's belated accession to the WTO. It removed a key obstacle to progress, namely, the political animosity between Moscow and Washington. It also smoothed the way by persuading other interested parties, such as Georgia, to reach an accommodation with Moscow.[17] The importance of incorporating Russia into an international rules-based regime should not be underestimated. Although the real test is whether it meets its WTO obligations—admittedly an unlikely prospect today (see chapter 3)—the reset at least created the opportunity for progress to be made in the future.

Generally speaking, Moscow and Washington sought to establish a more reliable basis for engagement. Although they continued to disagree strongly on many issues, both came to appreciate the virtues of a relative normality. There were moves toward the institutionalization of ties, notably through the Bilateral Presidential Commission with its twenty working groups.[18] Although much of the Commission's work was process-oriented, convening meetings and compiling worthy reports, its existence improved communication, at least at the level of senior officials. It could not magically transform Russia-U.S. relations. But it contributed at the margins, developing professional links, initiating a regular dialogue in key areas (for example, arms control), and opening up new, if modest, possibilities for cooperation.

Post-Crimea such progress has become badly tainted, and the Bilateral Commission a symbol of much that is wrong with the relationship: the emphasis on process over substance, the self-deception of "shared values" (what Lilia Shevtsova has called the "let's pretend" game);[19] and the sacrifice of principle to expediency.[20] These charges have some merit. At the same time, such institutionalization—nascent and imperfect as it is—is vital if there is to be any chance of restoring some level of constructive interaction between Moscow and Washington.

Finally, it is important to recognize the knock-on effect of the reset. It not only boosted Russia-U.S. relations, but also strengthened Moscow's ties with Europe. Without the reset, there would hardly have been a thaw with Warsaw between 2009 and 2012. While there were other contributing factors (see below), the reset provided a favorable backdrop. It also had a softening effect on Moscow's notoriously difficult interaction with the three Baltic states, and on the UK relationship, which attained a rough equilibrium after several years of precipitous decline.[21] Such achievements have since fallen by the wayside. But for a time, they did count for something—and were valued accordingly.

## Anatomy of a failed relationship

Much of the criticism of the reset has been based on a misunderstanding of its original purpose. It was never the intention, much less expectation, of the Obama administration that the reset would transform an often adversarial dynamic into a strategic partnership. As noted earlier, the objectives were far more limited. If an overarching purpose existed, then it was to secure Moscow's cooperation or compliance with selected American objectives: achieving major reductions in nuclear weapons; facilitating the passage of U.S. troops to and from Afghanistan; and strengthening the global nonproliferation regime by increasing the pressure on Iran. In these areas the reset fared surprisingly well—certainly better than many other initiatives of the Obama presidency.

What the reset could not do, however, was change the strategic culture of the Putin elite. It could not influence Moscow's proprietorial attitudes toward the post-Soviet space for the better, nor could it promote liberal democracy, the rule of law, and economic modernization in Russia. Most of all, it could not hope to sustain the illusion of common interests and shared values. Far from being a game changer, the reset was a metaphor for an interaction that has only rarely diverged from the dysfunctional mean. And its unfortunate fate was less the product of the White House's errors and misjudgments than of more deep-seated problems. The reset highlighted these with disconcerting clarity.

*Conflicting motivations and priorities.* There is a case for arguing that the reset was doomed from the outset because Moscow and Washington entered into it for entirely different reasons. The Putin regime believed that Obama had sought the reset out of weakness. U.S. support for Georgia had backfired; further NATO enlargement had been ruled out indefinitely; the president needed Russian assistance on Afghanistan and Iran; and the United States felt imperiled by the global financial meltdown and the rise of China.

Moscow also interpreted the reset as de facto acknowledgment of a Russian sphere of influence in the post-Soviet neighborhood,[22] and of Russia's status as a global power.

This reading was correct in some respects. Obama was keen to establish some kind of normal relationship after the setbacks of the Bush administration in eastern Europe and the Caucasus. And although this was not explicitly stated, he was prepared to soft-pedal on democracy promotion in Russia and the post-Soviet space in exchange for Moscow's support on Afghanistan, Iran, and strategic disarmament.

On most of the big issues, however, Moscow was wrong. The Obama administration did not seek the reset because it was weak. On the contrary, in early 2009 its confidence and international standing were sky-high; the foreign policy trials it was to suffer lay in the future. And although Washington wanted Russia's help, it was not prepared to pay any price for this. There was no recognition of a Russian sphere of influence, and no readiness to treat Russia as an international actor of equal standing to the United States. The latter prospect was especially improbable given that in 2009 Russia was the worst performing of all the G-20 economies.

These conflicting perceptions led to very different expectations of the reset. Putin craved an equal and global partnership with the United States—something to which he had aspired post-9/11 but that he had not achieved. Obama, on the other hand, envisaged Russia as a regional and niche ally. It would be useful in helping to achieve certain priorities, but it could not be a *global* partner—at least not anytime soon. This was less a problem of mistrust than of Russia's lack of heft beyond its neighborhood. Far from sharing Putin's view of Russia as one of the leading actors in the international system, the Obama administration treated it as an instrument of U.S. foreign policy.[23] And while the existence of the Bilateral Commission hinted at a more strategic view of the relationship, attention toward Russia in Washington was sporadic and driven by events.

Indeed, Obama's approach was closer to that of Bush post-9/11 than many would care to admit. It was also consistent with the overall pattern of Russia-U.S. relations since the end of the USSR—that is, unequal and lopsided, with plenty of arrogance, resentment, and feelings of entitlement thrown in. The reset reflected this history. With considerable luck and political will, it might have enjoyed a longer run of success. But it was asking a tremendous amount for it to transcend past and present realities.

*A tired agenda.* From the outset, the reset was dominated by leftover business and traditional security priorities, such as strategic disarmament and missile defense. As such, it was not so much a reset as a patch-up job.[24] Even cooperation on Afghanistan was about addressing a discrete need—ensuring the smooth passage of U.S. personnel and equipment—rather than being a project of long-term relationship-building.

Much of the zeitgeist of the reset was of acquiescence and the wish to "do no harm." Thus Russia did not veto a NATO no-fly zone over Libya in 2011, while the United States adopted a lower profile with the former Soviet republics.[25] To a certain extent this mutual forbearance suited both sides. Moscow and Washington disagreed about many things—missile defense, Syria, the Kremlin's approach to the post-Soviet space, and Eurasian integration. But so long as there was no immediate crisis—no U.S.-led military operation in Syria, no further NATO enlargement eastward, and no Russian formal annexation of Abkhazia and South Ossetia—these differences were manageable. Both sides identified an interest in sidestepping troublesome issues and suspending disbelief, as if operating on the principle of "you pretend to agree with us, and we pretend to believe you."[26]

Such an approach was by its very nature unsustainable. Once past business had been dealt with or shelved, Moscow and Washington needed to find a new basis for cooperation. Without a fresh agenda, the relationship would, and did, stagnate. And with stagnation, many of the differences that had been set aside inevitably resurfaced, leading to a further downturn.[27] At no stage during the reset did a forward-looking agenda emerge. The issues that might have formed the basis of one were either secondary priorities for Washington and (especially) Moscow, such as climate change and development assistance, or areas where cooperation was hindered by deep mistrust—Syria, WMD proliferation, and counterterrorism. Even the success of the NDN was limited in time and scope; its utility diminished rapidly with the drawdown in U.S. and other NATO combat troops from Afghanistan. In these circumstances, Moscow reverted to its previous mode: viewing the remaining American force presence in central Eurasia more as a geopolitical threat than as an instrument for preserving regional security.[28]

Part of the problem was that Russia and the United States had few common interests outside security cooperation. One can say that they should have focused more on economic engagement, but the possibilities here were limited. Although companies such as Boeing and Pepsi were able to tap into sectoral markets, the overall presence of American manufacturing companies in Russia was very small compared with that of their European counterparts. With economic ties so thin, there was a limited constituency in the United States to support a more comprehensive and resilient partnership with Russia.[29] The contrast with the China lobby in Washington was striking.

Crucially, the United States had no requirement to import Russian energy, following the development of its own huge shale gas reserves. Individual companies, such as ExxonMobil, expanded their presence in Russia, notably through the agreement with Rosneft to develop Arctic energy resources.[30] However, this had little impact on the wider relationship. As an *international oil company* (IOC) driven by profit, ExxonMobil's priorities are different from those of the White House, and it has tended to distance itself from U.S. government policies.[31] This has meant that the company's success is largely its own, with few knock-on effects for state-to-state relations.[32] (That said, some diplomatic crises are so serious that they hurt even the most powerful IOCs. Western sanctions against Russia led in September 2014 to suspension of the company's operations in the Kara Sea.)[33]

*Major policy differences.* One of the flaws of the reset was the hope that bilateral problems might be resolved or at least managed if they could be discussed in a pragmatic, cooperative spirit. This underestimated the gravity and intractability of the two sides' substantive disagreements. For example, there was an unbridgeable gulf between Washington's insistence that its missile defense plans were directed against Iran, North Korea, and other "rogue" states, and Moscow's claim that these plans threatened Russian national security. One side's conviction in the existence of a universal danger was contradicted by the other's belief that the proposed solution was far worse than the original threat, and therefore reflected ulterior motives, namely, a plot to undermine Russia's "strategic parity."[34]

These differences made it impossible to build on the reset's early achievements. After START, the Obama administration had hoped to move to the next stage of nuclear disarmament—reductions in the numbers of tactical nuclear missiles, where Russia had a pronounced superiority.[35] But Moscow saw no reason to surrender its comparative advantage without obtaining a significant quid pro quo on missile defense.[36] Similarly, there was little prospect that the Kremlin would countenance tougher UN sanctions against Tehran "for free." Although Russia voted for UNSCR 1929, it did not do so because it shared American assessments about the seriousness of the Iranian nuclear threat, but because it still hoped to reap dividends elsewhere from the reset.[37] As relations deteriorated, such considerations became moot.

It became much harder to maintain a façade of consensus in the face of mounting evidence to the contrary. Moscow and Washington spoke of common security threats and challenges, but it was clear that they had different objectives when it came to the specifics of counterterrorism, nonproliferation, and conflict resolution. The disjunction between in-principle "agreement" and divergent policies was highlighted at the November 2010 NATO summit in Lisbon. Official statements suggested progress toward a joint missile defense system to protect the Euro-Atlantic space.[38] But real agreement proved elusive. Whereas the United States and its NATO allies envisaged two separate, if parallel, systems with some interoperability, the Russian government called for a single, pan-European missile defense system, in which it would be responsible for the east European "vector," in effect giving it a right of veto on command-and-control decisions. Moscow's position was completely unacceptable to NATO.[39] In this, as on many other issues, the Russia-U.S. policy divide became wider, more public, and increasingly bitter.

On Syria both sides wanted an end to the civil war, opposed Islamist extremism, and worried about the destabilization of the region. But they had polarized views on the future of President Assad. Whereas the U.S. political establishment demanded his removal as part of a broader peaceful settlement, Moscow saw his survival as critical to several major objectives: promoting Russian geopolitical influence; asserting the principle of national sovereignty in the face of Western moral interventionism; and discouraging grassroots democratic movements in the Middle East and closer to home. In this last connection, Moscow never understood why Washington promoted democracy and human rights when this undermined its own security interests—as in "liberating" Iraq to Iranian influence in 2003, or dumping its long-time ally Hosni Mubarak and permitting the Muslim Brotherhood to come to power in Egypt.[40]

*The "right" and "wrong" side of history.* These conflicting perceptions underscored the perennial problem of the values gap. Despite efforts to fudge this, it became an area of growing contention as the reset began to falter. Differences over Syria and the Arab Spring reflected a larger normative conflict between Russia and the United States—one side emphasizing the primacy of national sovereignty,[41] the other the universality of human rights.[42] There was discord too over the role of the United States as global conscience. Moscow accused Washington of hypocrisy and double standards, pointing to the continued existence of the Guantánamo detention facility and American support for authoritarian regimes such as Saudi Arabia and Bahrain.[43] Conversely, many in Washington noted that Russia showed little respect for the principles of national sovereignty and noninterference when it came to its ex-Soviet neighbors.[44]

By late 2011, the values gap was already poisoning the relationship. In October then U.S. secretary of state Hillary Clinton accused Russia (and China) of being on the "wrong side of history" over Syria, and two months later expressed public support for the anti-Putin protests in Moscow.[45] In December 2012, the U.S. Congress passed the Magnitsky Act, which included measures to identify Russian officials suspected of human rights abuses, deny them entry into the United States, and freeze their assets.[46] The Russian Duma (parliament) retaliated with the so-called "Dima Yakovlev" law, which, among its provisions, banned U.S. adoptions of Russian orphans.

By this time any hope of normative accommodation had evaporated. Putin not only challenged the right of the United States to undertake international action in the name of a higher good, but also revived the notion of a systemic ideological divide between Russia and the West. The schism was now between home-grown traditionalism and foreign liberalism, rather than between communism and capitalism.[47] But it was no less corrosive. The Kremlin had not only decided that Western liberal norms and values were unsuitable for Russia; it chose to proselytize its brand of moral and political conservatism across the post-Soviet space, through such devices as the Eurasian Union.

*"Who wins over whom (kto kogo)?"* In this fractious climate the reset became a hostage to political fortune, as policymakers on both sides struggled to justify its diminishing outcomes. Moscow complained that it had gained very little in return for cooperation on Afghanistan, Iran, and START. It drew analogies with the post-9/11 period, when Putin's support for the United States was "rewarded" with the latter's withdrawal from the 1972 ABM Treaty; American involvement in various color revolutions; failure to repeal the 1974 Jackson-Vanik amendment;[48] and Bush's decision to invade Iraq despite the objections of the UN. According to the growing number of reset critics, the United States under Obama was just as bad. Behind the pretense of constructive engagement, it was proceeding with missile defense; interfering in Russian domestic affairs; and behaving arbitrarily in international affairs.[49]

The complaints were similarly vocal on the American side. There it was alleged that Obama had given Russia a free pass over the Georgia war and its continuing illegal occupation of Georgian territory; done nothing to check Putin's authoritarian tendencies;[50] and allowed Moscow to reestablish its hegemony in the post-Soviet space.[51] In the 2012 U.S. presidential campaign, Republican candidate Mitt Romney described Russia as America's "number one geopolitical foe," and criticized Obama for going soft on Moscow.[52] Although he was ridiculed for overstating the Russia threat, his remarks highlighted a growing feeling that the reset no longer served any useful purpose.[53]

Underpinning all this was a sense of self-righteousness and unrequited virtue. Each side believed the other was not doing enough to sustain the reset. Viewed from Moscow, the Americans were behaving as arrogantly and duplicitously as ever, while many in Washington saw a regime whose mission in life seemed to be to make things as difficult as possible for the United States. The Kremlin's handling of the Snowden affair only strengthened suspicions about Russian mischief-making.[54]

Even the relative successes of Russia-U.S. cooperation, such as the initiative to remove chemical weapons from Syria in the fall of 2013, became spoiled. Much of the commentary at the time focused not on an important disarmament outcome—securing Damascus's cooperation in eliminating weapons stockpiles—but on how Putin had outmaneuvered Obama and embarrassed the United States.[55] Matters were not helped by Putin's letter in the *New York Times*, in which he pontificated on the virtues of peaceful dialogue, the primacy of international law, and the dangers of American exceptionalism.[56]

*Overdependence on personalities.* One of the reset's many vulnerabilities was that its fortunes were intimately linked to particular individuals. Senior figures in the Obama administration, including the president himself, encouraged a misleading dichotomy between the "authoritarian" Putin and the "liberal" Medvedev.[57] This polarizing approach repeated the mistakes of earlier periods—the "Bill and Boris" show in the 1990s[58] and the subsequent "George and Vlad" relationship—when a much-storied personal empathy substituted for (and sometimes detracted from) movement on policy.[59] Washington overinvested in Medvedev as the supposed proponent of modernization and the reset. In doing so, it misread the extent of both his influence and his reformist inclinations, while underestimating Putin's centrality in foreign as well as domestic policymaking.[60] Such misjudgments made it all the more difficult to arrest the deterioration in relations following the latter's return to the Kremlin.

The poorly disguised personal tension between Obama and Putin was not a deal-breaker in itself, since the reset was already in deep trouble. But it did nothing to defuse tensions. In 2012 Obama's decision to miss the APEC summit in Vladivostok and Putin's reciprocal no-show at the Chicago G-8 summit were widely interpreted as signaling a new downturn.[61] And when the two presidents did meet at the margins of the Los Cabos G-20 summit in June 2012, the coldness of their interaction seemed to epitomize a relationship that had lost all momentum and direction.

### The Ukraine crisis—reinforcing a negative-sum game

The annexation of Crimea, Moscow's ongoing destabilization of eastern Ukraine, the imposition of Western sanctions, and the shooting down of a Malaysian Airlines plane by Russian-supported separatists in July 2014 have all deepened the hostility between Moscow and Washington. In fact, this is the worst crisis in relations since the early 1980s.[62] It is difficult to find any redeeming features—perhaps the continued discussions over the Iranian nuclear program, the preservation (for now) of the NDN—and there are justified fears that some of the reset's achievements, such as the START agreement, could unravel. Cooperation may still be possible in the face of strategic shocks, for example the emergence of IS (Islamic State) in the greater Middle East. But the mindset on both sides is almost entirely negative and pessimistic.

It is tempting to see the Ukraine crisis as a game changer in Russia-U.S. relations. Although this may yet turn out to be the case, the fallout from the crisis is consistent with the pattern of the last few years. The problems that undermined the reset during 2009–11 have been exacerbated, but they are essentially *the same problems as before*. Take the issue of conflicting expectations and priorities. The Kremlin remains committed to thwarting Washington's alleged geopolitical ambitions in the post-Soviet space; challenging the legitimacy of U.S. international leadership; and asserting Russia as a global power, with inalienable rights in its neighborhood. Conversely, Washington is in no mood to respect Russia's claims to special consideration as a regional hegemon and global equal to the United States, and regards constructs such as spheres of influence as not only irrelevant, but unconscionable.

Both sides understand tacitly that any settlement of the conflict in Ukraine is contingent on finding a way to work together. But they are no closer to agreeing on what this cooperation should look like. Their experience of constructive engagement has been limited to areas where they have a long track record, as in arms control negotiations, or where the United States actively seeks Russian assistance more or less cap in hand, as with the NDN. The notion of positive-sum cooperation, in which both sides benefit equally, is a stranger to the relationship.

Putin, in particular, views the Ukraine crisis in overwhelmingly competitive terms. Failure to secure key Russian objectives—"autonomy" for the country's eastern regions; a Ukraine permanently excluded from EU (and, of course, NATO) membership—would be to suffer a direct and catastrophic defeat at Washington's hands. On the other hand, success in realizing these aims would represent a tremendous blow to the influence the United States has in Europe and to its global standing. More than anything, it would symbolize the transition from American unipolarity to a post-American world order.

The Ukraine crisis has confirmed the growing importance of the values gap in Russia-U.S. relations. The Obama administration's early approach of going easy on democracy promotion in exchange for Russian help on Afghanistan and Iran was already in trouble by 2011. Kremlin support for the openly brutal Assad regime left the White House little room for maneuver, which shrank to almost nothing following Putin's return to the presidency and subsequent domestic crackdown. During 2012 his embrace of an archaic conservatism as the embodiment of the "Russian national idea," and the vigorous promotion of the Magnitsky bill by the U.S. Congress, accelerated the normative divergence. Russian actions in Ukraine did not mark a sea change in this respect, but underlined just how irreconcilable the differences over values had become, and their destructive impact on bilateral cooperation.

Finally, the Ukraine crisis has worsened the problem of overpersonalization. In American eyes Putin is more than ever the embodiment of all that is wrong with Russia and its approach to the world. This view reflects a certain reality—namely, the personalized nature of the Russian political system, in which Putin is the supreme decisionmaker. But it underestimates and trivializes broader differences of perception, priorities, and interests. One of the more uncomfortable truths the West must face today is that Putin's aggressive conduct of foreign policy enjoys massive elite and public support—whether on Ukraine, Syria, or the abstract notion of a great and powerful Russia. In these circumstances, the "Putinization" of Russia-U.S. relations is yet another aggravating factor. Few in Washington believe there is much point in seeking cooperation from Moscow as long as Putin rules, while there is growing outrage in the Kremlin at the personal attacks against the Russian president, and the sanctions targeted at his inner circle.

## Outlook

The prospects for Russia-U.S. engagement are grim. All the signs point to a growing militancy on both sides. Far from being cowed by U.S.-led sanctions and a Russian economy in recession, Putin has become ever more defiant. He has injected regular Russian troops into the conflict in eastern Ukraine. He has stepped up efforts to use China as a geopolitical counterweight to American "hegemonism" and the BRICS as the vanguard of a non-Western world order. He plays on tensions between Washington and European capitals over sanctions and energy security. He promotes Russia as a notional alternative to the United States in countries such as Egypt.[63] And he is reaching out to governments in Central and South America, signing nuclear deals with Argentina and reopening the former Soviet military radar station at Lourdes in Cuba.[64] The very premise that cooperation is desirable has become suspect.[65] The Kremlin appears ready to settle for a rough equilibrium based on limited engagement in a few selected areas.[66] But if it is unable to achieve even this, then no matter—America stands to lose more.[67]

Meanwhile, U.S. antipathy toward Russia is at a three-decade high. Virtually every foreign policy action by Moscow is seen as anti-American in some degree. Putin's brand of authoritarian conservatism has become identified with a return to Soviet-era repression. Russian actions in Ukraine, such as providing the weapons that brought down the Malaysian Airlines plane, have led some to see it as a rogue actor. There is a growing political consensus in Washington in favor of containment: strengthening the NATO alliance; arming the Ukrainian military; engaging more closely with other ex-Soviet republics, such as Moldova and Georgia; stiffening European resolve on energy diversification; and undermining Sino-Russian cooperation wherever possible.[68] Engagement with Putin's Russia has become anathema to Democrats and Republicans alike. And the situation is likely to get worse. Whoever succeeds Obama as president in 2017 will have minimal scope to be flexible, whether it is on missile defense, developments in the post-Soviet space, or a new Euro-Atlantic security framework.[69]

Interaction between Moscow and Washington is sliding into a state of mutually assured noncooperation. However, this is hardly stable, but will increase the risks of an adversarial relationship becoming openly confrontational. A Russia resigned to the unfeasibility (or undesirability) of cooperation with the United States is likely to become more interventionist in the ex-Soviet republics; systematically harass the Baltic states; step up authoritarian control at home; and take every opportunity to remind Washington of its capacity to cause trouble if its interests are not "respected." In this, it will act on the principle that it is better to be disliked than to be ignored.[70]

## The New/Old Europe

Russian elite attitudes toward Europe have changed radically over the course of the Putin era. Gone is the desperation to be accepted in the European mainstream, and the inferiority complex that imbued this aim. The Kremlin feels emboldened to challenge the assumption that the EU, with its values, rules, and institutions, stands for Europe and "European-ness." In its place, it has promoted three alternative, loosely interrelated constructs.

The first is a revamped Concert of Europe. Its defining feature is an enhanced role for the leading continental powers—Germany, France, and of course Russia.[71] Such a Concert is more a set of understandings than a formal arrangement. Moscow envisages a regional oligarchy, analogous to the "global oligarchy" of the multipolar world order.[72] Under certain circumstances, it is willing to see this elite group include other parties, such as Italy, Poland, and the European Commission.[73] But even an expanded grouping would retain certain features: Russia would be a central player; the arrangement would be the principal decisionmaking framework on the European continent; and the role of "outsiders"—above all the United States, but also its close ally the United Kingdom—would be circumscribed.

The second conception favored by Moscow is less exclusive, but is likewise intended to undermine the EU's normative monopoly (embodied by the *acquis communautaire*) and accord Russia a pivotal status in Europe. This is the notion of a larger European civilization, in which the emphasis moves from a codified, rules-based Europe to one where to feel European is to be European. The attraction of this model is threefold. It serves as an instrument of national self-affirmation; it entails no concrete obligations; and it places no constraints on Russia becoming a regional and global power on its own terms. On the contrary, it offers a useful launchpad from which to project its influence farther afield. Russia can simultaneously be a European civilization, a Eurasian power, a bridge between East and West and North and South, and one of the centers in the polycentric system of international relations. Moreover, at a time when much of European civilization is falling into a "systemic crisis," Russia has the opportunity to lead efforts to give it new vigor and purpose.[74]

Third, Putin has been publicizing the idea of a European economic space from Lisbon to Vladivostok, in which a Moscow-led Eurasian Union would be the co-equal of the EU.[75] Although he depicts a "Greater Europe united by shared values of freedom, democracy, and market laws," this vision is overwhelmingly interests-based. It emphasizes a "harmonized community of economies," with a common free trade zone and "coordinated policies in industry, technology, the energy sector, education, science, and also eventually to scrap visas."[76] Such a Greater Europe would place Russian interpretations of norms and values on the same footing as the *acquis*, remove political conditionalities from commercial cooperation and technological transfers, and grant full legitimacy to his Eurasian Union project.[77]

In practice these various visions have translated into a Russian approach to Europe that is selective, conditional, and fragmented. One can no longer speak of Moscow pursuing a "European strategy" or seeking to implement "European values" (of one kind or another). Instead, it engages with different countries and institutions on an individual basis, emphasizing key bilateral relationships at the expense of cooperation with the EU and other pan-European bodies, such as the OSCE, the Council of Europe, and the European Court of Human Rights. This bilateralist bias—and corresponding dislike of multilateralism—emerges clearly when we examine Russia's diverse interactions on the European continent.

*Growing tensions with Brussels*

To members of the Putin elite the EU encapsulates much that is wrong with modern Europe. They see an institution that is overlarge, crippled by process, and, with the addition of new member-states from central and eastern Europe, congenitally anti-Russian. They resent its intrusiveness and assumed superiority.[78] And although they still take it seriously as an economic bloc (and Russia's number one trading partner), there is little respect for its political stature.[79]

These perceptions and prejudices have been strengthened by the global financial crash and the eurozone crisis. Russian leaders see no reason to listen to lectures about the benefits of market liberalization and good governance when so many EU member-states have failed to manage their own affairs. For Moscow the principal lesson is that the only worthwhile engagement in Europe is direct cooperation with the few countries that know what they want and are able to achieve it.

Even before events in Ukraine, the so-called strategic partnership with the EU had been stagnating for years. Indeed, this is putting a gloss on things. There are fundamental contradictions in institutional culture, where Moscow's partiality to great power diplomacy clashes with the EU's consensual decisionmaking;[80] in political values, where Putin's authoritarian conservatism is the polar opposite of European democratic capitalism; and in acrimonious disagreements on specific issues. There has been minimal progress toward a successor framework to the Partnership and Cooperation Agreement (PCA),[81] while the vision of a "common economic and humanitarian space from the Atlantic to the Pacific"[82] is as distant as ever. Russia-EU summits have become painful exercises in managing tensions and glossing over lack of achievement.

Moreover, both sides are becoming desensitized to the need for active cooperation. Moscow has given up hope of achieving real concessions from Brussels, such as liberalization of the Schengen visa regime, while the EU no longer believes in the prospect of Russia's convergence with core European values—at least not while Putin is in power. At a time when member-states are preoccupied with serious internal problems, they are unwilling to devote time and resources to what many regard as a fruitless endeavor. This lassitude extends to relatively apolitical areas, such as the "partnership for modernization," which has been rendered meaningless by conflicting interpretations of what it should entail. Initial hopes in Brussels that such a partnership would encourage reforms in Russia have crumbled with the realization that, for Putin, the whole point is to facilitate the importation of European technology and know-how without any conditionalities.[83]

Meanwhile, there are three problems that have the potential to condemn Russia-EU relations to long-term, systemic crisis. They are clashing perceptions of energy security; the continuing conflict between the EU's Eastern Partnership (EaP) program and Moscow's Eurasian Union; and the struggle over the future of Ukraine.

*Energy security.* For much of the past decade, Moscow has operated on the premise that its European gas customers were incapable of working together owing to their competing national interests. It disregarded Brussels, and concentrated its efforts instead on expanding Gazprom's ties with leading European energy companies, such as E.ON-Ruhrgas in Germany, Total in France, and ENI in Italy. At the same time, it played hardball with the Ukrainians, and with a number of central and east European countries, in particular Poland and the Baltic states. This behavior proceeded from two assumptions: gas prices would continue to climb indefinitely, and Russia would always hold the whip-hand in its energy relations with Europe.

However, Moscow underestimated the capacity of the Europeans to unite in response to arbitrary interruptions of their gas supply, such as occurred in January 2006 and January 2009 as a result of disputes between Moscow and Kyiv.[84] These crises had the effect, metaphorically speaking, of knocking European heads together. The outcome was the EU's Third Energy Package, with its rules on the "unbundling" of gas supply and distribution, and measures to promote competition. It changed the rules of the game—and the geo-economic balance of power. Since 2009, Gazprom has found itself repeatedly outmaneuvered, as EU customers have exploited a buyer's market and their newfound unity to renegotiate supply agreements at lower prices.[85] The European Commission's launching of an anti-trust suit against Gazprom in September 2012 testified to the change in fortunes and growing European confidence vis-à-vis Russia.[86] This was vital in stiffening the resolve of EU member-states to introduce sanctions against Moscow over Ukraine. Fear of the consequences of gas cutoffs, while still present, was notably less than a few years earlier.

The issue is not just about prices, but also about different ways of doing business. As noted in chapter 3, the Kremlin looks at gas exports to Europe through a geopolitical as well as commercial lens—as the most effective means of projecting Russian influence. By contrast, EU member-states see the question more in market and energy security terms. They believe, no less self-interestedly, that gas prices should reflect the current global glut; they doubt the reliability of Russian supply; and they are keen to reduce their energy dependence by diversifying to other sources. These conflicting perspectives highlight a more general problem of mistrust between Moscow and

Brussels. Well before events in Ukraine, each accused the other of bad faith and of politicizing energy ties, with neither willing to give ground.[87]

Developments during 2014 suggest these disagreements will become more intense. The Ukraine crisis has obvious implications for Russian gas exports to Europe; despite construction of the Nordstream pipeline, 55–60 percent of these exports still transit Ukrainian territory.[88] Brussels also blocked construction of the South Stream gas pipeline, by leaning on member-states through which it would have passed—Bulgaria, Serbia (currently a candidate for EU membership), Hungary, and Austria.[89] This move, along with the collapse in global oil prices, slumping European gas demand, and recession in Russia, led Putin to cancel the project altogether in December 2014.[90] Perhaps most important, the Sino-Russian gas agreement of May 2014 makes it likely that Moscow will ratchet up the rhetoric about redirecting gas exports to Asia. Although this threat is bogus, it will give further impetus to European efforts to diversify supply, and raise the political temperature between Moscow and Brussels.

*Eastern Partnership versus Eurasian Union.* Moscow has been so dismissive of EU soft power in recent times that it is surprising that it should be concerned about a program whose performance—and budget—has been so modest.[91] But that is to miss the main point. The Eastern Partnership program has become symbolic of a much wider contest for influence between the EU and Russia, and the six Eastern Partnership countries—Ukraine, Belarus, Azerbaijan, Georgia, Moldova, and Armenia—a battleground for competing economic interests, rival political allegiances, and contrasting normative visions.

Notwithstanding disclaimers on both sides, Brussels and Moscow view this competition in zero-sum terms. The EU reiterates that the EaP countries cannot abide by the provisions of DCFTAs (Deep and Comprehensive Free Trade Areas) and Association Agreements with Brussels, and still join Moscow-led groupings such as the Customs Union and Eurasian Economic Union. As the then EU commissioner for enlargement and neighborhood policy, Stefan Fule, put it in September 2013, "You cannot at the same time lower your customs tariffs as per the DCFTA and increase them as a result of the Customs Union membership."[92]

For its part Moscow portrays moves toward DCFTAs and Association Agreements as overtly anti-Russian acts, all the more serious against the backdrop of its deteriorating relations with the West. In the lead-up to the Vilnius Eastern Partnership summit in November 2013, it threatened several EaP countries with retaliatory measures if they concluded (or initialed) agreements with Brussels. Its main deterrent effort was centered on Ukraine, and the interests of President Yanukovych and other oligarchs, but it also targeted Chisinau, suspending imports of Moldovan wine and spirits on spurious sanitary grounds and threatening to destabilize Transnistria.[93]

Although the competition between the EaP and the Eurasian Union has since been overshadowed by developments in Ukraine and the larger crisis in Russia-U.S. relations, it has not gone away. Ukraine as an issue may have graduated beyond the narrow confines of the EaP/Eurasian Union dichotomy, but this is less true of Moldova and Georgia. Their efforts to pursue a pro-European orientation via Association Agreements are meeting fierce resistance from the Kremlin, which is determined to counter the subversive influence of liberal ideas in Russia's neighborhood.

*The future of Ukraine.* The unfolding of the Ukraine crisis has confirmed Russian perceptions of the EU as divided, weak, and increasingly irrelevant. The reluctance of some member-states to agree on meaningful sanctions against Moscow has encouraged the Kremlin's natural tendency to bilateralize relations with Europe, sidestepping Brussels as far as possible. To some extent this disengagement is reciprocated, with the EU focusing much more on eurozone priorities, such as the bailout negotiations with the Syriza government in Greece.

Nevertheless, Ukraine will remain a blight on Russia-EU relations. The reasons have less to do with its own future than with the fact that it will be a magnet for all sorts of other tensions. Developments there will have a major bearing on European energy security, given the pipelines that cross its territory. It will be a battleground in the struggle between opposing visions of European security, values, and institutions. And its precarious situation over the next few years will severely complicate Russia-EU cooperation across the board, and consolidate the trend of mutual alienation.

### The primary importance of Germany

The relationship with Germany is the kernel of Russia's European direction. Germany is critical above all because it is the dominant political and economic force on the European continent. There are also compelling bilateral reasons for close engagement. In Europe it is Russia's main trading partner (US$76.5 billion in 2013) and source of foreign investment (accounting for 21.9 percent of FDI projects in 2012).[94] It is a primary energy customer, whose demand for Russian gas may grow as it phases out nuclear power.[95] It opposes further NATO enlargement, and Western military intervention in Syria. And for much of the past decade it has taken a soft line on democratization and the rule of law in Russia. The German political class retains strong feelings of guilt for the Nazi invasion of the Soviet Union, while there is abiding gratitude to Mikhail Gorbachev for allowing German reunification. There are personal factors too that should favor a good relationship. Putin speaks excellent German, having served as a KGB officer in Dresden in the second half of the 1980s,[96] while Matthias Warnig has been a member of Putin's inner circle for more than two decades.[97]

The Kremlin views a good relationship with Berlin as integral to strengthening Russia's position in Europe (and beyond). It hopes that Germany will help counterbalance American geopolitical influence; dampen efforts to reduce European energy dependence on Russia;[98] open the way to missile defense cooperation on Moscow's terms; and be a conduit for the flow of advanced technology. In this last connection, it counts on the goodwill of the German business lobby, which, for much of the Putin era, has adopted a supportive and sometimes collusive stance toward the Kremlin.

In the past few years, however, things have become very difficult. While Chancellor Angela Merkel is a fluent Russian speaker, she has been much less compliant than her predecessor, Gerhard Schröder, who fitted the Kremlin's ideal of a European leader—partial toward Russia and dismissive of the concerns of smaller neighbors.[99] Merkel has been openly critical of authoritarian trends in Russia, as well as of Moscow's foreign policy, and the whole mood of the relationship has changed. In November 2012, Andreas Schockenhoff, then Germany's commissioner for German-Russian coordination, noted that "Moscow has a different conception of modernization than we do," and that "the police, courts, and lawmakers now rely on intimidation and repression of civil society."[100] Although Schockenhoff has since given way to the more well-disposed Gernot Erler, this does not get around the larger problem, for Moscow, of Merkel's more robust approach to the relationship.

Crucially, she has not indulged Putin's attempts to sidestep the EU. Berlin has not only bought into the Third Energy Package, but also responded to the eurozone crisis by pushing for closer fiscal and political coordination. By supporting more effective multilateralism in Europe, it is acting at direct cross-purposes to Moscow. The conventional view of Germany as Russia's best advocate in the West is no longer valid.[101] Although German business interests remain relatively sympathetic, attitudes among the political elite and general public have become very negative. According to a Transatlantic Trends Survey of September 2012, Russia's approval rating in Germany plummeted from 48 percent in 2011 to 32 percent one year later—a fall that coincided with Putin's return to the presidency, the Pussy Riot case, and the raft of anti-protest legislation instigated by the Kremlin.[102]

The Ukraine crisis has accentuated these trends. Merkel was outspoken in condemning the annexation of Crimea; has been consistently critical of Russian behavior since then; and was instrumental in the imposition of EU sanctions.[103] Foreign Minister Frank-Walter Steinmeier, previously seen as an enthusiastic advocate of *Ostpolitik*,[104] has not proved the soft touch that many thought he would be.[105] German policy toward Russia is more questioning than at any time in the past two decades. And the notion that there can be a meeting of minds between Moscow and Berlin has become discredited. Unsurprisingly, Russia's actions have resulted in a further deterioration of its public image in Germany; a 2014 Pew Global Attitudes survey found that its "favorable" rating had fallen to an all-time low of 19 percent versus 79 percent "unfavorable."[106]

It is difficult to see the bilateral relationship improving soon, given the probability that Merkel and Putin will dominate their countries' national politics for some years yet. Berlin will sustain its efforts to develop a more cohesive and disciplined European Union, and remain a vocal critic of authoritarian trends in Russia. The strongest area of the relationship will be the commercial side, although there is potential for trouble here as well. German manufacturing exports are vulnerable to Russia's slumping economic fortunes and enhanced geopolitical risks,[107] while Berlin's emphasis on renewables and energy efficiency has longer-term implications for imports (and prices) of Russian gas.[108]

### Europe's second power

The case of France differs from Germany's in several respects. French public discourse has been more vocal in criticizing human rights abuses and pseudo-democracy in Russia.[109] The economic relationship, including energy cooperation, is less significant. And Paris has been much more activist than Berlin on broader international questions. In 2011 then president Nicolas Sarkozy led the charge in NATO and the UN for military intervention against Gaddafi (in contrast to Merkel's decision to abstain on the Security Council Resolution). Sarkozy's response to the Arab Spring in general revealed clear differences with Moscow on issues of sovereignty and the "responsibility to protect."

Despite this, the Franco-Russian relationship has historically been strong. Paris and Moscow have taken the view that they can—and must—do business with each other. This stems, in the first instance, from a shared great power tradition. As a member of the P5, G-8, and G-20, and, after Germany, the leading player in the EU, France is unquestionably a major power, as well as one of the world's largest economies. Its leaders are accustomed to seeing international relations from a realist perspective, and this has been conducive to a degree of commonality with the Kremlin, particularly on the notion of a multipolar order.[110] For their part the Russians admire the French tradition of strategic independence, associated in particular with the iconic figure of Charles de Gaulle.[111] There is in both countries a strong streak of anti-Americanism and a keenness to ensure that the United States is not allowed to dominate world affairs. Both also have a deep respect for each other's culture and civilization.

Until recently Moscow saw France's foreign policy as pragmatic, driven by a keen sense of its national interests. The 2011 deal for the sale of the Mistral-class helicopter assault vessels exemplified a state-to-state relationship less encumbered than most by normative concerns.[112] Like Germany, France backed a more central role for Russia in Euro-Atlantic security.[113] But unlike Germany, it showed little inclination to speak out in support of smaller nations, whether within the EU or in the post-Soviet space.[114] The French government, as opposed to the French media, was inclined to downplay the sometimes uncomfortable politics of the relationship, and emphasize economic diplomacy instead.

The victory of François Hollande in the 2012 presidential elections cast a shadow over some of these assumptions. Although there were no significant changes to France's Russia policy, the Hollande administration signaled its commitment to building a more muscular European Union and intervening actively in Syria.[115] As with Germany, the Kremlin's hopes that it could peel France away from broader European positions became increasingly unrealistic, especially as French public perceptions of Russia—and Putin—worsened. Russia's "favorable" rating dropped by nearly half, from 56 percent in 2011 to 31 percent in 2012.[116]

Events in Ukraine have widened the divide between Moscow and Paris. Hollande initially attempted to insulate French commercial interests from the effects of Western sanctions. But this position became untenable as evidence of direct Russian military involvement in Ukraine accumulated. The Mistral deal was suspended in September 2014,[117] amid a general hardening of French policy. There is some speculation that Hollande is looking to do a deal with Putin on Ukraine. However, his very weak domestic position means that he is unable to pursue a more independent (and compliant) French line, but is instead tied to Merkel's tougher approach. Against this backdrop, one of the principal hopes of the Kremlin's European policy—a Moscow-Berlin-Paris troika—has become defunct.

### Old enemies, new differences

I alluded earlier to the initial impetus the reset gave to ties between Russia and Poland. This relationship has long been hugely problematic, weighed down by all sorts of unresolved issues—from the Polish invasion of Muscovy in the sixteenth century and the Russian Empire's role in three partitions of Poland at the end of the eighteenth century, to the more recent memory of the NKVD's massacre of Polish army officers at Katyn, Stalin's alleged complicity in the crushing of the 1944 Warsaw uprising, and Russian suzerainty over Poland during the cold war.

Polish-Russian interaction has remained difficult throughout the post-Soviet period. The reservoir of mistrust on both sides is daunting. The Poles routinely accuse the Kremlin of retaining imperial ambitions, while many in Moscow see Warsaw as determined to destroy any prospect of a reasonable relationship between Russia and Europe. These animosities have been fueled by a series of bitter disagreements: Polish accession to NATO in the 1990s, Russian energy policy, the deployment of U.S. missile defense batteries to Poland, and Warsaw's support for the Orange Revolution.

The course of relations has followed the fortunes of the U.S.-Russia reset. During 2009–10, when the reset enjoyed some momentum, Warsaw and Moscow took important steps toward normalization. Polish Prime Minister Donald Tusk's Civic Platform was much more conciliatory toward Russia than its predecessor, the Law and Justice Party, headed by the Kaczyński brothers. Putin won praise for his compassionate reaction to the Smolensk air disaster in April 2010, which killed President Lech Kaczyński and other senior Polish figures;[118] he offered a public apology and display of contrition for the Katyn massacre; and he appeared ready to condemn some of Stalin's crimes.[119] Significantly, though, the Russian moves were the result not of a historical or moral epiphany but of political calculation. They arose out of the larger improvement in relations with the United States and the West, and reflected Putin's appreciation of the growing importance of Poland within the EU and across Europe.[120]

This de facto linkage meant that the improvement in relations could not be sustained. Instead, it suffered severe collateral damage from the downturn between Russia and the West after 2011. Moscow reverted to standard positions. It not only inveighed against "attempts to rewrite history . . . and revise the outcomes of World War II,"[121] but insisted that the countries of eastern Europe, including Poland, owed Russia a timeless debt of gratitude for ending Nazi occupation.

The revival of history as a negative factor in the relationship was accompanied by renewed differences over specific bilateral and regional issues. The report of the Russian investigating commission into the Smolensk crash, which blamed the Polish military crew, provoked an angry reaction in Poland and accusations of a Russian cover-up. These suspicions were heightened by

Moscow's reluctance to return the remnants of the plane.[122] Geopolitically the Kremlin regarded Warsaw as the prime mover in the EU's efforts to wean Eastern Partnership states from Russian influence.[123]

The latest Ukraine crisis has brought their simmering confrontation out into the open. Warsaw's support for the Maidan revolution, its condemnation of the annexation of Crimea, and determined advocacy of tougher EU sanctions highlight a changed strategic and political reality.[124] There is no longer any pretense, in Warsaw or Moscow, about common interests. Poland's position as the strongest supporter of the Poroshenko administration in Kyiv sets it at odds with the Kremlin. Relatedly, Warsaw's demands for an enhanced NATO military presence in Poland and the Baltic states signal a return to the traditional view of Russia as an existential threat. In this picture, NATO's primary function is no longer the postmodern one of "promoting stability" in the Euro-Atlantic space, but the adversarial duty of countering Russia.

Against this negative tide, there are very few sources of comfort. The economic relationship is of diminishing value to both sides. Although Poland still imports significant volumes of Russian gas, it is developing its own shale gas reserves as part of a broader effort to reduce energy dependence on Russia. In trading terms, it looks much more to Germany, and two-way Polish-Russian investment has sunk to negligible levels.[125] It is difficult to see how or where the bilateral relationship will improve, unless as part of a broader rapprochement between Russia and the West. But this is a flimsy basis for constructive engagement, and the most plausible prognosis must be for a further deterioration on multiple fronts.

### A split relationship

Given that the United Kingdom and Russia are both nuclear weapons powers, P5 members, and among the world's leading economies, there has been remarkably little to their state-to-state relationship over the years. By contrast, trade has been significant (US$23.2 billion in 2012),[126] while the UK was, until recently, one of the largest sources of foreign direct investment into Russia, led by BP's nearly 20 percent equity in Rosneft.[127]

Today the Russia-UK relationship is as dysfunctional as any. The two governments disagree on virtually every high-profile issue—Ukraine, NATO, the fate of Assad, missile defense, U.S. global leadership. They have highly antagonistic perceptions of each other. Reports in September 2013 that Putin's spokesman Dmitry Peskov had described Britain as "a small island no one listens to" may have been apocryphal, but, if true, should not have come as a surprise.[128] To many in Moscow, the UK is an irritating junior partner of the

United States, largely alienated from the rest of Europe and with little independent influence in international affairs.

As with Poland, the reset had an early positive impact on Russia-UK relations. It facilitated, most notably, the resumption of dialogue following the lengthy diplomatic hiatus caused by the Litvinenko affair.[129] What it could not do, however, was bridge the differences between the two sides over Litvinenko or invest real content into their political and security relationship. Moscow and London established a "2+2" format for meetings of their respective foreign and defense ministers, but even at their best, official ties remained cool and insubstantial.

The Ukraine crisis has nullified even that modest progress, and frozen the relationship once again. London has followed Washington's hard line on sanctions and seized the opportunity to reassert the United Kingdom's position as an essential player in Euro-Atlantic security. As host of the 2014 NATO summit in Newport, Wales, Prime Minister David Cameron was instrumental in establishing an alliance Rapid Reaction Force, of which British troops are to make up one-fourth.[130] Compared with these priorities, the relationship with Russia is of peripheral importance. London's decision in July 2014 to proceed with a public inquiry into Litvinenko's death signaled that it no longer cared about Moscow's sensitivities, nor believed in the feasibility of worthwhile cooperation anytime soon.[131]

### Europe's twin outsiders

The relationship between Russia and Turkey presents many synergies. Both regard themselves as civilizations rather than "ordinary" nation-states. They have a similar mix (or confusion) of identities—European, Eurasian, traditionalism versus modernity. And following the end of the cold war, they have struggled to adapt to, and be accepted by, an EU-centered Europe. Turkey may be a frontline member of NATO, and Russia a predominantly Christian country, but both feel their outsider status keenly, and share a strong sense of victimhood vis-à-vis mainstream Europe (and Brussels in particular).[132]

The similarities do not stop there. Turkish President Recep Erdoğan and Vladimir Putin subscribe to similar principles of political and moral conservatism: a dominant role for the state; growing restrictions on independent institutions (NGOs, the media); and the reassertion of national and cultural relativism in opposition to Western-led universalism. In Turkey they speak of the Putinization of Erdoğan, while Putin has been described as a Kemalist (after the founder of modern Turkey, Kemal Atatürk).[133] The economic relationship is crucial. After the EU, Russia is Turkey's largest trading partner (US$33 billion in 2013) and accounts for 55 percent of its gas imports.[134] It is a major source of foreign investment in the Turkish economy, a presence reinforced by flagship projects such as the US$20 billion Akkuyu nuclear power plant. Turkey is also the largest foreign destination for Russian tourists, with more than four million visits in 2013.[135]

But behind these positive indicators, there are some problems. The most salient is disagreement over how to deal with Assad. Whereas Moscow is determined to protect the Syrian president, Ankara is among the most active advocates of regime change.[136] There are also tensions arising from Turkey's position as a front-line member of NATO; one specific Russian concern is that the deployment of an integrated missile defense system in Europe will involve Ankara's participation at some stage. Even the outlook for economic ties is by no means cloudless. Turkey is anxious about the widening trade imbalance (imports are three times more than exports), and keen to reduce its vulnerability to disruptions in gas supply. It is also involved in various infrastructural projects that will bypass Russian territory, such as the Trans-Adriatic Pipeline (TAP) and Trans-Anatolian Natural Gas Pipeline (TANAP).[137]

These differences do not mean that the relationship is necessarily headed for trouble. Erdoğan and Putin have adopted a constructive approach toward each other. The latter, especially, has been concerned to insulate bilateral ties from the Syrian conflict, as reflected in his fire-fighting visit to Ankara in December 2012,[138] and then again in December 2014. And the crisis over Ukraine has only encouraged him to keep reaching out to Erdoğan. Nevertheless, this remains a fragile relationship, susceptible to spiraling tensions in the region and the further deterioration of Russia-NATO relations.

## A new constituency?

There has been much discussion lately about emerging pro-Kremlin constituencies in a number of European countries. These constituencies side openly with Moscow on issues such as the Eastern Partnership, non-intervention in Syria, and Ukraine. They are hostile to an EU-centered wider Europe. And they subscribe to similar conservative and authoritarian values. As a result, they are sometimes seen as a fifth column in a Kremlin strategy to undermine European unity, discredit democratic liberalism, and diminish Europe's regional and international weight.[139]

These perceptions are not without some basis. However, the real picture is more complicated. While certain European governments, political parties, and interest lobbies look benignly upon Russian foreign and domestic policy, they do so for very different reasons: narrow self-interest, political likemindedness, and historical, religious, and cultural affinities. The ties that bind may be of recent provenance, as with Viktor Orban's Fidesz party in Hungary and

Marine Le Pen's Front National in France. Or they may have a deeper foundation, as in a historical pan-Slavism (Bulgaria and Serbia) or shared Orthodox faith (Bulgaria, Serbia, and Greece).

The extent of pro-Moscow sympathy also varies from country to country. It may arise out of a broad political and popular consensus (Greece and Serbia again), or be the subject of considerable contention, as in the case of the Czech Republic.[140] Sometimes the chief driver of "pro-Moscow" attitudes is not so much active support for Russia as anti-U.S. and anti-Brussels sentiment—either in response to the negative consequences of economic globalization, or as part of a more generalized resentment.[141]

Given rising tensions between Russia and the West, there is understandable anxiety about the Kremlin's footprint. Sympathetic or collusive groups within European elites could weaken the resolve of governments to resist external aggression—as happened in the lead-up to World War II. That said, we should not exaggerate Putin's successes in suborning these elites. To do so would be to undersell Europe's continuing strengths, encourage the self-seeking Russian narrative of a West in decline, and confuse cause and effect.

In the case of Greece, for example, a 2014 Pew Global Attitudes survey found that 61 percent of respondents viewed Russia in a favorable light—a figure barely affected by the annexation of Crimea and events in eastern Ukraine. But such ratings appear to have little to do with Putin; the same survey noted that only 41 percent of respondents were confident that he would do the "right thing regarding world affairs," compared with 57 percent who had no such confidence. This suggests that pro-Russian sentiment in Greece, and in countries such as Bulgaria, is due to factors that have little to do with Kremlin policy. Greece has a long tradition of left-wing, anti-American political opposition, while the eurozone crisis has had devastating consequences for its population. Despite that, most Greeks wish to remain in the EU and to retain the euro. There is no desire to gravitate toward a (nonexistent) "Russian model."

Hungarian Prime Minister Orban is widely portrayed as Putin's new best friend: opposing EU sanctions against Moscow, cooperating with Gazprom in restricting Ukraine's access to imported Russian gas, and concluding a major agreement to modernize the Paks nuclear plant. Yet such moves are motivated overwhelmingly by self-interest—ensuring access to Russian resources and nuclear technology—rather than normative convergence.[142] Orban's well-documented authoritarian tendencies owe much more to indigenous Hungarian nationalism than to Putinism.

No case highlights the limits of Kremlin influence better than Serbia. In most respects, it is the most obvious candidate to be a client-state. It not only has close ties with Russia going back centuries, but also compelling reasons to dislike the West—the NATO bombing campaign in 1999 and the subsequent secession of Kosovo. Nevertheless, Belgrade continues to push hard for Serbia's accession to the EU. While it would like to retain a foot in both camps, and has made concessions to Moscow to this purpose,[143] it regards European integration, not Russia, as the key to its future.

In sum the Kremlin would like to develop a network of friends and partners in Europe, particularly in the south and east. And it has succeeded insofar as there are influential groups that act, purposefully or otherwise, to further Russian interests. Yet this is a long way from representing a cohesive Kremlin constituency. Talk of governments in central and eastern Europe favoring Russia over Europe is wide of the mark. While some of them strive to keep channels open with Moscow, their European choice is unmistakable.

### The limitations of bilateralism

Moscow's bilateralist approach toward Europe highlights the disjunction between its preconceived view of the international system and often confusing regional realities. On the one hand, it sees a Europe crippled by internal divisions and excess.[144] It believes that the major European powers, led by Germany, run the continent's affairs—all the more so since the eurozone crisis. And it has no respect for Europe's brand of democratic multilateralism, as embodied by the EU.

On the other hand, the Kremlin is discovering that matters are not so straightforward. In the first place, EU member-states are more united on Russia than they have been for years. Although the Ukraine crisis has highlighted disagreements over the appropriate level of sanctions, there has been a surprising degree of consensus in condemning Russia's behavior in Crimea and eastern Ukraine—certainly far greater than the Kremlin anticipated. In other areas, Russian attempts to split or otherwise manipulate EU member-states have been largely ineffectual. Although Moscow made some early inroads with the South Stream countries (see above), EU energy policy is more cohesive these days. Putin's announcement of the cancellation of the South Stream project in December 2014 was tacit acknowledgment of this fact.

Second, Berlin and Paris have not succumbed to Russian blandishments. In particular, Merkel has proved an altogether more demanding proposition than Putin's favorite European leader, Gerhard Schröder. Third, and relatedly, small states matter. The idea that Germany and/or France can (or would even try to) browbeat, say, Estonia is nonsensical. Many of the smaller European countries are demonstrating a real independence of purpose, and a much improved ability to utilize multilateral mechanisms to their advantage.

Finally, the EU's rules-based vision of Europe remains the preeminent narrative on the continent. Tales of Putin's tactical brilliance over Ukraine overlook that European influence in that country is now much stronger than before. Brussels may have misplayed the modalities of the Eastern Partnership, but subsequent developments in Ukraine and other ex-Soviet republics, such as Georgia, testify to the enduring appeal of its message.

The Kremlin's facile views of European realities have also caused it to mishandle other continent-wide issues, notably relations with NATO. To Russian policymakers, the alliance is at best "a relic of the cold war," but more often an "enemy" organization.[145] They see it not as an alliance between America and Europe, but as a geopolitical instrument of the United States *in* Europe. This perception was evident during negotiations on European missile defense. When Medvedev emerged from the NATO Lisbon summit in November 2010 with what he thought was in-principle agreement, Moscow assumed that a deal could quickly be finalized with Washington, and that the Europeans would meekly follow suit. In fact, it was wrong on both counts: the Americans refused to countenance the devolution of command-and-control functions, and the Europeans were vehemently opposed to the idea.[146]

Such misperceptions have been reprised in relation to Ukraine. Moscow accuses the United States of overweening geopolitical ambition in eastern Europe, and of seeking regime change in Russia.[147] But prior to Crimea the Obama administration had shown very little interest in Ukraine. The irony is that Russian actions have brought a renewed sense of purpose in Washington and unity to an alliance that had previously been exhibiting signs of major decay.

Moscow has been slow to adapt to a postmodern, multilateral Europe because this is so much at odds with Russian strategic culture and its emphasis on hard power, geopolitical priorities, and great power collusion. It has also been misled by its experience with an earlier, more compliant generation of European leaders, such as Schröder, former French president Jacques Chirac, and ex–Italian prime minister Silvio Berlusconi. Yet it does not appear to be exercised by this deficit of understanding. Far from seeking to engage more actively with European institutions, it continues to circumvent them—except on the rare occasions when it is enlisting support for a discrete political objective, as with the OSCE and the "federalization" of Ukraine (see chapter 4).

### A depressing prognosis

Europe is a more natural partner for Russia than the United States. It is geographically closer, much more important commercially, less judgmental on the whole, and it poses no geopolitical threat. Nevertheless, relations are unlikely to improve over the next few years. Moscow's lack of respect for political Europe ensures that it is functioning mainly on autopilot, while European leaders (and publics) are losing interest in Russia as a partner. Few believe in the prospect of rule of law and economic modernization under Putin, and they are weary of pandering to Kremlin sensitivities. With hindsight Merkel's criticism, at the 2012 St. Petersburg Dialogue, of the disproportionate sentences handed out to the Pussy Riot members represented a watershed in changing European attitudes.[148]

National governments will continue to engage politically with Russia, while the EU will remain the latter's largest source of trade and foreign investment for probably the next decade at least. But illusions about Russia's "European-ness" and a common European vision have given way to a deep feeling of alienation. Putin's Russia has become as foreign as China, while being a far less attractive partner. The outlook is just as gloomy on the Russian side. Even in the 1990s when Europe was riding high, there was already a strong Americacentric bias in Moscow.[149] Today, ideas of a Union or Alliance of Europe, marrying the EU's soft power with Russia's hard power capabilities, appear hopelessly utopian. With many in the Russian policy community identifying Europe as the greatest casualty of shifting international trends, there is no influential constituency in favor of abandoning (or diluting) Moscow's country- and power-based approach to European affairs.

## The Place of the West in Putin's Foreign Policy

The demise of the reset and the deterioration of relations with Europe raise questions about the larger position of the West in Moscow's worldview. It would be natural to conclude from recent developments that Russian foreign policy is finally shedding its Westerncentric bias. Just as the global financial downturn has acted as a catalyst for power shifts in the world, so the Ukraine crisis is stimulating Russia's reorientation.

Strangely, though, the Putin regime has in some respects become more, rather than less, Westerncentric. It is important to understand why this is so, since it not only belies Moscow's pronouncements about a "turn to the East," but also runs against the grain of contemporary international politics.

### Foreign policy conservatism

The previous chapter considered why Russia has failed to make its mark in Asia. One explanation was the predispositional influence of historical, geographical, and civilizational factors, which has translated into an enduring Westerncentrism. But no less important is a deeply conservative mentality that militates against significant change *of any kind*. In a very real sense, Moscow's continuing Westerncentrism stands as a metaphor for a Russia stuck in a time warp, seemingly incapable and unwilling to adapt to a world in transformation.

The United States and Europe represent the known. Relations with them can sometimes be extremely difficult, as today. But when Russian policymakers engage with their Western counterparts, they resort to a well-rehearsed repertoire of behaviors, negotiating tactics, and policy positions.[150] By contrast, interaction with the Chinese and other Asians is a more unfamiliar enterprise, requiring revised assumptions and different approaches. The Chinese have proved especially challenging partners, notwithstanding the upward trajectory of their relationship. The reasons are not linguistic, but cultural in the wider meaning of the term.[151]

The dichotomy between the familiar and unfamiliar applies above all to the sphere of security. Although Moscow talks up the dangers of missile defense, condemns NATO's appropriation of Euro-Atlantic security, and warns of American unipolarity and exceptionalism, there is a reassuring routine about threats from the West. The issues appear readily comprehensible, and not to require imaginative solutions. This applies also to larger international problems, such as the Syrian conflict. The Kremlin sees no great mystery in the workings of U.S. foreign policy, even while it regards it as dangerous and ill-intentioned. With the Chinese, everything is so much more ambiguous. There is discomfort, not about the gravity or immediacy, but the elusiveness of the challenges posed by China's rise.

## Selective engagement

There are perfectly rational arguments to support Russia's continuing Westerncentrism. As the world's only truly global power, the United States has an enormous material and psychological impact on Kremlin decisionmaking. Europe is Russia's closest neighbor and most important economic partner. And despite the supposed decline of the West, the world is still dominated by Western governments, institutions, and norms.

In Russia as elsewhere, the West is identified with advanced economic development, first-rate technology, and high living standards. If Russia is to become internationally competitive in industry, services, and agriculture, it needs to engage with the West—often in direct competition with China, India, and other emerging economies.[152] Silicon Valley, not Skolkovo Management School or Chinese technology parks, is the external benchmark—a reality recognized by the 40,000 Russians reportedly working there.[153] Despite relations with the United States sinking to a post–cold war nadir, it is Exxon-Mobil, not CNPC, that the Kremlin really desires as a partner in developing energy resources in the Arctic and Russian Far East.

One should also not underestimate the cultural and normative pull of the West. Contrary to the simplistic claim that ordinary Russians prefer author-itarian leadership to democracy, the evidence shows that they are partial to the expansion of individual liberties and to political choice, ideals usually associated with the liberal West.[154] The most eloquent illustration of the Russ-ian population's abiding Westerncentrism is not the anti-Putin protest move-ment of 2011–12, but the lifestyle of its middle class, which is more disposed than ever to embrace "Western" habits. And despite the rise of Asia, the brain drain of young, ambitious Russians is to the United States and Europe, not to China and India.

In the meantime, members of the ruling elite operate according to a barely concealed double standard. They excoriate the West, and particularly Europe, as soft and clapped-out. Yet they send their children to be educated at Euro-pean and American universities; buy property in London; invest their money in Western banks and hedge funds; and pursue legal redress in British courts. In doing so, they act on the tacit—but unmistakable—assumption that the "West is best." It is revealing that the Eurasian Economic Union, a counter-Western integration project, nevertheless borrows heavily from the EU's *acquis communautaire* as the model of international best practice on norms and standards.[155] And the EEU's bureaucratic apparatus, the Eurasian Eco-nomic Commission, is a copy of the European Commission in Brussels.

Since late 2013 Putin has been promoting the "de-offshorization" of Russ-ian capital and property, ostensibly to make Russian interests less vulnerable to outside (read: Western) pressure, but mainly to bolster his political control. So far, however, this has had limited effect. The business interests of the elite are intertwined with the West, and the fragile state of the Russian economy suggests this will not change soon. Capital flight from Russia in 2013 was esti-mated at US$63 billion, and this figure was exceeded in the first quarter of 2014 (US$65–70 billion).[156] In September that year, former finance minister Alexei Kudrin estimated that US$110 billion had left the country since the start of the Ukraine crisis.[157]

That said, it is important to distinguish between Westerncentrism and pro-Westernism. Like many of his predecessors over the past 300 years, Putin looks at the West as both resource *and* threat.[158] It is a resource for economic devel-opment and elite enrichment. But it is a threat when viewed through the prism of political models and geopolitical balancing. It also serves as a vital mobi-lizational tool for the Kremlin.[159] The tactic of identifying an external public enemy has been especially evident during the Ukraine crisis, but it has long historical antecedents and a seductive rationale. It provides an easy alibi for failures of policy and governance, and the justification for repressive measures, such as tighter controls over the media, NGOs, and political opposition.

What is emerging, then, is a process of selective, or à la carte, engagement with the West, marked by the compartmentalization of interests. Russia's rulers are distancing themselves from Western political values while still hoping to attract large-scale European (and even American) technical assistance. They want to keep open their personal access to the West, while vigorously resisting the penetration of liberal ideas into Russian society. They pay lip service to the rule of law, accountable government, combating corruption, and building a civil society, but do everything possible to consolidate existing power relations.[160] Ultimately they seek not convergence or integration with the West, but cooperation and acquiescence *by* the West.

## The Reaffirmation of Russian Foreign Policy

Putin appears to have drawn three broad conclusions from Russia's relations with the West over the past decade. The first is that one cannot trust in the good intentions of the Western powers, the United States principally. Behind the disingenuous moralizing about democracy and global governance, they pursue their interests with a ruthless purpose and disregard of others. Russia must therefore see the West (and the world) for what it is.[161]

The second conclusion is that his conduct of foreign policy has been overwhelmingly successful. Under his watch the humiliated nation of the 1990s has metamorphosed into a resurgent global power, "one of the influential and competitive poles in the modern world."[162] It is more independent, more indispensable, more self-confident, and more influential than at any time since the fall of the Soviet Union.

Third, as Putin sees it, Russia is in a position to dictate, or at least control, the terms of its engagement with the West. The days of being told what to do and how to do it are over. It can decide when and where to cooperate, or whether to cooperate at all. Today the West needs Russia more than ever: in international conflict management; as a geopolitical counterweight to China; as a bulwark against Islamist extremism; and, in the case of Europe, as a primary supplier of energy. The onus is therefore on the West to adjust to Russia, not the other way round—and this means, in the first instance, treating it as an equal and respected partner.

Russia's relationship with the West is not a self-standing phenomenon, but reflects—and reinforces—the overall orientation and mindset of its foreign policy. Notwithstanding talk of adapting to "profound changes in the geopolitical landscape," and to international relations that are "increasingly complex and unpredictable,"[163] there has been no structural shift in regime thinking about the world and Russia's place in it. In the Kremlin's worldview, events (and crises) come and go, requiring tactical dexterity and sometimes policy adjustments, but principles and strategic culture are permanent.

Consequently the Putin era has seen the consolidation of core tenets of Russian foreign policy, influenced more by the realpolitik of the nineteenth-century diplomat Prince Alexander Gorchakov than by the realities of the twenty-first century.[164] These tenets include an abiding self-perception as one of the world's premier powers, an unshakable faith in the primacy of hard power, and the conviction that Russia will always play a leading role in international affairs. If there is an overarching lesson to be learned from dealings with the West, then for Putin it lies in the value of reaffirmation over reinvention: sticking to one's beliefs, resisting alien notions of right and wrong, and defending national interests even in the face of the strongest opposition. In his neo-Hobbesian vision of the world, in which the strong thrive and the "weak get beaten," there can be no other way.

All this indicates that Russia's interaction with the West will become more problematic over the next few years. The list of fundamental disagreements of policy and principle is truly formidable. Add to this Putin's mixture of triumphalism and aggrieved righteousness, and it is difficult to see a way out of the current adversarial paradigm. Although Moscow is not solely responsible for this state of affairs, there will be no improvement in relations as long as the Kremlin identifies missile defense, the Third Energy Package, and an independent Ukraine as greater threats to Russia than WMD proliferation and Islamist extremism.

It may take a major strategic shock, or series of shocks, to arrest the overall trend of negative continuity. One such shock might be the emergence of a recklessly expansionist China. Another, more probable scenario is a region-wide conflagration across the Middle East. Even so, it would be unwise to count on the emergence of a new spirit of cooperation, given the baggage that keeps accumulating between Russia and the West. At a minimum, there would need to be a return to realism on all sides: ditching the pretense of commonalities that are anything but; eschewing quasi-mystical ambitions of world order; and focusing on concrete priorities. Only then can there be a better fit between expectations, possibilities, and outcomes.

# Part III

# Possibilities

# seven

# A New Foreign Policy for a New Russia

He who shows himself is not conspicuous;
He who considers himself right is not illustrious;
He who brags will have no merit;
He who boasts will not endure.

LAO TZU, SIXTH CENTURY BCE

This chapter is based on a premise that many will find very hard to accept: namely, that a new Russian foreign policy is not only necessary, but also possible. Recent trends appear to confirm that "Russia is what it is," defined by the characteristics that have shaped its development since it emerged as a continental power in the eighteenth century. These features include an abiding sense of greatness and strategic entitlement; suspicion toward outside influences; an imperial mentality; and a profound political and moral conservatism. For supporters and critics alike of the Putin regime, the nature of Moscow's engagement with the world will remain essentially unaltered, even if there is some adjustment to individual policies from time to time.

The case against reform is reinforced by the experience of the post-Soviet era. Many in the ruling elite, including Putin himself, harbor a profound sense of grievance toward the West. They claim that Moscow has on numerous occasions stretched out the hand of friendship, only to be rebuffed, humiliated, and exploited. The lesson they have drawn is that Russia should not seek to meet the self-interested prescriptions of others, but stay true to its great power destiny and play to its strengths.

Such thinking is all the more persuasive when most Russians, including some liberals, regard Putin's foreign policy as highly successful. They recognize that Russian actions are often unpopular in the West, but for them this matters less than the restoration of national self-respect and strategic independence. They contrast Putin's resolve with the vacillation of Western governments. They recall how military intervention against the despised Saakashvili regime in Tbilisi turned the geopolitical tables against the Americans, and killed off NATO enlargement for the foreseeable future.[1] And they rejoice in the annexation of Crimea and the evident discomfiture of a once dominant West. Why, given all this, should Russia look to change anything?

Meanwhile, the domestic circumstances and mood of the Putin elite militate against reforms. There has been a battening down of the ideological and institutional hatches. Putin is striving to expand his already considerable personal authority, amid speculation about a fourth presidential term beyond 2018.[2] The economy revolves more than ever around centralized rent-seeking in energy and other natural resources. The state is increasingly intrusive, reaching into people's private as well as public lives. And a mass program of moral and historical education has been initiated, rooted in an ultra-traditionalism that bears uncomfortable parallels with Tsar Nicholas I's holy trinity of *samoderzhavie*, *pravoslavie*, and *narodnost* (autocracy, Orthodoxy, nationhood). All this represents a most unpromising context from which a new Russian foreign policy might emerge. There appears to be neither motive nor opportunity.

## Challenging Pessimism

However, if the obstacles to the formation of a new Russian foreign policy are undoubtedly formidable, we should avoid lapsing into a lazy fatalism. It would be a mistake to rule out significant change on the basis that today's conditions will necessarily prevail tomorrow. Or to believe that what is improbable now will always be so. Change, if and when it comes, may not be linear and evolutionary. To assume this is to underestimate two critical factors: the mutability and suddenness of history and a world in the midst of unprecedented transformation.

At the end of chapter 1 I alluded to tectonic shifts in Russia's history— from despotic principality to mainstream European power, from continental to global power, and from adversarial to cooperative engagement. Many of these shifts occurred with remarkable speed. Peter the Great, Joseph Stalin, and Mikhail Gorbachev brought about *revolutionary* change in just a few years, in settings that were arguably less conducive to reform than Russia today. Who would have predicted, for example, that the Soviet Union would transmogrify from the weakling of European politics in the 1920s into a global superpower in only two decades? Or that the cold war and the communist world would end as suddenly as they did? Such spectacular reversals of fortune are not flukes, but have occurred countless times in history— witness the transformation of China post-Mao, the rise of the European Union out of the devastation of World War II, and the overthrow of well-entrenched authoritarian regimes as a result of the Arab Spring. Moreover, it is historically unsound to conclude that such dramatic change can happen only under extreme circumstances. There was nothing inevitable about the sudden collapse of the Soviet Union, China's economic and social liberalization under Deng Xiaoping, or the ejection of Arab dictators who had misruled their peoples for decades. Alternative outcomes—more conservative and "predictable"—were at least as plausible.

The case for long-term stasis is all the more suspect given that far-reaching change is all around us. Authoritarian regimes yearn for control—to stem the flow of ideas and to manage events. But this is infinitely more difficult these days. Instead, they find themselves hostage to circumstances, often forced to respond in ways they never anticipated, and struggling in vain to hold on to illusions of stability, greatness, and power.[3]

As noted at the beginning of the book, the central challenge facing the Putin regime is to reconcile its preconceptions about the way of the world and Russia's place in it with regional and global realities that defy many core assumptions. Previous chapters have argued that Moscow has yet to come to terms with this task, as measured by its performance in four key areas of foreign policy: global governance, the post-Soviet space, relations with Asia, and engagement with the West. This chapter addresses the classic revolutionary question of "what is to be done" (*chto delat*).[4] How might Russia develop a foreign policy that responds more ably to the demands of the new world disorder? What form could this take, what would be its guiding principles, and how might it play out in specific areas?

## The Imperative of Change

In thinking about a new Russian foreign policy in a rapidly evolving international context, it is helpful to divide the question in terms of "why," "what," and "how": *why* Russia should adapt and even reinvent itself; *what* it needs to change; and *how* it should go about it.

The "why" of change is perhaps the easiest question for outsiders to answer, and the hardest for many Russians to recognize. One of the most striking phenomena of the post–cold war period has been Russia's strategic decline from second superpower to a regional actor with some global interests. Of course, much of this decline has been unavoidable and, in some respects at least, good for both Russia and international society. The end of the Soviet empire and cold war confrontation resulted in a considerably less threatening profile. During the 1990s the task of post-Soviet reconstruction implied a primary focus on the enormous challenges of domestic reform, along with substantial foreign policy retrenchment.

The point is not that Russia is less powerful than the Soviet Union, but that its importance and influence have fallen further and longer than warranted. Notwithstanding the drumbeat of national resurgence under Putin, Russia's weight in international affairs is feeble given its physical extent, extensive resources, and inherited capabilities. It has enjoyed the odd high-profile victory, such as the 2008 war against Georgia and the 2014 annexation of Crimea, as well as the diplomatic intervention that forestalled U.S. military action against Assad over the use of chemical weapons. But such "wins" have tended to be fleeting, rather than game changers for its position in the world. Russia aspires to be an equal of the United States and China, yet it plays only a peripheral role in shaping a twenty-first-century agenda. Dmitri Trenin rightly notes that "for Moscow to become a recognized purveyor of regional and global public goods, a long and hard slog lies ahead."[5] In areas where it has traditionally been strong, such as strategic disarmament and energy security, its imprint has become noticeably weaker. Visions of Russia as an energy power are increasingly suspect in light of the shale revolution, the rationalization of EU energy policy, growing strategic dependence on China, and the discovery of new sources of fossil fuels around the world.

Putin seeks to reassert Russian influence in the post-Soviet space through various devices, such as the Eurasian Economic Union (EEU) and the Collective Security Treaty Organization (CSTO). But with few exceptions this influence is declining, and is likely to fall further as the ex-Soviet republics consolidate their sovereignty, and China and various regional powers become more active. For all Putin's "successes" in annexing Crimea and destabilizing eastern Ukraine, Russian leverage on Kyiv is at a post-Soviet low. Even in the maximalist scenario of de facto partition between a Russian sphere of influence in the east and a Europe-oriented west, Moscow's position would be weaker than before the Maidan revolution or even in the aftermath of the Orange Revolution ten years earlier.

Elsewhere Russia's footprint is either contracting or remains insignificant. It has limited itself to a disruptive role in Euro-Atlantic security. It offers little in helping to manage various conflicts in the Middle East. On the contrary, its steadfast support for the Assad regime has been a major factor in the intensification and radicalization of the war in Syria, and the rise of Islamic State (IS). Its geopolitical and economic presence in Asia is very modest, despite the "turn to the East." From time to time, Russian actions and statements provoke a flurry of interest, but almost invariably in a negative context.

Its preventative influence can still be formidable, as we have seen in Ukraine, Georgia, and Syria. But its will and capacity to create remain unproven.

It is indicative of this reduced situation that international interest in Russia itself is sporadic and superficial—in the non-West as well as the West. As the "lonely power,"[6] it has few friends in the world, and most of those tend to be regimes with dubious reputations—Belarus, Venezuela, Nicaragua, Syria, Zimbabwe, Sudan. It maintains sound relations with countries such as China and India, but here, too, Russia rates as a secondary priority. Beijing, for example, is significantly more committed to engagement with the United States, East Asia, and the European Union than it is to Sino-Russian "strategic partnership"—energy deals notwithstanding.

Moscow routinely insists that Russia is an integral part of European civilization, a Euro-Pacific power, and a global player. Yet it has struggled to gain recognition for any of these identities. Washington does not see Russia as more than a regional partner at best. European policymakers regard it as a destructive, almost delinquent actor. And Asians view it as an outsider. Russia retains a residual status as the world's second nuclear weapons state, but this carries much less weight than it once did. It is symptomatic of Russia's trials that the one major institution in which it is indubitably an insider—the UN Security Council—is experiencing a crisis of credibility, as its composition and modus operandi are widely condemned as anachronistic.[7]

Naturally there are risks to change. Putin has become accustomed to reinforcing regime legitimacy through the image of a wronged Russia reasserting itself against a malign West. To accept and act on the need for change would be to acknowledge that his conduct of international relations has been flawed. Such an admission would not only be personally discomfiting but also potentially destabilizing, even in a country where foreign affairs generally holds little interest for the population. Putin's handling of the Ukraine crisis highlights the risks. Having surfed a wave of nationalist sentiment to boost his popularity, he is finding that this restricts his room for maneuver; he is under constant pressure to show strength.[8]

It is also difficult to separate changes in foreign policy from domestic reforms. Gorbachev recognized this when he wrote about "new thinking for our country *and* the world,"[9] and the Putin generation feels the nexus no less keenly. For conservatives and reformers alike, a new foreign policy in an old political system is unimaginable. It would call into question many of the pillars that sustain the regime: opaque, non-accountable governance; institutionalized corruption on a grand scale; and an obsolescent economic model. It would contribute to the demystification of the *vlast* (the ruling authority), whose hold on power has depended as much on aura as on performance. And on a more materialistic level it would undermine vested interests in key sectors such as energy.

But the risks of sticking to the tried and familiar are greater still, if less immediate. As the Italian writer Giuseppe di Lampedusa once observed, "if we want things to stay as they are, things will have to change."[10] Russia will struggle to remain *any kind* of major power—traditional or modern, military or economic, hard or soft—if it pursues a foreign policy driven more by a sense of entitlement than a purposeful appreciation of its national interests. In a world that has rarely been more fluid, and where everything is to play for, it has the possibility to redefine itself as a global player. But it cannot do so by adhering to the static precepts that governed relations between the European great powers in the nineteenth century. A Russia that fails to adapt to the demands of the new world disorder will remain backward, in comparison not only with the developed West, but also with a rising non-West. It would be less actor than acted upon, unable to defend its interests against the competing agendas of others. Such an outcome would be more than merely unfortunate; it would represent a terrible betrayal of Russia's vast potential, and of the unprecedented opportunities offered to it by the current international context.

## The Substance of Change

If the imperative of change in Russian foreign policy should not be in doubt, it is more challenging to identify *what* Moscow must change. There is a facile assumption in North America and Europe that Russia should just follow the "good" example set by the leading Western powers and become a "normal" country with a "normal" foreign policy: pro-Western, post-imperial, sincerely multilateralist, and having shed the last vestiges of its great power mentality.

This is impractical. For one thing, the West is hardly in a strong position to dictate international good practice to others. The past decade has witnessed spectacular failures in U.S. and European foreign policy, while the global financial crash has badly damaged the West's moral and economic standing. More important, Russia needs to reform its foreign policy not by blindly following some external template, but taking into account its own strengths and limitations. Although the concept of a Russian "specificity" (*spetsifika*) has been much overplayed in the past, it retains some validity. The most "modern" foreign policy must proceed from the reality that Russia occupies more than a tenth of the earth's land mass spread across two continents; retains several thousand nuclear weapons; is a member of the P5; and possesses abundant natural resources. It must also factor in demographic pressures;[11] a declining industrial base; and the existence of multiple weak states in its neighborhood.

The primary, indeed only appropriate, criterion in devising a new Russian foreign policy is *effectiveness*, as defined by: (1) the pursuit of objectives whose realization will enhance the welfare of the Russian people; and (2) the development of capabilities that will facilitate the achievement of those objectives. Everything else is secondary. Thus the purpose of cooperation with the United States, Europe, or China is not to garner status, or to be liked, but to contribute materially to Russia's national security, sustainable economic growth, and political and social stability.

### Prioritizing substance

The greatest failing of Russian diplomacy has been a preoccupation with form over substance. Although all governments are guilty of this, in Russia it has assumed exceptional proportions. Posturing about "indispensability"; strident demands for respect; the proliferation (and consequent devaluation) of "strategic partnerships"; and the propagating of myths such as BRICS solidarity—all speak of an obsession with abstractions. Such grandstanding has highlighted the disjunction between an overweening sense of entitlement and the modesty of Russia's actual contributions.

The first task, then, of a new Russian foreign policy is to focus much more on delivering concrete outcomes. There have been occasional signs of improvement, but too few and poorly coordinated. Chapter 5 noted that Russian participation in Asian multilateral structures had become more high-level, yet progress here remains unimpressive. Similarly, over the years Moscow has undertaken various initiatives, such as Medvedev's proposal for a new European security architecture. Unfortunately, these have suffered from a lack of content and the unsubtle intrusion of ulterior motives. Despite repeatedly calling for a "Helsinki-II" to update the original 1975 Helsinki Accords, the Kremlin took more than a year to come up with the flimsiest of documents. It was no surprise, then, that Western governments should view the Russian ideas with suspicion—as an attempt to undermine NATO rather than as a sincere effort to build a better Euro-Atlantic security system.[12]

The Medvedev project revealed that Moscow is often more concerned with the anticipated resonance of a proposal than with its practicality. The combination of inadequate substance and over-politicization ensures that such initiatives often fail to get to first base, let alone progress further. The problem of form over substance is also a serious drag on Russia's bilateral relationships.

The plethora of framework agreements and memorandums of understanding (MOUs) often acts as a placebo, masking the inability—and sometimes lack of commitment—to achieve substantive deals. This failing was well illustrated by the decade-long saga of Sino-Russian gas negotiations.

Such shortcomings are not only irritating distractions but have concrete consequences for Russian interests. The delays over the gas deal (and other energy agreements, such as construction of the ESPO branch pipeline) were instrumental in pushing Beijing to turn to Central Asia, where it quickly negotiated *and implemented* long-term agreements with Turkmenistan, Kazakhstan, and Uzbekistan. This, in turn, led to China becoming the principal economic player in Central Asia and an emerging strategic actor there (see chapter 5).

The larger challenge for Russian policymakers might be summed up as one of "talking less, walking more." A public commitment to closer engagement with Asia is commendable, but useless without proper follow-up. Instead of speaking in generalities such as a "polycentric system of international relations" and "non-institutionalized mechanisms of global governance,"[13] Moscow would be better off concentrating on the specifics of economic interaction with China, India, Brazil, and other parts of the non-Western world. A more businesslike approach is essential if Russia is to dispel the damaging perception that it is more interested in status than results.

### Promoting a positive agenda

One of the features of Russian foreign policy under Putin (and previously Yeltsin) has been its pursuit of an "anti-agenda," in which the main thrust is less to advance Russian national interests than to block those of other players. Over the years it has devoted strenuous efforts to countering American "unilateralism," undermining NATO, dividing the Europeans on energy security, and preventing the former Soviet states from developing closer ties with the West.

To some extent an anti-agenda is part of every country's foreign policy. This is particularly true of states that have been weakened or are in relative decline—both considerations that apply to Russia. Nevertheless, there is almost no area of foreign policy where Moscow has conceived, much less pursued, a constructive agenda. Its contribution to global governance centers largely on ritualistic assertions about the primacy of international law; it views the post-Soviet space through a zero-sum lens; its turn to the East has contributed nothing to security-building or economic integration in the Asia-Pacific region; and its relations with the United States and Europe, even in better times, are more competitive than cooperative.

The EEU might appear to be the exception to the rule. However, Moscow's "positive" agenda here is highly conditional. The main goal is not to promote Eurasian integration as a mutually beneficial good, but to preserve Russia's position as the leading strategic actor in the post-Soviet space; it has no interest in any integration model that it does not direct and closely control.[14] The creation of an internal Eurasian space is a *defensive* measure in the face of sundry challenges: Islamist extremism, Western liberal influences, Chinese economic and political penetration, and resurgent feelings of independence among the ex-Soviet republics.

The adverse impact of an anti-agenda is most strongly felt in Russia's relations with the United States. There are many reasons why their interaction has been difficult for all but brief periods. But one critical element is that for much of this time Moscow has been fixated on preventing Washington from achieving its aims, rather than attempting to advance a program of its own. This negative approach has been evident not only in the usual areas, such as NATO enlargement and missile defense, but also where Russian interests are less apparent or actually stand to gain from U.S. actions: WMD counterproliferation in relation to Iran and North Korea; counterinsurgency in Iraq and Afghanistan (pre-reset); and American security cooperation with Japan, South Korea, and various ASEAN member-states.

Such behavior is often explained as a product of visceral anti-Americanism and a "culture of envy."[15] More charitably one can argue that Russia's domestic challenges in the post-Soviet era have not permitted decisionmakers the luxury of developing an active strategy of their own.[16] Whatever the explanation, it has contributed to the widespread perception, in the non-West as well as the West, that Russia has little to offer beyond naysaying.[17]

Putin's diplomatic stroke in September 2013 over Syria's chemical weapons challenged this narrative. For the first time, Moscow was credited with initiating a constructive course of action to resolve a serious international problem. By securing Assad's consent to the removal of weapons stockpiles, Putin appeared to position Russia as a key contributor to the global commons: in countering WMD proliferation, in promoting regional stability, and in reinforcing international norms. But from the outset, there was skepticism about the Kremlin's motives. Was Putin's initiative driven by a commitment to uphold international norms, such as the Chemical Weapons Convention, or was the real purpose to constrain America's actions and undermine its influence? These aims are not mutually exclusive, of course, but the larger challenge for Moscow, as elsewhere, is to ensure that positive outcomes from Russian diplomacy are more than just by-products of geopolitical maneuvering.

*Playing to strengths*

One of the principal challenges Russia faces is to reestablish itself as a leading player in a world where past pedigree counts for little in determining a country's stature and influence. Accordingly, it will need to find ways of maximizing its strengths, rather than taking them for granted.

*Territory.* Russia's most important trump is its sheer geographical extent, which offers unparalleled opportunities to influence an enormous range of states, governments, and societies. The world—or at least the Eurasian continent—is Russia's oyster. But this potential is double-edged. An advanced, enlightened Russia would represent a model for good governance, rule of law, civil society, and business entrepreneurship. Conversely, a Russia living off past glories, demanding rather than earning respect, is likely to find its physical size a constant source of anxiety to itself and others.

The Russian Far East illustrates this dichotomy. On the one hand, the fact that so much of Russia's territory lies in Asia is a great advantage in engaging with the most dynamic region of the world, Pacific Asia. There is no intrinsic reason why Vladivostok cannot revert to being the open, cosmopolitan trading city it was before World War I and in the early years of the Revolution.[18] And the RFE (and Siberia as a whole) has considerable promise as a development area for natural resources, infrastructure, and, eventually, food and water security. On the other hand, none of this will happen as long as Russia's eastern regions remain a byword for bad governance, corruption, and neglect. In this event they would be a magnet for all kinds of insecurities, from fear of Chinese economic dominion to the consequences of demographic decline. Size, in other words, is only an advantage when backed up by the will and capacity to embrace change. This will require more than hosting an APEC summit in Vladivostok, building a shiny new bridge and university campus,[19] or embarking on grand infrastructural projects such as the upgrading of the Trans-Siberian and BAM (Baikal–Amur Mainline) railways.

*Resources.* Another obvious Russian strength comes from energy and other natural resources. Again this is a mixed blessing. For much of the Putin era these riches have been a hindrance to reform—an endless source of rents to a corrupt elite, and of funds to sustain moribund sectors of the economy. Cushioned by the boom in global commodity prices from 2003, the Putin regime did not feel the need to make difficult policy choices, such as implementing the rule of law, improving the quality of state and corporate governance, and introducing essential economic and social reforms.

Used intelligently, Russia's resources could be the springboard for its global reemergence. Instead of substituting for structural and institutional reform, the energy sector could become the foundation of best practice across the economy—from good corporate governance to enhanced cooperation with foreign partners and the incorporation of cutting-edge technology. And instead of energy being associated with the more unpleasant aspects of Russian diplomacy, Moscow could reestablish a reputation as a reliable energy supplier. One of the ironies is that misuse of the so-called "energy weapon" has actually weakened Russian influence in Europe, Asia, and the post-Soviet space. Spooked by the fear of gas cutoffs, the EU has pushed through unbundling and interconnectivity reforms, while looking to alternative sources of supply. The ex-Soviet republics have sought, with some success, to reduce their reliance on Russian energy imports and pipelines. And China and other prospective Asian customers have responded to supply uncertainties by seeking greater diversification.

Fortunately for Moscow, the consequences of mishandling its energy relations are not terminal. Europe will still need Russian oil and gas in large quantities, and Western companies remain interested in developing new resources in the Russian energy sector. China will look to build on the oil and gas agreements of 2013–14, and participate in other projects—the latest prospective venture being a 10 percent equity stake in the huge Vankor oil field in Krasnoyarsk *krai*.[20] There is potential too with other Asian countries, such as Japan, the ROK, and Vietnam. What Russia cannot afford to do, however, is to assume that abundant natural resources automatically equate to international influence.

*Identity.* Russia's multiplicity of identities is key to reasserting itself as a global player. It can legitimately claim an interest in developments in many regions and on many issues. At the same time, there is a danger of breadth at the expense of focus, and of pursuing ambitious objectives without marshaling the requisite commitment and capacity to support them in earnest.

In the new world disorder, Russia's identities work on a use it or lose it basis. There is little point in promoting itself as a Euro-Pacific power if it plays no meaningful role in Asian affairs, or as a bridge between civilizations when neither Europe nor Asia sees it fulfilling such a role. The same is true of pretensions to be the geopolitical balancer between the United States and China, or the setter of "new" global norms when it shows minimal interest in frameworks such as the G-20. Self-identification of one kind and another is only persuasive when substantiated by a demonstrable ability to achieve results.

*Brains.* Culture and education frequently come up in discussions about Russia's comparative advantages. Even at the height of the cold war, these were viewed in a generally positive light by the West. And it was the same story in China, despite the deterioration of Sino-Russian relations from the late 1950s. Today, when foreign attitudes toward the Kremlin are often very negative, Russian writers, musicians, scientists, and chess players continue to be held in high esteem.

The challenge is to develop these invaluable resources while it is still possible. For decades Russia has claimed a superior educational system, fostering the most advanced scientific research, and raising a highly skilled workforce. This is now under serious threat.[21] Russia is falling ever farther behind not just the West, but also China and India. In the most recent (2014) Shanghai Academic Ranking of World Universities, only two Russian universities, Moscow State (MGU) and St. Petersburg State, made the top 500.[22] Russian scientists continue to dazzle, but they do so in Europe and the United States.[23]

Russian students are studying in ever larger numbers abroad, and then choosing to stay rather than return to what many see as a country without a future.[24] According to Rosstat, the Federal Statistics Agency, the number of Russians moving abroad was five times greater in 2013 (186,372) than in 2010 (33,578).[25] These emigrants—and non-returnees—are exactly the people Russia needs if it is to be internationally competitive. But this will not happen until Moscow addresses deep-seated problems such as endemic corruption within the education system and in society more broadly.

### Building a reputation

Russia has had a poor international reputation for centuries,[26] aggravated by the cold war and the difficulties of post-Soviet transition. Preconceptions about "imperialist ambitions" and a "Soviet mindset" would have been hard to shift at the best of times. But in the fraught 1990s many Western observers were inclined to interpret Russian missteps as evidence of a deeper malevolence.

Such adverse perceptions have been reinforced over the course of the Putin era. The Kremlin has only rarely succeeded in portraying Russia in a positive light, despite the hiring of Western PR firms, the establishment of organizations such as RT and Russkii Mir, and the vast sums lavished on prestige projects such as the Sochi Winter Olympics (US$51 billion) and the Vladivostok APEC summit (US$22 billion).[27]

Tellingly, negative perceptions of Russia are not restricted to the West, but are prevalent in non-Western countries as well. Its "favorable" ratings are predictably low in the Middle East,[28] but they are also unimpressive in fellow BRICS countries such as Brazil (24 percent favorable versus 59 percent unfavorable in 2014) and South Africa (25-51), and, perhaps most surprisingly, in much of Latin America.[29] The conspicuous exception to the overall trend is China (66–23), whose leaders have consistently talked up Sino-Russian partnership, and where many people admire Putin's toughness in the face of Western (and especially U.S.) "arrogance."[30]

Addressing the problem of reputational damage is ultimately a challenge of effective policymaking; no amount of spin can undo the damage caused by bad decisions.[31] That said, Moscow has not helped itself by resorting to intemperate rhetoric and menaces. These have resulted in Russia almost invariably being depicted as the aggressor, even when it is not the only guilty party. It was a failure of communication as much as policy shortcomings, for example, that resulted in Russia receiving the lion's share of the blame for the 2006 gas cutoff to Ukraine and the 2008 Georgia war.

Apparent PR successes, such as the initiative in September 2013 to eliminate Syrian chemical weapons, have been partial at best—and not just because they have been overtaken by subsequent events. As noted elsewhere, Putin's open letter to the *New York Times* was much resented in the United States as an obvious display of Schadenfreude. And while Russia gained some kudos for persuading Assad to give up his chemical weapons, its standing has been undermined by its passivity in the face of Damascus's wanton slaughter of civilians. (The reputational damage to Russia would have been still greater but for events beyond the Kremlin's control, namely the distraction of the IS insurrection in Iraq and eastern Syria.)

Most recently the Ukraine crisis has highlighted the successes and failures of Russia's information offensive. Domestically, this has been very effective. Putin has exploited images of the "enemy West," Ukrainian "fascists," and disloyal Russian liberals to boost his popularity ratings to unprecedented levels. The Kremlin's campaign has also enjoyed some success in southeast Ukraine—although not to the extent it hoped. The local population is hostile toward the Poroshenko administration and the West, yet there is little enthusiasm for "independence" or for joining the Russian Federation.[32]

The biggest PR defeat, however, has been internationally. As in other cases, the problem lies more with Moscow's actions than in deficiencies of public presentation. Nevertheless, the latter have been significant. Excesses of language, crude disinformation, and the refusal to take any responsibility for the shooting down of Malaysian Airlines flight MH17 by Moscow-backed "separatists" have contributed to an image of Russia as aggressive and increasingly reckless. This impression has been reinforced by a sharp increase in overflights by Russian combat aircraft, leading to several near-misses with passenger planes.[33]

The contrast with China is striking. Although Beijing has been highly assertive in pursuing its claims in the East China Sea and South China Sea, it has not been demonized to anything like the same extent. This is partly because of its global importance, partly because its actions have been more cautious (it has not actually occupied the Senkaku/Diaoyu islands), but also because Beijing has been relatively restrained in its rhetoric. It has been careful, for example, to portray the United States more as a partner than an enemy, despite their considerable differences.[34]

### Taking long views

Russian foreign policy in the post-Soviet era has lacked strategic purpose. Decisionmakers have conceived of grand schemes—a multipolar world order, Russia as a bridge or balancer between East and West, Russia as the indispensable power, and so forth—and responded tactically to individual events. However, there has been no coherent or systematic approach toward advancing Russia's interests.

The hyper-reactiveness of Russian foreign policy militates against the pursuit of long-term objectives. In the Asia-Pacific region, Moscow's instrumentalism and lukewarm engagement have undermined efforts to establish Russia as a significant player. With the United States it has been torn between a desire to position itself as Washington's principal partner and the fear of being too accommodating. Conceptually too there has always existed a critical tension between an almost pathological need for acceptance by others and asserting itself as an independent center of global power.

If Russia is to be a major player in an emerging world order, it will need to concern itself less with point-scoring and "brilliant" coups, and more with what it wants to achieve in the long run. On Syria, does it want to be part of a larger international solution or is it more comfortable with a condition of "manageable" conflict that guarantees it a pivotal role? In the post-Soviet space, does it see its primary interest in the emergence of functional, stable states on its periphery or does it prefer them to be vulnerable and, it hopes, more susceptible to its dictates? In Euro-Atlantic security, will it raise the stakes on missile defense, or find a way to defuse the issue even while it continues to disagree on the details? The answers to some of these questions may not necessarily be clear-cut. What is evident, however, is that the fixation on short-term gains is counterproductive for Russia's strategic interests.

This is illustrated by its policy toward Ukraine, which has been portrayed by some as a string of victories. Force Yanukovych to pull out of the Association Agreement negotiations? Check. Take over Crimea and destabilize eastern Ukraine? Check. Embarrass the West? Check. Boost Putin's domestic standing? Check. And yet the upshot of all this is that Russia—and Putin—finds itself in a much weaker position than if it had adopted a more restrained and far-sighted approach. Moscow could have exploited the steady buildup of disappointed expectations between Yanukovych and Brussels in the course of 2013. It could have waited for the EU and key member-states to lose interest in Ukraine and the Eastern Partnership, signs of which were already unmistakable.[35] It could have exploited the fact that Obama was distracted by pressing business at home and abroad. It could have relied on Ukraine's slumping GDP and energy dependence to strengthen Russian leverage. And it could have done all this at virtually no risk.

## The Specifics of Change

Changes in overall approach and principle require a transformation in the mentality of the ruling elite, something that, even in an optimistic scenario, may take several decades. There are, however, a number of relatively specific steps the Putin leadership could take to make its conduct of international relations more effective. They are a mixture of crisis management and long-term capacity-building. In some cases the benefits would be felt almost immediately, in others it will take years for tangible results to emerge. But together these measures are aimed at facilitating Russia's emergence as a globally influential actor, at ease with itself and its neighbors, and better able to respond to the diverse challenges of the modern world.

### Accommodation with Ukraine

The great French statesman Talleyrand might have said of Moscow's Ukraine policy that "it is worse than a crime, it is a mistake."[36] The damage done to Russia's strategic interests has already been mentioned. The question today is whether there is a way out for Putin, and what form this might take. Can he row back on Russian military operations in eastern Ukraine and the rise of ultra-nationalism at home, or is he condemned by the exigencies of political survival to pursuing a path of confrontation?

The most important task for the Kremlin should be to step away from military escalation and, above all, to avoid a full-scale intervention by Russian troops. Comparisons with the Soviet invasion and occupation of Afghanistan may seem far-fetched but are relevant in underlining that such an intervention would be protracted, extremely costly, and debilitating on just about every level imaginable. Once committed, Russia would find it virtually impossible to extricate itself without incurring severe collateral damage; for a modern-day parallel, see the U.S. retreats from Iraq and Afghanistan. Worse still, Ukraine would continue to pose a major existential challenge as an immediate and highly unstable neighbor.

Despite many miscalculations, the Kremlin retains a number of important cards. The first is that the Poroshenko government in Kyiv has no choice but to come to some sort of accommodation with Moscow. Without Russian cooperation, eastern Ukraine will be ungovernable for a very long time. This reality alone will maintain the pressure for the decentralization of decision-making powers, guarantee a lasting (if reduced) Russian influence in the country, and consolidate the status of Russian as an official language—an important face-saver for Moscow.

Second, Ukraine faces enormous challenges over the next few years. These include nation-building (or nation-mending), economic recovery and modernization, developing the rule of law, and establishing relations with Russia and Europe on a more stable footing. It would be no surprise if Kyiv failed to address these challenges successfully. Ukrainian difficulties would increase the opportunities for Russian leverage, not just in obvious areas such as energy, but across the board.

Third, it is doubtful whether the United States and Europe (aside Poland) have the will to sustain a long-term commitment to Ukraine. Before the shooting-down of MH17, Berlin and Paris had been pressuring Kyiv to compromise with Moscow on decentralization, Russian language status, and non-membership in NATO. Short of a further major escalation by the Kremlin, they are likely to resume such efforts after a decent interval. In reality, they (and most other European capitals) just want the problem of Ukraine to go away. While the Obama administration has been vocal in its support for Kyiv, its investment in Ukraine's future is also suspect, given the pressure of so many competing domestic and foreign policy priorities. An already reluctant engagement would be further undermined if the Ukrainian authorities fail to perform. In that event the West's "Ukraine-fatigue," increasingly in evidence in dealings with Yanukovych during 2013, would soon reappear.

All this suggests that a more cooperative and patient approach by Moscow would pay ample dividends. In lieu of military escalation, the open destabilization of Poroshenko, and the denigration of Ukrainian national identity,[37] the Kremlin would exploit Russia's comparative advantages: the continuation of close ties with the Ukrainian elite, the interdependency of heavy (especially military) industry,[38] a pivotal position as the primary energy supplier (while resisting the temptation to blackmail Kyiv), and an abiding interest in the future of Ukraine. In short, it would prioritize active engagement with Kyiv instead of being distracted by the West's (nonexistent) geopolitical ambitions in eastern Europe.

There are also compelling tactical arguments in favor of moderation. By appearing more reasonable, Moscow would limit Kyiv's room for maneuver, dilute Western interest, and minimize the reputational damage to Russia caused by past policy mistakes. If, as seems very possible, Ukraine becomes more dysfunctional in coming years, Russia's hand will have been strengthened for having exercised restraint. And in the less probable event that Ukraine emerges as a functional state and prosperous economy, Russia would still profit from having a stable neighbor and reliable economic partner. Either way, Moscow stands to gain much by playing a long game.

### Developing Eurasian multilateralism

In the past, Putin's attempts to promote regional structures, such as the Customs Union and the CSTO, as instruments of Russian influence have been constrained by the concerns of the ex-Soviet republics for their sovereignty. The credibility of these organizations has also been damaged by their failure to tackle regional security and economic problems, an example being the CSTO's negligible role during the 2010 crisis in Kyrgyzstan.

Since 2011 the Customs Union has developed some institutional momentum, reflected in its evolution into the Eurasian Economic Union. Kremlin impatience could, however, jeopardize the EEU's prospects. The more vigorously Moscow promotes its larger vision of Eurasian integration, the more it is suspected of pursuing a neoimperialist project—especially in the wake of developments in Ukraine. Kazakhstan and Belarus are already bucking against the "politicization" of integration.[39] And there is considerable resentment at Moscow's efforts to enforce collective discipline on its counter-embargo against EU sanctions.

It would pay the Kremlin to be sensitive to such concerns. The danger in forcing others to make tough choices is that it encourages them to find ways of mitigating Russian pressure—most obviously, reaching out to the EU and China. Instead, Moscow could take steps to sweeten participation in its preferred regional structures, including more equitable representation at the working level. As of April 2015, three-fourths of the department heads of the Eurasian Economic Commission were Russian.[40] While some imbalance is unavoidable, given the different levels of national expertise, too large a disproportion conveys the impression that the EEU is essentially a Russian proxy. Moscow could also bend a little more on common tariffs. Manufacturing in Kazakhstan has suffered badly from having to raise the prices of many goods to uncompetitive levels owing to the increased cost of inputs from outside the EEU. As a result, local items are being squeezed out by Russian imports.[41]

Another idea to improve the reputability of Moscow-led organizations is to broaden their membership. Thus the CSTO would no longer be just a CIS-type body, with the negative connotations this carries, but would become pan-Eurasian. Moscow could involve other parties—China, India, Turkey, Iran, and even, in time, the EU—either as full or associate members, or as observers. While an early transformation of the CSTO is improbable, a gradual expansion of its geographical remit might be possible, somewhat akin to the development of ASEAN. Similarly, extending the membership in the EEU beyond the former Soviet Union could generate important economic and security dividends: boosting regional trade, enhancing the prospects for large-scale infrastructural projects, and acting as a broader confidence-building measure across Eurasia.

Finally, Moscow would benefit from being more tolerant to "rival" multilateral structures such as the Eastern Partnership program. In this, it would proceed from the knowledge that the EaP and the various Association Agreements and DCFTAs are far from being a panacea for all the ills that dog its partner-members in the post-Soviet space—poor governance, high levels of corruption, and moribund industries. A less allergic approach would be more likely to reap dividends, helping to allay the nervousness of EaP countries about Russian intentions, and reducing some of the animus in relations with Brussels.

### Stabilizing relations with Europe

Russia's fortunes in the current world disorder, and the international system that eventually emerges from it, will depend in large part on whether it is able to rebuild functional relations with the West. Contrary to the belief of nationalist voices in Moscow, there is no "Eastern" or home-grown alternative in the event of failure. Instead, Russia would find itself increasingly isolated and backward, ill-equipped to deal with a vast array of domestic and external challenges. The Ukraine crisis has highlighted its acute vulnerability to international energy and currency markets.

It makes sense for Moscow to concentrate on Europe, rather than the United States, for a couple of reasons. First, the policy agenda is reasonably substantial. Economic interdependence offers no guarantee of a smooth ride, as we have seen, but it does supply the motivation and basis for a working relationship in the future. Second, a Europe-first approach would facilitate Russia's objectives in the post-Soviet neighborhood. Despite growing annoyance at Putin's actions, the Europeans are nevertheless inclined to reach an accommodation. In particular, the Kremlin can rely on key European players, including Germany and France, to block EU (and especially NATO) membership for Ukraine, Moldova, and Georgia.

Naturally such assumptions start to look unsafe when Putin steps up military operations in Ukraine, threatens the Baltic states, increases the pressure on Moldova and Georgia, and ratchets up the rhetoric on energy issues and the Eastern Partnership. But if he were to follow a policy of "do no harm"—that is, avoid further provocative and confrontational actions—things would become easier, albeit gradually. Most EU member-states are looking for an excuse to do the minimum, whether over Ukraine, strengthening the NATO alliance, or increasing their own defense spending. They are keen to seize on any signs of reasonableness to lower the temperature with Moscow and restore a degree of normality.

In energy relations, Russia's priority should be to reestablish its reputation as a reliable supplier. This in no way precludes developing new markets in the Asia-Pacific region (and elsewhere), or minimizing the problems of gas transit through Ukraine by expanding Nordstream in due course. But it does entail a less politicized and emotional approach: toning down the complaints about the EU's unbundling provisions, desisting from threats to divert Russian gas from Europe to Asia, and delinking (as far as is possible) commercial ties with Ukraine from ongoing political and security tensions.[42]

### International security cooperation

The intractability of the Syrian civil war and the challenge of managing Iran's nuclear development program will ensure that Russia continues to play a role in international security governance. The question, as noted in chapter 3, is what kind of role. It is unrealistic to expect Moscow to have a transformative impact on decisionmaking in Damascus and Tehran; it does not possess that kind of clout. It could, however, maximize its influence by showing greater flexibility.

On Syria, the Kremlin has aligned itself unconditionally with Damascus, not only allowing the latter to manipulate the terms of their engagement but also causing Russia serious reputational damage in the Middle East. Maintaining a more even-handed position would enhance Russia's chances of playing the part of honest broker; contain the fallout on key relationships in the region, such as Turkey; and ensure that it receives greater credit when things do work, such as with the removal of chemical weapons.

There are areas of international security cooperation where Moscow can take the lead. One is to build on the very specific success of the Northern Distribution Network to address the broader challenge of security management in central Eurasia. Much will depend here on the commitment of other players. But the Kremlin's willingness to move from conventional geopolitical calculus to a more positive-sum approach will be critical. Paradoxically, a significant U.S. presence in the region would serve Russian interests. It could facilitate Russian access to Afghanistan, and help contain the threat of the Taliban and the spread of Islamist extremism. It could also ease anxieties about the growth of Chinese influence. Given that Russia is unlikely to regain its former hegemonic position in Central Asia, it has a vested interest in the emergence of a "polycentric" regional environment in which no single power is able to dominate.

More concretely, there is considerable scope—and need—to improve intelligence-sharing on terrorism and other transnational crime, such as narcotics trafficking. The latter has emerged as a particular threat. Whereas Russia was once principally a transit country, it is now a primary destination for drugs coming out of Afghanistan, with an estimated three million heroin users.[43] Given the gravity of this problem, Moscow should look to resume counter-narcotics cooperation with Washington, and involve the Central Asian governments in these efforts. And although there is an understandable reluctance to become entangled in the task of nation-building in Afghanistan, a modest level of involvement could be sustained in technical areas, such as police training and equipment, where it has already made a start.

Against the background of sharply deteriorating relations with the United States, there have been growing calls for Russia to pull out of various arms control agreements, such as START and the Intermediate-range Nuclear Forces (INF) agreement signed by Ronald Reagan and Mikhail Gorbachev in 1987. Yet Moscow can ill afford the unraveling of the international nuclear weapons regime. A new arms race would destroy the Russian economy, and very possibly lead to the collapse of the Putin system (or worse). It would be the very embodiment of "suicidal statecraft."[44]

Relatedly, Russian interests would benefit from a calmer response to American missile defense plans. Shrill statements about the threat this poses to national security have only hardened attitudes in Washington, and limited Obama's room for maneuver with his domestic critics.[45] The reality is that it will be decades—if ever—before the United States is able to mount even a notional challenge to Russia's strategic defense capabilities.[46] Instead of threatening retaliation in response to a nonexistent danger, Moscow could focus on reinforcing the nuclear nonproliferation regime in other, more accessible ways. This might include the coordination of measures to assist a civilian nuclear energy program in Iran (taking advantage of a more enlightened regime in Tehran); a less compliant approach toward Pyongyang; and greater intelligence-sharing, involving the development of joint early warning systems.

## Embracing Asia

Russia is unlikely to be a major player in East Asia for at least the next decade. But it can profit from the increasingly diffuse character of Asian affairs to advance its interests.

The most plausible route is to become a primary supplier of energy. Now that it has concluded major oil and gas agreements with China, and allowed Chinese companies into upstream projects, the outlook for large-scale cooperation is more promising. Nevertheless, it will require an immense amount of work to translate these agreements into practical reality.

It is therefore vital that Russia develop options with other Asian countries, such as Japan, South Korea, and Vietnam, and also protect energy ties with its primary European customers. Although the Sino-Russian partnership has grown in recent years, and has been boosted by the Ukraine crisis, Moscow would be foolhardy to rely on Chinese demand. Even if the political relationship remains intact, economic circumstances can and do change. Diversifying markets would help to reduce Russia's exposure.

On diversification more generally, resumption of the rapprochement with Tokyo would be of significant benefit to Russian interests. Although Japan participated in the G-7 sanctions post-Crimea, it did so with noticeable reluctance—and only because it was obliged, as the United States' principal ally in East Asia, to support Washington. Given half a chance, Tokyo will look to resume the process of normalization with Moscow as soon as possible, including through the 2+2 ministerial process. For Moscow, such engagement would lay the groundwork for a more comprehensive, less China-dependent, approach toward Asia. But not if it attempts to use closer ties with Tokyo as leverage against Beijing, or Sino-Russian partnership to squeeze the Japanese on the territorial question. Real rapprochement will only happen if engagement is valued on its own terms.

Being serious about Asia means addressing two other priorities as a matter of urgency. One is to enhance Russia's multilateral diplomacy, especially at the working level. This is partly about improving its networking. But it is also about exhibiting a greater commitment to the region, for example in areas such as energy development or food and water security. Some of Moscow's ideas might struggle to gain traction initially, but the messaging itself would be important. It would signify a more professional and committed attitude and give impetus to the turn to the East.

In the end, however, everything hinges on the condition of Russia's eastern regions. Nothing would do more to improve Russia's position in Asia than to resolve the chronic problems of misgovernment and backward development in the RFE and Eastern Siberia. This will be a vast project spanning several decades, requiring immense political will, financial capital, and external investment. The difficulties are truly intimidating. But until Moscow is prepared to tackle this *national* task over the long haul, Russia will continue to be a backwater in the Asia-Pacific region.

## What Can and Should the West Do?

This is a book about Russian foreign policy, rather than Western policy toward Russia, which merits a volume all to itself. That said, it is worth briefly discussing the implications for decisionmakers in North America and Europe. What conclusions should they draw from Putin's actions, not just in Ukraine, but also in other areas of foreign (and domestic) policy? And what are the possibilities and limits of Western action?

### The virtues of soft power

The most important lesson is that the amount of "hard" leverage Western governments can exert on Moscow is limited. Although its economy is suffering, Russia does not face the prospect of early implosion. It possesses the world's third-largest gold and foreign currency reserves; it has a very low sovereign debt-to-GDP ratio; and it enjoys a large trade surplus. The imposition of sanctions was important in signaling Western opposition to Russian actions in Crimea and eastern Ukraine. However, there is no evidence to suggest that direct economic pressure will lead to a softening of the Putin regime's approach. On the contrary, sanctions have reinforced an already strong siege mentality.[47] As a number of commentators have observed, Russia's capacity to absorb pain is considerably greater than the ability (and desire) of Western countries to inflict it.[48] This equation may change over time, but not soon. As long as Putin continues to enjoy sky-high ratings at home, he will remain defiant abroad. Meanwhile, the willingness of the Europeans to adhere to a robust line—and make sacrifices— is open to question. Even a slight softening of Russian tactics might be enough to undermine consensus.

At the same time, Western "soft" influence retains a powerful pull on Russian society. Notwithstanding Putin's determined efforts to establish a "new" national idea based on traditionalism and conservatism, survey after survey reveals that the public, especially but not only the younger generation, appreciates "Western" values, such as the rule of law, political pluralism, media freedoms, and an independent judiciary.[49] It admires the West's technological achievements, and envies its quality of life.

In other words, while Russians are cynical about the morality and intentions of Western policymakers, they remain susceptible to Western influence writ large. They support Putin on Ukraine and subscribe to notions of Russian greatness. But they also want to experience and absorb much of what people in the West take for granted. It is this continuing allure of Western soft power that governments need to factor in when developing policy toward Russia. It suggests that positive incentives, such as visa liberalization and student scholarships, are likely to be more effective than Magnitsky-type legislation and various sanctions in influencing Russia's future course.

## A new realism

In the previous chapter, I referred to the "let's pretend" game—the tendency of Western policymakers in the past to delude themselves that they shared common interests and understandings with the Putin regime.[50] It has been evident for some time that they do not. This has been graphically borne out not just by events in Ukraine, but also by Putin's turn toward authoritarian traditionalism since early 2012. The main problem between Moscow and Western capitals is not a failure of communication, although this does not help. The divergence is much more fundamental and deep-rooted. Not only is there disagreement over Russia's role in the world; there is also a widening chasm on global governance, international law, and even on what constitutes acceptable state behavior.

These differences have been exacerbated by developments over the past quarter of a century. Yet they have always existed in one form or another. There is little basis for the assertion that things would have been very different if only the West had been "nicer"—less triumphalist and more generous—toward Russia in the 1990s. Such claims underestimate the influence of the long-term structural factors that have shaped Russian strategic culture (as discussed in chapters 2 and 3).

In this unpromising context, there is no viable alternative to implementing the well-tried formula of "cooperate where you can, and compete when you must." The danger for Western policymakers lies in thinking that Putin is committed to cooperation *for its own sake*. In fact, this is only of interest if it serves the Kremlin's particular, often narrowly self-interested goals. It is essential to keep this in mind when discussing ways of stabilizing the situation in eastern Ukraine, preventing the nuclear weaponization of Iran, or managing the security environment in Afghanistan and Central Asia.

Western governments need to be more committed and less apologetic in defense of their national interests, even if this leads to regular episodes of unpleasantness. Attempting to ingratiate oneself with Moscow is not only immoral, it is ineffectual. It is naïve to imagine that "understanding" Russia's "legitimate concerns" will somehow result in a more reasonable, accommodating approach in the Kremlin. On the contrary, vacillation and half-heartedness, seasoned with fatalism, encourage Putin to strive for more, secure in the knowledge that he has greater stomach for the struggle—whether it is over the sovereignty of the ex-Soviet republics, energy relations, the future of European security, or the rules of global governance.

In this connection a misplaced historical guilt, notably over NATO enlargement, serves no useful purpose. It is largely thanks to NATO (and the EU) that the countries of central and eastern Europe have enjoyed unparalleled security and prosperity over the past two decades, and that the Baltic states have managed to preserve their independence.[51] Measures to strengthen NATO's presence in Poland and the Baltic states through the regular rotation of troops, and the establishment of a Rapid Reaction Force, have been condemned in Moscow.[52] But they signal at least that the alliance is starting to get serious about its mutual defense commitments. The alternative—wishing Russian aggression away under the guise of "engagement"—is asking for trouble: the effective demise of NATO, the steady degradation of the Euro-Atlantic security environment, and the delegitimation of Western institutions and norms.

### Pursuing a positive agenda

Just as Russian foreign policy has been guilty of an obsessive America-centrism, so some Western leaders are prone to conducting relations with third countries through a distorted Russia lens. Such behavior has often taken the form of acute anxiety about how Moscow might react to particular Western actions—from NATO enlargement to missile defense and Magnitsky-type legislation. Although it would be overstating things to say that the Kremlin has exercised a de facto veto over Western decisionmaking, the latter has on occasion flirted perilously close to appeasement.

But it also works the other way round; some Western politicians appear to be motivated more by a desire to oppose Russia than to prosecute a positive agenda of their own. This was evident over Georgia, with the lionizing of Saakashvili, and especially with Yanukovych in Ukraine. Much of the push to conclude an Association Agreement with Kyiv in 2013 was intended to counter Russian geopolitical interests in the shape of the Customs Union, rather than uphold European norms and values, much less build a stronger Europe.[53] To this end certain EU member-states advocated a complaisant attitude toward Yanukovych's failure to meet EU preconditions, in particular the release of former prime minister Yulia Tymoshenko.

The dangers of such an unprincipled approach are clear. In opening itself up to manipulation by a clientelist elite, the EU was in danger of selling its principles down the river. Arrangements of convenience with regimes whose sole virtue is an ability to frustrate Putin discredit and undermine the European project. Policymakers should not make the same mistake as Moscow by pursuing a geopolitically driven anti-agenda.[54] Accelerating NATO membership for certain ex-Soviet republics would, for example, be counterproductive— not because it would provoke Putin, but because it would overstretch the alliance's capabilities and hence weaken European security.

Such considerations are especially relevant to the future of Ukraine post-Maidan. The main thrust of Western policy should not be to punish Russia so much as to support Ukraine, ideally in cooperation with Moscow but if necessary without it. Unlike sanctions, which are often a facile substitute for more difficult measures, this enterprise will require sustained political commitment, substantial resources, and abundant patience—qualities not easily found in the post–financial crisis West. It will also mean holding the government in Kyiv to its commitments on political and economic reform, even as there is understanding that Ukraine's problems will not be solved quickly.

Ultimately, Western governments need to determine what it is they are trying to achieve, and then commit themselves properly to the task. If there is no serious intention to help build a viable Ukraine, then it would be better to turn their attention to something they do believe in. For in this case, as in so many others, a half-baked policy is worse than no policy at all.[55]

## Heal thyself

The West will be able to engage effectively with Russia only if it is able to put its own house in order. Although the era of their domination is over, Western countries and organizations still exert a powerful influence in the world. This is likely to continue for many decades, provided, of course, that they address some of the shortcomings that have diminished them in recent years.

There are some positive signs. The U.S. economy is growing steadily, and European unity is no longer quite the oxymoron it appeared a few years ago. But it will take much more to restore the credibility of Western-led norms and institutions. It is difficult to make the case for the United States' moral leadership when its domestic politics are so flawed and have such adverse consequences for its foreign relations.[56] And unless European countries are able to articulate and implement a forward-looking vision, they will find themselves marginalized in the international system that eventually emerges from today's world disorder. In this event Europe's much-fabled soft power would shrink into mere self-parody.

One immediate area for improvement is to get serious about European security. For too long, European members of NATO have outsourced responsibility for this to the United States. There has been endless talk of burden-sharing, but only five out of the twenty-eight members of NATO have reached the two percent of GDP threshold for defense spending recommended by the alliance.[57] As a result, NATO has lost much of its credibility, not only within Europe, but also with Russia and other non-Western countries, notably China. The Ukraine crisis has shaken this complacency, but for how long is unclear. There is a danger that if and when relations with Russia stabilize, most NATO members will revert to old habits.

One can draw a larger conclusion from all this. There is no meaningful soft power without at least a reliable element of hard power. Economic development, technological advancement, and cultural power are more effective than military strength in projecting long-term influence in the contemporary international environment. But this does not mean that military strength has become redundant. Unfortunately, most European governments seem to labor under this misapprehension.

## Looking Ahead

There are few grounds for believing that the Putin regime will subscribe to a progressive foreign policy vision for Russia anytime soon. It remains convinced that its conduct of external relations has been successful, that the principles underpinning it are sound, and that Russia's international fortunes are on the up. It sees little reason, therefore, to moderate its sense of great power entitlement, or to change its approach toward contentious areas such as the post-Soviet neighborhood and interaction with the West.

The Kremlin also faces a conundrum. Russia's long-term future is contingent on the transformation of many aspects of its political life, economy, and society. Such seismic changes are intrinsically destabilizing and would call into question many of the pillars that currently sustain the regime. The ruling elite would have to balance between short-term expediency and eventual necessity—to see beyond its own immediate interests and embrace the wider national good. Short of being compelled by an existential crisis or external strategic shocks, it is very unlikely to make such a choice. Today the outlook is for continuing military buildup, mounting pressure on Russia's neighbors, alienation from Europe, and open antagonism with the United States.

On a more positive note, such a confrontational course is hard to maintain over a long period, especially given Russia's mounting economic difficulties. While Putin's popularity is riding high following the annexation of Crimea, the challenge for him will be to preserve popular legitimacy after the memory of a "short, victorious war" begins to fade, and the public's attention turns once again to more prosaic priorities such as living standards, housing, and social services. It is all very well to speak of preserving "stability,"[58] but Russia's domestic and international context scarcely permits the luxury of a static conservatism.

This brings us back to modernization, an idea that has become practically extinct since Putin's return to the Kremlin. Russia's ability to tackle various foreign policy challenges hinges on its willingness to change *inside*. A Russia that fails to mend a sclerotic political system, the absence of rule of law, rent-seeking on an epic scale, and the exodus of intellectual capital is hugely handicapped. Comprehensive modernization is the sine qua non of a modern foreign policy—and the key to ensuring that Russia occupies an influential position in the international system. The point of reforms is not so that Russia can look like the United States or Europe, but to create a more secure and capable nation *in its own right*. Only through modernization will Russia be attractive to its neighbors, become a credible player in Asia, and advance its interests with the United States and Europe. Such a Russia would be in a position to shape regional and global governance, and to receive the respect it craves.

There are of course many paths to modernization. The experience of China in the post-Mao period is radically different from that of its Asian neighbors, or the countries of central and eastern Europe. But there is one common denominator. In the end, modernization is about the readiness to be flexible and nondoctrinaire, to abandon or at least renovate tired conceptions of identity and strategic culture, and to stimulate the growth of a dynamic society at home and a fresh vision of one's place in the world.

This drive for change has been the hallmark of every emergent global power in the modern era—Great Britain in the late eighteenth century, America in the late nineteenth and early twentieth centuries, and China post-Mao. Over the next ten to fifteen years, the tension between the perceptual world of Putin's Kremlin and the actual world in which Russia must operate will become increasingly stark. In those circumstances Russia's rulers may come to realize that true power and greatness come not from historical tradition or a sense of destiny, but from the Darwinian ability to adapt to an ever-changing external environment.

# eight
# Russia and the World in 2030

> The beginnings and endings of all human undertakings are untidy.
> JOHN GALSWORTHY, 1933

Russian foreign policy has experienced numerous fluctuations over the past two decades. There have been periods of buoyancy—Putin's second presidential term, the immediate aftermath of the Georgia war, and following the diplomatic intervention over Syria's chemical weapons in September 2013. And then there have been other times when Moscow's conduct of international relations has been chaotic and ineffective, as during much of the Yeltsin presidency.

The Putin era has seen political consolidation, economic growth, and social order. Yet even during this time of relative domestic stability, Russian foreign policy has passed through different stages that appear to have little correlation with one another. These have included an initial rapprochement with Europe in 2000–01; Putin's "strategic choice" in favor of the United States post-9/11; the gathering crisis of Russia-West relations after 2003, culminating in the Georgia war; the heyday of the reset during 2009–10; the reassertion of Russian traditionalism and anti-Americanism from 2011; and the current crisis in Russia-West relations.

Such vicissitudes have diverse causes. Broad international trends, such as the boom in global energy and commodity prices after 2004, the continuing rise of China, and the world economic downturn, have exerted a critical influence. Russian foreign policy has also been shaped by more discrete developments—the wars in Iraq and Afghanistan and the grassroots movements of the Arab Spring. And events closer to home have had a tremendous impact, notably the Orange Revolution, the anti-Putin protests of 2011–12, and the toppling of Yanukovych.

Leaders of all countries, not just Russia, like to speak about strategic vision and long-term thinking. But real decisionmaking is a far messier affair, reflecting the influence of many random and unpredictable factors. When one surveys Putin's foreign policy, it is difficult to make the case that it has been any more strategic, or less reactive, than under his predecessor. In earlier chapters I identified a number of recurrent themes: an abiding sense of "great power-ness"; Russia as an independent center of global power; the notion of indis-pensability; and the belief in civilizational uniqueness. However, although these ideas have been highly influential, they do not offer a fail-safe guide to Kremlin policy. As the Ukrainian revolution has shown, events constantly intrude to upset and reshape the supposedly natural order of things.

Perhaps the only reliable conclusion one can draw is that Russian foreign policy has always been marked by stark contradictions and "accidents." And that the mythology of permanent national interests is as suspect today as it has always been. What is left instead is a confusing hybrid of the conservative, the atavistic, and the sometimes pragmatic.

## Four Scenarios

The presence of so many variables makes it unwise to offer confident predic-tions about the future course of Russian foreign policy. It makes sense instead to sketch out four scenarios looking ahead to 2030. As noted in the Prologue, their purpose is not predictive, but suggestive—to think about some of the ways in which Russian foreign policy might develop given different contexts. Some of the scenarios will seem more probable than others, but they are all possible. And what eventually transpires may combine elements from several of them.

The first scenario, "soft authoritarianism," is characterized by a compara-tively benign stasis, similar to the "stagnation" (*zastoi*) of the late Brezhnev era.[1] The second scenario, "hard authoritarianism," envisions a strengthening of personalized, nondemocratic power, many elements of which have appeared since Putin's return to the Kremlin in 2012. Third, "regime fractur-ing" considers what might happen if there were to be a breakdown of politi-cal authority, along with economic crisis and social disorder. Finally, "second-wave liberalism" imagines a Russia undergoing a genuine process of modernization and democratization. Together, these four scenarios encom-pass many of the main principles and influences that are likely to shape Russ-ian foreign policy over the next fifteen years.

### Soft authoritarianism

This scenario is in some degree retrospective. It posits that Russia in 2030 will resemble the Russia of much of the Putin era. The political system would be one of semi- or soft authoritarianism, headed by a preeminent but not absolutist personality. Despite the formal existence of a political opposition, there would be only one real center of power, and attempts to challenge it would be firmly rebuffed. The economy would look much as it did under the Putin-Medvedev tandem. There would be limited attempts at diversification and modernization, highlighted by a few marquee projects, like the Skolkovo Innovation Center. But energy and natural resources would remain dominant—at once vital sources of national (and personal) wealth and instruments of power projection.

In foreign policy we would see the entrenchment of traditional interpretations of Russian identity, norms, and values. Moscow would retain a patrimonial mentality toward the ex-Soviet republics, and look to contain the influence of other external actors, above all the United States and China. At the same time, it would be chary of assuming imperial burdens, such as sustaining unpopular regimes in the face of political protest and economic penury. Its approach would be defined by a "semi-imperialism" or patrimonialism on the cheap—one that aims to extract whatever advantages it can at minimum cost and risk. There would be occasional red lines, for example in the event of a renewed push for Georgian or Ukrainian membership in NATO. But on the whole Moscow would steer clear of confrontation.

It would be a similar story in relation to Asia. A politically stagnant Russia in 2030 would adopt a circumspect approach, inhibited by both lack of capacity and strategic apprehension. Decisionmakers would continue to emphasize partnership with Beijing, strive to maximize resource exports, and participate halfheartedly in Asian multilateral bodies. Despite occasional flirtations with Japan, India, and Vietnam, there would be no significant rebalancing of Russian policy within Asia. On the contrary, this would become more China-dependent. In many areas Moscow would be left hoping for the best—that Beijing sticks to the border settlement; that there is no major conflict on the Korean peninsula; that Sino-American tensions are contained; and that Islamist extremism does not lead to the collapse of authoritarian regimes in Central Asia. It would attempt to exploit opportunities as they arise, but the dream of Russia becoming a Euro-Pacific power would remain notional.

Russia-West relations under this scenario would be a mixed bag. The ruling elite would continue to view the United States as the strategic benchmark, but have no expectations of partnership. It might occasionally feel disposed to remind Washington of Russia's presence. But it would be careful to avoid a deterioration of relations of the magnitude that occurred during 2004–08 and again since early 2014. In fact, Washington and Moscow could arrive at a certain understanding. Rather than straining to invest substance in their bilateral ties, they might be content with a rough predictability and the absence of conflicts, and cooperate on discrete issues such as arms control and combating Islamist extremism.

Moscow could react to the prospect of growing American indifference by turning more toward Europe, focusing in particular on economic cooperation. However, a long-term rapprochement between Russia and the EU would be unlikely. The inertial thinking that characterizes the strategic culture of the Putin elite would be a feature of a stagnating Russia in 2030. Moscow would retain a globalist and America-centric outlook, especially if Europe is unable to restore its international standing to the level of the 1990s. The emphasis on bilateral relationships with leading European players, such as Germany and France, would be even more pronounced than it is today.

Under the soft authoritarian scenario it is difficult to envisage anything other than a steady decline of Russia's international position. Not only would it fail to keep up with China, but there is every possibility that, as we approach 2030, it would fall behind other non-Western powers—India, Brazil—as well as rising regional actors such as Turkey and Indonesia. Far from being an emerging or "emerged" economy,[2] it could enter the ranks of the world's regressing nations. Fast forward to 2030, and the gap between the mythology of Russia as a born-again great power and the reality of its declining influence would be stark. It would find itself marginalized in international decisionmaking, and could struggle to exercise effective sovereignty over parts of its own territory, such as the Russian Far East and the North Caucasus. The regime would continue to feed off the trappings rather than substance of influence, and look to maintain its longevity within its own self-contained world.

There are two obvious difficulties with the soft authoritarian scenario. One is that the necessary suspension of disbelief—both within the elite and the general population—may only be sustainable for a short time. The hardening of the Putin system since early 2012 would seem to suggest that the idea of a "stable" stagnation is a mirage. At most it would be a temporizing phase between eras defined by more committed systems of authoritarianism and democracy. The other objection to this scenario is that Russia, much as the Kremlin might wish to insulate it from subversive external influences, is not an island. It will inevitably be affected by regional and global trends, from climate change to the technological revolution, and by the shifting realities of international power. In these dynamic circumstances stasis is hardly an option. The external pressures on decisionmakers to do something—anything—will intensify. And this raises the question of "what next?"

## Hard authoritarianism

One possible resolution is the emergence of an overtly authoritarian system. This scenario could arise in circumstances similar to Germany in the 1930s: economic breakdown and hyperinflation; political fracturing; social disintegration; and foreign policy humiliations. There would be a general hankering for the restoration of stability, and hopes would be invested in a "strong leader."

However, it seems more probable that a hard authoritarian system in Russia would come about as a result of the steady accumulation of political, economic, and social tensions. A leader—charismatic or otherwise—might identify the need and opportunity to pursue a more dictatorial approach to government: concentrating political authority through a rigorously applied "vertical of power" (*vertikal*); reasserting tight state control over the economy; clamping down on media and NGO activity; and building up the security and military establishment. Many of these measures have already been taken since Putin's return to the presidency. In the hard authoritarian scenario they would be reinforced and become more intrusive, extending deep into the private domain.

There would, however, be an underlying basis of moderation. We are talking here about authoritarianism rather than totalitarianism. This regime would be repressive in many respects, but it would also resort to co-optation and accommodation—again, similar to the Kremlin's modus operandi at the time of writing. It would be reluctant to resort to open tyranny, if only because this is expensive and debilitating to maintain.

It is generally assumed that a more authoritarian Russia would engender an aggressive foreign policy—a nexus all the more persuasive given Moscow's actions in Ukraine and its confrontation with the West. There would be a heightened emphasis on Russia's "rights" in the international system, geopolitical balancing, open hostility toward outside involvement in the post-Soviet neighborhood, continued military buildup, and an ultra-allergic response to foreign "interference" in Russia's domestic affairs. A reversion to the battle lines of the cold war might occur—a lasting structural divide along geopolitical and ideational lines.

Nevertheless, a strongly authoritarian regime would still have to operate within certain parameters, and be mindful of two critical considerations. The first centers on the limits of power. A "strong leader" might well harbor a vision of Russia as a global power but be hamstrung by the lack of capacity to realize this ambition. As noted elsewhere, a large nuclear arsenal and standing army do not, in themselves, equate to significant power projection capabilities.

Similarly, Moscow might find that the geopolitics of energy security meant that, for all Russia's abundance of resources, it had diminishing leverage over its neighbors. Much would depend on the state of global energy and commodity markets.

Second, an authoritarian regime would need to balance the political and financial costs of an aggressive foreign policy against the imperative of preserving its domestic position. It would face difficult spending choices—for example, whether to bankroll an expensive foreign adventure to project Russian power or to ensure that pensions stayed ahead of the cost of living. The level of commodity prices would again be a crucial variable, determining the economic affordability of an activist approach to external relations. There is also the matter of strategic risk. Russia would lose in an arms race with the United States and possibly, in time, China—a defeat that could lead to regime collapse. This is likely to give pause for thought to the most bullish of leaders.[3]

The colossal expense and other difficulties of resurrecting an empire suggest that Russia, even under a hard authoritarian leadership, might behave with relative restraint in its neighborhood. It is worth reiterating that Putin's favored approach to reasserting Russian influence in Ukraine post-Maidan has been to employ proxies and engage in hybrid warfare, rather than commit regular troops in large numbers. By 2030 the former Soviet republics will have enjoyed four decades of independence and developed a close network of ties with various other actors—not just the United States and China, but also Turkey, Iran, India, Pakistan, and the Europeans. Moscow would react vigorously to moves by Georgia and Ukraine to gain membership in NATO or the EU. However, for the most part it would concentrate on exercising influence through nonmilitary means, including, if necessary, the threat of economic sanctions and energy cutoffs.

The hardening of authoritarian tendencies would complicate relations with the West, and the United States in particular—as we have seen in Putin's second term, during the post-2011 domestic crackdown, and over Ukraine. However, the possibility of a compartmentalization of anti-Westernism in Russia should not be excluded. An authoritarian regime would reject liberal democratic values and assert national greatness. But it might simultaneously seek functional relations with certain Western governments, encourage Western companies to invest capital and advanced technology, and support human contacts—not only tourism, but also scientific, cultural, and sporting exchanges.[4] It would hope to maintain a broadly cooperative interaction—"selective engagement"—on the basis of being seen as a vital partner in meeting a common external threat, such as a serious escalation in Islamist extremism.[5]

Ordinary logic suggests that such a Russia would be likely to have a good relationship with China. The recent expansion of bilateral cooperation has coincided with a strengthening of authoritarian control in both countries, as Putin and Xi Jinping have sought a level of political dominance not seen since Stalin and Mao, respectively. Yet there is another future that is at least as plausible. Sino-Russian partnership could turn out to be the biggest casualty from the emergence of an openly authoritarian regime in Moscow. Already very active in the Far East and Central Asia, China by 2030 may well be the number one external actor in post-Soviet Eurasia—an outcome clearly incompatible with the archetypal authoritarian vision of Russian greatness. It is no accident that some of the more fearful voices in recent years regarding Chinese intentions have come from advocates of Russia's "great power" mission (*derzhavniki*).[6]

Disappointment with the turn to the East could also lead the Kremlin to step up efforts at post-Soviet integration through the Eurasian Union, or turn back to Europe. This is not to say that it would seek confrontation with Beijing or withdraw from Asia. But Russia's struggles for acceptance could result, somewhat accidentally, in a rapprochement with European institutions and states, on the basis that its future lies with the West even in an "Asian century." This would be less a case of positive attraction than of a common interest in counterbalancing or mitigating Chinese power. Just as Moscow has looked to Beijing to counter the United States, so it may seek partners to counter a potential new hegemon—one with which it shares a long border and an often troubled history.

Notwithstanding attempts to present a confident façade, an authoritarian Russia would feel profoundly insecure. Sensitive to its own frailties, it might opt for an inward-looking, almost minimalist foreign policy. This would focus on a limited number of essential priorities: strengthening nuclear and conventional capabilities to meet direct security threats; safeguarding economic sovereignty through autarkic practices such as import substitution; and managing or quarantining regional conflicts. Such a Russia would be prone to excesses of language and might occasionally lash out, but for the most part would look to act circumspectly. After all, the first and last objective of any authoritarian regime is self-preservation, and this will require a relatively benign international environment in the longer term.

The biggest threat to such a regime would come from its inability to adapt to, or contain, external (and internal) influences. Its conundrum would be the same as in the first scenario—the practical impossibility of insulating Russia from the world around it. In this, one may draw a parallel with the USSR, which imploded when its people realized that the system they were living in had lost all utility and legitimacy, especially by comparison with a confident, prosperous West. In 2030 such contrasts could be multiplied many times over, with the benchmarks coming not only from the usual suspects, but also from emerging and established non-Western powers.

## Regime fracturing

Although it does not seem especially plausible today, one of the scenarios that should be considered is regime fracturing, marked by acute political instability and civil disorder. It could result from a combination of factors: a sustained slump in global commodity prices; the demise or incapacitation of Putin; internecine rivalries within the elite; and crippling socioeconomic problems.

Developments could unfold in several ways under this scenario. We might see the Weimarization of Russia: genuine pluralism, civic activism, and economic and cultural liberalization, coexisting uneasily with feeble institutions, macroeconomic instability, and ultranationalism.[7] Another grim possibility is territorial disintegration involving the secession of all or part of the North Caucasus, and the loss of political as well as economic sovereignty over the Russian Far East. It is improbable that Russia would be reduced to a modern-day Muscovy, but the very principle of a Russian Federation could be subjected to considerable strain.

There could also be an outpouring of democratic feeling that leads to regime change, as in Georgia in 2003 and Ukraine in 2004 and 2013–14. In the case of Georgia, a chaotic situation gave way relatively smoothly to a functional government, which was able to implement significant reforms. In Ukraine, however, the Orange Revolution soon lost its sense of purpose, leaving in place a dysfunctional and corrupt polity—a cycle that could well be repeated in the post-Maidan era.

In these confused circumstances Russian foreign policy would be highly erratic. To get an idea of how it might play out, it is useful to recall the early years of the Yeltsin period, around 1992–93, when there were several competing foreign policy strands—liberal Westernizers, *derzhavniki*, imperialists, and so-called pragmatists[8]—all interacting against the backdrop of fears about the further breakup of Russia. The outcome of these tensions was a lowest common denominator foreign policy.[9] Decisionmaking was dictated by immediate imperatives, such as Yeltsin's preoccupation with staying in power, rather than longer-term objectives. Such problems would be magnified many times over in the event of the erosion or breakup of the Russian Federation; the proliferation of independent or near-autonomous actors would kill off any chance of a cohesive foreign policy.

Certain themes tend to recur during periods of political and economic instability. One is the rise of nationalism or hyper-nationalism, which taps into people's insecurities and promises easy solutions.[10] Today the main targets of nationalist sentiment in Russia are the United States and, at the popular level, Muslim migrant workers from Central Asia and Azerbaijan, and these are likely to remain the scapegoats of choice in 2030 under the fracturing scenario. The United States would still be the world's leading power, Muslims will comprise an ever larger share of Russia's population, and Islam will remain the dominant religion among many of its neighbors. Anxieties about the loss of a core Slavic identity would become more acute. China too could find itself the object of nationalist prejudice as it completes its transformation into a global power.

One probable consequence of regime disintegration would be the end of Russia's imperial ambitions. The kind of nationalism that emerges under conditions of acute instability would be largely defensive, seeking less to project power than to repel foreign influences. By 2030 Russia would have lost the capacity to intervene effectively in its neighborhood. There might be occasional populist outbursts, over, say, the treatment of ethnic Russian minorities. But it is doubtful whether Moscow would be inclined to pursue any kind of comprehensive imperial project in the post-Soviet space.

It is natural to assume that anarchy would exacerbate anti-Western feelings. Strangely, though, it could have the opposite effect: reviving interest in Western norms and values. The unraveling of the Putin system would discredit both authoritarianism and the thesis that Russia can follow its "own path" of development. By 2030 the long-time association of democracy with kleptocracy and national humiliation may have faded, giving way to a renewed belief that political pluralism and Western-style rule of law are not only feasible, but essential to a functioning society.

That said, this "pro-Westernism," if one can use such a simplistic term, would be a most fragile phenomenon. In the late 1980s and 1990s, democratic ideals were unable to take root in an alien and volatile environment, and quickly gave way to reactionary sentiments—particularly among the political elite. History could repeat itself if domestic stability remains elusive, and if engagement with Europe and the United States does not deliver tangible dividends.

Under the fracturing scenario, Russia would cease to be a significant player, including in Eurasia, and would become instead a theater and object of international politics. One can assume that other actors would look to exploit its weakness. China, in particular, could expand its influence across Eurasia—not only in Central Asia but also further west into the Caucasus and beyond—as well as strengthen its economic domination of the Russian Far East. Beijing may even hope to regain territories lost as a result of the "unequal treaties,"[11] although it is unlikely to risk the use of force to this end.

The adverse consequences of a "poor and unhappy" Russia—politically hamstrung, economically enfeebled, and socially demoralized—would not be limited to it alone. One can hardly imagine a more destabilizing development than Russia's descent into chaos, violence, and disintegration. Such a Russia would be a huge headache for Western and Asian policymakers. Not only would it be unable to cooperate effectively in countering major threats, such as Islamist extremism and WMD proliferation, but it could become the epicenter of a deteriorating global environment far more worrying than even today's world disorder.

### Second-wave liberalism

This scenario is based on the presumption that Russia will eventually undergo a major process of modernization. Faced with the prospect of its continuing regression, both in absolute terms and relative to emerging superpowers such as China, the Kremlin would finally get serious about reform. The principal driver here would not be a Damascene conversion to Western democratic capitalism, but rather an implicit recognition that it had run out of options. By this stage stagnation would have proved unsustainable, authoritarianism ineffectual, and anarchy abhorrent. Political and economic liberalization might be the only course left.[12]

This version of liberalism would differ substantially from mainstream American and European understandings. To adapt Deng Xiaoping's famous phrase, it would be "liberalism with Russian characteristics,"[13] and might well be viewed by some as semi-liberalism at best. Nevertheless, there would be real progress in implementing modernizing reforms, involving political pluralism, genuine (if imperfect) rule of law, functioning institutions, a competitive economy, and a developing civil society.

The type of foreign policy that arises out of this "second wave" of Russian liberalism[14] would be Western-oriented, but internationalist. It would involve major changes to operating principles, including reconceptualizing notions of greatness and power. Russia would move beyond its traditional emphasis on military might and geopolitical balancing toward a more active involvement in multilateral processes. It would take advantage of its natural resources, but do so in a way that highlighted its reliability as well as influence. And, most important of all, it would aim to realize the vision, articulated by Dmitri Trenin, of being a great country as well as a major power—accepting that the second will scarcely be possible without the first.[15]

The scenario of second-wave liberalism could see a policy of post-imperial reengagement, one that recognizes the ex-Soviet republics as fully sovereign entities. The latter would lose their "special" status within Russian foreign policy, and the closeness of bilateral ties would depend on their individual relevance and utility to Moscow's objectives. Instead of pursuing broad aspirations, such as Eurasian integration, Moscow would focus on specific projects—in energy, infrastructure, telecommunications, and agriculture—with key states such as Ukraine, Kazakhstan, Uzbekistan, and Azerbaijan. And it would scale down its activities in countries where Russian interests were no longer so compelling.

Such a "liberal" approach could lead to Russia being squeezed out of the post-Soviet space by other major actors, namely the United States, China, and the EU. But in fact the opposite is more plausible. Under the liberal scenario Moscow could pursue an active policy of engagement, in which the accent was on getting Russia in rather than keeping others out. An unambiguously post-imperial approach would serve over time to allay suspicions in the ex-Soviet republics about a hegemonic agenda.[16] It would reflect a more equitable, interests-based attitude to cooperation. Many of Russia's inherited trumps—commonalities of language and culture, inter-elite networks, and close economic ties—would still count for something in 2030. To its neighbors such a post-imperial Russia would represent a more appealing, and less threatening, partner than an economically and strategically assertive China or a morally intrusive West.[17]

The advent of a liberal regime might help to establish Russia's relations with the United States and Europe on a more stable footing. The convergence of values would aid confidence-building and enable misunderstandings to be better managed. Such a Russia would be more likely to reach a consensus in areas such as WMD counterproliferation, global financial governance, and international conflict resolution. The primary focus of Moscow's interest in the West would shift from the United States to Europe, as "partnerships for modernization" with the EU and individual member-states acquired proper substance.

That said, Russia-West relations should not be idealized under this scenario. Even allowing for a "perfect" set of circumstances—an enlightened, progressive regime in Moscow, a responsive administration in Washington, and a reinvigorated and engaged Europe—it could take several decades to achieve a sustainable, well-balanced interaction. It would be especially naïve to assume that Moscow would tamely acquiesce in Western aims and interests. There would continue to be conflicting priorities, significant policy differences, and sometimes very public disagreements. The most liberal-minded Russian politician would still give priority to Russian interests, and criticize Western actions that were seen to undermine these. The behavior of a more liberal and democratic regime might not differ that much from that of the Yeltsin administration during the first half of the 1990s. It could turn out to be a hugely frustrating partner for the West—erratic, hyper-sensitive, and sometimes downright contrary. Worse still, it might seek refuge in a populist nationalism, driven by the need to bolster its domestic legitimacy.[18]

Given the often jaundiced attitudes of Russian liberals toward China, Moscow and Beijing might be expected to have a problematic relationship. However, although a liberal regime would undoubtedly prioritize cooperation with Europe and the United States, and be wary of Chinese intentions, it would still recognize the value of maintaining good ties with Beijing.[19] By 2030 China may be the primary customer for Russian oil and gas and for a number of other commodities as well. The two countries will continue to share a long border and retain a strong interest in a stable Central Asia and Northeast Asia. These commonalities suggest that Moscow would avoid provoking a deterioration in relations with Beijing, even if the normative gap between them were to widen—which is no certainty in light of the pressures for political liberalization in China.

Moscow would, however, pursue a more diversified approach in Asia, based on closer ties with Tokyo, New Delhi, and other capitals. To this end, it might look to cut a deal with Japan over the disputed islands. It would be more inclined to engage with the United States as an Asia-Pacific power and possible counterweight to China, and it would participate more actively in Asian multilateral forums. Such interaction would not only be important for its relations within Asia, but also encourage a more geographically balanced approach overall. Although Moscow's outlook would remain Western-oriented, Russian foreign policy in practice would reflect the emergence of the Asia-Pacific region as the primary center of global political and economic activity.

A liberal Russian foreign policy might turn out to be the most confident and assertive of all the 2030 scenarios. It offers the best prospects for bona fide modernization, a fresh approach toward the ex-Soviet republics, a more positive relationship with Europe and the United States, and more diverse and substantial engagement in Asia. Coming on the back of the failures of other forms of governance, it might also enjoy greater popular legitimacy and benefit from international goodwill. In short, it would have a fighting chance of success.[20]

Yet there is no guarantee that a second wave of liberalism would be any more successful than the first, or than other forms of rule that have been attempted and found wanting. Two caveats come immediately to mind. First, a new liberal regime could ill afford to repeat the mistakes—and arrogance—of the 1990s. It would need to be smarter in grasping political realities; more inclusive in developing consensus within the elite and among the population; less naïve in its expectations of the West; and more professional in pursuing cooperation with a range of foreign partners.

Second, by the time liberalism returned to Russia, the international system would have moved on. Russia might find that others no longer viewed it as a leading power, except in a few niche areas. In that event it would have to rebuild its position and influence virtually from scratch. Unable to lean on historical reputation, it would need to demonstrate its credentials through sheer weight of performance. This would present considerable psychological as well as policy challenges, and the most liberal of regimes could struggle to reconcile the pursuit of Russian interests with a continuing cooperative mindset toward the world.

## Conclusion

This book has set out to address three questions. First, what are the implications for Russia of a fluid and uncertain international context, aka the new world disorder? Second, how is Putin's foreign policy responding to changing regional and global realities? And third, what are Russia's possibilities in the international system over the next ten to fifteen years?

It is, of course, difficult to come up with definitive answers. Many of the issues are still being played out, and their outcomes will remain unclear for a long time. Nevertheless, we can venture some preliminary judgments on the basis of developments during the Putin era, and particularly in the period following the global financial crash of 2008.

The first conclusion is the most self-evident: Russia faces a very challenging international environment, which imposes tremendous demands on its ability to prosper in coming decades. Conventional wisdom has it that the United States and Europe, and Western norms and institutions, are the greatest casualties of a world in transition. But in fact the most likely victims are those states, organizations, and societies—wherever they may be—that are either unwilling or unable to adapt.

A complacent, non-modernizing Russia is as vulnerable as anyone. Its vast territory, great natural resources, and multiplicity of identities are potential strengths, but also sources of weakness. Although it does not face an immediate existential threat, the specter of a long decline at home and gradual marginalization in international society is real. In key respects, Russia is less equipped than leading Western nations to adjust to decline. There is, in a manner of speaking, "less fat to lose," which increases the chances of more drastic and unpleasant outcomes. If the Putin system were to unravel, there could be a breakdown in political authority *of any kind*.[21] If the economy were to suffer a prolonged crisis, the consequences for political and social stability could be disastrous. And if Russia's strategic fortunes were to fall further, it would become prey to the geopolitical ambitions of others, and a primary source of regional and global insecurity.

Second, the Putin regime has yet to grasp the enormity of the task that confronts it. It has shown no sense of urgency in implementing the reforms Russia needs in order to become a competitive economy and dynamic society, and influential international actor in the longer term. It has focused on the troubles of the United States and Europe, but, as the scripture says, failed to see the beam in its own eye. The Kremlin identifies dysfunctional politics, recession, and loss of moral authority in the West, but not that its own economic model is exhausted, or that its political system and values are unsustainable. It derives enormous satisfaction from various *succès d'éclat*, such as the annexation of Crimea, but fails to recognize the adverse consequences of such actions for Russia's strategic interests. It acts as if Russia's difficulties are temporary—and generally the fault of others—and that the right response to challenges both domestic and external is to reinforce traditional institutions and habits.[22] Through all the shifts in direction over the years, the core principles and underlying culture of Russian foreign policy have remained essentially intact, functioning in their own looking-glass world.

Finally, "nothing is written." Past and present shortcomings do not mean that Russia is doomed to be a minor or weak player in a post-American century. Although several of its trumps are less important (and more double-edged) than before, it remains a "lucky" country in many respects.[23] It also enjoys the luxury of a window of opportunity in which it can begin to address some of the formidable domestic and foreign policy challenges it faces now and well into the future. The world is in such flux and confusion that all outcomes, the good as well as the bad, are possible. But success will depend on self-awareness and a real commitment to transformation. If Russia seizes the opportunities that are open to it, there is no reason why it cannot redefine itself as a modern great power—stable, prosperous, and globally influential. But if it continues to cling to the status quo and to illusions of timeless destiny, it will surely be left trailing by the march of history.

# Notes

## Prologue

*Epigraph:* Vladimir Putin, TV address to the nation after the Beslan massacre, September 4, 2004 (http://archive.kremlin.ru/eng/speeches/2004/09/04/1958_type 82912_76332.shtml). Putin's phrase is borrowed from a speech by Joseph Stalin to the First All-Union Conference of Leading Personnel of Socialist Industry on February 4, 1931: "Such is the law of the exploiters—to beat the backward and the weak. It is the jungle law of capitalism. You are backward, you are weak—therefore you are wrong; hence you can be beaten and enslaved. You are mighty—therefore you are right; hence we must be wary of you" (https://www.marxists.org/reference/archive/stalin/works/1931/02/04.htm).

1. Dmitri Trenin, *The End of Eurasia: Russia on the Border between Geopolitics and Globalization* (Carnegie Moscow Center, 2001), pp. 29–30, 311–12.

2. During his speech to the International Valdai Discussion Club (henceforth referred to as Valdai Club) on October 24, 2014, Putin spoke of "consolidating society based on traditional values and patriotism" (http://eng.news.kremlin.ru/transcripts/23137/print).

3. "You just don't in the 21st century behave in 19th century fashion by invading another country on [a] completely trumped up pretext"—U.S. Secretary of State John Kerry on *CBS Face the Nation*, March 2, 2014 (http://www.cbsnews.com/news/john-kerry-warns-of-consequences-for-russia-after-ukraine-invasion/).

4. Kishore Mahbubani was the originator of this now widely used expression—see *The New Asian Hemisphere: The Irresistible Shift of Power to the East* (New York: PublicAffairs, 2008). Interestingly, this book contains only a handful of references to Russia, none of them flattering. Russia is even more peripheral in Mahbubani's latest book, *The Great Convergence: Asia, the West, and the Logic of One World* (New York: PublicAffairs, 2013).

5. "Concept of the Foreign Policy of the Russian Federation" (henceforth referred to as 2013 Russian Foreign Policy Concept), approved by Vladimir Putin on February 12, 2013 (http://www.mid.ru/brp_4.nsf/0/76389FEC168189ED44257B2E0039B16D).

6. In remarks to the Valdai Club in September 2013, Putin spoke of "new strategies to preserve our identity in a rapidly changing world" (http://eng.kremlin.ru/news/6007).

7. There is some debate about whether the term "great power" is appropriate in the early twenty-first century, given its nineteenth-century connotations and the existence of a good alternative in "major power." However, its resonance in contemporary Russian political discourse means that it is useful in conveying the spirit of Putin's foreign policy.

8. Vladimir Putin, opening remarks to the Valdai Club, September 19, 2013 (http://eng.kremlin.ru/news/6007).

9. The original Concert grew out of the 1815 Congress of Vienna, when the victorious powers set out to consolidate their defeat of Napoleon by establishing a long-lasting authoritarian peace. This they did with some success until the outbreak of World War I. Although there were occasional conflicts involving the major powers, most notably the Crimean War of 1853–56, these were relatively limited in scope.

10. Fareed Zakaria, *The Post-American Century* (New York: W.W. Norton, 2009).

11. Sergei Karaganov, "Lucky Russia," *Russia in Global Affairs*, March 29, 2011 (http://eng.globalaffairs.ru/pubcol/Lucky-Russia-15154).

12. The term "besieged fortress" was used by Lenin in a "Letter to American Workers," published in *Pravda* on August 22, 1918 (https://www.marxists.org/archive/lenin/works/1918/aug/20.htm).

13. Remarks by Vladimir Mau at the Wilton Park Russia conference, March 2011 (used with his permission).

14. When Lord Macartney met with the Qianlong Emperor in 1793, China was still the greatest power in the world. By 1911, however, the Qing dynasty had subsided into oblivion.

15. Francis Fukuyama, *The End of History and the Last Man* (New York: Penguin Books, 1992); Robert Kagan, *The Return of History and the End of Dreams* (London: Atlantic Books, 2008). Although Kagan sought to refute Fukuyama's thesis about the triumph of liberal democracy, he identified a similar nexus between democracy/authoritarianism at home and cooperation/confrontation abroad.

16. Russia's share of global GDP in 2014 measured by purchasing power parity (PPP) was estimated at 3.3 percent—see http://www.economywatch.com/economic-statistics/Russia/GDP_Share_of_World_Total_PPP/.

17. 2013 Russian Foreign Policy Concept.

18. See Putin's annual address to the Federal Assembly, April 25, 2005. There is some debate about the correct translation of his words. The official English translation (http://archive.kremlin.ru/eng/speeches/2005/04/25/2031_type70029type82912_87086.shtml) speaks of "a major geopolitical catastrophe of the century," which reads oddly—a function largely of the non-use of articles in Russian. The Russian

transcript of the speech (*"krushenie Sovetskogo Soyuza bylo krupneishei geopolitich-eskoi katastrophoi veka"*) and its immediate context (http://archive.kremlin.ru/appears/2005/04/25/1223_type63372type63374type82634_87049.shtml) suggest, however, that Putin intended to say that the fall of the USSR was "the greatest" rather than simply "a major" catastrophe.

19. In this connection Putin's often quoted remark that "whoever does not regret the passing of the Soviet Union has no heart, whoever wants it back has no brain" reflects imperial regret rather than a post-imperial mindset.

20. Sergei Lavrov, "Vneshnyaya politika Rossii i novoe kachestvo geopoliticheskoi situatsii" [Russian Foreign Policy and a Qualitatively New Geopolitical Situation], *Diplomatic Yearbook of the Russian Ministry of Foreign Affairs*, December 15, 2008 (http://www.mid.ru/bdomp/brp_4.nsf/2fee282eb6df40e643256999005e6e8c/80f92fa1b96d767ec3257520002dd4ae!OpenDocument).

21. Vladimir Putin, "Russia and the Changing World," *Moskovskie novosti*, February 27, 2012 (http://valdaiclub.com/politics/39300.html).

22. Nikolay Spasskiy, "The Decline of Europe and Russia's Future," *Russia in Global Affairs*, June 23, 2012 (http://eng.globalaffairs.ru/number/The-Decline-of-Europe-and-Russias-Future-15572); Dmitry Babich, "Why the EU has lost the right to lecture Russia," Valdai Club website, November 29, 2012 (http://valdaiclub.com/europe/52080.html).

23. An early KGB evaluation of the young Putin described him as having a "reduced sense of danger," something which he admitted was deemed a "very serious shortcoming"—*Ot pervogo litsa: razgovory s Vladimirom Putinym* [From the First Person: Conversations with Vladimir Putin] (Moscow: Vagrius, 2000), p. 34.

24. Alexei Arbatov, "Real and Imaginary Threats," *Russia in Global Affairs*, April 15, 2013 (http://eng.globalaffairs.ru/number/Real-and-Imaginary-Threats-15925).

25. Ivan Krastev, "Would Democratic Change in Russia Transform its Foreign Policy?," Open Democracy, February 7, 2013 (http://www.opendemocracy.net/od-russia/ivan-krastev/would-democratic-change-in-russia-transform-its-foreign-policy).

## Chapter 1

1. The original quotation from *On War* is "war is nothing but a continuation of politics with the admixture of other means"—*The Oxford Dictionary of Quotations*, rev. 4th ed. (Oxford University Press, 1996), p. 205.

2. "Russia cannot be understood with the mind alone, No ordinary yardstick can span her greatness: She stands alone, unique—In Russia, one can only believe."

3. Archie Brown, *The Myth of the Strong Leader: Political Leadership in the Modern Age* (London: Basic Books, 2014), pp. 46–48.

4. "Pochemu v Rossii nevozmozhno postroenie demokratii" [Why It Is Impossible to Build Democracy in Russia], *Svobodnaya pressa*, February 21, 2011 (http://svpressa.ru/society/article/39132).

5. Dmitri Trenin and Bobo Lo, *The Landscape of Russian Foreign Policy Decision-making* (Carnegie Moscow Center, 2005).

6. Igor Torbakov, "'What Does Russia Want?'—Investigating the Interrelationship between Moscow's Domestic and Foreign Policy," *DGAP Analyse*, May 1, 2011, p. 9.

7. Sechin has also acted as Putin's personal envoy to Latin America, no doubt chosen for this purpose because of Venezuela's importance as an oil exporter—see Alexander Bratersky, "Sechin to Visit Venezuela amid Speculation about Chavez's Health," *Moscow Times*, January 30, 2013 (http://www.themoscowtimes.com/news/article/sechin-to-visit-venezuela-amid-speculation-about-chavezs-health/474701.html).

8. Vladimir Putin, remarks to the Valdai Club, September 19, 2013 (http://eng.kremlin.ru/news/6007). See also Maria Snegovaya, "How Putin's Worldview May Be Shaping His Response in Crimea," *Washington Post*, March 2, 2014 (http://www.washingtonpost.com/blogs/monkey-cage/wp/2014/03/02/how-putins-worldview-may-be-shaping-his-response-in-crimea/).

9. Much has been made of the influence of the ultra-nationalist Alexander Dugin on Putin's Eurasian direction. But evidence for this is sketchy. Dugin has been a peripheral figure for much of the Putin era, and Putin himself has not acknowledged any intellectual debt. It is difficult, also, to square Dugin's warnings about the "China threat" with Putin's commitment to strategic convergence with Beijing.

10. They are especially committed to maintaining the principle of "strategic parity" with the United States—see comments by Deputy Defense Minister Anatoly Antonov in the 2012 BBC documentary "Putin, Russia, and the West."

11. As of December 2013, Rossiya Segodnya (Russia Today) replaced RIA-Novosti. Putin's public affairs spokesman Dmitry Peskov explained the change as the need to promote Russia more aggressively—"propaganda in the good sense of the word" (http://en.ria.ru/russia/20131219/185718548-print/Russia-Needs-Propaganda-Putin-Spokesman.html). Since then, RT and Rossiya Segodnya have benefited from massive injections of public funds. See Gabrielle Tétrault-Farber, "Looking West, Russia Beefs Up Spending on Global Media Giants," *Moscow Times*, September 23, 2014 (http://www.themoscowtimes.com/news/article/looking-west-russia-beefs-up-spending-on-global-media-giants/507692.html).

12. Bobo Lo, *Vladimir Putin and the Evolution of Russian Foreign Policy* (Oxford: Chatham House and Blackwell, 2003), p. 3.

13. Rent-seeking occurs when monopolistic companies (for example, Rosneft or Gazprom) use their privileged positions within the ruling elite to maximize their share of existing wealth, rather than to generate new wealth.

14. See Matthew Evangelista, "Putin: a New de Gaulle?," PONARS Policy Memo 253, October 2002.

15. It has been speculated that those in the loop included Sergei Ivanov, chief of the Presidential Administration; Nikolai Patrushev, secretary of the Security Council; and Aleksandr Bortnikov, director of the Federal Security Service (FSB). All were former KGB colleagues of Putin. See Steven Lee Myers, "Russia's Move into Ukraine Said to be Born in Shadows," *New York Times*, March 7, 2014 (http://www.nytimes.com/

2014/03/08/world/europe/russias-move-into-ukraine-said-to-be-born-in-shadows.html?
_r=0).

16. "I consider that the unipolar model is not only unacceptable but also impossible in today's world . . . the model itself is flawed because at its basis there is and can be no moral foundations for modern civilization"—Putin's speech at the Munich Conference on Security Policy, February 10, 2007 (http://eng.kremlin.ru/transcripts/8498).

17. Andrew Wilson, *Ukraine's Orange Revolution* (Yale University Press, 2005), pp. 94–95.

18. Yushchenko was Ukrainian prime minister from 1998 to 2001.

19. Although Medvedev was the nominal commander-in-chief, few were in any doubt that the decision to go to war was Putin's.

20. The author was told in an off-the-record conversation in November 2014 that neither CNPC nor Gazprom was happy about the terms of the deal, but both were instructed at the highest level to finalize it.

21. Comments made to the author by a prominent banker close to the Kremlin.

22. Peter Duncan, "Batman and Robin? Exploring Foreign Policy Differences between Putin and Medvedev during the Medvedev Presidency," CEPSI (Centre for European Politics, Security & Integration) Working Paper, March 2013, p. 17.

23. Roy Allison, *Russia, the West, and Military Intervention* (Oxford University Press, 2013), p. 194. Dmitri Trenin is more unequivocal, asserting that "it was definitely Putin who ordered the Russian delegation to abstain from voting in the UN Security Council"—"Vladimir Putin's Fourth Vector," *Russia in Global Affairs*, June 30, 2013 (http://eng.globalaffairs.ru/number/Vladimir-Putins-Fourth-Vector-16048).

24. See Thomas Grove, "Mysterious YouTube Video Accuses Russia's Medvedev of Treason," Reuters, February 1, 2013 (http://www.reuters.com/article/2013/02/01/net-us-russia-medvedev-video-idUSBRE9100Z720130201).

25. The juxtaposition of "good Tsar, bad boyars [nobles]" dates back to the time of Ivan the Terrible in the late sixteenth century.

26. There have been several pithy descriptions of the relationship between Putin and Medvedev. A leaked cable from John Beyrle, U.S. ambassador in Moscow, referred to the tandem as "Batman and Robin"—see "US Embassy Cables: 'Tandem Politics' of Medvedev and Putin," *The Guardian*, December 1, 2010 (http://www.theguardian.com/world/us-embassy-cables-documents/178955). Another description is of Putin as the supreme mafia don (*capo di tutti capi*) and Medvedev as the "nephew who went to Harvard." In some respects, the public dynamic between the two is not so different from that of Yeltsin and his long-time prime minister Viktor Chernomyrdin during the 1990s. Then it often seemed that Chernomyrdin's main job was to take the heat for the Kremlin's failures.

27. *Vedomstvennost* referred to the practice of placing the interests of one's department or ministry above the greater good, be it that of the Communist Party, the Soviet state, or the people.

28. Fiona Hill and Clifford Gaddy, *Mr. Putin: Operative in the Kremlin,* 2nd ed. (Brookings, 2015), p. 207.

29. Richard Connolly and Philip Hanson, "Russia's Accession to the World Trade Organization: Commitments, Processes, and Prospects," *Eurasian Geography and Economics,* vol. 53, no. 4, 2012, p. 479.

30. Lavrov has been foreign minister since 2004. This still leaves him some way behind Gromyko, who held the position for 28 years in the Soviet Union, from 1957 to 1985.

31. Ekaterina Stepanova, "The Syria Crisis and the Making of Russia's Foreign Policy," PONARS Eurasia Policy Memo 199, June 2012, p. 5.

32. Sergei Ivanov was a high-flying colleague of Putin in the KGB. He served as defense minister from 2001 to 2007 and then as first deputy prime minister until he was demoted to deputy prime minister in May 2008, in which capacity he worked until December 2011. His current position, Chief of the Presidential Administration, makes him Putin's gatekeeper.

33. Don Jensen, "Sergei Ivanov Returns to Center Stage," *Institute of Modern Russia,* April 2, 2013.

34. Stephen Fortescue, "The Policy Process in Putin's Third Presidency," paper presented to the eleventh conference of the Australasian Association for Communist and Post-Communist States, University of Tasmania, February 7–8, 2013.

35. Hill and Gaddy have noted that there are "only vertical links up to Putin, even within the informal system, and no real horizontal ties. Everyone, no matter who, needs to check back with Putin or refer back to Putin to legitimate his own position, ideas, or general standing" (*Mr. Putin,* p. 219).

36. Trenin and Lo, *The Landscape of Russian Foreign Policy Decisionmaking,* p. 16.

37. As Hill and Gaddy put it, "Their collective experience has turned the Russian population into survivalists, people who constantly think of and prepare for the worst" (*Mr. Putin,* p. 77).

38. There were exceptions, of course, such as Tbilisi's attempts to recover Abkhazia and South Ossetia in 1992–93 and the civil war in Tajikistan.

39. This is true not only of the United Kingdom and France, but also of Italy, the Netherlands, Poland, and several other NATO member-states.

40. Putin's meeting with the Valdai Club, September 6, 2004—see Ariel Cohen, "U.S.-Russian Security Cooperation after Beslan," October 25, 2004, Heritage Foundation backgrounder 1809 (http://www.heritage.org/research/reports/2004/10/us-russian-security-cooperation-after-beslan).

41. "Russia PM Vladimir Putin Accuses US over Protests," BBC News, December 8, 2011 (http://www.bbc.co.uk/news/world-europe-16084743).

42. Nikolai Patrushev, "Ukraine Crisis—the View from Russia," interview in *Rossiiskaya gazeta,* October 24, 2014 (http://www.theguardian.com/world/2014/oct/24/sp-ukraine-russia-cold-war).

43. "Why Vladimir Putin Needs a Poor, Aggressive Russia," *New Republic*, March 2, 2014 (http://www.newrepublic.com/article/116824/why-vladimir-putin-needs-poor-aggressive-russia-crimea).

44. Even then, Yeltsin felt the need to make a token demonstration during the Kosovo conflict, sending 200 Russian paratroopers to briefly occupy Slatina airport outside Pristina: "I decided that Russia must make a crowning gesture, even if it had no military significance.... [It] was a sign of our moral victory in the face of the enormous NATO military, all of Europe, and the whole world"—Boris Yeltsin, *Midnight Diaries* (London: Phoenix, 2000), p. 266.

45. Lo, *Vladimir Putin and the Evolution of Russian Foreign Policy*.

46. Robert Coalson, "Russia: Why the Chekist Mind-set Matters," Radio Free Europe/Radio Liberty, October 15, 2007 (http://www.rferl.org/content/article/1078954.html).

47. This has been the author's experience from various meetings with senior regime figures, such as Sergei Ivanov and Vladimir Yakunin.

48. "McCain: When I Looked at Putin's Eyes I Saw 3 Letters: K G B," http://www.youtube.com/ watch?v=lAVIaIJWP-Q (uberpulse.com, July 18, 2007).

49. Hill and Gaddy, *Mr. Putin*, pp. 110, 115.

50. "Russia: Public Backs Putin, Crimea's Secession," Pew Global Attitudes survey, May 8, 2014 (http://www.pewglobal.org/2014/05/08/chapter-3-russia-public-backs-putin-crimeas-secession/).

51. Vladimir Putin, "Russia and the Changing World," *Moskovskie novosti*, February 27, 2012.

52. This tailoring of identity has been evident since the beginning of his presidency—see Lo, *Vladimir Putin and the Evolution of Russian Foreign Policy*, p. 4.

53. Konstantin Eggert, presentation at the International Council for Central and Eastern European Studies (ICCEES), Tampere, June 2000.

54. Torbakov, "'What Does Russia Want?'"; see also Putin's remarks to the Valdai Club, September 19, 2013 (http://eng.kremlin.ru/news/6007).

55. Dmitri Trenin, *The End of Eurasia: Russia on the Border between Geopolitics and Globalization* (Carnegie Moscow Center, 2001).

56. The Russian Far East has an estimated population of 6.3 million—less than that of Hong Kong for the fourth-largest territorial entity in the Asia-Pacific (after Canada, China, and the United States).

57. This attitude dates back to the 1920s, and was a major driver of Stalin's mass industrialization in the 1930s.

58. Isaiah Berlin, *Russian Thinkers* (Harmondsworth: Penguin, 1994), p. 118.

59. Russian leaders from Gorbachev to Putin have claimed that the West reneged on assurances given in 1989–90 that Germany would not be reunified, and that NATO would not expand into the Visegrad countries (then Czechoslovakia, Poland, and Hungary). In fact, it is unclear whether such assurances were ever made. The docu-

mentary record reveals no specific mention of these, although it cannot be ruled out that oral promises were offered and/or understood. See Angela Stent, *The Limits of Partnership: U.S.-Russian Relations in the Twenty-First Century* (Princeton University Press, 2014), p. 37.

60. The "century of humiliation" covers the period from the end of the First Opium War to the founding of the People's Republic of China.

61. The original Time of Troubles (*smutnoe vremya*) followed the death of Tsar Fyodor in 1598 and the establishment of the Romanov dynasty under Tsar Michael in 1613. During this time, Muscovy suffered repeated rebellions, famines and other natural disasters, and foreign occupation.

62. Putin's TV address after Beslan, September 4, 2004 (http://archive.kremlin.ru/eng/speeches/2004/09/04/1958_type82912_76332.shtml).

63. While serving as deputy head of mission at the U.S. Embassy in Moscow in 1944, George Kennan wrote of "the hope, latent in every Russian soul, that the scope and daring of the Russian mind will some day overshadow the achievements of the haughty and conventional West." I am indebted to Rodric Braithwaite for drawing my attention to this observation. Hill and Gaddy note that "every survived calamity reaffirms the special status of Russia in history" (*Mr. Putin*, p. 77).

64. See, for example, "Ronald Reagan: The Man Who Beat Communism," *The Economist*, June 10, 2004 (http://www.economist.com/node/2747709).

65. See Igor Ivanov, "What Diplomacy Does Russia Need in the 21st Century?," *Russia in Global Affairs*, December 29, 2011 (http://eng.globalaffairs.ru/number/What-Diplomacy-Does-Russia-Need-in-the-21st-Century-15420).

66. Brown, *The Myth of the Strong Leader*, p. 47.

67. 2013 Russian Foreign Policy Concept.

68. "Meeting with Young Academics and History Teachers," November 5, 2014 (http://eng.kremlin.ru/transcripts/23185).

69. Bobo Lo, *Russian Foreign Policy in the Post-Soviet Era: Reality, Illusion and Mythmaking* (Basingstoke: Palgrave Macmillan, 2002).

70. See Vyacheslav Glazychev, "The 'Putin Consensus' Explained," in Ivan Krastev, Mark Leonard, and Andrew Wilson (eds), *What Does Russia Think?* (London: European Council on Foreign Relations, September 2009), pp. 9–13.

71. It was testament to Putin's comfort level that he felt able to observe the letter of the constitution by allowing formal presidential succession to pass to Dmitry Medvedev in 2008.

72. Putin's speech at the Munich Conference on Security Policy, February 10, 2007 (http://eng.kremlin.ru/transcripts/8498).

73. Bobo Lo, "Russia's Crisis and What It Means for Regime Stability and Moscow's Relations with the World," CER Policy Brief.

74. Lilia Shevtsova, *Lonely Power: Why Russia Has Failed to Become the West and the West Is Weary of Russia* (Washington: Carnegie Endowment for International Peace, 2010), p. 77.

75. Oksana Antonenko and Igor Yurgens, "Toward a NATO-Russia Strategic Concept," *Survival*, vol. 52, no. 6, December 2010–January 2011, pp. 5–11. This article is interesting not only for its content, but also for its coauthorship; Yurgens was (and remains) the head of the Medvedev think tank, the Institute of Contemporary Development (INSOR).

76. See Irina Borogan and Andrei Soldatov, "The Kremlin Versus the Bloggers: The Battle for Cyberspace," Open Democracy, March 27, 2012.

77. The comparative prosperity of the Putin era does not change this broad assessment, but gives the regime some leeway; it is still "in credit."

78. "Crude Oil Price Summary," United States Energy Information Administration (http://www.eia.gov/beta/MER/index.cfm?tbl=T09.01#/?f=M&start=200001&end=2 01301&charted=0-6).

79. Ibid. Russia's international reserves fell from US$597 billion on July 31, 2008, to US$384 billion on April 30, 2009. There then followed a substantial and sustained rally, with reserves reaching US$538 billion by the end of 2012. They were still at US$524 billion as late as October 31, 2013, before suffering a new slump. See Russian Central Bank statistics (http://cbr.ru/eng/hd_base/default.aspx?Prtid=mrrf_m).

80. This led to the so-called "oil-for-loan" agreement, whereby the Chinese lent US$25 billion in return for guaranteed oil deliveries of 15 million tonnes per annum, and construction of the Daqing spur of the East Siberia–Pacific Ocean oil pipeline—see chapter 5.

81. Putin, "Russia and the Changing World."

82. In his annual news conference with the domestic and international media on December 18, 2014, Putin asserted that Russia's economic difficulties "were obviously provoked primarily by external factors." He claimed, further, that Western sanctions against Russia had been imposed "in violation of WTO rules, international law, and the UN Charter" (http://eng.kremlin.ru/transcripts/23406).

83. This is the main reason why Russia has been in denial about the shale revolution, since it seriously challenges this assumption—see chapter 3.

84. I am indebted to Tatiana Mitrova of the Russian Academy of Sciences' Energy Research Institute for this information.

85. Clifford Gaddy, "Will the Russian Economy Rid Itself of Dependence on Oil?," RIA-Novosti, June 16, 2011 (http://www.brookings.edu/research/opinions/2011/06/16-russia-economy-gaddy).

86. Harold Meyerson, "Conservatives Face Conflicting Corporate and National Interests," *Washington Post*, May 8, 2014 (http://www.washingtonpost.com/opinions/harold-meyerson-conservatives-face-conflicting-corporate-and-national-interests/2014/05/07/c12a1640-d5f3-11e3-95d3-3bcd77cd4e11_story.html).

87. "American Shale Gas Project Is a Bubble about to Burst—Gazprom CEO," RT, March 30, 2013 (http://rt.com/business/shale-gas-gazprom-us-088/).

88. Alan Riley, "Commission versus Gazprom: The Anti-Trust Clash of the Decade?," CEPS Policy Brief 285, October 31, 2012.

89. "You Can Forget Russia as a Democracy," interview with Vladislav Inozemtsev, *Spiegel Online*, November 21, 2012.

90. Anders Aslund, "An Assessment of Putin's Economic Policy," *CESifo Forum*, July 2008 (http://www.iie.com/publications/papers/paper.cfm?ResearchID=974).

91. Surkov defined sovereign democracy in the following obtuse terms: "While building an open society we don't forget that we are a free nation. And we want to be a free nation among other free nations and to cooperate with them proceeding from fair principles, we don't want to be managed from abroad."—"Surkov in His Own Words," *Wall Street Journal*, December 18, 2006 (http://www.wsj.com/articles/SB116646992809753610).

92. Nikita Khrushchev famously exhorted the Soviet Union to "catch up and surpass" (*dognat i peregnat*) the United States.

93. Dmitri Trenin and Boris Dolgin, "Russia's Foreign Policy: Modernize or Marginalize," Open Democracy and polit.ru, January 15–21, 2010.

94. Mikhail Dmitriev and Daniel Treisman, "The Other Russia," *Foreign Affairs*, vol. 91, no. 5, September/October 2012, pp. 59–72.

95. "Russians Back Protests, Political Freedoms," Pew Global Attitudes survey, May 23, 2012.

96. There are parallels here with Stalin's campaign against "cosmopolitanism"; in both cases the primary target was the urban liberal middle class.

97. "Novorossiya" covers the area adjoining the Black Sea from Rostov-na-Donu in the east to Transnistria in the west, including the major industrial regions of Donetsk and Luhansk. The Russian Empire conquered these territories from the Ottoman Empire at the end of the eighteenth century, and held them until the 1917 revolution. Subsequently, most of "Novorossiya" was subsumed into the Ukrainian Soviet Socialist Republic, and then in 1991 into the newly independent Ukraine. Although ethnic Russians moved into these areas in large numbers from the late 1920s, they still represented only a quarter of the local population according to the most recent (2001) Ukrainian census. See Ralph Clem, "What Exactly Is Putin's New 'New Russia'?," *Washington Post*, September 4, 2014 (http://www.washingtonpost.com/blogs/monkey-cage/wp/2014/09/04/what-exactly-is-putins-new-new-russia/).

98. The British ambassador, Tony Brenton, was subjected to sustained harassment in 2006–07. The Estonian ambassador, Marina Kaljurand, was likewise targeted after her government moved the Soviet war memorial in Tallinn.

99. Tatiana Stanovaya, "The Fate of the Nashi Movement: Where Will the Kremlin's Youth Go?," Institute of Modern Russia, March 26, 2013 (http://imrussia.org/en/politics/420-the-fate-of-the-nashi-movement-where-will-the-kremlins-youth-go).

100. Lyudmila Alexandrova, "Russian Government Embarks on Struggle with Illegal Migration," TASS, August 9, 2014 (http://itar-tass.com/en/opinions/763039); "Thousands of Russia's Labour Migrants Are Packing Bags," TASS, January 13, 2015 (http://itar-tass.com/en/opinions/770954).

101. In an October 2014 survey conducted by the All-Russian Public Opinion Research Center (VTsIOM), 79 percent of those polled thought that China would be

an "ally" or "close partner" in the twenty-first century, compared with 9 percent who envisaged it as a "dangerous neighbor/rival," and 1 percent as a "rival/enemy." In 2005 the respective figures were 48 percent, 25 percent, and 6 percent. See "Russia and China: From Hostility and Competitiveness towards Friendship and Cooperation," VTsIOM press release 1686, November 6, 2014 (http://www.wciom.com/index.php?id=61&uid=1023).

102. See Gabrielle Tétrault-Farber, "Putin to Meet Pope Francis as Church Relations Warm," *Moscow Times*, November 25, 2013 (http://www.themoscowtimes.com/news/article/putin-to-meet-pope-francis-as-church-relations-warm/490150.html).

103. It should be noted that the Russian Orthodox Church is by no means monolithic. While some figures supported the 2012 law banning foreign adoptions of Russian children, others criticized it as an inhumane response to the passing of the Magnitsky Act in the United States (discussed in chapter 6).

104. "Russians Want Church Out of Politics," RT, August 14, 2012 (http://rt.com/politics/orthodox-church-politics-poll-632/).

105. "Dieu le veult" was the orchestrated response of the crowd to Pope Urban II's call for the First Crusade in 1095.

106. Igor Zevelev, "A New Realism for the 21st Century," *Russia in Global Affairs*, December 27, 2012.

107. These measures included the Dima Yakovlev law on adoptions, the expulsion of USAID, and the termination of the Nunn-Lugar Cooperative Threat Reduction (CTR) program.

## Chapter 2

*Epigraph*: Thomas Hobbes, *Leviathan* (Harmondsworth: Penguin, 1968 [1651]), p.188. Hobbes clarifies that "the nature of War, consisteth not in actuall fighting; but in the known disposition thereto," p. 186.

1. Robert Massie, *Peter the Great: His Life and World* (New York: Ballantine Books, 1980), pp. 242–43.

2. 2013 Russian Foreign Policy Concept.

3. Jack Snyder, *The Soviet Strategic Culture: Implications for Nuclear Options* (Santa Monica: RAND, 1977), p. 9.

4. Hobbes, *Leviathan*, pp. 186–90. See also Hedley Bull, *The Anarchical Society: a Study of Order in World Politics*, 3d ed. (Basingstoke: Palgrave, 2002 [1977]), pp. 44–46.

5. Dmitri Trenin, *Post-Imperium: A Eurasian Story* (Washington: Carnegie Endowment for International Peace/Basingstoke: Palgrave Macmillan, 2010), pp. 217–18.

6. "Trust in the United States as the leader of the free world and the free economy, and confidence in Wall Street as the center of that trust, has been damaged, I believe, forever," Vladimir Putin—"Putin: US Image Damaged Forever over Economy Woes," *USA Today*, October 9, 2008 (http://usatoday30.usatoday.com/news/world/2008-10-09-1149101095_x.htm). American difficulties were also the butt of Russian

cartoons—see "Baffet: ekonomika SShA lezhit na obeikh lopatkakh" [Buffett: the U.S. Economy Is Flat on Its Back] (http://ria.ru/caricature/20081003/151835843.html) and "Analiticheskii prognoz: chto teriaiut SShA" [Analytical Forecast: What the U.S. Is Losing] (http://ria.ru/caricature/20081120/155545737.html).

7. Sergei Karaganov, "Security Strategy: Why Arms?," *Russia in Global Affairs*, October 26, 2012.

8. In 2013 expenditure was 4.2 percent of GDP, far outstripping the share of China (2.1 percent) and exceeding that of the United States (3.8 percent)—World Bank, "Military Expenditure (% of GDP)" (http://data.worldbank.org/indicator/ms.mil.xpnd.gd.zs_).

9. James Sherr, *Hard Diplomacy and Soft Coercion: Russia's Influence Abroad* (London: Chatham House, 2013).

10. Celeste Wallander describes this as "transimperialism"—"Russian Transimperialism and Its Implications," *Washington Quarterly*, vol. 30, no. 2, spring 2007.

11. Political parties said to be in receipt of Kremlin funding include the Front National in France and Hungary's Fidesz party—see chapter 6.

12. "Russian Influence Abroad: Non-State Actors and Propaganda," summary report of a Chatham House meeting on October 24, 2014. Soviet "active measures" covered a multitude of sins: manipulation of the media, information warfare (*informatsionnaya voina*) and disinformation (*disinformatsiya*), selective assassinations, and political repression.

13. As articulated by Joseph Nye, *Soft Power: The Means to Success in World Politics* (New York: PublicAffairs, 2004).

14. Consistent with this view of soft power as, in effect, "soft warfare," the 2013 Foreign Policy Concept warns against its "destructive and unlawful use [by others] . . . to exert political pressure on sovereign states, interfere in their internal affairs, destabilize their political situation, [and] manipulate public opinion."

15. Dmitri Trenin writes of "strategic independence" in foreign affairs, and "domestic independence," defined as "full sovereignty for the ruling elite"—"Of Power and Greatness," in Piotr Dutkiewicz and Dmitri Trenin (eds), *Russia: The Challenges of Transformation* (New York University Press, 2011), pp. 411–14.

16. Trenin, *Post-Imperium*, p. 29.

17. Francis Fukuyama, in *The End of History and the Last Man* (London: Penguin Books, 1992), wrote of the "unreality of realism," dismissing it as a "fitting view of international polities for a pessimistic century"—p. 252.

18. In the 1990s, then U.S. president Bill Clinton justified NATO enlargement principally on the grounds of "promoting stability" throughout the European continent.

19. See Putin, "Russia and the Changing World," *Moskovskie novosti*, February 27, 2012; also Nikolai Patrushev, "Ukraine Crisis—The View from Russia," *Rossiiskaya gazeta*, October 24, 2014 (http://www.theguardian.com/world/2014/oct/24/sp-ukraine-russia-cold-war).

20. Andrei Kozyrev, "Rossiya i Ssha: partnerstvo ne prezhdevremenno, a zapazdy-vaet [Russia and the USA: Partnership Is Not Premature, but Overdue]," *Izvestiya*, March 11, 1994, p. 3.

21. "Rossiya ishchet novoe mesto v mire" [Russia Seeks a New Place in the World], interview in *Izvestiya*, March 6, 1996, p. 3.

22. Sergei Lavrov, "Russia in the 21st Century World of Power," *Russia in Global Affairs*, December 27, 2012.

23. 2013 Russian Foreign Policy Concept.

24. In referring to Russia as one of the "centers of the new polycentric world," Lavrov writes that this status is due to Russia's "military, geographical and economic capabilities, its culture and human potential"—Lavrov, "Russia in the 21st Century World of Power."

25. The Chinese thinker Zheng Bijian coined the term "peaceful rise," but this came to be regarded as somewhat threatening, and so was jettisoned in favor of the more neutral expression "peaceful development"—see Susan Shirk, *China: Fragile Superpower* (Oxford University Press, 2007), pp. 108–09.

26. "The modern world is indeed multipolar, complex, and dynamic—this is objective reality. Any attempts to create a model of international relations where all decisions are made within a single 'pole' are ineffective, malfunction regularly, and are ultimately set to fail."—Putin interview with ITAR-TASS, July 15, 2014 (http://eng.kremlin.ru/transcripts/22667).

27. 2013 Russian Foreign Policy Concept.

28. Igor Zevelev, "A New Realism for the 21st Century," *Russia in Global Affairs*, December 27, 2012.

29. "The emergence of new global economic and political actors with Western countries trying to preserve their traditional positions enhances global competition, which is manifested in growing instability in international relations" (2013 Russian Foreign Policy Concept).

30. Putin's remarks to the Valdai Club, September 19, 2013 (http://eng.kremlin.ru/news/6007); see also Nikolai Spasskiy, "The Decline of Europe and Russia's Future," *Russia in Global Affairs*, June 23, 2012 (http://eng.globalaffairs.ru/number/The-Decline-of-Europe-and-Russias-Future-15572).

31. The May 2014 elections to the European Parliament were notable for the spectacular gains made by far-right parties, such as UKIP (United Kingdom Independence Party) and the Front National in France.

32. See, for example, Timofei Bordachev, "Political Tsunami Hits Hard—the European Union and Functional Disintegration," *Russia in Global Affairs*, June 30, 2013 (http://eng.globalaffairs.ru/number/Political-Tsunami-Hits-Hard-16054).

33. Sergei Karaganov, "The Map of the World: Geopolitics Stages a Comeback," *Russia in Global Affairs*, May 19, 2013 (ttp://eng.globalaffairs.ru/pubcol/The-Map-of-the-World-Geopolitics-Stages-a-Comeback-15974).

34. Lavrov, "Russia in the 21st Century World of Power."

35. 2013 Foreign Policy Concept.

36. Pavel Salin, "Russia and Asia, or Russia within Asia?," *Russia in Global Affairs*, September 24, 2011 (http://eng.globalaffairs.ru/number/Russia-and-Asia-or-Russia-within-Asia-15330).

37. 2013 Russian Foreign Policy Concept.

38. Fyodor Lukyanov argues that the Kremlin, whether under Yeltsin, Putin, or Medvedev, "has always sought to restore Russia's role as a leading player in the international arena. It was the circumstances and levers available to the head of state that changed"—"'Vigor, Toughness and Tolerance,'" *Russia in Global Affairs*, March 27, 2011 (http://eng.globalaffairs.ru/number/Vigor-Toughness-and-Tolerance-15152).

39. Bobo Lo, *Vladimir Putin and the Evolution of Russian Foreign Policy* (Oxford: Chatham House and Blackwell, 2003); Vyacheslav Nikonov, "The Putin Strategy," *Russia in Global Affairs*, February 8, 2005 (http://eng.globalaffairs.ru/number/n_4415).

40. The notion of "smart power"—combining hard and soft power—encapsulates this vision well. See Igor Ivanov, "What Diplomacy Does Russia Need in the 21st Century?," *Russia in Global Affairs*, December 29, 2011 (http://eng.globalaffairs.ru/number/What-Diplomacy-Does-Russia-Need-in-the-21st-Century-15420).

41. Andrei Kozyrev, "The Lagging Partnership," *Foreign Affairs*, vol. 73, no. 3, May/June 1994.

42. Leon Aron, "The Foreign Policy Doctrine of Postcommunist Russia and Its Domestic Context," in Michael Mandelbaum (ed.), *The New Russian Foreign Policy* (New York: Council on Foreign Relations,1998), p. 33.

43. Vyacheslav Volodin told a session of the 2014 Valdai Club conference that "any attack on Putin is an attack on Russia"—see "'No Putin, No Russia,' Says Kremlin Deputy Chief of Staff," *Moscow Times*, October 23, 2014 (http://www.themoscowtimes.com/news/article/no-putin-no-russia-says-kremlin-deputy-chief-of-staff/509981.html).

44. Trenin, "Of Power and Greatness," p. 407.

45. In 2000 Putin asked George Robertson, then secretary-general of NATO, why Russia had not been invited to join the alliance. Robertson replied that countries needed to apply and fulfill the membership criteria, whereupon Putin declared: "I am not standing in any queue with a lot of countries that don't matter"—Robertson's remarks at the Council on Foreign Relations, Washington, February 25, 2009 (http://www.cfr.org/nato/remarks-former-nato-secretary-general-lord-robertson/p18661).

46. Putin's remarks to the Valdai Club, September 19, 2013 (http://eng.kremlin.ru/news/6007).

47. Putin's remarks to the Valdai Club, October 24, 2014 (http://eng.kremlin.ru/news/23137).

48. Henry Kissinger, *Diplomacy* (New York: Touchstone, 1994), pp. 703–32; Bobo Lo, "Russia, China and the United States—from Strategic Triangularism to the Post-Modern Triangle," *Proliferation Papers* 32, Winter 2010/*Russie.NEI Visions* 47, February 2010 (http://www.ifri.org/?page=contribution-detail&id=5860).

49. "Rossiya ishchet novoe mesto v mire."

50. Yeltsin–Jiang Zemin joint declaration "On a Multipolar World and the Formation of a New International Order," April 23, 1997 (http://www.fas.org/news/russia/1997/a52—153en.htm).

51. Peter Ferdinand, "The Positions of Russia and China in the UN Security Council in the Light of Recent Crises," European Parliament Briefing Paper, March 2013, p. 6.

52. Pavel Salin, "Russia's Three Roads to Asia," *Russia in Global Affairs*, December 27, 2012 (http://eng.globalaffairs.ru/number/Russias-Three-Roads-to-Asia-15818).

53. Now known as the "One Belt, One Road" initiative.

54. The theme of a "dialogue between civilizations" has been around for some time. Since 2003 Vladimir Yakunin, head of Russian railways and one of Putin's closest confidants, has hosted a series of conferences on this theme on the Greek island of Rhodes.

55. Victor Larin, "Russia's Eastern Border: Last Outpost of Europe or Base for Asian Experiment?," *Russian Expert Review*, vol. 18, no. 4, October 2006.

56. Ronald Suny, "Provisional Stabilities: the Politics of Identities in post-Soviet Eurasia," *International Security*, vol. 24, no. 3, Winter 1999/2000; Samuel Huntington, *The Clash of Civilizations and the Remaking of World Order* (New York: Touchstone, 1998), p. 138.

57. Salin, "Russia's Three Roads to Asia."

58. Lilia Shevtsova, *Lonely Power: Why Russia Has Failed to Become the West and the West Is Weary of Russia* (Washington: Carnegie Endowment for International Peace, 2010).

59. Alexei Fenenko, "APEC Remains an American Project," Valdai Club website, September 13, 2012 (http://valdaiclub.com/asia/48800.html).

60. Roderic Lyne, "My Neighbor's Cow: Russia in Post-Cold War Europe," lecture at the annual conference of the Centre for Russian and East European Studies, University of Birmingham, June 3, 2011; see also Julian Lindley-French, "What Does Russia Want?," *Russia in Global Affairs*, June 22, 2011 (http://eng.globalaffairs.ru/number/What-Does-Russia-Want-15238).

61. In this, there are parallels with the Chinese concept of a "harmonious world," whereby the leadership hopes that a favorable external context will assist domestic political and economic goals.

62. Xi Jinping first unveiled the concept of "a new type of relationship between major countries in the 21st century" at a speech in Washington on February 15, 2012 (https://www.ncuscr.org/content/video-vice-president-xi-jinping-policy-address). This would be based on four principles: (i) increasing mutual understanding and strategic trust; (ii) respecting each other's "core interests and major concerns"; (iii) deepening mutually beneficial cooperation; and (iv) enhancing international cooperation. This became formalized as a "new model of great power relations" at the Obama–Xi summit in Sunnylands, California, in June 2013.

63. Putin's remarks to the Valdai Club, October 25, 2012 (http://eng.kremlin.ru/transcripts/4564).

64. Zevelev, "A New Realism for the 21st Century."

65. Sergei Karaganov, "Mir stanovitsya vse menee prozapadnym" [The World Is Becoming Ever Less Pro-Western], interview with *Rossiiskaya gazeta*, April 23, 2014 (http://www.rg.ru/2014/04/23/karaganov-site.html).

66. Francis Fukuyama, "The End of History?," *The National Interest*, Summer 1989, pp. 3–18.

67. Ken Jowitt, *New World Disorder: The Leninist Extinction* (Berkeley: University of California Press, 1992), p. 264.

68. Ivan Krastev and Mark Leonard employed the term "peaceful disorder" in *The Spectre of a Multipolar Europe*, European Council on Foreign Relations, October 2010 (http://ecfr.3cdn.net/d294639d029f24c751_ilm6y7pbp.pdf).

69. LSE Professor Barry Buzan is especially critical of the indiscriminate use of the term "international community" (conversation with the author).

70. See Steven Pinker, "Violence Vanquished," *Wall Street Journal*, September 24, 2011 (http://www.wsj.com/articles/SB100014240531119041067045765832035894080). This essay summarizes his book, *The Better Angels of Our Nature* (New York: Viking, 2011). See also *Human Security Report 2013* (Vancouver: Simon Fraser University).

71. Jowitt, *New World Disorder*, p. 264.

72. See, for example, Kishore Mahbubani, *The New Asian Hemisphere: The Irresistible Shift of Global Power to the East* (New York: PublicAffairs, 2008).

73. Robert Service, "Putin's Czarist Folly," *New York Times*, April 6, 2014 (http://www.nytimes.com/2014/04/07/opinion/putins-czarist-folly.html?_r=0).

74. Sergei Karaganov, "Lucky Russia," *Russia in Global Affairs*, March 29, 2011 (http://eng.globalaffairs.ru/pubcol/Lucky-Russia-15154).

75. Zbigniew Brzezinski, *The Grand Chessboard: American Strategy and its Geostrategic Imperatives* (New York: Basic Books, 1997), p. 24.

76. Perhaps the clearest definition of soft power today is offered by James Sherr: "the ability to influence the preferences and behaviour of others through affinity or attraction" (*Hard Diplomacy and Soft Coercion*, p. 15).

77. According to a poll from October 2014 conducted by the Democratic Initiatives Foundation in Kyiv, 54 percent of Ukrainians supported EU membership compared with 22 percent who backed Moscow's Customs Union; previously, the numbers had been roughly equal. The same poll found that 44 percent favored Ukrainian membership in NATO, compared with 22 percent supporting nonaligned status, and 15 percent in favor of military alliance with Russia. In March 2012, the respective figures had been 13 percent, 42 percent, and 26 percent. See Chris Dunnett, "Ukrainians' Public Opinions: Pro-Europe, Skeptical of Moscow," Ukraine Crisis media center, October 21, 2014 (http://uacrisis.org/ukrainians-public-opinions-pro-europe-skeptical-moscow/).

78. Poland has decided to acquire national air and missile defense capabilities—Lukasz Kulesa, "Poland and Ballistic Missile Defense: the Limits of Atlanticism," *Proliferations* 14, 2014, Institut Français des Relations Internationales (http://www.ifri.org/en/publications/enotes/proliferation-papers/poland-and-ballistic-missile-defense-

limits-atlanticism). In November 2013, Poland and the Baltic states hosted NATO's biggest military exercises ("Steadfast Jazz") for seven years—Matt Millham, "NATO Wraps up Major Exercise in Poland, Baltics," *Stars and Stripes*, November 12, 2013 (http://www.stripes.com/news/nato-wraps-up-major-exercise-in-poland-baltics-1.252512).

79. Putin's remarks to the Valdai Club, September 19, 2013 (http://eng.kremlin.ru/news/6007).

80. As of June 2014, China held more than US$1.8 trillion in U.S. securities, of which US$1.26 trillion were treasury securities—"Preliminary Report on Portfolio Holdings of U.S. Securities at End-June 2014" (http://www.treasury.gov/ticdata/Publish/shlprelim.html).

81. World Bank, "Poverty Head Count Ratio at $2 a Day (PPP), (% of Population)" (http://data.worldbank.org/indicator/SI.POV.2DAY).

82. As of March 2015, the United States' public debt was $US18.2 trillion.

83. Revealingly, China has not fought a war since 1979 when an attempted incursion in northern Vietnam ended in frustration and a somewhat humiliating retreat.

84. Beijing's declaration in November 2013 of an Air Defense Identification Zone (ADIZ) around the disputed islands led the Japanese and South Koreans to set aside their differences temporarily in the face of a greater anxiety.

85. Joshua Cooper Ramo, *The Age of the Unthinkable: Why the New World Disorder Constantly Surprises Us* (New York: Back Bay Books, 2009), pp. 75–81.

86. "The Views and Opinions of South-Eastern Regions Residents of Ukraine: April 2014," Kyiv International Institute of Sociology. Support for joining Russia was higher in Luhansk (30.3 percent) and Donetsk (27.5 percent) than in other parts of southeast Ukraine, but still significantly less than opposition to the idea (50.9 percent and 52.2 percent, respectively) (http://kiis.com.ua/?lang=eng&cat=reports&id=302&page=1).

87. Oswald Spengler, *The Decline of the West*, abridged version (Oxford University Press, 1991 [1923]).

88. Margaret Macmillan, *Nixon and Mao: The Week that Changed the World* (New York: Random House, 2008).

89. The United States still accounts for around a quarter of global GDP, compared with a peak share of 32 percent in 1985.

90. In 2010 the United States accounted for 49 percent of patents issued by the United States Patent and Trademark Office. Although China's share more than tripled after 2004, it was still under 3 percent six years later—National Center for Science and Engineering Statistics (NCSES), "Science and Engineering Indicators 2012" (http://www.nsf.gov/statistics/seind12/c0/c0s9.htm).

91. This trend is so strong that despite much tougher border controls, the U.S. population continues to grow rapidly. The U.S. Census Bureau estimates that this will increase from 315 million today to 400 million by 2050—"U.S. Census Bureau Projections Show a Slower Growing, Older, More Diverse Nation a Half Century from Now" (http://www.census.gov/newsroom/releases/archives/population/cb12-243.html).

92. Nigerian Central Bank Governor Lamido Sanusi complained that "China takes from us primary goods and sells us manufactured ones. This was also the essence of colonialism." Sun Yun, "China's Increasing Interest in Africa: Benign but Hardly Altruistic," Brookings, April 5, 2013 (http://www.brookings.edu/blogs/up-front/posts/2013/04/05-china-africa-sun). See also Brian Winter and Caroline Stauffer, "Chinese Investors Sour on Brazil, and Projects Melt Away," Reuters, November 1, 2013 (http://www.reuters.com/article/2013/11/01/us-brazil-china-investment-insight-idUSBRE9A004920131101).

93. The China hand Clinton Dines has aptly encapsulated Beijing's desire for status without responsibility: "the Chinese want to sit in the front seat of the car, but they don't want to drive."

94. Comments by Jia Qingguo at the panel on "China's Role in the World: Global Citizen or Mercantile Bully," Lennart Meri Conference, Tallinn, Estonia, May 14, 2011.

95. The phrase "leadership from behind" has been subjected to considerable ridicule. Yet it is underpinned by a certain logic—as "the empowerment of other actors to do your bidding or, as in the case of Libya, to be used as cover for a policy that would be suspect in the eyes of other nations if it's branded as a purely American operation." See Ryan Lizza, "Leading from Behind," *New Yorker*, April 26, 2011 (http://www.new yorker.com/news/news-desk/leading-from-behind).

96. I am indebted to Erik Jones for this insight.

97. Bobo Lo and Lilia Shevtsova, *A 21st Century Myth: Authoritarian Modernization in Russia and China,* Carnegie Moscow Center, 2012 (http://carnegie.ru/publications/?fa=49116).

98. "Russians Back Protests, Political Freedoms," Pew Global Attitudes survey, May 23, 2012 (http://www.pewglobal.org/2012/05/23/russians-back-protests-political-freedoms-and-putin-too/).

99. Dmitri Simes, "How Obama Is Driving Russia and China Together," *National Interest*, June 24, 2014 (http://nationalinterest.org/feature/how-obama-driving-russia-china-together-10735).

100. Nancy Birdsall and Francis Fukuyama, "The Post-Washington Consensus," *Foreign Affairs*, vol. 90, no. 2, March/April 2011, pp. 45–53.

101. The "Sinatra doctrine" was shorthand to describe Gorbachev's decision to allow the Warsaw Pact countries to manage their own affairs. The phrase was first used by MFA spokesman Gennady Gerasimov in October 1989.

102. Sultan Akimbekov, "Needless Rush," *Russia in Global Affairs*, March 21, 2014 (http://eng.globalaffairs.ru/number/Needless-Rush-16499).

103. See Richard N. Haass, "The Age of Nonpolarity," *Foreign Affairs*, May/June 2008; also Ian Bremmer and Nouriel Roubini, "A G-Zero World," *Foreign Affairs*, March/April 2011.

104. Irked by Yanukovych's maneuvering between Moscow and Brussels, Sergei Karaganov complained that Ukraine's elite lacked "any sense of orientation except to suck at two mothers"—"A Lop-Sided Power," *Russia in Global Affairs*, December 26, 2013 (http://eng.globalaffairs.ru/number/A-Lop-Sided-Power-16279).

## Chapter 3

*Epigraphs:* Vladimir Putin, "A Plea for Caution from Russia," *New York Times*, September 11, 2013 (http://www.nytimes.com/2013/09/12/opinion/putin-plea-for-caution-from-russia-on-syria.html?pagewanted=all&_r=0). Daniel Treisman, "Russia as a Global Policy Leader," *Russia in Global Affairs*, June 30, 2013 (http://eng.globalaffairs.ru/number/Russia-as-a-Global-Policy-Leader—16052).

1. "One of the main goals of Russian foreign policy is making the international system fair, democratic, and, ideally, self-regulating—Sergei Lavrov, "Russia in the 21st Century World of Power," *Russia in Global Affairs*, December 27, 2012 (http://eng.globalaffairs.ru/number/Russia-in-the-21st-Century-World-of-Power-15809).

2. This has been the gist of many of the author's conversations with Asian interlocutors over the years.

3. In a 2011 interview with *The Guardian*, Francis Fukuyama described Russia as "hopeless—if they didn't have energy, they'd be a totally inconsequential country." See Stephen Moss, "Francis Fukuyama: 'Americans Are Not Very Good at Nation-Building,'" *The Guardian*, May 23, 2011 (http://www.theguardian.com/books/2011/may/23/francis-fukuyama-americans-not-good-nation-building).

4. 2013 Russian Foreign Policy Concept.

5. See Putin's speech to the Munich Security Conference, February 10, 2007 (http://archive.kremlin.ru/eng/speeches/2007/02/10/0138_type82912type82914type82917type84779_118123.shtml).

6. "In trying to resolve the crisis in southeast Ukraine, the OSCE is playing a very positive role," Putin's remarks to the Valdai Club, October 24, 2014 (http://eng.kremlin.ru/news/23137).

7. Keir Giles, "Putin Celebrates Victory," Chatham House Expert Comment, May 11, 2014 (http://www.chathamhouse.org/expert/comment/14293).

8. Catherine Belton, "Voloshin Trawls for Iraq Deals," *Moscow Times*, February 26, 2003 (http://www.themoscowtimes.com/sitemap/free/2003/2/article/voloshin-trawls-for-iraq-deals/240141.html).

9. 2013 Russian Foreign Policy Concept.

10. Kishore Mahbubani, *The Great Convergence: Asia, the West, and the Logic of One World* (New York: PublicAffairs, 2013), p. 114.

11. The resolution was passed 100 votes for, 11 against, with 58 abstentions. In addition to Russia, those opposing it were North Korea, Belarus, Armenia, Syria, Zimbabwe, Sudan, Cuba, Nicaragua, Venezuela, and Bolivia—see http://www.un.org/en/ga/68/resolutions.shtml.

12. Andrei Tsygankov uses the term "multipolar multilateralism"—"Russia and Global Governance in the Post-Western World," *Russian Analytical Digest* 114, June 4, 2012, pp. 7–9.

13. Dmitri Trenin, "Of Power and Greatness," in Piotr Dutkiewicz and Dmitri Trenin (eds), *Russia: The Challenges of Transformation* (New York University Press, 2011), p. 414.

14. Non-attributable meeting with the Valdai Club, September 2006.

15. Carlo Davis, "Russia Threatened to Nix the Iran Talks: Does It Really Have that Power?," *New Republic*, March 21, 2014 (http://www.newrepublic.com/article/117116/russia-threatens-p51-iran-talks-does-it-really-have-power); also Alireza Noori, "Russia and Iran's Nuclear Dossier in Rouhani's Tenure: the Need for Change," *Iran Review*, July 4, 2013 (http://www.iranreview.org/content/Documents/Russia-and-Iran-s-Nuclear-Dossier-in-Rouhani-s-Tenure-The-Need-for-a-Change.htm).

16. "Concept of Participation of the Russian Federation in BRICS" (http://eng.news.kremlin.ru/media/events/eng/files/41d452b13d9c2624d228.pdf).

17. "Sixth Summit: Fortaleza Declaration and Summit Plan," July 15, 2014 (http://brics6.itamaraty.gov.br/media2/press-releases/214-sixth-brics-summit-fortaleza-declaration).

18. Putin faced withering criticism and even ridicule at the Brisbane G-20 summit—see "Ukraine Crisis: Putin under Pressure at G-20 Summit," BBC News, November 15, 2014 (http://www.bbc.co.uk/news/world-australia-30067612).

19. 2013 Concept of the Participation of the Russian Federation in the BRICS.

20. "Putin Says BRICS Should Focus on Key World Issues," RIA-Novosti, March 22, 2013 (http://en.ria.ru/politics/20130322/180174140/Putin-Says-BRICS-Should-Focus-on-Key-World-Issues.html).

21. Consistent with such image-making, the official theme of the 2011 St. Petersburg International Economic Forum—the Russian government's flagship corporate gathering—was "Emerging Leadership for a New Era," a conference that coincided with the visit of Hu Jintao to Moscow and St. Petersburg.

22. Much has been made of the New Development Bank. However, the funds allocated to it are very modest. Each of the five BRICS is to contribute US$10 billion over the next seven years, although the actual commitments are said to be even less. To put the NDB into perspective, China's *promised* allocation is the same as the sum it lent to SCO member-states in June 2009 to tide them over the global financial crisis.

23. Remarks by Chinese participants at the Stockholm China Forum, August 30, 2014 (author was present).

24. See chapter 2, note 62 (https://www.ncuscr.org/content/video-vice-president-xi-jinping-policy-address).

25. Ashley Tellis, *Opportunities Unbound: Sustaining the Transformation in US-Indian Relations* (Washington: Carnegie Endowment for International Peace, 2013), pp. 4–8 (http://carnegieendowment.org/files/opportunities_unbound.pdf).

26. The political values of modern India are far closer to Western liberal norms than they are to the authoritarianism of Putin's Russia or the monopoly rule of the Chinese Communist Party. Conversely, the Chinese economy is notably more open and liberal than its Indian and Russian counterparts.

27. The origins of the EEU are somewhat unclear. Astana highlights Nazarbaev's suggestion in 1994 for a Eurasian trading bloc, but others trace it back to a 1993 Russian proposal for an Economic Union roughly based on the EU. The initial institutional breakthrough was the signing by Russia, Kazakhstan, and Belarus of a treaty on

the formation of a customs union (January 1995). In October 2000, this led to the creation of the Eurasian Economic Community (EEC), and then the Customs Union in 2010. The Single Economic Space (SES) was established on January 1, 2012, and the Eurasian Economic Commission followed six months later. The EEU in its latest form began life on January 1, 2015. See Rilka Dragneva and Kataryna Wolczuk, "Russia, the Eurasian Customs Union and the EU: Cooperation, Stagnation or Rivalry?," Chatham House Briefing Paper, August 2012.

28. Fyodor Lukyanov, "G8: Does Russia Stand among the Great Nations?," *Russia Beyond the Headlines*, May 17, 2013 (http://rbth.co.uk/opinion/2013/05/17/does_russia_stand_among_the_great_nations_26051.html).

29. The Soviet leadership originally attempted to secure "independent" representation for all fifteen republics of the USSR. In the end, it settled for two—the Ukrainian SSR and Byelorussian SSR.

30. Olga Shumylo-Tapiola, "The Eurasian Customs Union: Friend or Foe of the EU?," Carnegie Endowment for International Peace, October 3, 2012 (http://carnegieendowment.org/2012/10/03/eurasian-customs-union-friend-or-foe-of-eu/dyir#).

31. Julian Cooper describes Moscow's approach as one of "hegemonic bilateralism"—see "Russia's trade relations within the Commonwealth of Independent States," in Elana Wilson Rowe and Stina Torjesen (eds), *The Multilateral Dimension in Russian Foreign Policy* (Abingdon: Routledge, 2012), pp. 179–80.

32. Kazakhstan's contribution to the RRF is the most substantial of the other CSTO member-states. It currently contributes an air assault brigade and a marine forces battalion.

33. The Eurasian Economic Community became defunct following the formal establishment of the EEU on January 1, 2015.

34. The sale of the first 50 percent of Beltransgaz was agreed in principle in 2006, and completed in 2010 at a cost of US$2.5 billion—Andrew Wilson, *Belarus: The Last European Dictatorship* (Yale University Press, 2011), p. 200.

35. See chapter 4.

36. Vladimir Putin, "A New Integration Project for Eurasia: the Future in the Making," *Izvestiya*, October 3, 2011 (http://www.russianmission.eu/en/news/article-prime-minister-vladimir-putin-new-integration-project-eurasia-future-making-izvestia-3-). It is worth noting that Ukraine was central to Putin's earlier (2003) project of a Single Economic Space.

37. "Considering the completion of the active military stage of the antiterrorist operation in Afghanistan, the member states of the Shanghai Cooperation Organization consider it necessary that respective members of the antiterrorist coalition set a final timeline for their temporary use of [ground infrastructure] and stay of their military contingents on the territories of the SCO member states"—Declaration of Heads of Member States of SCO, Astana, July 5, 2005 (http://www.chinadaily.com.cn/china/2006-06/12/content_6020345.htm).

38. Most notoriously, the Dushanbe SCO summit in August 2008 refused to support Russia in recognizing Abkhazia and South Ossetia as independent states.

39. Both countries are set to become full members of the 2015 SCO summit in Ufa, Russia.

40. Zhao Huasheng, "China-Russia Relations in Central Asia," ASAN Forum, November 22, 2013 (http://www.theasanforum.org/china-russia-relations-in-central-asia/).

41. The Russian government has moved to reduce its exposure; the current figure is the lowest since 2008. In October 2013, Russian holdings of U.S. treasury securities stood as high as US$150 billion (http://www.treasury.gov/ticdata/Publish/mfh.txt). Although the sharp deterioration in relations with Washington has been a major factor behind the sell-off, the main reason is the need to access ready cash in order to fund essential programs at home—Howard Amos, "Russia Dumps $22 Billion in U.S. Bonds to Slow Economy's Slide," *Moscow Times*, February 19, 2015 (http://www.themoscowtimes.com/business/article/russia-dumps-22-billion-in-us-bonds-to-slow-economys-slide/516265.html).

42. Comments by Minister of the Economy Alexei Ulyukayev—see Stepan Kravchenko and Scott Rose, "Russia Forecasts Losing Ground in Global Economy by 2030," Bloomberg News, November 7, 2013 (http://www.bloomberg.com/news/2013-11-07/russia-forecasts-losing-ground-in-global-economy-by-2030.html).

43. Russia's performance as the G-20 chair in 2013 was widely derided. Although it had some excellent experts at the working level, the absence of high-level political interest in financial reform was a more telling factor. Revealingly, throughout its membership in the G-8 (1998–2014), Russia remained excluded from the grouping's financial discussions.

44. See, for example, Putin's remarks to the Valdai Club, September 19, 2013 (http://eng.kremlin.ru/news/6007).

45. Dmitry Medvedev, speech at the St. Petersburg International Economic Forum, June 18, 2010 (http://eng.kremlin.ru/transcripts/456). For an excellent summary of the difficulties in realizing such a vision, see Dmitry Abramov, Stanislav Polezhaev, and Mikhail Sherstnev, "Moscow as International Financial Center: Ideas, Plans and Perspectives," *Journal of Eurasian Studies* (Hanyang), vol. 2, 2011, pp. 144–52 (http://www.sciencedirect.com/science/article/pii/S1879366511000121).

46. The most obvious recent example was the 2008 Georgia war.

47. Richard Connolly and Philip Hanson, "Russia's Accession to the World Trade Organization: Commitments, Processes, and Prospects," *Eurasian Geography and Economics*, vol. 53, no. 4, 2012, pp. 488–89. Compared to Russia's hard road to accession, countries such as Kyrgyzstan were shoehorned into the WTO in order to encourage democracy and capitalism there.

48. Alexei Portansky, "Russia's Accession to the WTO: External Implications," *Russia in Global Affairs*, June 22, 2011 (http://eng.globalaffairs.ru/number/Russias-Accession-to-the-WTO-External-Implications-15239). Although Moscow reversed its

position in October 2009, the initial action resulted in a severe loss of negotiating momentum.

49. Andrew Kramer, "In Outburst, Putin Says WTO Rules Don't Apply," *New York Times*, April 8, 2011 (http://www.nytimes.com/2011/04/09/business/global/09wto.html?_r=1&).

50. Connolly and Hanson, "Russia's Accession to the World Trade Organization," p. 496; Gleb Bryanski, "Putin Says Russia's Economy to Suffer from WTO Entry," Reuters, November 21, 2012 (http://www.reuters.com/article/2012/11/21/us-russia-putin-wto-idUSBRE8AK14W20121121).

51. In 2012 Peter Rutland identified the Communists and nationalists in particular, but also significant elements in the Just Russia (Spravedlivaya Rossiya) and majority United Russia (Edinaya Rossiya) parties—"Journey's End: Russia Joins the WTO," *Russian Analytical Digest* 111, April 2, 2012, p. 4.

52. Such estimates were, however, conditional on significant improvements in Russia's business climate (Connolly and Hanson, "Russia's Accession to the World Trade Organization," p. 492).

53. According to Nikolai Petrov, "managed democracy" was characterized by a strong presidency, weak institutions, state control of the media and of the elections process, and "visible short-term effectiveness and long-term inefficiency"—"The Essence of Putin's Managed Democracy," summary of meeting at the Carnegie Moscow Center, October 18, 2005 (http://carnegieendowment.org/2005/10/18/essence-of-putin-s-managed-democracy/2a3).

54. Clifford Gaddy, "Russia and the World Trade Organization: Not the End but the Beginning," *Brookings Up Front*, December 16, 2011 (http://www.brookings.edu/blogs/up-front/posts/2011/12/16-russia-wto-gaddy).

55. At the 2013 Gaidar Forum, former WTO director-general Pascal Lamy insisted that Russia could not pick and choose which WTO obligations it wanted to implement—Ivan Tchakarov, "Gaidar Forum Highlights the Problem with Russia," *Business New Europe*, January 18, 2013 (http://www.bne.eu/story4424/COMMENT_Gaidar_Forum_highlights_the_problem_with_Russia). See also Joshua Chaffin, "Europe Cools on Russia's WTO Accession," *Financial Times*, December 5, 2012, available online by subscription (http://www.ft.com/cms/s/0/ff524424-3eff-11e2-9214-00144feabdc0.html#axzz2qJVjN4kW).

56. Alexei Portansky, "WTO Membership—Easier Said than Done," *Russia in Global Affairs*, March 21, 2014 (http://eng.globalaffairs.ru/number/WTO-Membership—Easier-Said-Than-Done-16505); "You Can Forget Russia as a Democracy," interview with Vladislav Inozemtsev, *Spiegel Online*, November 21, 2012 (http://www.spiegel.de/international/world/important-medvedev-advisor-warns-russia-will-not-progress-under-putin-a-868562.html).

57. "Embracing Isolationism: Russia's New Protectionism," *Global Counsel Insight*, November 6, 2014 (http://www.global-counsel.co.uk/system/files/publications/Global_Counsel_Embracing%20isolation_Russias_new_protectionism.pdf); Richard

Connolly, "Economic Modernization in Russia: the Role of the World Trade Organization," *European Politics and Society*, vol. 16, no. 1, 2015, p. 41.

58. Tom Miles, "Russian Memo to WTO says U.S. Sanctions Are Illegal," Reuters, April 24, 2014 (http://www.reuters.com/article/2014/04/24/us-ukraine-crisis-russia-wto-idUSBREA3N0QS20140424).

59. Although Moscow claims that the rules and practices of the EEU are WTO-compatible, there is compelling evidence that it is severely restricting Central Asian imports of Chinese goods—see Nargis Kassenova, Alexander Libman, and Jeremy Smith, "Discussing the Eurasian Customs Union and Its Impact on Central Asia," *Central Asia Policy Forum* 4, February 2013 (http://037eabf.netsolhost.com/wordpress/wp-content/uploads/2013/10/Policy_Forum_4_February_2013.pdf).

60. The term "energy security" can mean very different things. For the customer it means security of supply, but for a major energy supplier such as Russia it is about security of demand.

61. John Lough, "Russia's Energy Diplomacy," Chatham House Briefing Paper, May 2011, p. 15.

62. Ibid., pp. 2–3.

63. "European Union: Trade with Russia," August 27, 2014 (http://trade.ec.europa.eu/doclib/ docs/2006/september/tradoc_113440.pdf); Observatory of Economic Complexity data regarding "Products that Russia Exports to China (2012)" (http://atlas.media. mit.edu/explore/tree_map/sitc/export/rus/chn/ show/2012/) (both accessed February 4, 2015).

64. Clifford Gaddy and Barry Ickes emphasize the crucial role of the energy sector in sustaining systemic inefficiencies throughout the economy—"Caught in the Bear Trap," Legatum Institute, November 2013, p. 13.

65. Under a take-or-pay arrangement, the customer is obliged to pay for the full contracted amount of gas regardless of whether it is needed or used.

66. Paul Stevens, "The 'Shale Gas Revolution': Developments and Changes," Chatham House Briefing Paper, August 2012, p. 10.

67. The Third Energy Package hits hardest at vertically integrated companies, such as Gazprom.

68. Moscow's moves against Nabucco included tying up gas at source (in Azerbaijan and Turkmenistan), discrediting the project's viability among potential customers (Turkey and southern Europe), and developing its own spoiling project in the form of South Stream.

69. The Nordstream project links Russia directly to Germany via the Baltic Sea. Unlike South Stream, it has an undoubted commercial and geoeconomic logic, above all because it reduces Russia's dependence on transit states such as Ukraine.

70. Tatyana Mitrova (head, Energy Research Institute, Russian Academy of Sciences) notes that Gazprom reviewed 58 supply contracts with 39 clients during 2009–14.

71. Catherine Belton, Alex Barker, and Joshua Chaffin, "Kremlin Shields Gazprom from EU Probe," *Financial Times*, September 11, 2012, available online by subscription (http://www.ft.com/cms/s/0/fcdbe0e4-fc31-11e1-ac0f-00144feabdc0.html#axzz2qJVjN4kW).

72. "American Shale Gas Project Is a Bubble about to Burst—Gazprom CEO," RT, March 30, 2013 (http://rt.com/business/shale-gas-gazprom-us-088/). More recently, Igor Sechin has suggested that shale could go the way of the dotcom collapse—"US Shale Oil Boom Could Become Next 'Dotcom Bubble,' Says Russian Oil Boss," *The Guardian*, February 10, 2015 (http://www.theguardian.com/business/2015/feb/10/us-shale-oil-next-dotcom-bubble-russia-rosneft-igor-sechin-opec).

73. Sergey Pravosudov, "Lack of Russian Gas Strangles China," Gazprom website, June 19, 2013 (http://www.gazprom.com/press/reports/2013/china-suffocates/). Gazprom is strongly suspected of funding anti-fracking protests in Europe—see James Burgess, "Gazprom Funds Anti-fracking Campaigns in Europe?," *Oil Price*, October 1, 2012 (http://oilprice.com/Latest-Energy-News/World-News/Gazprom-Funds-Anti-Fracking-Campaigns-in-Europe.html).

74. Press conference at the summit of the Gas Exporting Countries Forum (GECF), July 1, 2013 (http://eng.kremlin.ru/transcripts/5666).

75. Vadim Koptelov, "Russia and Norway in the Arctic," Russian International Affairs Council, May 28, 2012 (http://russiancouncil.ru/en/inner/?id_4=436#top).

76. Paragraph 10 of the 2009 National Security Strategy lists terrorism, WMD proliferation, the "global information struggle," nationalism and xenophobia, demography, the environment, "uncontrolled and illegal migration," human and narcotics trafficking, and pandemics—"National Security Strategy of the Russian Federation to 2020" (http://rustrans.wikidot.com/russia-s-national-security-strategy-to-2020).

77. The notion of the "three evils" (terrorism, separatism, extremism) is ever present in Sino-Russian and SCO statements.

78. Katia Moskvitch, "Climate Change Summit Leaves Russia Cold," BBC News, December 16, 2009 (http://news.bbc.co.uk/1/hi/8415166.stm).

79. Anna Korppoo, Jacqueline Karas, and Michael Grubb (eds), *Russia and the Kyoto Protocol: Opportunities and Challenges* (London: Chatham House, 2006).

80. Nina Tynkkynen notes that "the main obstacle to greater Russian commitment to climate policy actions is that the damage caused to the country is not understood at all in Russia. Accordingly, Russia has not initiated any adaptation plans or policies"—"Russia and Global Climate Governance," *Russie.Nei.Visions* 80, September 2014, p. 16.

81. Dmitry Medvedev, speech at the Copenhagen Climate Change Conference, December 18, 2009 (http://archive.kremlin.ru/eng/speeches/2009/12/18/1840_type 82912type82914_223431.shtml). Russia's target was a modest concession, both because it was contingent on other countries making similar commitments and because in 2007 (that is, before the financial crisis) Russia emitted 32 percent fewer greenhouse gases than before the fall of the Soviet Union—Igor Istomin, "Nothing

New on the Climate Front?," *Russia in Global Affairs*, December 25, 2010 (http://eng.globalaffairs.ru/ number/Nothing-New-on-the-Climate-Front-15083).

82. Consistent with its emphasis on gas as clean energy, the Russian government has also committed itself to reducing the flaring of excess gas—see Gleb Bryanski and Vladimir Soldatkin, "Putin Warns Oil Firms: Cut Flaring or Pay Fines," Reuters, November 10, 2009 (http://www.reuters.com/article/2009/11/10/us-russia-oil-gas-idUSTRE5A94VD20091110).

83. See Andrei Tsygankov, "Russia's Afghanistan Debate: Managing Fear of and in the West," *Problems of Post-Communism*, vol. 60, no. 6, November/December 2013, pp. 29–41.

84. Vitaly Naumkin, "Russia Focuses on Eliminating Middle East Terrorist Threat," *Russia in Global Affairs*, September 9, 2014 (http://eng.globalaffairs.ru/book/Russia-focuses-on-eliminating-Middle-East-terrorist-threat-16953).

85. Ivan Safranchuk, "Afghanistan in Search of Balance," *Russia in Global Affairs*, October 7, 2012 (http://eng.globalaffairs.ru/number/Afghanistan-in-Search-of-Balance-15691).

86. Glenn Kates, "Conspiracies, West-bashing, and Sympathy—Russia Reacts to Charlie Hebdo Attack," Radio Free Europe/Radio Liberty, January 9, 2015 (http://www.rferl.org/content/charlie-hebdo-russia-reaction-terrorism-violence/26785081.html); also Neil MacFarquhar, "Conspiracy Theories Mix with Official Condolences," *New York Times*, January 12, 2015, available online by subscription (http://www.nytimes.com/2015/01/13/world/europe/conspiracy-theories-mix-with-official-condolences.html?_r=0).

87. In 2004 in response to a question from the author, then defense minister Sergei Ivanov claimed that the real threat posed by Iran was not nuclear, but ballistic, specifically the potential for intermediate-range missiles to hit targets in the Don and Volga basins (meeting with the Valdai Club, September 2004).

88. "Lavrov: No Need for European Missile Defense Shield if Iran Deal a Success," RT, November 25, 2013 (http://rt.com/news/lavrov-missile-shield-iran-265/).

89. Richard Weitz describes this aptly as "leverage maximization"—"Russia and Iran: a Balancing Act," *The Diplomat*, November 21, 2013 (http://thediplomat.com/2013/11/russia-and-iran-a-balancing-act/). Interestingly, Iranian President Hassan Rouhani has in the past accused Russia and China of exploiting their ties with Tehran for leverage vis-à-vis the United States—see M.K. Bhadrakumar, "Foreign Policy Priorities of Iran's Rouhani," Valdai website, June 18, 2013 (http://valdaiclub.com/asia/59320.html).

90. Marie Mendras, in "Talking Point: the Logic of Russian Foreign Policy," Open Democracy debate with Fyodor Lukyanov, December 13, 2012 (http://www.open-democracy.net/od-russia/oliver-carroll-fyodor-lukyanov-marie-mendras/talking-point-logic-of-russian-foreign-policy).

91. Author's conversations with American officials and analysts.

92. Jason Lyall, "Farewell, Manas!," *Washington Post*, October 22, 2013 (http://www.washingtonpost.com/blogs/monkey-cage/wp/2013/10/22/farewell-manas/).

93. "Russia Attacks NATO Afghanistan Withdrawal Plan," *The Guardian*, April 19, 2012 (http://www.theguardian.com/world/2012/apr/19/russia-criticises-nato-afghanistan-withdrawal).

94. Chris Rickleton, "Central Asia: Cold-War Attitudes Hindering Drug War," Eurasianet, February 6, 2013 (http://www.eurasianet.org/node/66513).

95. The Magnitsky Act of December 2012 listed Russian officials suspected of the ill-treatment and death of the lawyer Sergei Magnitsky, put them on a U.S. entry blacklist, and outlined measures to freeze their assets—see chapter 6.

96. Treisman, "Russia as a Global Policy Leader."

97. Igor Ivanov, "What Diplomacy Does Russia Need in the 21st Century?," *Russia in Global Affairs*, December 29, 2011 (http://eng.globalaffairs.ru/number/What-Diplomacy-Does-Russia-Need-in-the-21st-Century-15420).

98. Under UN Security Council Resolution 1674 of April 28, 2006, "The Protection of Civilians in Armed Conflict" (http://www.un.org/en/ga/search/view_doc.asp?symbol=S/RES/1674%282006%29).

99. Kenneth Rapoza, "Russia's Medvedev says Gadaffi [*sic*] Must Go," Forbes, May 27, 2011 (http://www.forbes.com/sites/kenrapoza/2011/05/27/russias-medvedev-says-gadaffi-must-go/).

100. Roy Allison, *Russia, the West, and Military Intervention* (Oxford University Press, 2013), pp. 194–95.

101. Mikhail Margelov, "Russia's vision for the Middle East and North Africa," Chatham House, London, December 10, 2013 (http://www.chathamhouse.org/sites/files/chathamhouse/home/chatham/public_html/sites/default/files/101213Russia.pdf).

102. Ibid., pp. 6–7.

103. Vladimir Putin, "Russia and the Changing World," *Moskovskie novosti*, February 27, 2012 (http://valdaiclub.com/politics/39300.html).

104. Saudi Arabia, moreover, stands accused of aiding IS—see Josh Rogin, "America's Allies Are Funding ISIS," *The Daily Beast*, June 6, 2014 (http://www.thedailybeast.com/articles/2014/06/14/america-s-allies-are-funding-isis.html).

105. See, for example, Simon Shuster, "Russian Realpolitik: Inside the Arms Trade with Syria," *Time*, July 1, 2012 (http://world.time.com/2012/07/01/russian-realpolitik-inside-the-arms-trade-with-syria/).

106. Putin's remarks to the Valdai Club, September 19, 2013 (http://eng.kremlin.ru/news/6007).

107. "Kiev is the mother of the Russian cities, Russian language, Russian religion . . . we do not consider ourselves foreigners . . . we have been one nation for more than 300 years, even before that. The Slavs brought their religion there more than 1,000 years ago"—Sergei Lavrov interview with Bloomberg TV, May 14, 2014 (http://www.mid.ru/bdomp/brp_4.nsf/e78a48070f128a7b43256999005bcbb3/fc216870be040e3c44257cd900491440!OpenDocument).

108. Germany abstained on UNSCR 1973 over Libya, and at the 2013 G-20 summit in St. Petersburg refused to sign a U.S.-drafted declaration blaming Assad for the chemical weapons attack at Ghouta—Ian Traynor, "Merkel Sides with Unlikely Allies

over Syria," *The Guardian*, September 9, 2013 (http://www.theguardian.com/world/german-elections-blog-2013/2013/sep/09/merkel-unlikely-allies-syria).

109. Moscow supported the appointment of former secretary-general Kofi Annan as UN special envoy on Syria, although it did little to ease his hugely unenviable task—see Rick Gladstone, "Resigning as Envoy to Syria, Annan Casts Wide Blame," *New York Times*, August 2, 2012 (http://www.nytimes.com/2012/08/03/world/middleeast/annan-resigns-as-syria-peace-envoy.html?pagewanted=all); also Vladimir Solntsev, "Missiya Annana nevypolnima?" [The Annan Mission Unfulfilled?], *Vek*, August 3, 2012 (http://wek.ru/missiya-annana-nevypolnima).

110. Operation Enduring Freedom has already lasted longer than the Soviet occupation of Afghanistan (1979–89). Meanwhile, more than a decade after the overthrow of Saddam Hussein Iraq remains a violent, politically dysfunctional, and ethnically and religiously divided country.

111. Thomas Friedman, *The World Is Flat: A Brief History of the Globalized World in the Twenty-First Century* (London: Penguin, 2006).

112. Treisman, "Russia as a Global Policy Leader."

## Chapter 4

*Epigraph*: *Three Kingdoms: A Historical Novel*, attributed to Luo Guanzhong (Beijing: Foreign Languages Press/University of California Press, 2003 [fourteenth century CE]), p. 5.

1. One of the more difficult challenges in discussing the issues in this chapter is that of terminology. "Near Abroad" (*blizhnee zarubezhe*) and "Post-Soviet space" (*post-sovetskoe prostrantsvo*) are Russia-centric and proprietorial in tone, and are consequently disliked by many of the ex-Soviet republics. But satisfactory alternatives are hard to find. "Commonwealth of Independent States" (CIS) is a dated term, and in any case often refers to the institution of the CIS. "Newly Independent States" (NIS) is meaningless, since these states have been independent for more than two decades. Finally, Eurasia (*Evraziya*) is confusing, since it can either refer to the Eurasian continent from Lisbon to Vladivostok, or *post-Soviet* Eurasia—in which case we are back to the problem of Sovietism.

2. President Medvedev's interview with Russian TV channels on August 31, 2008. He defined "regions in which Russia has privileged interests" as "home to countries with which we share special historical relations and are bound together as friends and good neighbors" (http://archive.kremlin.ru/eng/speeches/2008/08/31/1850_type82912type82916_206003.shtml).

3. Vladimir Putin, "Russia and the Changing World," *Moskovskie novosti*, February 27, 2012 (http://valdaiclub.com/politics/39300.html).

4. Adam Michnik, "Putin Is Trying to Reconstruct the Russian Empire," *New Republic*, July 21, 2014 (http://www.newrepublic.com/article/118790/after-malaysia-flight-17-we-should-call-putin-shameless-thug); "Russia and Ukraine: the Home

Front," *The Economist*, March 15, 2014 (http://www.economist.com/news/europe/21599061-kremlins-belligerence-ukraine-will-ultimately-weaken-russia-home-front).

5. Dmitri Trenin, "Of Power and Greatness," in Piotr Dutkiewicz and Dmitri Trenin (eds), *Russia: The Challenges of Transformation* (New York University Press, 2011), p. 410.

6. Dmitri Trenin, *Post-Imperium* (Washington: Carnegie Endowment for International Peace, 2011); see also Fyodor Lukyanov, "Kremlin's Imperial Ambitions Ended in 2010," *Moscow Times*, December 23, 2010 (http://www.themoscowtimes.com/opinion/article/kremlins-imperial-ambitions-ended-in-2010/427658.html).

7. Ross Terrill, *The New Chinese Empire—and What It Means for the United States* (New York: Basic Books, 2003), p. 3.

8. James Sherr notes that recent versions of Russia's Military Doctrine reflect "the revival of the view of states as sovereign 'spatial-geographical phenomena' engaged in a struggle to dominate 'space'"—*Hard Diplomacy and Soft Coercion: Russia's Influence Abroad* (London: Chatham House, 2013), p. 12.

9. In recent years Moscow has pressured the Baltic states in various ways, including through cyberattacks, energy cutoffs, import bans, allegations over the mistreatment of Russian-speaking minorities, and harassment of diplomats serving in Moscow.

10. "Vneshnyaya politika Rossii i novoe kachestvo geopoliticheskoi situatsii" [Russian Foreign Policy and a Qualitatively New Geopolitical Situation], *Diplomatic Yearbook of the Russian Foreign Ministry of Foreign Affairs*, December 15, 2008 (http://www.mid.ru/bdomp/brp_4.nsf/2fee282eb6df40e643256999005e6e8c/80f92fa1b96d767ec3257520002dd4ae!OpenDocument).

11. Putin's Speech to the Federal Assembly of the Russian Federation, April 25, 2005 (http://archive.kremlin.ru/appears/2005/04/25/1223_type 63372type63374 type82634_87049.shtml).

12. Russkii Mir ("Russian world") was established in June 2007 to promote Russian language and culture (http://www.russkiymir.ru/fund/). James Sherr notes that the Kremlin's cultural policy challenges the integrity and authenticity of other national cultures of the former Soviet Union—*Hard Diplomacy and Soft Coercion*, pp. 111–12.

13. "Russia's ideology in the 21st century should be liberal capitalism with the aim of creating a liberal empire"—"Anatoly Chubais: Russia Should Aim to Create a Liberal Empire in CIS," Pravda.ru, September 25, 2003 (http://english.pravda.ru/news/russia/25-09-2003/52757-0/).

14. Chubais has reportedly backtracked on the idea of a "liberal empire," claiming that it was essentially a slogan to persuade Yeltsin to pursue market rather than statist solutions to Russia's economic problems—author's correspondence with a confidential source, June 2013. In his original remarks Chubais spoke about a "ring of great democracies in the 21st century, including the U.S., a united Europe, Japan and Rus-

sia at the centre of a liberal empire" (http://english.pravda.ru/news/russia/25-09-2003/52757-0/).

15. That said, Moscow has invested several billion dollars in propping up break-away regions, such as Abkhazia, South Ossetia, and Transnsistria—William Schreiber, "The Hidden Costs of a Russian Statelet in Ukraine," *The Atlantic*, March 4, 2014 (http://www.theatlantic.com/international/archive/2014/03/the-hidden-costs-of-a-russian-statelet-in-ukraine/284197/).

16. Jeffrey Mankoff, *Russian Foreign Policy: The Return of Great Power Politics*, 2d ed. (Lanham, Md.: Rowman and Littlefield, 2012), p. 6.

17. Comments at a seminar in Australia in 2014.

18. For example, Trenin, *Post-Imperium*.

19. In 1997 Russia concluded landmark agreements extending the Black Sea fleet's lease in Sevastopol by twenty years and recognizing Ukraine's territorial integrity, including Crimea.

20. Yeltsin made only one official visit to Central Asia, which was curtailed because of illness—"Yeltsin Rests after Cutting Short Central Asian Tour," BBC News, October 13, 1998 (http://news.bbc.co.uk/1/hi/world/europe/192407.stm).

21. Under the Pereyaslav agreement of 1654, the Zaporozhian Cossacks submitted Ukraine to the rule of Muscovy. Soviet leaders such as Nikita Khrushchev and Leonid Brezhnev regarded themselves as both Ukrainian and Russian. Even Yeltsin, the execu-tor of the demise of the USSR, stated that "without Ukraine, it is impossible to imag-ine Russia"—*Midnight Diaries* (London: Phoenix, 2000), p. 243.

22. Putin's remarks to the Valdai Club, September 19, 2013 (http://eng.krem-lin.ru/ news/6007).

23. In 2014 Ukraine's direct imports of Russian gas fell 40 percent to 14.5 billion cubic meters—Elena Mazneva, "Russian 2014 Gas Export Seen Lowest in Decade as Demand Falls," Bloomberg, January 13, 2015 (http://www.bloomberg.com/news/articles/2015-01-13/russia-2014-gas-exports-seen-lowest-in-decade-as-nations-cut-use).

24. These steps included tight restrictions on the activities of "political" non-governmental organizations, that is, those promoting democracy and the rule of law; the creation of Nashi to foster pro-regime sentiment; and further controls on the mainstream electronic media.

25. The same was true of the Orange Revolution. Putin actively campaigned on behalf of Yanukovych in the 2004 presidential elections, visiting Kyiv on numerous occasions, so Yushchenko's victory was an especially bitter blow.

26. Sergei Goryachko, "Vladimira Putina priznali nezameninym: Rossiyane gotovy vybrat ego prezidentom v chetverty raz" [Vladimir Putin Recognized as Irreplaceable: Russians Ready to Elect Him President for a Fourth Time], *Kommersant.ru*, May 15, 2014 (http://www.kommersant.ru/doc/2470499).

27. Clifford Gaddy and Barry Ickes, "Ukraine: a Prize Neither Russia nor the West Can Afford to Win," Brookings, May 22, 2014 (http://www.brookings.edu/research/articles/2014/05/21-ukraine-prize-russia-west-ukraine-gaddy-ickes).

28. See chapter 2, note 77 (http://uacrisis.org/ukrainians-public-opinions-pro-europe-skeptical-moscow/).

29. "Khoteli kak luchshe, a poluchilos kak vsegda."

30. Alexander Bogomolov and Oleksandr Lytvynenko, "A Ghost in the Mirror: Russian Soft Power in Ukraine," Chatham House Briefing Paper, January 2012, pp. 6, 9.

31. John Besemeres, "Ukraine: Time to Cut a Deal?," *Inside Story*, May 30, 2014 (http://inside.org.au/ukraine-time-to-cut-a-deal/).

32. PfP is a defense cooperation program between NATO and individual Euro-Atlantic countries. Its activities vary depending on the country's needs, but typically cover defense reform, defense policy and planning, and civil–military relations. Aside from the three Baltic states, which are full members of NATO, all 12 of the ex-Soviet republics, including Russia, have participated in the PfP, although their commitment to it differs hugely.

33. "NATO's Relations with Ukraine," December 16, 2014 (http://www.nato.int/cps/en/natolive/topics_37750.htm?selectedLocale=en).

34. Smitta Purushottam, "Ukraine's Flirtation with China and Russia's Quest for a Eurasian Union," IDSA Issues Brief, November 4, 2011, pp. 5–6; also Stephen Blank, "Why China Courts Eastern Europe," *The Diplomat*, February 25, 2012 (http://thediplomat.com/2012/02/why-china-courts-eastern-europe/).

35. Oleksandr Okhrymenko, "Ukraine Opens New Era in Relations with China," *EurActiv*, December 11, 2013 (http://www.euractiv.com/europes-east/ukraine-opens-new-era-relations-analysis-532288/).

36. See Slawomir Matuszak, *The Oligarchic Democracy: The Influence of Business Groups on Ukrainian Politics*, OSW Studies 42, September 2012, Center for Eastern Studies, Warsaw.

37. "Ukraine to Slash 2013 Gas Imports from Russia," RIA-Novosti, November 16, 2012 (ttp://en.ria.ru/news/20121116/177515276.html).

38. There were reports in 2013 of the Kremlin backing its own man, Viktor Medvedchuk, for the 2015 Ukrainian presidential elections (Yevhen Solonyna, "Russia's Plan for Ukraine: Purported Leaked Strategy Document Raises Alarm," Radio Free Europe/Radio Liberty, August 20, 2013 (http://www.rferl.org/content/russia-ukraine-leaked-strategy-document/25081053.html). This was a long shot, given Medvedchuk's very low popularity (1 percent), the complications in promoting a "fifth column" figure, and the risk—subsequently proven—that Yanukovych's ouster could open the way to a more liberal and pro-European administration. That said, the Kremlin sees Medvedchuk as useful in the post-Maidan Ukraine: as a figurehead for various Cossack and Slavic-Orthodox groups, and as a "mediator" in the OSCE-brokered Trilateral Contact Group on Ukraine. See Vladimir Socor, "The Contact Group in Ukraine Weighted toward Russia," *Eurasia Daily Monitor*, vol. 11, no. 131, July 18, 2014 (http://www.jamestown.org/single/?tx_ttnews[tt_news]=42645&no_cache=1#.VGX WAMl0V-0).

39. The Kremlin started doing this just before Yanukovych was toppled, indicating the extent of its concern over his failure to suppress the Maidan movement. See "Sergei Glazyev, 'Federalization—Not an Idea, but a Clear Need,'" interview in *Business New Europe*, February 6, 2014 (http://newseurope.me/2014/02/06/sergei-glazyev-federalization-idea-clear-need/). The term "federalization" has gone in and out of fashion, sometimes being superseded by labels such as "decentralization." The meaning, however, remains the same—devolution of decisionmaking powers from Kyiv to the eastern regions under the Kremlin's control.

40. See chapter 2, note 86.

41. "The War Next Door: Can Merkel's Diplomacy Save Europe?," *Spiegel Online*, February 14, 2005 (http://www.spiegel.de/international/europe/minsk-deal-represents-and-fragile-opportunity-for-peace-in-ukraine-a-1018326.html); Keir Giles, "Putin Celebrates Victory," Chatham House Expert Comment, May 11, 2014 (http://www.chathamhouse.org/expert/comment/14293).

42. "Ukraine Troops Retreat from Key Town of Debaltseve," BBC News, February 18, 2005 (http://www.bbc.co.uk/news/world-europe-31519000); Shaun Walker and Oksana Grytsenko, "Ukraine Forces Admit Loss of Donetsk Airport to Rebels," *The Guardian*, January 21, 2015 (http://www.theguardian.com/world/2015/jan/21/russia-ukraine-war-fighting-east).

43. "Presidential Administration Chief Describes Ukrainian Developments as 'Genocide,'" ITAR-TASS, June 19, 2014 (http://itar-tass.com/en/old-russia/736809). In a similar vein, Putin has subsequently claimed that Kyiv's cutting of gas supply to the Donetsk region "sounds like genocide," February 25, 2015 (http://eng.kremlin.ru/transcripts/23648).

44. Potential scenarios include the annexation of Luhansk and Donetsk; implementation of the Novorossiya project, which would see the takeover of the whole Black Sea coastline from Donetsk to Transnistria; absorption of the major eastern Ukrainian cities of Kharkiv (only 40 km from the Russian border) and Dnepropetrovsk; and even the occupation of the whole of Ukraine east of the Dnieper, resulting in its partition between a European west and Russian east. If this last scenario came to pass, it would recall the various partitions of Poland in the second half of the eighteenth century, in which Catherine the Great was a principal player.

45. Zbigniew Brzezinski, *The Grand Chessboard: American Primacy and its Geostrategic Imperatives* (New York: Basic Books, 1997).

46. "Putin prigrozil Kievu 'zashchitnymi merami' v sluchae torgovogo partnerstvo s ES" [Putin Threatens Kiev with "Defensive Measures" if There Is a Trade Partnership between Ukraine and the EU], NEWSru.com, August 22, 2013 (http://www.newsru.com/finance/22aug2013/ukr_print.html).

47. Roger McDermott, "Karimov-Nazarbayev Summit Signals Shift in Central Asian Security," *Eurasia Daily Monitor*, June 18, 2013 (http://www.jamestown.org/programs/edm/single/?tx_ttnews[tt_news]=41034&tx_ttnews[backPid]=685&no_cache=1#.VSgiwpPAr9o).

48. After 9/11, for example, Nazarbaev simultaneously kept Moscow happy by not hosting a U.S. base in Kazakhstan, and Washington onside by facilitating the transit of U.S. forces and matériel into Afghanistan.

49. "European Union: Trade with Kazakhstan," August 27, 2014 (http://trade.ec.europa.eu/doclib/docs/2006/september/tradoc_113406.pdf).

50. Valikhan Tuleshov, "Kazakhstan Will Play Key Role in Russia's Foreign Policy," Valdai website, June 13, 2012 (http://valdaiclub.com/near_abroad/44361.html).

51. Nazarbaev will be seventy-five on July 6, 2015.

52. Tuleshov, "Kazakhstan Will Play Key Role in Russia's Foreign Policy"; see also Sultan Akimbekov, "Needless Rush: Another Look at Eurasian Integration," *Russia in Global Affairs*, March 21, 2014 (http://eng.globalaffairs.ru/number/Needless-Rush-16499).

53. Other areas include health, education, science, culture, and legal issues—see Kazakhstan Ministry of Foreign Affairs, *Astana Calling*, no. 336, January 10, 2014, p. 4.

54. European Union External Action Fact Sheet, "EU-Kazakhstan Enhanced Partnership and Cooperation Agreement," October 9, 2014 (http://www.eeas.euro–a.eu/statements/docs/2014/141009_01_en.pdf).

55. "President Vladimir Putin of Russia on Kazakhstan and Its Future," *Tengri News*, August 30, 2014 (http://en.tengrinews.kz/politics_sub/President-Vladimir-Putin-of-Russia-on-Kazakhstan-and-its-future-255793/); see also "Kazakhstan May Leave EEU if Its Interests Are Infringed: Nazarbayev," *Tengri News*, August 27, 2014 (http://en.tengrinews.kz/politics_sub/Kazakhstan-may-leave-EEU-if-its-interests-are-infringed-Nazarbayev-255722/).

56. James Marson, "Putin to the West: Hands Off Ukraine," *Time*, May 25, 2009 (http://content.time.com/time/world/article/0,8599,1900838,00.html).

57. Moscow has already acted to prevent Kazakhstan (and Belarus) from taking advantage of its counter-embargo on agricultural imports from the EU—Dosym Satpaev, "Kazakhstan and the Eurasian Economic Union: the View from Astana," European Council on Foreign Relations, January 12 , 2015 (http://www.ecfr.eu/article/commentary_kazakhstan_and_the_eurasian_economic_union_view_from_astana395).

58. *CIA World Factbook*, table on "FSU-12 Nation Building: Ethnic Russian Populations."

59. On October 1, 2013, the Central Bank's foreign reserves were only sufficient to cover two months' worth of imports—"Positive Incentives Prop Moscow's Ties with Minsk, Kiev," *Oxford Analytica*, October 15, 2013.

60. As emphasized by the title of Andrew Wilson's book, *Belarus: The Last European Dictatorship* (Yale University Press, 2011).

61. Wilson, *Belarus*, pp. 227–29; Alex Nice, "Playing Both Sides: Belarus between Russia and the EU," *DGAP Analyse*, no. 2, March 2012, p. 9. Lukashenko's imprisonment of rival presidential candidates in 2010 ended these illusions for the time being. Remarkably, though, EU officials appear to be falling for the same trick again—Charles Grant, "The Slow Dance between Minsk and Brussels," *CER Insight*, April 10, 2015 (http://www.cer.org.uk/insights/slow-dance-between-minsk-and-brussels).

62. "Russia to Open New Su-27 Airbase in Belarus Next Year," Airforce-Technology.com, October 16, 2014 (http://www.airforce-technology.com/news/newsrussia-to-open-new-su-27-airbase-in-belarus-next-year-4406164).

63. In 2011 Moscow was finally able to secure Gazprom's acquisition of the second 50 percent of Beltransgaz (the Belarus state gas company), in return for a US$3 billion loan from EurAsEC to Minsk—see chapter 3, note 34.

64. As Alex Nice has pointed out, behind the façade of "virtual integration" with Russia, Lukashenko has been pursuing a consistent state-building policy—"Playing Both Sides," p.10.

65. Economic relations between the EU and Belarus have grown rapidly in recent years. In 2013, the EU accounted for 26.2 percent of total Belarus trade, second only after Russia (49.5 percent)—"European Union: Trade with Belarus" (http://trade.ec.europa.eu/doclib/ docs/2006/september/tradoc_113351.pdf).

66. See Ronald Asmus, *A Little War That Shook the World: Georgia, Russia, and the Future of the West* (Basingstoke: Palgrave Macmillan, 2010).

67. Nikita Petrov, "Russia Army's Weaknesses Exposed during War in Georgia," RIA-Novosti, September 9, 2008 (http://en.ria.ru/analysis/20080909/116657490.html).

68. The Bucharest summit communique declared that Ukraine and Georgia "will become members of NATO." Significantly, however, it did not put a timeline on this, and decided against a Membership Action Plan (MAP) by which they might eventually have joined the alliance (http://www.nato.int/cps/en/natolive/official_texts_8443.htm).

69. Asmus, *A Little War That Shook the World.*

70. According to the deputy head of the Federal Migration Service, one million Georgians were working in Russia in late 2007, nearly all of them illegally—*Singled Out: Russia's Detention and Expulsion of Georgians*, Human Rights Watch Report, vol. 19, no. 5, October 2007, p. 32.

71. Chinese MFA briefing, August 2008. See also Yu Bin, "China-Russia Relations: Guns and Games of August: Tales of Two Strategic Partners," *Comparative Connections*, October 2008, pp. 1–4 (http://csis.org/files/media/csis/pubs/0803qchina_russia.pdf).

72. Nina Kurashvili, "Georgia's New Leaders Seek Fresh Start with Russia," Institute of War and Peace Reporting, November 16, 2012 (http://iwpr.net/report-news/georgias-new-leaders-seek-fresh-start-russia).

73. One way of doing this would be for them to "elect" to join the Russian Federation as "autonomous republics," with status and prerogatives similar to those of Chechnya or Crimea.

74. Luke Harding, "Georgia Angered by Russia-Abkhazia Military Agreement," *The Guardian*, November 24, 2014 (http://www.theguardian.com/world/2014/nov/25/georgia-russia-abkhazia-military-agreement-putin)

75. "EU, U.S. Condemn Russia South Ossetia 'Treaty,'" Radio Free Europe/Radio Liberty, March 18, 2015 (http://www.rferl.org/content/european-union-washington-russia-south-ossetia-/26906742.html).

76. European Commission press release, "EU and Georgia Conclude Talks on Deep and Comprehensive Free Trade Area" (http://europa.eu/rapid/press-release_IP-13-721_en.htm).

77. Alexi Petriashvili, Georgian minister for European and Euro-Atlantic Integration, "Association with Georgia Stands to Boost EU Role in Region, Growth and Security," *EurActiv*, June 25, 2014 (http://www.euractiv.com/sections/europes-east/association-georgia-stands-boost-eu-role-region-growth-and-security-303059).

78. "Georgians 'Strongly Support' European Integration, NDI Survey Reveals," *Agenda.ge*, August 25, 2014 (http://agenda.ge/news/20035/eng).

79. The Southern Gas Corridor is a European Commission initiative to facilitate gas supply from Central Asia and the Caspian to Europe. The term can be used more generically to cover any oil and gas pipelines that circumvent Russian territory.

80. "Georgian Patriarch Ilia II Visits Moscow, Meets Putin," Democracy and Freedom Watch, July 27, 2013 (http://dfwatch.net/georgian-patriarch-ilia-ii-visits-moscow-meets-putin-41150).

81. The legal dispute over the Caspian Sea centers on whether it should be considered a "sea" or a "lake." If it is regarded as a sea, there is no formal impediment to individual countries building energy pipelines across it. If, however, it is considered a lake, then in key respects it belongs equally to the five Caspian Sea littoral states (Russia, Azerbaijan, Kazakhstan, Turkmenistan, and Iran). In practice, Russia and Iran have strongly supported the second definition—Russia because it wishes to prevent the construction of pipelines that go around its territory; and Iran because it would otherwise only have access to a modest share of the Caspian Sea's resources. See Eka Siradze and Otabek Suleimanov, "Legal Status of Caspian Sea," *Natural Gas Europe*, August 6, 2013 (http://www.naturalgaseurope.com/legal-status-of-caspian-sea).

82. James Nixey, "The Long Goodbye: Waning Russian Influence in the South Caucasus and Central Asia," Chatham House Briefing Paper, June 2012, p. 4.

83. According to Aliyev, Azerbaijan's annual defense budget is US$3.7 billion—nearly twice Armenia's total government budget, and a twenty-three-fold increase from a decade ago. See Shahla Sultanova and Yekaterina Poghosyan, "Neighbourhood Watches as Azerbaijan Arms Up," Institute of War & Peace Reporting, July 25, 2013 (http://iwpr.net/report-news/neighbourhood-watches-azerbaijan-arms).

84. "If an aggression is committed against one of the States Parties by any state or group of states, it will be considered an aggression against all the States Parties to this treaty . . . [and] all the other States Parties will render it necessary assistance, including military . . ." (http://www.odkb.gov.ru/start/index_aengl.htm).

85. Rovshan Ibrahimov, "Russia's Borders: Azerbaijan Benefits from Not Offending Its More Powerful Neighbour," *The Conversation*, December 10, 2014 (http://the-conversation.com/russias-borders-azerbaijan-benefits-from-not-offending-its-more-powerful-neighbour-35221); also Sergei Markedonov, "The Caucasian Factor in Eurasian Integration," *Russia in Global Affairs*, March 21, 2014 (http://eng.globalaffairs.ru/number/The-Caucasian-Factor-in-Eurasian-Integration-16500).

86. Zulfugar Agayev, "Azeri-Russian Arms Trade $4 Billion amid Tension with Armenia," Bloomberg, August 13, 2013 (http://www.bloomberg.com/news/2013-08-13/azeri-russian-arms-trade-4-billion-amid-tension-with-armenia.html); also Joshua Kucera, "Again Testing Armenia's Loyalty, Russia Offers More Tanks to Azerbaijan," Eurasianet, May 25, 2014 (http://www.eurasianet.org/node/68405).

87. "European Union: Trade with Azerbaijan" (http://trade.ec.europa.eu/doclib/docs/2006/september/ tradoc_113347.pdf).

88. Indeed, in February 2015 Azerbaijan applied for observer status in the SCO.

89. Joshua Kucera, "The Great Caspian Arms Race," *Foreign Policy*, June 22, 2012 (http://www.foreignpolicy.com/articles/2012/06/22/the_great_caspian_arms_race).

90. From a Russian perspective, the decision of the Azerbaijan state oil company SOCAR to select this route instead of the EU's Nabucco-West to transport gas from the Shah Deniz field was the lesser of two evils—Shahin Abbasov, "Azerbaijan: When It Comes to Pipelines, It's Not Personal, It's Strictly Business," Eurasianet, July 19, 2013 (http://www.eurasianet.org/node/67277).

91. As the commentator Arkady Dubnov puts it, "President Karimov, known for his political pragmatism (which many of his partners call, at best, double-dealing)"— "Tashkent Goes, Problems Stay," *Russia in Global Affairs*, October 7, 2012 (http://eng.globalaffairs.ru/number/Tashkent-Goes-Problems-Stay-15692).

92. "Tashkent's foreign policy can be compared to pendulum motion: every two to three years, Uzbekistan turned away from Russia and other CIS partners and moved closer to the West, and vice versa"—Murat Laumulin, "Virtual Security of Central Asia," *Russia in Global Affairs*, October 7, 2012 (http://eng.globalaffairs.ru/number/Virtual-Security-of-Central-Asia-15694). Of course, it can be reasonably argued that Tashkent's balancing policy is the most logical way of maximizing its strategic independence and sovereignty.

93. It had previously withdrawn from the CSTO in 1999, before rejoining the organization in 2006. It later blocked the intervention of a Russia-led CSTO force to quell riots in the southern Kyrgyzstan city of Osh in 2010.

94. Dubnov, "Tashkent Goes, Problems Stay."

95. On May 13, 2005, Uzbekistan's security forces fired on a demonstration in the eastern city of Andijon. Estimates of the number of killed vary from the government's count of 187 to several hundred. In the wake of the massacre and Western condemnation, Karimov terminated the U.S. lease on the base in Karshi-Khanabad.

96. Tom Balmforth, "Kremlin Calm as China's Clout Rises in Russia's Backyard," Radio Free Europe/Radio Liberty, September 12, 2013 (http://www.rferl.org/content/russia-calm-china-central-asia-influence/25104383.html).

97. In a 2009 conversation with Under Secretary of State Bill Burns, Karimov reportedly "dwelled obsessively on Russian 'imperial ambitions' in Central Asia and warned the U.S. not to 'make deals with Russia behind our backs'"—cable from U.S. Embassy Tashkent, July 22, 2009, WikiLeaks (http://www.cablegatesearch.net/

cable.php?id=09TASHKENT1271). Similar complaints have since become a matter of public record.

98. Laumulin, "Virtual Security of Central Asia."

99. A 2013 report by the Russian International Affairs Council (RIAC) observed that the "entire political system . . . is designed in such a way that the President is the primary and, at the same time, backbone figure. . . . All decisions are made by the President and a narrow circle of his associates. The current balance among the elites can be easily upset because clear mechanisms of a successor choice are yet unavailable."— *Russia's Interests in Central Asia: Contents, Perspectives, Limitations*, RIAC Report 10, June 25, 2013, p. 11.

100. Alexey Malashenko describes it aptly as "a symbiosis of Eastern despotism and totalitarianism"—"Turkmenistan: Has There Been a Thaw?," Carnegie Moscow Center Briefing, vol. 14, no. 4, September 2012, p. 2.

101. "Russia Blamed for Pipeline Blast," BBC News, April 10, 2009 (http://news.bbc.co.uk/1/hi/world/asia-pacific/7993625.stm); see also Malashenko, "Turkmenistan," p. 7.

102. Author's conversation with a Turkmenistani representative of a leading Western multinational energy company, September 2013.

103. This thinking is not entirely logical. Chinese access to Turkmenistani and other Central Asian gas weakened Gazprom's negotiating position with CNPC over their gas agreement (see chapter 5).

104. RIAC, *Russia's Interests in Central Asia*, pp. 13–14.

105. The alleged threat of Moldovan goods undermining domestic producers is absurd, since they comprise less than 0.25 percent of Russia's total trade—comments by Andrei Suzdaltsev, in Gabrielle Tétrault-Farber, "EU Association Agreements Not Seen as Threat to Russian Economy," *Moscow Times*, June 26, 2014 (http://www.themoscowtimes.com/news/article/eu-association-agreements-not-seen-as-threat-to-russian-economy/502590.html).

106. Nicu Popescu and Leonid Litra, "Transnistria: a Bottom-up Solution," European Council on Foreign Relations Policy Brief 63, September 2012, pp. 4–5.

107. These amount to more than US$4 billion. "Russia Uses Transnistrian Gas Debt as Political Weapon against Moldova," interview with Emmet Tuohy, Moldova.org, July 26, 2013 (http://www.moldova.org/ russia-uses-transnistrian-gas-debt-as-political-weapon-against-moldovainterview-238043-eng/).

108. For a comprehensive account of the Transnistrian conflict and various mediation efforts, see William Hill, *Russia, the Near Abroad, and the West: Lessons from the Moldova-Transdniestria Conflict* (Washington: Woodrow Wilson Center, 2012).

109. That said, dealings with Tiraspol have become more awkward, as a result of the surprise victory of Yevgeny Shevchuk in the 2012 Transnistrian presidential elections. Shevchuk has proved something of an irritant to Moscow, which neither trusts his political orientation nor his efforts to develop more cooperative ties with Chisinau—Popescu and Litra, "Transnistria," p. 6.

110. To this purpose, the Kremlin is backing former president Vladimir Voronin and his Party of the Communists of the Republic of Moldova (PCRM) in the hope that a new administration will pull Moldova back from European integration and toward Moscow.

111. Fyodor Lukyanov, "Kremlin's Imperial Ambitions Ended in 2010," *Moscow Times*, December 23, 2010 (http://www.themoscowtimes.com/opinion/article/kremlins-imperial-ambitions-ended-in-2010/427658.html).

112. Samuel Charap and Alexandros Petersen, "Reimagining Eurasia," *Foreign Affairs*, August 20, 2010 (http://www.foreignaffairs.com/articles/66542/samuel-charap-and-alexandros-petersen/reimagining-eurasia).

113. David Trilling, "Letter from Bishkek: How Did Kurmanbek Bakiyev's Presidency Fail?," *Foreign Affairs*, April 12, 2010 (http://www.foreignaffairs.com/features/letters-from/letter-from-bishkek).

114. See chapter 3.

115. The building of the Naryn dam has become a sore point in both Kyrgyzstan-Uzbekistan and Russia-Uzbekistan relations—"Russian Control of Central Asian Dams 'Risks Full Conflict with Uzbekistan,'" *acquaNOW.info*, September 27, 2012 (http://www.ooskanews.com/daily-water-briefing/russian-control-central-asian-dams-risks-full-conflict-uzbekistan_24527).

116. Alexey Malashenko, "Kyrgyzstan: A White Ship amidst the Ice of Post-Soviet Authoritarianism," Carnegie Moscow Center Briefing, vol. 14, no. 2, March 2012, pp. 7–8.

117. Chinese President Xi Jinping's visit to Bishkek in September 2013 saw Beijing commit US$3 billion to various projects, including the Kyrgyzstan section of a gas pipeline from Turkmenistan to China (http://www.azernews.az/region/59416.html).

118. Gazprom alone has promised to invest more than US$600 million to modernize Kyrgyzstan's energy infrastructure—George Voloshin, "Kyrgyzstan Draws Closer to Eurasian Union amid Crisis in Russia," *Eurasia Daily Monitor*, vol. 12, no. 5, January 9, 2015 (http://www.jamestown.org/programs/edm/single/?tx_ttnews%5Btt_news%5D=43386&cHash=f6538a1c4b81e5dfc112a0ec6d693c27#.VNOoQy69FXs).

119. "Russia Gets 30-Year Extension for Base in Tajikistan," BBC News, October 5, 2012 (http://www.bbc.co.uk/news/world-asia-19849247).

120. Alexey Malashenko, "Tajikistan: Civil War's Long Echo," Carnegie Moscow Center Briefing, vol. 14, no. 3, April 2012, p. 9.

121. Eleanor Dalgleish, "Goodbye Lenin: Tajikistan's Historical Narrative," Open Democracy, April 3, 2013 (http://www.opendemocracy.net/od-russia/eleanor-dalgleish/goodbye-lenin-tajikistans-new-historical-narrative).

122. Nixey, "The Long Goodbye," pp. 4–5.

123. In 2013 the EU accounted for 27.9 percent of Armenia's total trade, compared with Russia's 24.3 percent—"European Union: Trade with Armenia" (http://trade.ec.europa.eu/ doclib/docs/2006/september/tradoc_113345.pdf).

124. Celeste Wallander, "Russian Transimperialism and Its Implications," *Washington Quarterly*, vol. 30, no. 2, 2007.

125. Andrew Wood, "A Russian Requiem," Chatham House Expert Comment, April 8, 2014 (https://www.chathamhouse.org/media/comment/view/198918).

126. Back in 1989 Paul Kennedy wrote that "there is nothing in the character and tradition of the Russian state to suggest that it could ever accept imperial decline gracefully"—*The Rise and Fall of the Great Powers: Economic Change and Military Conflict from 1500 to 2000* (London: Fontana, 1989), p. 664. In 2010 the Levada Center conducted a poll that asked the question, "Do you think that Russia should restore its status as a great empire?" An astonishing 78 percent of respondents answered in the affirmative. See Alexei Levinson, "A Smaller Empire?," *Russia in Global Affairs*, March 27, 2011 (http://eng.globalaffairs.ru/number/The-Notion-of-Empire-as-Applied-to-Todays-Russia-15142).

127. "Clinton Calls Eurasian Integration an Effort to 'Re-Sovietize,'" Radio Free Europe/Radio Liberty, December 7, 2012 (http://www.rferl.org/content/clinton-calls-eurasian-integration-effort-to-resovietize/24791921.html).

128. The 201st motor rifle division has been crucial in shoring up the Rakhmon regime in Tajikistan.

129. Igor Torbakov observes that "it is precisely the policy of propping up the post-Soviet authoritarian rulers that puts a brake on any potential integration process: authoritarian power is *indivisible*: it cannot be transferred or delegated to any supra-national bodies"—"'What Does Russia Want?' Investigating the Interrelationship between Moscow's Domestic and Foreign Policy," *DGAP Analyse*, no. 1, May 2011, p. 11.

## Chapter 5

*Epigraph:* Du Qiwen, president of the Association of Diplomatic History of the PRC, is quoted in "'There Is No Russian Pivot to Asia,'" interview with Du Qiwen and Evans Revere, Geneva Centre for Security Policy, September 2014 (http://www.gcsp.ch/Regional-Development/Programme-News/There-is-no-Russian-pivot-to-Asia).

1. In 1992 Boris Yeltsin was already advocating "a full-scale foreign policy with multiple vectors. While developing our relations with Western countries . . . we must work with equal diligence in the eastern direction"—"Chto skazal Eltsin Rossiiskim diplomatam" [What Yeltsin Said to Russia's Diplomats], *Rossiiskie vesti*, October 29, 1992, p. 1.

2. See Bobo Lo, *Axis of Convenience: Moscow, Beijing, and the New Geopolitics* (Brookings and Chatham House, 2008), pp. 18–19.

3. Fyodor Lukyanov, "Povorot na vostok," Council on Foreign and Defense Policy, February 15, 2010 (http://old.svop.ru/mm/2010/mm25.htm).

4. 2013 Russian Foreign Policy Concept.

5. Andrei Tsygankov argues that although Russia "has become stronger and more confident since 2000, it is not a rising power given the growing international competition and domestic constraints on its development. It is catching up with some European economies, but is unable to narrow a widening gap with China and India." See

"The Heartland No More: Russia's Weakness and Eurasia's Meltdown," *Journal of Eurasian Studies*, vol. 30, 2011, p. 5.

6. See Vladimir Putin, "Russia and the Changing World," *Moskovskie novosti*, February 27, 2012 (http://valdaiclub.com/politics/39300.html).

7. Igor Zevelev, "A New Realism for the 21st Century," *Russia in Global Affairs*, December 27, 2012 (http://eng.globalaffairs.ru/number/A-New-Realism-for-the-21st-Century-15817).

8. Ibid.

9. In the United States and Australia, the description "Indo-Pacific" has become quite common—see "Russia and the Indo-Pacific," ANU Centre for European Studies Briefing Paper (Canberra, Australia), vol. 3, no. 11, September 2012.

10. See Dmitri Trenin, *The End of Eurasia: Russia on the Border between Geopolitics and Globalization* (Washington: Carnegie Endowment for International Peace, 2002).

11. In 1919 the father of modern geopolitical theory, Halford Mackinder, wrote in *Democratic Ideals and Reality* that "who rules East Europe commands the Heartland; who rules the Heartland commands the World-Island; who rules the World-Island controls the world."

12. According to the Russian National Committee of the Council for Security Cooperation in the Asia-Pacific (CSCAP), "21st century imperatives offer a new view of Russia as a Euro-Pacific country, not merely European or Eurasian"—"Going East: Russia's Asia-Pacific Strategy," *Russia in Global Affairs*, December 25, 2010 (http://eng.globalaffairs.ru/number/Going-East-Russias-Asia-Pacific-Strategy-15081).

13. There were several border clashes in 1969, but direct confrontation was surprisingly infrequent, given the massive buildup of forces on both sides of the Sino-Soviet border. In 1980 the Red Army had forty-five divisions in the Soviet Far East.

14. The most serious attempt was Mikhail Gorbachev's speech in Vladivostok on July 28, 1986, in which he promised to "give dynamism" to the Soviet Union's relations with countries of the Asia-Pacific region—*Izbrannye rechi i stati* [Selected Speeches and Articles] (Moscow House of Political Literature, 1987), vol. 4, pp. 26–32.

15. The expression "unbreakable friendship" was first employed by Stalin in a letter to Mao, dated September 2, 1951 (https://www.marxists.org/reference/archive/stalin/works/1951/09/02.htm).

16. Bobo Lo, "Russia, China and the United States: from Strategic Triangularism to the Post-Modern Triangle," IFRI, *Proliferation Papers* 32, Winter 2010/*Russie-CEI Visions* 47, February 2010, pp. 12–13.

17. Yeltsin–Jiang Zemin joint declaration "On a Multipolar World and the Formation of a New International Order," April 23, 1997 (http://www.fas.org/news/russia/1997/a52—153en.htm).

18. Bobo Lo, *Russian Foreign Policy in the Post-Soviet Era* (Basingstoke: Palgrave Macmillan, 2002), p. 108.

19. *China's Peaceful Rise: Speeches of Zheng Bijian, 1997-2005* (Brookings, 2005).

20. Author's conversations with representatives of APEC member economies.

21. Igor Ivanov, "What Diplomacy Does Russia Need in the 21st Century?," *Russia in Global Affairs*, December 29, 2011 (http://eng.globalaffairs.ru/number/What-Diplomacy-Does-Russia-Need-in-the-21st-Century-15420).

22. "In the eyes of . . . Russian leaders, the Eastern countries are only there to act as strategic cards to be played when it gets into trouble with the Western countries"— Yang Cheng, "The Vladivostok APEC Summit and Chinese-Russian Cooperation under Russia's Far Eastern Strategy," Valdai website, September 20, 2012 (http://valdaiclub.com/asia/49140.html).

23. Author's conversation with Ji Zhiye, China Institute of Contemporary International Relations (CICIR), Beijing, May 2007.

24. Russia-Japan trade rose from US$3.9 billion in 1998 to US$21.2 billion in 2007 (http://www.mofa.go.jp/region/europe/russia/pdfs/trade_volume.pdf).

25. A brief summary of the ESPO saga may be found in Lo, *Axis of Convenience*, pp. 143–46.

26. Yevgeny Primakov first broached this idea during a visit to New Delhi in December 1998—Nikolai Pakhlin, "Treugolnik Moskva-Pekin-Deli" [Moscow–Beijing–New Delhi Triangle], *Rossiiskaya gazeta*, December 22, 1998, p. 7.

27. Comments by Russia's APEC ambassador, Gennady Ovechko—in Eleonore Dermy, "Russia Asserts Pacific Power at APEC Summit," AFP, September 4, 2012 (https://www.chinapost.com.tw/commentary/afp/2012/09/05/353297/Russia-asserts.htm).

28. Sergei Blagov, "Russia Seeks Increased Trade with China," *Eurasia Daily Monitor*, vol. 9, no. 57, March 21, 2012 (http://www.jamestown.org/programs/edm/single/?tx_ttnews[tt_news]=39159&tx_ttnews[backPid]=587&no_cache=1#.Ut600bTFKUk).

29. "European Union: Trade with Russia" (http://trade.ec.europa.eu/doclib/docs/2006/september/ tradoc_113440.pdf, accessed February 25, 2015). Russia exported nearly as much to the Netherlands as to *the whole of Asia*—see *The Russian Eagle: Russia's Pivot to Asia: Evolution, Not Revolution*, Sberbank report, June 2014, p. 10.

30. *Russia 2013: Shaping Russia's Future*, Ernst and Young's Attractiveness Survey, pp. 22–23.

31. The EU alone accounted for 80 percent of Russian oil exports, 70 percent of gas exports, and 50 percent of coal exports (http://eeas.europa.eu/delegations/russia/press_corner/all_news/news/2013/20131118_2_en.htm).

32. It is only fair to note that reputable economists have debunked these claims— see Vladimir Mau, "Russian Economic Reforms as Perceived by Western Critics," Bank of Finland Economies in Transition (BOFIT), no. 12, 1999, p. 6.

33. Bobo Lo and Lilia Shevtsova, *A 21st Century Myth: Authoritarian Modernization in Russia and China* (Carnegie Moscow Center, July 2012).

34. Putin's two daughters studied in Germany. The elder lived in the Netherlands until the furor over the downing of MH17 forced her to leave; the younger is said to still reside in Munich. Medvedev's son has permanent residence status in the United Kingdom. Lavrov's daughter studied at Columbia University, New York, and is still living in the United States. For a comprehensive list of the Putin elite and their personal

connections with the West, see Aisen Tacho, "The Western Choice of the Russian Government," *Euromaidan*, April 25, 2014 (http://euromaidanpr.com/2014/06/09/the-western-choice-of-the-russian-government/); also "The Kremlin Kids Love the West," Picture.Dot.News, November 27, 2014 (https://picturesdotnews.wordpress.com/2014/11/27/the-kremlin-kids-love-the-west/).

35. Seweryn Bialer, "Russia and China: the Young vs Old Leaders. Two Communist Systems—but How Different," *Christian Science Monitor*, January 12, 1987 (http://www.csmonitor.com/1987/0112/elead-f.html).

36. See Minxin Pei, "China and Russia: Best Frenemies Forever?," *Fortune*, March 28, 2013 (http://management.fortune.cnn.com/2013/03/28/china-russia-us-frenemies/); also Tsuneo Akaha, "A Distant Neighbor: Russia's Search to Find Its Place in East Asia," *Global Asia*, vol. 7, no. 2, Summer 2012 (http://www.ct2014.com/Issue/Article Detail/206/a-distant-neighbor-russias-search-to-find-its-place-in-east-asia.html).

37. "Going East: Russia's Asia-Pacific Strategy" (http://eng.globalaffairs.ru/number/Going-East-Russias-Asia-Pacific-Strategy-15081). Although CSCAP-Russia started out as a nongovernmental organization, its institutional home has since moved to the Foreign Ministry's Second Asia Department.

38. Leonid Grigoriev, "Will Russia Reorient Its Energy Exports from Europe to Asia?," Valdai website, June 17, 2011 (http://Valdaiclub.com/economy/27020.html).

39. See Putin and Xi press comments, March 22, 2013 (http://eng.kremlin.ru/transcripts/5160); also Sino-Russian summit declaration, May 20, 2014 (http://news.kremlin.ru/ref_notes/1642/print).

40. Although "core interests" is a Chinese expression, it is especially apt to describe Russian priorities in Ukraine.

41. See Gilbert Rozman, "Asia for the Asians: Why Chinese-Russian Friendship Is Here to Stay," *Foreign Affairs*, October 29, 2014 (http://www.foreignaffairs.com/articles/142305/gilbert-rozman/asia-for-the-asians); Charles Krauthammer, "Who Made the Pivot to Asia? Putin," *Washington Post*, May 22, 2014 (http://www.washington-post.com/opinions/charles-krauthammer-who-made-the-pivot-to-asia-putin/2014/05/22/091a48ee-e1e3-11e3-9743-bb9b59cde7b9_story.html); also Dmitri Simes, "How Obama Is Driving Russia and China Together," *National Interest*, June 24, 2014 (http://nationalinterest.org/feature/how-obama-driving-russia-china-together-10735).

42. Ivan Nechepurenko, "Yakunin Lashes Out against West, Says Russia Will Turn East," *Moscow Times*, May 23, 2014 (http://www.themoscowtimes.com/ business/article/yakunin-lashes-out-against-west-says-russia-will-turn-east/500800.html).

43. Comments by Sergei Karaganov at the Valdai conference on "Developing Asia-Pacific's Last Frontier: Fostering International Cooperation in Russia's Siberia and Far East," Singapore, December 17, 2013 (attended by author).

44. Gazprom's exploratory ventures in the South China Sea have caused some ructions in Beijing—"Russia's Mixed Signals in South China Sea," *Global Times* editorial, April 13, 2012 (http://www.china.org.cn/opinion/2012-04/13/content_25138042.htm). However, these tentative steps scarcely point to a reorientation of Russian policy in East Asia.

45. Putin's address at the APEC business summit, September 7, 2012 (http://eng.kremlin.ru/news/4371); also post-summit press conference, September 9, 2012 (http://eng.kremlin.ru/transcripts/4386).

46. In April 2015 the two sides reached agreement on the S-400 missile system. Negotiations are ongoing for the sale of Su-35 multipurpose fighters and Lada-class submarines.

47. "East, Not West, Russia's Top 5 Trade Partners in Asia," RT, May 6, 2014 (http://rt.com/business/157092-east-west-russia-trade/).

48. Amrutha Gayathri, "China Warns ASEAN against Discussing South China Sea Tensions, Rebuffing Clinton's Call for Resolution," *International Business Times*, July 11, 2012 (http://www.ibtimes.com/china-warns-asean-against-discussing-south-china-sea-tensions-rebuffing-clintons-call-resolution).

49. Following the sinking of the South Korean corvette *Cheonan* in March 2010, the Russian report on the incident adhered to the Chinese line that it had resulted from an accidental collision with a floating mine.

50. Su Xiaohui, "Don't Misinterpret China-Russia Relationship," *China & US Focus*, March 25, 2013 (http://www.chinausfocus.com/foreign-policy/dont-misinterpret-china-russia-relationship/).

51. Such praise reflects the reality that Putin is personally very popular in China, particularly among women—Yu Bin, "Pivot to Eurasia and Africa: Xi's Style," *Comparative Connections*, May 2013, p. 3.

52. "Both Moscow and Beijing are well aware that our countries have not exhausted their potentials. We have a way to go," Putin interview, RT, May 18, 2014 (http://rt.com/news/159804-putin-china-visit-interview/).

53. "European Union: Trade with China" (http://trade.ec.europa.eu/doclib/docs/2006/september/ tradoc_113366.pdf, accessed December 3, 2014).

54. Between 2001 and 2006, the share of manufacturing in Russian exports to China fell from nearly 30 percent to 1.5 percent—Ji Zhiye, "China-Russia Bond," *Contemporary International Relations*, vol. 17, no. 1, Jan./Feb. 2007, pp. 13–14. This share has fallen further over the past decade—see http://atlas.media.mit.edu/explore/tree_map/sitc/export/rus/chn/show/2012/.

55. Vladimir Milov, "Rossiya lozhitsya pod Kitai" [Russia is Lying Down under China], *Ekho Moskvy*, May 20, 2014 (http://www.echo.msk.ru/blog/milov/1323818-echo/). Other commentators reach the same diagnosis, but are somewhat more phlegmatic (or fatalistic) about the nature of the economic relationship—see Vladislav Inozemtsev, "My uzhe davno podseli na kitaiskuyu iglu" [We Got Hooked on China Long Ago], interview in *Novaya gazeta*, October 17, 2014 (http://www.novayagazeta.ru/economy/65738.html?print=1).

56. According to Russia's senior trade representative in Beijing, Sergei Tsyplyakov—see Blagov, "Russia Seeks Increased Trade with China."

57. Chinese participation in the construction of a new branch to the Moscow Metro is an exception to the rule, although this was jeopardized as a result of the plummeting ruble in late 2014—Alexander Panin, "Russia's Weak Ruble Puts China's

Moscow Development Projects on Hold," *Moscow Times*, November 17, 2014 (http://www.themoscowtimes.com/business/article/russia-s-weak-ruble-puts-china-s-moscow-development-projects-on-hold/511300.html). More promising, in May 2015 the two sides signed an agreement to build a high-speed rail link between Moscow and Kazan—"Chinese Company Wins $390mn Contract to Develop Russian High-Speed Railway," RT, May 13, 2015 (http://rt.com/business/258241-china-russia-railway-construction/).

58. It took fifteen years for the 1,030-kilometer ESPO branch line to be built. By contrast, the far more controversial Nordstream gas pipeline to Germany via the Baltic Sea was completed quite quickly, despite strenuous objections from several neighboring countries.

59. Jake Rudnitsky and Stephen Bierman, "Russia's $270 Billion Oil Deal Set to Make China Biggest Market," Bloomberg News, June 21, 2013 (http://www.bloomberg.com/news/2013-06-21/rosneft-s-270-billion-oil-deal-set-to-make-china-biggest-market.html).

60. See Lo, *Axis of Convenience*, pp. 245–46, note 29.

61. *China Country Analysis Brief*, U.S. Energy Information Administration, updated February 4, 2014 (http://www.eia.gov/countries/cab.cfm?fips=CH). Paradoxically, Russia's share of Chinese oil imports was highest before construction of the ESPO branch line. In 2006 it exported 15 million tonnes, accounting for 11 percent of Chinese imports.

62. It has been claimed that the deal could triple Russian oil exports to China. Given the latter's rapidly expanding import requirements, however, the increase in Russia's share is likely to be relatively modest—particularly if Iranian oil (and gas) becomes more freely available.

63. Keun-Wook Paik, "With China Deal, Russia Stands at Centre of Energy Geopolitics," Chatham House Expert Comment, May 23, 2014 (http://www.chatham-house.org/expert/comment/14563).

64. According to the agreement, Russia will supply an annual volume of 38 billion cubic meters (bcm) to China over a period of thirty years, beginning in 2018. The price per thousand cubic meters (mcm) is thought to be about US$350, compared with a European average in 2014 of US$370. Putin has also suggested that the price will be indexed to global oil prices, similar to Russia's agreements with European gas companies. The gas is to be delivered through the Power of Siberia pipeline, which has yet to be built, and whose construction will require a minimum investment of US$55 billion on the Russian side and US$20 billion from China. In fact, the amounts needed are likely to be far greater, and may climb to US$150–200 billion—see Ilya Zaslavsky, "Insiders Benefit from Gazprom–CNPC Deal, but Russia's Budget Loses," Chatham House Expert Comment, June 2, 2014 (http://www.chathamhouse.org/expert/comment/14633).

65. *The Russian Eagle*, p. 25. Rosneft apparently believes that the first gas will not come through until 2025 at the earliest (author's conversation, March 2015).

66. James Marson, "Gazprom Refuses to Use US Benchmark in China Gas Deal," *Wall Street Journal*, September 5, 2013 (http://blogs.wsj.com/emergingeurope/2013/09/05/gazprom-refuses-to-use-u-s-benchmark-in-china-gas-deal/).

67. This is why Russian attempts to revive the "western route" through the Altai region are unlikely to gain much traction in Beijing, notwithstanding the signing of a framework agreement in November 2014.

68. Mathieu Boulegne, "Xi Jinping's Grand Tour of Central Asia: Asserting China's Growing Economic Clout," Central Asia Economic Paper 9, October 2013, pp. 2–3; and "Central Asia Supplies Close to Half of Chinese Gas Imports in 2013," *Business New Europe*, Eurasian Development Bank, June 18, 2014 (http://www.bne.eu/content/central-asia-supplies-close-half-chinese-gas-imports-2013).

69. Ksenia Kushkina and Edward Chow, "The 'Golden Age' of Gas in China," *Russian Analytical Digest* 119, October 21, 2012, pp. 4–6.

70. "'Rosneft privekla kitaitsev dlya osvoeniya Dalnego Vostoka'" [Rosneft Enticed the Chinese into Developing the Far East], lenta.ru, October 18, 2013 (http://lenta.ru/news/2013/10/18/cnpc/); Rakteem Katakey and Will Kennedy, "Russia Lets China into Arctic Rush as Energy Giants Embrace," Bloomberg News, March 25, 2013 (http://www.bloomberg.com/news/2013-03-25/russia-cuts-china-into-arctic-oil-rush-as-energy-giants-embrace.html).

71. Author's conversation with a senior executive of a leading IOC.

72. Ministry of Foreign Affairs of the People's Republic of China, "Chinese and Russian Heads of State Exchange New Year Greetings," press release, December 31, 2014 (http://www.fmprc.gov.cn/mfa_eng/zxxx_662805/t1225579.shtml).

73. See note 41 above.

74. The scholar Yan Xuetong, a vocal critic of American policy, has nevertheless described the U.S.-China relationship as the only truly global relationship—"Constructing a new framework for a new Great-Power relationship between China and the United States," Carnegie-Tsinghua Global Dialogue, Beijing, December 4, 2013.

75. For an excellent summation of the pivot, see Kenneth Lieberthal, "The American Pivot to Asia: Why Obama's Turn to the East Is Easier Said than Done," *Foreign Policy*, December 21, 2011 (http://www.foreignpolicy.com/articles/2011/12/21/the_american_pivot_to_asia).

76. Yang Cheng, "The Vladivostok APEC Summit"; author's private conversations with Chinese interlocutors at the Stockholm China Forum, August 30, 2014.

77. The Russia Strategy-2020 document, which reflects liberal economic views within the Putin elite, observed that "the main risks to Russia, linked with the emergence of new centers of power, are rooted in the growth of China's economic potential and international status"—Fyodor Lukyanov, "Uncertain World: Russia-China: Change of Course?," RIA-Novosti, March 22, 2012 (http://sputniknews.com/analysis/20120322/172305525.html).

78. Alexei Arbatov and Vladimir Dvorkin, *The Great Strategic Triangle*, Carnegie Moscow Center Report, April 1, 2013 (http://www.carnegie.ru/2013/04/01/great-strategic-triangle/fvbx).

79. Victor Larin, "Russia-China Relations and the Russian Far East," chapter presentation at a conference on "New Perspectives on Sino-Russian Relations," Institute for Defence Studies, Oslo, September 22, 2014.

80. Rilka Dragneva and Kataryna Wolczuk, "Russia, the Eurasian Customs Union and the EU," Chatham House Briefing Paper, August 2012, pp. 9–11.

81. These included an agreement to expand gas deliveries from Turkmenistan to 65 bcm by 2020; CNPC's acquisition of an 8.33 percent share in Kazakhstan's massive Kashagan oil field; US$15 billion's worth of agreements in energy, infrastructure, and transport with Uzbekistan; and deals amounting to US$3 billion with Kyrgyzstan—Boulegne, "Xi Jinping's Grand Tour of Central Asia," pp. 2–3.

82. Alexander Cooley, *Great Games, Local Rules: The New Great Power Contest in Central Asia* (Oxford University Press, 2012), pp. 70–71; also chapter presentation by Yang Cheng, "China, Russia, and Central Asia post-2014," conference on "New Perspectives in Sino-Russian Relations," Institute for Defence Studies, Oslo, September 23, 2014.

83. Examples of such "betrayal" include Putin's decision to support the U.S.-led intervention in Afghanistan post-9/11; Russian recognition of the breakaway Georgian republics of Abkhazia and South Ossetia as independent states in August 2008; and the Geneva initiative with the United States to remove chemical weapons from Syria. In all these cases, the Chinese were either informed very late or not at all.

84. At the Yalta peace conference, Stalin promised Churchill and Roosevelt that the Soviet Union would enter the war against Japan three months after the end of the war in Europe. He used this opportunity to take over Sakhalin and the entire Kurile chain, including the southernmost islands of Kunashir, Etorofu, Shikotan, and the Habomais. As a result of this annexation, Russia and Japan have never signed a formal peace treaty, and remain technically in a state of war.

85. This pro-Japan lobby included Sergei Yastrzhembsky, head of the Presidential Administration, and First Deputy Prime Minister Boris Nemtsov. They were opposed by the MFA, among many others.

86. The Yeltsin-Hashimoto plan envisaged cooperation in six priority fields: investment; Russia's integration into the international economy; economic reform in Russia; business training for Russian executives; energy dialogue; and the civilian nuclear sector. See Mitsuko Nashima, "Hashimoto-Yeltsin Plan Stimulates Bilateral Economic Ties," *Japan Times*, April 15, 1998 (http://www.japantimes.co.jp/news/1998/04/15/national/hashimoto-yeltsin-plan-stimulates-bilateral-economic-ties/#.UuKUubTFKUk).

87. Hiroshi Kimura, *Japanese-Russian Relations under Gorbachev and Yeltsin* (Armonk, N.Y.: M.E. Sharpe, 2000), vol. 2, p. 220.

88. Under this formula, Russia would give up Shikotan and the Habomais in return for a peace treaty. One major flaw of the idea is that the returned islands comprise only 7 percent of the disputed territories.

89. Author's conversations in Moscow at that time.

90. In the late 1990s, Primakov as foreign minister was already arguing that economic cooperation would create a favorable climate in which the dispute might be resolved by "future generations"—Australia-Russia pol-mil discussions in October 1998, attended by the author.

91. Such ideas were initially floated during the "no neckties" diplomacy between Hashimoto and Yeltsin, and have resurfaced from time to time—Togo Kazuhiko, "Negotiations between Japan and USSR/Russia on the Northern Territories: Lessons for the Abe-Putin Renewal Talks," ASAN Forum, August 2, 2013 (http://www.theasan-forum.org/negotiations-between-japan-and-ussrrussia-on-the-northern-territories-lessons-for-the-abe-putin-renewal-of-talks/); see also "No Deal on Island Dispute," BBC News, September 5, 2000 (http://news.bbc.co.uk/1/hi/world/asia-pacific/910760.stm).

92. Putin alleged that the Japanese had misled him about their willingness to agree to a compromise on this basis. As he saw it, he had gone out on a political limb, only to be betrayed—remarks to the Valdai Club in September 2006 (author was present).

93. In the six years between Koizumi's departure and Shinzo Abe's second premiership, there were six prime ministers: Shinzo Abe (first time), Yasuo Fukuda, Taro Aso, Yukio Hatoyama, Naoto Kan, and Yoshihiko Noda.

94. Such anxieties led to an agreement in September 2012 to set up a second U.S. missile defense system on Japanese territory.

95. Fiona Hill, "Russia and Japan Make a Play for the Pacific," *Foreign Affairs*, November 27, 2013 (http://www.foreignaffairs.com/articles/140288/fiona-hill/gang-of-two); Cécile Pajon, "Japan–Russia: Toward a Strategic Partnership?," *Russie.NEI. Visions* 72, September 2013.

96. Nissan declared its intention to capture 10 percent of the Russian market by 2016—Nissan press release, May 21, 2012 (http://www.nissan-global.com/EN/NEWS/2012/_STORY/120521-03-e.html). The Renault-Nissan strategic partnership also included an agreement to take over half of Avtovaz. Toyota has a big plant in St. Petersburg, which produces the fourth best-selling SUV in Russia.

97. In 2012 Russia accounted for 10 percent of Japanese imports of crude oil. Japan also imported 8.3 million tons of LNG, up from 6 million tons in 2010—Akihiro Iwashita, "The Northern Territories and Russo-Japan Relations," *Russian Analytical Digest* 132, July 11, 2013, p. 2.

98. Shinji Hyodo, "Japan-Russia Relations in Triangular Context with China," ASAN Forum, November 22nd, 2013 (http://www.theasanforum.org/japan-russia-relations-in-triangular-context-with-china/)

99. Iwashita, "The Northern Territories," pp. 3–4.

100. The Hashimoto government was similarly guilty of misplaced optimism in the late 1990s, as was Koizumi in the early 2000s.

101. Moscow declared its intention to deploy its recently purchased Mistral-class amphibious assault vessels against this wholly improbable "threat"—"Russia Plans to Send First Mistral Ships to Protect Kurils," RIA-Novosti, February 9, 2011 (http://en.ria.ru/military_news/20110209/162525263.html).

102. "'India, Russia Trade May Touch $15 Billion by 2015': Federation of Indian Export Organisations," *Economic Times*, September 28, 2014 (http://articles.economic times.indiatimes.com/2014-09-28/news/54400415_1_india-show-russia-trade-russian-market).

103. Rama Lakshmi and Simon Denver, "Protests Disrupt India's Nuclear Energy Plan," *Washington Post*, September 15, 2012 (http://www.washingtonpost.com/world/asia_pacific/protests-disrupt-indias-nuclear-energy-plan/2012/09/15/ec75ca58-fdad-11e1-98c6-ec0a0a93f8eb_story.html); "Defective Russian Nuclear Reactor in India Tripped after 18 Days of Commercial Ops," *Mining Awareness Plus*, January 19, 2015 (https://miningawareness.wordpress.com/2015/01/19/defective-russian-nuclear-reactor-in-india-tripped-after-18-days-of-commercial-ops/).

104. In the period 2007–11, Indian arms purchases from Russia amounted to US$12.7 billion (80 percent of its total arms imports)—S.D. Pradhan, "Indo-Russian Relations in the Context of the Arms Procurement Policy," *Times of India*, April 30, 2013 (http://blogs.timesofindia.indiatimes.com/ChanakyaCode/entry/indo-russian-relations-in-the-context-of-the-arms-procurement-policy). In 2011 the two sides agreed on a deal for the sale of forty-two Su-30 multipurpose fighters, worth US$15 billion. Over the same period, there were virtually no new arms deals between Moscow and Beijing—Richard Weitz, "Why China Snubs Russia Arms," *The Diplomat*, April 5, 2010 (http://thediplomat.com/2010/04/why-china-snubs-russian-arms/?allpages=yes).

105. There are similar problems with the idea of a gas pipeline from Altai to northern India via China's Xinjiang province—"India Turns to Russia and China for Energy Security," *Oxford Analytica* Daily Brief, June 2, 2014.

106. There were various reasons for the delays: unreadiness of the carrier, problems with spare parts, and a price that continued to climb. One Indian commentary noted that New Delhi was "very unhappy with Russian sloppiness in handling large projects," and described the aircraft carrier deal as a "financial disaster for India"—"Procurement: How Russia Lost India," *StrategyPage*, August 24, 2013 (http://www.strategypage.com/htmw/htproc/articles/20130824.aspx).

107. Tanvi Madan, "Mr Putin Goes to India: Five Reasons Why the Russian President Will Be Welcomed There," *Brookings Up Front*, December 9, 2014 (http://www.brookings.edu/blogs/up-front/posts/2014/12/09-5-reasons-putin-will-be-welcomed-in-india-madan).

108. For an excellent analysis of the limitations of such triangularism, see Harsh Pant, "The Moscow–Beijing–Delhi 'Strategic Triangle': an Idea Whose Time May Never Come," *Crossroads*, vol. 5, no. 2, 2005, pp. 19–46.

109. Ashley Tellis, "The U.S.-India Strategic Dialogue: Forging the Next Stage of Cooperation," Carnegie Endowment for International Peace, June 20, 2013 (http://carnegieendowment.org/2013/06/20/u.s.-india-strategic-dialogue-forging-next-phase-of-cooperation/gb93); and "Triumph in New Delhi," *Foreign Policy*, November 16, 2010 (http://carnegieendowment.org/2010/11/16/triumph-in-new-delhi/zac).

110. China has developed naval facilities at Gwadiar in Pakistan and Hambantota, Sri Lanka.

111. Kishore Mahbubani accuses the P5 of behaving "as unelected dictators who did not tolerate any kind of democratic transparency or accountability for their

actions"—*The Great Convergence: Asia, the West, and the Logic of One World* (New York: PublicAffairs, 2013), p. 114.

112. Russian defense minister Sergei Shoigu visited Islamabad in November 2014. This followed the lifting of a Russian embargo on arms sales to Pakistan and discussions about the possible sale of Mi-35 helicopters. Sudha Ramachandran, "New Era in Russia-Pakistan Relations?," *The Diplomat*, December 3, 2014 (http://thediplomat.com/2014/12/new-era-in-russia-pakistan-relations/).

113. See Fahd Humayun, "Changing State of Play," Jinnah Institute, February 26, 2015.

114. Rajeev Sharma, "Dwindling Arms Sales Put India, Russia Military Partnership in Rough Patch," *Global Times*, July 29, 2013 (http://www.globaltimes.cn/content/799919.shtml#.UjuI3z-E7wE ). In 2012 New Delhi chose the French Rafale fighter over the MiG-29K, the Eurofighter, and the US F-16. Despite this setback for Washington, U.S. arms exports to India have grown from virtually nothing in 2008 to US$8 billion in 2013—Andrea Shallal, "US Aims to Expand Arms Trade to India by 'Billions of Dollars,'" Reuters, April 19, 2013 (ttp://in.reuters.com/article/2013/04/18/usa-india-weapons-idINDEE93H0F220130418).

115. This was a regular complaint of Russian officials and academics when the author served as an Australian diplomat in Moscow during the second half of the 1990s. There was particular annoyance at Russia's exclusion from the Korean Energy Development Organization (KEDO), whose purpose was to build light-water reactors for the DPRK in order to provide it with peaceful nuclear energy as an inducement to abandon its nuclear weapons program.

116. In 1961 the Soviet Union and North Korea concluded the Treaty of Friendship, Cooperation and Mutual Assistance. The treaty, which expired in 1996, committed each side to come to the aid of the other in the event of war (Article 1). The treaty Putin signed in 2000—"Friendship, Good Neighborliness, and Cooperation"—removed this controversial article. Seung-Ho Joo, "DPRK-Russian Rapprochement and Its Implications for Korean Security," *International Journal of Korean Unification Studies*, vol. 8, no. 1, 2000, pp. 4–7.

117. This view was especially pronounced in the MFA and the Institute of Oriental Studies (Institut vostokovedeniya), Russian Academy of Sciences.

118. Artyom Lukin, "Russia Shows Little Concern over North Korean Nukes (for Now)," *East Asia Forum*, March 2, 2013 (http://www.eastasiaforum.org/2013/03/03/russia-shows-little-concern-over-north-korean-nukes-for-now/).

119. This is the main reason why proposals such as a Russia-DPRK-ROK gas pipeline are unlikely to get off the ground. Although Moscow hopes to play the "Korea card" to strengthen its position with Beijing, its chances of doing so are minimal given the DPRK's near-total economic dependence on China.

120. "European Union: Trade with Russia" (http://trade.ec.europa.eu/doclib/docs/2006/september/tradoc_113440.pdf).

121. Yeu Soong-Ki, "S. Korea, Russia Share Views on Eurasian Union, Expand Investment in DPRK," Xinhua, November 13, 2013 (http://news.xinhuanet.com/english/world/2013-11/13/c_132884857.htm).

122. Keun-Wook Paik with Glada Lahn and Jens Hein, "Through the Dragon Gate? A Window of Opportunity for Northeast Asian Gas Security," Chatham House Briefing Paper, December 2012, pp. 9–10.

123. The 2013 Pew Global Attitudes survey on Russia showed a 53 percent "favorable" rating versus 33 percent "unfavorable"—better than in China (49–39) and especially Japan (27–64). Events in Ukraine have, however, had a negative impact. The 2014 Global Attitudes survey returned a 43–48 result for the ROK, in striking contrast to the upsurge in Russia's popularity in China (66–23) (http://www.pewglobal.org/2014/07/09/russias-global-image-negative-amid-crisis-in-ukraine/#).

124. Although Moscow maintained a reduced presence at the naval base in Cam Ranh, Vietnam, until 2002, it decided to close this after the Vietnamese demanded an annual rent of US$200 million.

125. Nga Pham, "Vietnam Orders Submarines and Warplanes from Russia," BBC News, December 16, 2009 (http://news.bbc.co.uk/1/hi/world/asia-pacific/ 8415380.stm). Since 2014 Russian tanker aircraft have been using the facilities at Cam Ranh to refuel TU-95 strategic bombers flying patrols near American bases in Guam—David Brunnstrom, "U.S. Asks Vietnam to Stop Helping Russian Bomber Flights," Reuters, March 11, 2015 (http://www.reuters.com/article/2015/03/11/us-usa-vietnam-russia-exclusive-idUSKBN0M71NA20150311).

126. In 2013 Russia and Vietnam were not ranked in each other's top ten trading partners. By comparison, China ranked second behind the EU in Russia's overseas trade, and first in Vietnam's (trade.ec.europa.eu/doclib/docs/2006/september/tradoc_113463.pdf; trade.ec.europa.eu/doclib/html/113440.htm).

127. Putin, "Russia and the Changing World"; 2013 Russian Foreign Policy Concept.

128. In 2012 Russia sold weapons to sixty-six different countries—"Putin Says Russia's Arms Exports up 12% in 2012," RIA-Novosti, April 3, 2013 (http://en.ria.ru/military_news/20130403/180422031.html).

129. Dmitri Trenin, *True Partners? How Russia and China See Each Other*, Centre for European Reform report, February 2012, p. 27.

130. Jeffrey Mankoff and Oleg Barabanov, *Prospects for US-Russia Cooperation in the Asia-Pacific Region: The United States and Russia in the Pacific Century*, Working Group on the Future of US-Russia Relations, Working Group Paper 3, July 2013, p. 5.

131. Alexei Fenenko, "APEC Remains an American Project," Valdai website, September 13, 2012 (http://valdaiclub.com/asia/48800.html).

132. "Going East: Russia's Asia-Pacific Strategy" (http://eng.globalaffairs.ru/number/Going-East-Russias-Asia-Pacific-Strategy-15081).

133. See Pavel Salin, "Russia's Three Roads to Asia," *Russia in Global Affairs*, December 27, 2012 (http://eng.globalaffairs.ru/number/Russias-Three-Roads-to-Asia-15818).

134. Oksana Antonenko, "Russia Emerges as a Big Player in Asia-Pacific, *Moscow Times*, June 9, 2011 (http://www.themoscowtimes.com/opinion/article/russia-emerges-as-a-big-player-in-asia-pacific/438528.html).

135. Putin gave particular emphasis to participation in projects such as the Trans-Siberian and Baikal-Amur Mainline (BAM) railways—see his address to APEC CEOs on October 7, 2013 (http://eng.kremlin.ru/news/6086), and press conference (http://eng.kremlin.ru/transcripts/6093) the following day.

136. Russia's substandard performance at Asian multilateral meetings is a particular complaint among ASEAN representatives—author's private conversations, August 2014.

137. Some experts, such as Victor Larin, use the term "Pacific Russia" to distinguish the Russian regions adjoining Northeast Asia (Primorye, Khabarovsk) from the vast hinterland of Eastern Siberia. The Russian government, however, has made little practical distinction, as its various development programs indicate.

138. One of the most striking contrasts is on either side of the Sino-Russian border. Whereas in the 1990s Chinese accounted for most of cross-border travel, today it is a very different story. Russian day-trippers travel in large numbers to Chinese border cities such as Heihe for tourism and especially shopping—Luke Harding, "Russia Fears Embrace of Giant Eastern Neighbour," *The Observer*, August 2, 2009 (http://www.theguardian.com/world/2009/aug/02/china-russia-relationship).

139. Natasha Kuhrt presents the choice in terms of "dual integration" with the Asia-Pacific region and the rest of Russia versus "double periphery," isolation from both—"The Russian Far East in Russia's Asia Policy: Dual Integration or Double Periphery?," *Europe-Asia Studies*, vol. 64, no. 3, May 2012, pp. 478, 482.

140. Victor Larin, "External Threat as a Driving Force for Exploring and Developing the Russian Pacific Region," Carnegie Moscow Center Working Materials, October 2013, pp. 4–5.

141. I am indebted to Victor Larin for these figures.

142. Energy resources alone comprised 55 percent of RFE exports to China in the first half of 2014—Victor Larin, "Russia-China Relations and the Russian Far East."

143. Putin's remarks at the APEC CEO Summit, Bali, October 7, 2013 (http://eng.kremlin.ru/transcripts/6086).

144. "Putin Ready to Revive Russia's Far East Mega Plan," RIA-Novosti, November 29, 2012 (http://en.ria.ru/business/20121129/177822312.html). Putin subsequently sacked Viktor Ishaev, the minister for Far Eastern Development (and formerly longtime governor of Khabarovsk *krai*).

145. "Medvedev to Oversee Business in Russia's Far East and Siberia," RIA-Novosti, January 15, 2014 (http://en.ria.ru/russia/20140115/186555060.html).

146. In this connection, Vladivostok was of a piece with the 2014 Winter Olympics in Sochi, the most expensive games of all time at an eye-watering US\$51 billion (compared with US\$40 billion for the 2008 Beijing Summer Olympics).

147. Arkady Moshes, "'Pacific Russia' Is Still a Dream: an APEC Summit Alone Will Not Make the Country a Top Player in the Region," *FIIA Comment*, Finnish Institute of International Affairs, September 2012, p. 1.

148. "Probe Shows Multi-Million-Dollar Fraud in Vladivostok APEC Summit," *Moscow Times*, December 27, 2013 (http://www.themoscowtimes.com/news/article/probe-shows-multi-million-dollar-fraud-in-vladivostok-apec-summit/492122.html); "Russia's Audit Chamber: $500 Million of APEC Summit Funds Stolen," *Eurasian Law*, November 13, 2012 (http://eurasian-law-breaking-news.blogspot.co.uk/2012/11/russias-audit-chamber-500-mln-stolen-on.html).

149. Kirill Muradov, "Russia's Pivot to Eurasia and the Battle for Ukraine," *East Asia Forum*, September 17, 2013; Fenenko, "APEC Remains an American Project"; Bobo Lo, "Russia's Eastern Direction—Distinguishing the Real from the Virtual," *Russie.NEI Reports* 17, IFRI.

150. Victor Larin, "Siberian Temptation: Imminent Struggle for World Treasury or the Chance for Advanced Partnership?," presentation at the Valdai conference on "Developing Asia Pacific's Last Frontier: Fostering International Cooperation in the Development of Russia's Siberia and Far East," Singapore, December 17, 2013.

151. Oleg Barabanov and Timofei Bordachev, "Realism Instead of Utopia: Siberia and the Far East as a Path to Russian Globalization," *Russia in Global Affairs*, December 28, 2012 (http://eng.globalaffairs.ru/number/Realism-Instead-of-Utopia-15821).

152. Author's conversations with Chinese and other Asian scholars. See also "'Kitaitsy ponimayut, chto Rossiya degradiruet iz-za korruptsii i neeffektivnogo upravleniya'" [The Chinese understand that Russia is becoming degraded because of corruption and ineffective management], interview with Alexander Gabuev (chair of the Russia in the Asia-Pacific program, Carnegie Moscow Center), lenta.ru, April 30, 2015 (http://m.lenta.ru/articles/2015/04/29/gabuev/).

153. It is indicative that in her famous article "America's Pacific Century" Hillary Clinton did not mention Russia at all. See *Foreign Policy*, October 11 2011 (http://www.foreignpolicy.com/articles/2011/10/11/americas_pacific_century). See also Kuhrt, "The Russian Far East in Russia's Asia Policy," p. 477.

154. Fyodor Lukyanov, "Will Russia Become Part of the West?," *Russia in Global Affairs*, May 31, 2012 (http://eng.globalaffairs.ru/redcol/Will-Russia-Become-Part-of-the-West-15559).

155. Reflected in the extravagant claim that "Russia has turned into the world's third greatest power"—Sergei Karaganov, "Lucky Russia," *Russia in Global Affairs*, March 29, 2011 (http://eng.globalaffairs.ru/pubcol/Lucky-Russia-15154).

## Chapter 6

*Epigraph:* X (Kennan), "The Sources of Soviet Conduct," *Foreign Affairs*, July 1947 (http://www.mtholyoke.edu/acad/intrel/coldwar/x.htm).

1. Dmitri Trenin, "'Osennii marafon' Vladimira Putina: k rozhdeniyu Rossiiskoi vneshnepoliticheskoi strategii" [Vladimir Putin's "Autumn Marathon": Toward the

Birth of a Russian Foreign Policy Strategy], Carnegie Moscow Center Briefing Paper, November 20, 2001, p. 6.

2. "Issues Paper on Relations with Russia," prepared by the Foreign Affairs Council of the European External Action Service (EEAS) for High Representative Federica Mogherini, January 19, 2015 (http://blogs.ft.com/brusselsblog/files/2015/01/Russia.pdf). For a clinical dissection of the paper, see Kadri Liik, "The Real Problem with Mogherini's Russia Paper," European Council on Foreign Relations, January 20, 2015 (http://www.ecfr.eu/article/commentary_the_real_problem_with_mogherinis_russia_paper402).

3. Dmitri Trenin, "Welcome to Cold War II," *Foreign Policy*, March 4, 2014 (http://www.foreignpolicy.com/articles/2014/03/04/welcome_to_cold_war_ii). The term "a new Cold War" was invented by the journalist Edward Lucas in the aftermath of the 2008 Georgia war. An updated version of his book *The New Cold War: Putin's Threat to Russia and the West* (Basingstoke: Palgrave Macmillan) was published in mid-2014.

4. Ivan Krastev, "Putin's World," Project Syndicate, April 1, 2014 (http://www.project-syndicate.org/commentary/ivan-krastev-blames-the-west-s-weak-response-in-crimea-for-empowering-russia#vaMwzSEzzhjPFQOD.99).

5. In *Ot pervogo litsa: razgorovy s Vladimirom Putinym* [From the First Person: Conversations with Vladimir Putin] (Moscow: Vagrius, 2000), Putin described Russia as a part of Western European civilization (p. 156).

6. "An Open Letter to the Obama Administration from Central and Eastern Europe," *Wyborcza gazeta*, July 15, 2009 (http://www.rferl.org/content/An_Open_Letter_To_The_Obama_Administration_From_Central_And_Eastern_Europe/1778449.html4); signatories included Václav Havel, Alexander Kwasniewski, and Lech Wałesa.

7. "The last few years have seen a dangerous drift in relations between Russia and the members of our Alliance [NATO]. It is time . . . to press the reset button and to revisit the many areas where we can and should be working together with Russia"— remarks by Vice President Biden at the 45th Munich Security Conference, February 7, 2009 (http://www.whitehouse.gov/the-press-office/remarks-vice-president-biden-45th-munich-conference-security-policy).

8. According to Ron Asmus, the "Principals Committee" of the U.S. National Security Council (which included the president, vice president, and national security adviser) briefly considered the option of American military involvement in the Georgia war. It seems, however, that this was a straw-man: "The president recognized that if the United States started down the path of anything military, they had to be prepared for an escalation and thus, in the end, for fighting Russia. There was a clear sense around the table that almost any military steps could lead to a confrontation with Moscow, the outcome of which no one could predict, and which was not in the US interest"—Ron Asmus, *A Little War That Shook the World: Georgia, Russia, and the Future of the West* (Basingstoke: Palgrave Macmillan, 2010), p. 187.

9. "Otnoshenie rossiyan k drugim stranam" [Attitudes of Russians toward other countries], Levada Center poll, December 8, 2014 (http://www.levada.ru/08-12-2014/otnoshenie-rossiyan-k-drugim-stranam).

10. "Russia's Global Image Negative amid Crisis in Ukraine," Pew Global Attitudes survey, July 9, 2014 (http://www.pewglobal.org/2014/07/09/russias-global-image-negative-amid-crisis-in-ukraine/).

11. Angela Stent likens the "prudent expectations management" of the Obama administration to the cautious approach of George H. W. Bush, in contrast to the bullishness of Bill Clinton and George W. Bush—*The Limits of Partnership: US-Russian Relations in the Twenty-First Century* (Princeton University Press, 2014), p. 217.

12. SORT was an unsatisfactory compromise between the Bush administration's reluctance to conclude any treaty at all and Moscow's desire for an agreement that would ensure the destruction, as opposed to mere decommissioning, of surplus warheads (http://www.nti.org/treaties-and-regimes/strategic-offensive-reductions-treaty-sort/).

13. The limits under the 2010 START agreement are: 700 in total of ICBMs (intercontinental ballistic missiles), SLBMs (submarine-launched ballistic missiles), and heavy bombers equipped with nuclear weapons; 1,550 deployed warheads; and 800 deployed and non-deployed ICBM launchers, SLBM launchers, and nuclear-equipped heavy bombers (http://www.state.gov/t/avc/newstart/index.htm).

14. U.S.-Russia Relations Fact Sheet, Bureau of European and Eurasian Affairs, U.S. Department of State, December 14, 2012 (http://www.state.gov/r/pa/ei/bgn/3183.htm).

15. This followed the U.S. raid on the Bin Laden compound in Abbottabad.

16. The cancellation of the S-300 deal certainly damaged Russia-Iran relations. Tehran threatened to take the case to international arbitration, while Moscow responded that it might shift to a hard-line position within the P5+1—Dmitry Gorenburg, "Iran's S-300 Lawsuit against Russia May Backfire," *Russian Military Reform*, December 13, 2012 (http://russiamil.wordpress.com/2012/12/13/irans-s-300-lawsuit-against-russia-may-backfire/).

17. Ellen Barry, "Russia Declares Deal to Join Trade Group," *New York Times*, November 3, 2011 (http://www.nytimes.com/2011/11/03/world/europe/russia-says-it-will-join-wto-in-deal-with-georgia.html?_r=0).

18. Until the fall of 2014, these included working groups on arms control and international security, energy, counterterrorism, counternarcotics, cyber, and space and military cooperation. But with the aggravation of tensions over Ukraine, many of the commission's activities have been suspended—see U.S. Department of State website (http://www.state.gov/p/eur/ci/rs/usrussiabilat/index.htm [accessed April 10, 2015]).

19. Lilia Shevtsova, "Vladimir Putin Offers the West a Faustian Bargain," *Washington Post*, May 8, 2014 (http://www.washingtonpost.com/opinions/vladimir-putin-offers-the-west-a-faustian-bargain/2014/05/08/47acffb0-d604-11e3-95d3-3bcd77cd4e11_story.html).

20. Before it was disbanded in January 2013, the working group on civil society was regarded by some as a cynical device to mask Obama's decision to go easy on political and civil rights abuses in Russia—David Kramer, "America's Silence Makes Us Complicit in Russia's Crimes," *Washington Post*, September 20, 2010 (http://www.washingtonpost.com/wp-dyn/content/article/2010/09/19/AR2010091902893.html).

21. There was even short-lived speculation about a UK-Russia reset—Vladimir Borisov, "Moscow Prepares for UK 'Reset' ahead of David Miliband's Visit," *Russia Now*, October 28, 2009 (http://www.telegraph.co.uk/sponsored/rbth/6454457/Russia-Now-Moscow-prepares-for-UK-reset-ahead-of-David-Milibands-visit.html).

22. The March 2011 Valdai report, "The U.S.-Russia Relations after the 'Reset': Building a New Agenda. A View from Russia" (http://vid-1.rian.ru/ig/valdai/US-Russia%20relations_eng.pdf), observed that "US policy—for the first time since the mid-1990s—does not undermine Russia's vital interests (for example, in the post-Soviet space,)" p. 5.

23. Stent, *The Limits of Partnership*, p. 258.

24. Or, as the 2011 report by the Valdai Club puts it, "clearing up the debris" of the 1990s and 2000s—"The U.S.-Russia Relations after the 'Reset,'" p. 23.

25. It is revealing that Obama did not invite Saakashvili to the White House for four years after the Georgia war.

26. This derives from the old Soviet joke "We pretend to work, and they pretend to pay us."

27. Dmitri Trenin puts it pithily: "Unless the U.S.-Russia relationship goes up, it will go down"—in "The World on Obama," *New York Times*, November 7, 2012 (http://www.nytimes.com/2012/11/07/opinion/the-world-on-obama.html?pagewanted=all&_r=0).

28. Dmitry Suslov, "Russia-US 'Reset' Over, What Next?," Valdai Club website, February 11, 2013 (http://valdaiclub.com/usa/54760.html); see also Leon Aron, "A Russian 'Frenemy,'" *Los Angeles Times*, March 5, 2013 (http://articles.latimes.com/2013/mar/05/opinion/la-oe-aron-russia-pause-20130305).

29. Stent, *The Limits of Partnership*, pp. 261–62.

30. The Rosneft-ExxonMobil agreement was wide-ranging, but centered on the joint exploration and development of three blocks in the Kara Sea (Arctic).

31. Lee Raymond, CEO of ExxonMobil, previously Exxon, from 1993 to 2005, summed up this attitude when he said: "I am not a U.S. company . . . and I don't make decisions based on what's good for the U.S."—Steve Coll, *Private Empire: Exxon/Mobil and American Power* (New York: Penguin, 2012), p. 71. Coll notes that "Raymond would manage Exxon's global position . . . as a confident sovereign, a peer of the White House's rotating occupants. . . . He did not manage the corporation as a subordinate instrument of American foreign policy; his was a private empire," p. 19.

32. Stephen Bierman, "Exxon's Russia Ambitions Show Oil Trumps Obama-Putin Spats," *Bloomberg News*, January 2, 2014 (http://www.bloomberg.com/news/2014-01-02/exxon-s-russia-ambitions-show-drilling-trumps-obama-putin-spats.html).

33. Clifford Kraft, "Exxon Halts Oil Drilling in Waters of Russia," *New York Times*, September 19, 2014 (http://www.nytimes.com/2014/09/20/business/exxon-suspending-700-million-drilling-operation-in-russian-waters.html?_r=0).

34. "'Strategic Balance Being Disrupted'—Putin," RIA-Novosti, February 27, 2013 (http://en.ria.ru/russia/20130227/179712595.html). In fact, as Dmitry Suslov has pointed out, the "threat" to Russia is not existential, but geopolitical: "Strategic parity with the United States . . . is what distinguishes Russia from the other power poles, including new ones, and what makes it a key player in big-time politics by definition."—"Cancellation of the Chicago Summit Suits Russia, US Interests," Valdai website, April 19, 2012 (http://valdaiclub.com/usa/41380.html).

35. Indeed, this was a key condition for congressional agreement to ratify the START treaty.

36. Deputy Prime Minister Dmitry Rogozin, cited in "Russia Sceptical over Obama's New Nuclear Reduction Proposal," RIA-Novosti, June 19, 2013 (http://en.ria.ru/russia/20130619/181755868.html).

37. Even then, Moscow condemned the United States and EU for supplementing UNSCR 1929 with their own sanctions to block investment in Iran's oil and gas industry—Howard LaFranchi, "As US and EU Slap on More Iran Sanctions, Russia is Miffed," *Christian Science Monitor*, June 17, 2010 (http://www.csmonitor.com/USA/2010/0617/As-US-and-EU-slap-on-more-Iran-sanctions-Russia-is-miffed).

38. "Breaking the 'Cold Spell' in Russia-NATO Relations," RT, November 22, 2010 (http://rt.com/politics/nato-russia-lisbon-summit/); "Russia to Work with NATO on Missile Defence Shield," BBC News, November 20, 2010 (http://www.bbc.co.uk/news/world-europe-11803931). The wording of the NATO-Russia Council (NRC) statement was rather more reserved: "We agreed to discuss pursuing missile defence cooperation. We agreed on a joint ballistic missile threat assessment and to continue dialogue in this area. The NRC will also resume Theatre Missile Defence Cooperation. We have tasked the NRC to develop a comprehensive Joint Analysis of the future framework for missile defence cooperation."—NATO-Russia Council Joint Statement, November 20, 2012 (http://www.nato.int/cps/en/natolive/news_68871.htm).

39. "[Our] territorial defence system will be part of our collective defence framework. We cannot outsource our collective defence obligations to non-NATO members," speech by NATO Secretary-General Anders Fogh Rasmussen at the Royal United Services Institute, London, June 15, 2011 ("NATO: Defending against Ballistic Missile Attack"—http://www.nato.int/cps/en/natolive/opinions_75473.htm).

40. Mikhail Margelov, "Russia's Vision for the Middle East and North Africa," transcript of speech at Chatham House, December 10, 2013 (http://www.chatham-house.org/sites/files/chathamhouse/home/chatham/public_html/sites/default/files/101213Russia.pdf), p. 7.

41. Vladimir Putin, "Russia and the Changing World," *Moskovskie novosti*, February 27, 2012 (http://valdaiclub.com/politics/39300.html); see also Putin's remarks to the Valdai Club, September 19, 2013 (http://eng.kremlin.ru/news/6007).

42. Thus Obama called for the UN Security Council to "stand against the Assad regime's relentless brutality and to demonstrate that it is a credible advocate for the universal rights that are written into the UN Charter," February 4, 2012 (http://www.cfr.org/syria/obamas-statement-syria-february-2012/p27292).

43. See remarks by Alexei Pushkov (chairman of the Duma's International Affairs Committee), cited in Fred Weir, "So Many Nyets: Why the Chasm between US, Russia Is So Hard to Bridge," *Christian Science Monitor*, February 21, 2013 (http://www.csmonitor.com/World/Europe/2013/0221/So-many-nyets-Why-the-chasm-between-US-Russia-is-so-hard-to-bridge).

44. Ariel Cohen and Stephen Blank, "'Reset' Regret: Russian 'Sphere of Privileged Interests' in Eurasia Undermines US Foreign Policy," Heritage Foundation, August 3, 2011 (http://www.heritage.org/research/reports/2011/08/reset-regret-russian-global-strategy-undermines-us-interests).

45. "Russia, China Should Explain Their Veto to the Syrians: Hillary Clinton," *The Nation*, October 6, 2011 (http://www.nation.com.pk/international/06-Oct-2011/Russia-China-should-explain-their-veto-to-Syrians-Hillary-Clinton). See also Hillary Rodham Clinton, *Hard Choices* (London: Simon & Schuster, 2014), pp. 235–60. The theme of "right" (and "wrong") side of history was used by Bill Clinton in endorsing Obama as the Democratic Party's candidate for the 2008 presidential elections— "Clinton: Barack Obama Is the Man for This Job," CNN International, August 27, 2008 (http://edition.cnn.com/2008/POLITICS/08/27/bill.clinton.transcript/index.html?iref=nextin).

46. The Magnitsky Act replaced the 1974 Jackson-Vanik amendment (see note 48 below). It covers not only officials suspected of involvement in the ill-treatment and death of Magnitsky, but also those implicated in other cases of human rights abuses. The U.S. Senate passed the bill by a crushing 92–4 in December 2012.

47. In his remarks to the Valdai Club in September 2013 Putin claimed that "many of the Euro-Atlantic countries are actually rejecting their roots, including the Christian values that constitute the basis of Western civilization." He contrasted this to Russia's identity as a "state civilization, reinforced by the Russian people, Russian language, Russian culture, Russian Orthodox Church, and the country's other traditional religions" (http://eng.kremlin.ru/news/6007).

48. The original Jackson-Vanik amendment denied Most Favored Nation trading status ("normal trade relations") to the Soviet Union for its failure to allow the free emigration of Jews. The amendment was overridden on an annual basis through the device of a presidential waiver. Although its original rationale has been obsolete for decades, Jackson-Vanik was consistently used by Congress as leverage to promote democracy and human rights in Russia. For a good analysis of the various issues, see Julie Ginsberg, "Reassessing the Jackson-Vanik Amendment," Council on Foreign Relations, July 2, 2009 (http://www.cfr.org/trade/reassessing-jackson-vanik-amendment/p19734).

49. Many of these points were made by Putin himself in an address to Russia's diplomats on July 9, 2012 (http://eng.kremlin.ru/transcripts/4145).

50. David Kramer and Lilia Shevtsova, "Here We Go Again: Falling for the Russian Trap," *American Interest*, February 21, 2013 (http://www.the-american-interest.com/articles/2013/02/21/here-we-go-again-falling-for-the-russian-trap/).

51. Cohen and Blank, "'Reset' Regret."

52. Mitt Romney interview with Wolf Blitzer, CNN, on March 26, 2012 (http://www.huffingtonpost.com/2012/03/26/mitt-romney-russia-geopolitical-foe_n_1380801.html).

53. Author's conversations in Washington, April 2013.

54. In 2013 the former CIA employee and NSA contractor Edward Snowden leaked a vast number of NSA and other intelligence files to various media sources. The leaked information revealed the extent of U.S. intelligence operations against allied countries, such as France and Germany. Snowden managed to elude arrest by flying to Hong Kong from his home in Hawaii, taking refuge in the Russian consulate there, and then escaping to Moscow. After some hesitation the Russian government granted him a one-year temporary asylum status, renewable annually. For an excellent account of the Snowden affair and its impact on Russia-U.S. relations, see Angela Stent, *The Limits of Partnership* (2nd ed., forthcoming 2015).

55. Julia Ioffe, "The Syria Solution: Obama Got Played by Putin and Assad," *New Republic*, September 10, 2013 (http://www.newrepublic.com/article/114655/obama-syria-policy-octopus-fighting-itself). Obama had previously declared that Assad's use of chemical weapons against the rebels would cross a "red line," and suggested that this would generate a U.S. armed response. But following the sarin attack on Ghouta on August 21, 2013, he decided to seek congressional approval for military action, although he was under no obligation to do so. It became clear that Congress would not grant its assent, at which point the Russian government offered to intercede with the Syrians.

56. Vladimir Putin, "A Plea for Caution from Russia," *New York Times*, September 11, 2013 (http://www.nytimes.com/2013/09/12/opinion/putin-plea-for-caution-from-russia-on-syria.html?pagewanted=all&_r=0).

57. The most notorious comment came from Obama himself in an interview on the eve of a summit in Moscow. After extolling his "very good" relationship with Medvedev, he described Putin as having "one foot in the old ways of doing business and one foot in the new." However, he would meet Putin because "he still has sway"— Chris McGreal and Luke Harding, "Barack Obama: Putin Has One Foot in the Past," *The Guardian*, July 2, 2009 (http://www.theguardian.com/world/2009/jul/02/obama-putin-us-russia-relations). In fairness, others had a clearer understanding of the tandem. Then U.S. ambassador John Beyrle observed in a cable to Washington that Medvedev was very much the junior member, with Putin remaining the ultimate decisionmaker—"US Embassy Cables: 'Tandem Politics' of Medvedev and Putin," *The Guardian*, December 1, 2010 (http://www.theguardian.com/world/us-embassy-cables-documents/178955).

58. The personalization of relations was also a feature of Soviet times, notably between Roosevelt and Stalin, and later between Reagan and Gorbachev.

59. In his meetings with the Valdai Club, Putin spoke warmly about George W. Bush, while lamenting that he was being let down by those around him.

60. Obama administration officials claim they tried to stay in touch with Putin during the tandem years, but were repeatedly rebuffed—see Stent, *The Limits of Partnership*, p. 217. That said, some of the statements emerging out of the White House were unhelpful, such as the (admittedly true) observation that Putin had "one foot in the old ways of doing business" (see note 57 above).

61. Ariel Cohen, "Putin and Obama Won't Visit Each Other Any More," Heritage Foundation, May 17, 2012 (http://dailysignal.com/2012/05/17/putin-and-obama-wont-visit-each-other-any-more/); Nikolai Gvosdev, "The Realist Prism: a Closer Look at U.S.-Russia 'Summit-gate,'" *World Politics Review*, May 18, 2012 (http://www.worldpoliticsreview.com/articles/11965/the-realist-prism-a-closer-look-at-u-s-russia-summit-gate).

62. In 1983 the NATO military exercise "Able Archer" provoked such alarm in Moscow that the Soviet armed forces were readied for an imminent nuclear strike—see Robert Service, *How They Ended the Cold War* (Palgrave Macmillan, forthcoming 2015).

63. Patrick Kingsley, "Vladimir Putin's Egypt Visit Sends Message to US," *The Guardian*, February 9, 2015 (http://www.theguardian.com/world/2015/feb/09/vladimir-putin-egypt-visit-message-us-russia).

64. Alec Luhn, "Russia to Reopen Spy Base in Cuba as Relations with the US Continue to Sour," *The Guardian*, July 16, 2014 (http://www.theguardian.com/world/2014/jul/16/russia-reopening-spy-base-cuba-us-relations-sour).

65. Alexei Pushkov, "Russia Grows Strong; Europe and the USA Weaken," Valdai Club website, January 9, 2014 (http://valdaiclub.com/near_abroad/66060.html); Andranik Migranyan, "The US in a Time of Change: Internal Transformations and Relations with Russia," *Russia in Global Affairs*, April 15, 2013 (http://eng.global affairs.ru/number/The-US-in-a-Time-of-Change-Internal-Transformations-and-Relations-with-Russia-15927).

66. Suslov, "Russia-US 'Reset' Over: What Next?"

67. This attitude was encapsulated by Putin's dismissive response to the third round of EU sanctions imposed against Russia in April 2014: "We all know . . . that no sanctions can be effective in the modern world." He went on to claim that sanctions would even bring certain benefits, such as consolidating people's savings and assisting de-offshorization—remarks at the First Media Forum of Independent Regional and Local Media, St. Petersburg, April 24, 2014 (http://eng.kremlin.ru/transcripts/7075).

68. There are some dissenting voices, notably advocates of traditional realpolitik such as Henry Kissinger, John Mearsheimer, and Dmitri Simes. But their influence on Obama's Russia policy has been minimal.

69. In an unguarded moment, Obama suggested to Medvedev in March 2012 that he would have greater scope to show "flexibility" on missile defense once he was re-elected—David Goodman, "Microphone Catches a Candid Obama," *New York*

*Times*, March 26, 2012 (http://www.nytimes.com/2012/03/27/us/politics/obama-caught-on-microphone-telling-medvedev-of-flexibility.html).

70. A variation of Niccolò Machiavelli's famous aphorism in *The Prince*: "It is better to be feared than loved, if you cannot be both."

71. In his February 2012 article "Russia and the Changing World," Putin wrote that Russia had a stake in ensuring a strong EU, "as envisioned by Germany and France." See also Yevgeny Shestakov, "Why We Have Finally Fallen Out of Love with Europe," Russia Beyond The Headlines, December 20, 2011 (http://rbth.ru/articles/2011/12/20/untitled_resource_14055.html).

72. This idea has its roots in the notion of European "collective security," conceived in the 1930s by Maxim Litvinov, People's Commissar for Foreign Affairs (1930–39). It also underpinned Medvedev's "new European security architecture."

73. In March 2009, the author attended a conference in Rome hosted by the Institute of Strategic Dialogue, entitled "Exploring New Vehicles for Strategic Engagement with Russia." The purpose of the conference was to consider mechanisms for more effective Russia-EU interaction, in particular, the idea of a Contact Group of six, comprising Germany, France, the UK, Italy, Poland, and the European Commission. Consideration was given to adding some others, such as the Netherlands and Sweden. Unsurprisingly, the idea came under heavy fire from a number of participants, and did not develop further. See http://www.strategicdialogue.org/events/items/ameurus-meeting-march2009 for the original position paper by Lord (David) Owen.

74. Nikolay Spasskiy, "The Decline of Europe and Russia's Future," *Russia in Global Affairs*, June 23, 2012 (http://eng.globalaffairs.ru/number/The-Decline-of-Europe-and-Russias-Future-15572). Spasskiy argues that the only way out for Europe is by "enhancing the role of the state," learning in particular from the Lee Kuan Yew model in Singapore.

75. "'From Lisbon to Vladivostok': Putin Envisions a Russia-EU Free Trade Zone," *Spiegel Online*, November 25, 2010 (http://www.spiegel.de/international/europe/from-lisbon-to-vladivostok-putin-envisions-a-russia-eu-free-trade-zone-a-731109.html). Igor Yurgens had previously proposed a "Union of Europe" as early as 2008—"Towards a Union of Europe," *Rossiiskaya gazeta*, November 6, 2008 (http://www.insor-russia.ru/en/_news/analytics/3303).

76. Vladimir Putin, "A New Integration Project for Eurasia: the Future in the Making," *Izvestiya*, October 10, 2011 (http://www.russianmission.eu/en/news/article-prime-minister-vladimir-putin-new-integration-project-eurasia-future-making-izvestia-3-).

77. Sergei Markov, "How Russia and EU Can Build a Greater Europe," *Moscow Times*, December 3, 2013 (http://www.themoscowtimes.com/opinion/article/how-russia-and-eu-can-build-a-greater-europe/490718.html).

78. Dmitry Babich, "Why the EU Has Lost the Right to Lecture Russia," Russia Beyond the Headlines, November 28, 2012 (http://rbth.co.uk/articles/2012/11/28/why_the_eu_has_lost_the_right_to_lecture_russia_20503.html).

79. Putin once memorably compared the EU to a hamster that was constantly stuffing its cheeks with food it was then unable to digest—"Putin Compares EU with Hamster," *Baltic News Network*, November 14, 2011 (http://bnn-news.com/putin-compares-eu-hamster-41214).

80. The EU's success in brokering a cease-fire in the 2008 Russia-Georgia war was due largely to the fact that France held the Union presidency at the time. Sarkozy was the only European leader, other than Merkel, who could have secured a cease-fire.

81. The PCA has technically expired, and is being rolled over on a year-to-year basis.

82. 2013 Russian Foreign Policy Concept.

83. Arkady Moshes, "Russia's European Policy under Medvedev: How Sustainable Is a New Compromise?," *International Affairs* (London), vol. 88, no. 1, 2012, pp. 20–21.

84. European countries were not primary parties to these disputes, but were affected because of Ukraine's position as a transit state for their imports of Russian gas. When Gazprom cut off Ukraine's supply, the Ukrainians reacted by siphoning off the gas intended for Europe, which in turn led to a general shutdown for several days in 2006 and again for two weeks in 2009.

85. See chapter 3, note 70.

86. Alan Riley, "Commission v. Gazprom: The Antitrust Clash of the Decade?," CEPS Policy Brief 285, October 31, 2012.

87. Andrey Konoplyanik and Alan Riley, "EU versus Gazprom: the Substance and Implications of the Antitrust Clash," presentations at a Chatham House seminar, London, November 27, 2013.

88. The figure was 80 percent pre-Nordstream—see "16 Percent of Natural Gas in Europe Flows through Ukraine," *Today in Energy*, United States Energy Information Administration, March 14, 2014 (http://www.eia.gov/todayinenergy/detail.cfm?id=15411, accessed July 22, 2014).

89. Stanley Reed, "A Conduit for Russian Gas, Tangled in Europe's Conflicts," *New York Times*, June 30, 2014 (http://www.nytimes.com/2014/07/01/business/international/south-stream-pipeline-project-in-bulgaria-is-delayed.html); see also John Lough, "The EU's Tough Gas Game with Russia," Chatham House Expert Comment, June 12, 2014 (www.chathamhouse.org/expert/comment/14874).

90. Nick Thorpe, "Was Russia's South Stream Too Big a 'Burden' to Bear?," BBC News, December 3, 2014 (http://www.bbc.co.uk/news/world-europe-30289412); Elena Mazneva, "Russia 2014 Gas Export Seen Lowest in Decade as Demand Falls," Bloomberg, January 13, 2015 (http://www.bloomberg.com/news/articles/2015-01-13/russia-2014-gas-exports-seen-lowest-in-decade-as-nations-cut-use).

91. When the Eastern Partnership was established in 2009, it was allocated €600 million for the period 2010–13 (http://eeas.europa.eu/ eastern/faq/index_en.htm). In fact, actual funding is somewhat more generous under the European Neighbourhood and Partnership Instrument (ENPI)—€2.5 billion for the period 2011–13 (http://www.consilium.europa.eu/uedocs/cms_Data/docs/pressdata/EN/foraff/ 139765.pdf).

92. Statement to the European Parliament, Strasbourg, September 11, 2013 (http://europa.eu/rapid/press-release_SPEECH-13-687_en.htm).

93. Nikolaj Nielsen, "Russia Bans Moldova Wine ahead of EU Summit," *EU Observer*, September 11, 2013 (http://euobserver.com/foreign/121388); "EU Warns Russia over Trade 'Threats' to ex-Soviet Bloc," BBC News, September 12, 2013 (http://www.bbc.co.uk/news/world-europe-24061556).

94. *Russia 2013: Shaping Russia's Future*, Ernst and Young's Attractiveness Survey, p. 22.

95. Russia supplies a third of Germany's gas imports (http://www.eon.com/en/business-areas/gas-supply-and-production/sources-of-supply/russia.html). The 2011 Fukushima nuclear disaster led to a decision to phase out nuclear power by 2022.

96. For an excellent analysis of Putin's posting in Dresden (1985–89), see Fiona Hill and Clifford Gaddy, *Mr. Putin: Operative in the Kremlin,* 2nd ed. (Brookings, 2015), pp. 110–15.

97. Putin's inner circle is almost exclusively Russian, with two notable exceptions: Warnig and former chancellor Schröder. The background to the relationship between Putin and Warnig is predictably murky, with stories that they knew each other in a professional capacity during Putin's KGB posting in Dresden. Officially, their relationship dates from 1991, when Putin was deputy mayor of St. Petersburg in charge of foreign relations, and Warnig was the Dresdner Bank's representative in the city. Warnig's official position as of early 2015 is CEO of Nordstream. However, this sinecure hardly reflects his real importance to Putin.

98. Principally by supporting the expansion of Nordstream and watering down proposals for alternative pipelines bypassing Russia, such as Nabucco.

99. In September 2005, Schröder signed a US$4.7 billion deal to build Nordstream, just before losing the Bundestag elections to Merkel. Two months later, he was appointed chairman of the board of Nordstream—Craig Whitlock and Peter Finn, "Schroeder Accepts Russian Pipeline Job," *Washington Post*, December 10, 2005 (http://www.washingtonpost.com/wp-dyn/content/article/2005/12/09/AR2005120901755.html).

100. "'A Sign of Alienation': Sharp Words Define German-Russian Relations," *Spiegel Onlin*e, November 1, 2012 (http://www.spiegel.de/international/europe/interview-commissioner-for-german-russian-coordination-schockenhoff-a-864566.html).

101. Stefan Meister, "An Alienated Partnership: German–Russian Relations after Putin's Return," FIIA (Finnish Institute of International Affairs) Briefing Paper 103, May 10, 2012 (http://www.fiia.fi/en/publication/263/#.UkHpMj-E7wE).

102. "European and American Views of Russia Turned from Favorable to Unfavorable" (http://trends.gmfus.org/views-of-russia-turned-from-favorable-to-unfavorable/).

103. John Lough, "Ukraine Crisis Prompts a Sea Change in Germany's Russia Policy," Chatham House Expert Comment, November 24, 2014 (http://www.chatham house.org/expert/comment/16320).

104. The literal translation of *Ostpolitik* is "Eastern policy," but it really means reaching out to Russia and establishing an accommodation of interests.

105. Author's conversation with a European foreign minister, May 2014.

106. "Russia's Global Image Negative amid Crisis in Ukraine," Pew Global Attitudes survey, July 9, 2014 (http://www.pewglobal.org/2014/07/09/russias-global-image-negative-amid-crisis-in-ukraine/).

107. "German Manufacturing Orders Slump in June," *Business Spectator*, August 6, 2014 (http://www.businessspectator.com.au/news/2014/8/6/economy/german-manufacturing-orders-slump-june).

108. Meister, "An Alienated Partnership."

109. Marie Mendras, "Russia-France: a Strained Political Relationship," *Russian Analytical Digest* 130, July 1, 2013, p. 7.

110. Thomas Gomart, "France's Russia Policy: Balancing Interests and Values," *Washington Quarterly*, vol. 30, no. 2, Spring 2007, p. 147.

111. Mendras, "Russia-France," p. 2. See also Vyacheslav Nikonov, "Back to the Concert," *Russia in Global Affairs*, November 16, 2002 (http://eng.globalaffairs.ru/number/n_12); "Toward an Alliance of Europe," Analytical Report by the Russian Group of the International Valdai Discussion Club, September 2010, p. 4.

112. "No Plans to Suspend Mistral Deal over Syria—France," RIA-Novosti, August 29, 2012 (http://en.ria.ru/world/20120829/175498868.html).

113. Arnaud Dubien, "Socialist President in France and Future of Russian-French Relations," Valdai Club website, May 25, 2012 (http://valdaiclub.com/europe/43320.html).

114. Mendras, "Russia–France."

115. For example, Paris supported Turkey's request for the deployment of NATO Patriot missiles on its border with Syria.

116. Transatlantic Trends Survey of September 12, 2012 (http://trends.gmfus.org/views-of-russia-turned-from-favorable-to-unfavorable/). Although in 2013 there was a slight recovery to 36 percent, the Ukraine crisis has precipitated a further decline to 26 percent (versus 73 percent "unfavorable")—see "Russia's Global Image Negative amid Crisis in Ukraine."

117. "Ukraine Crisis: France Halts Warship Delivery to Russia," BBC News, September 3, 2014 (http://www.bbc.co.uk/news/world-europe-29052599).

118. On April 10, a TU-154 carrying President Kaczyński and a large official entourage crashed on its approach to Smolensk airport. They had been due to attend an event marking the 70th anniversary of the massacre at Katyn (19 km from Smolensk). In addition to the president and his wife, other high-profile fatalities included former president Ryszard Kaczorowski, the chief of the Polish General Staff, and the president of the National Bank of Poland.

119. Michael Schwirtz, "Putin Marks Massacre of Polish Officers," *New York Times*, April 7, 2010 (http://www.nytimes.com/2010/04/08/world/europe/08putin.html?_r=0); Benjamin Bidder, "Remembering the Katyn Massacre: Putin Gesture Heralds New Era in Russian–Polish Relations," *Spiegel Online*, April 8, 2010 (http://www.spiegel.de/international/europe/remembering-the-katyn-massacre-putin- gesture-heralds-new-era-in-russian-polish-relations-a-687819.html).

120. Dmitri Trenin, "Russia and Poland: a Friendship That Must Not Fail," Open Democracy, December 2, 2010 (http://www.opendemocracy.net/od-russia/dmitri-trenin/russia-and-poland-friendship-that-must-not-fail).

121. 2013 Russian Foreign Policy Concept.

122. "Interview with [Polish Foreign Minister] Radoslaw Sikorski: Polish-Russian Relations Are on the Rise, but Complicated Issues Need to be Solved," *Interfax*, December 18, 2012 (http://www.interfax.com/interview.asp?id=383765).

123. Pawel Wisniewski, "Poland's Strategy for Dealing with Russia's Human Rights Record," Carnegie Moscow Center, March 1, 2013 (http://www.carnegie.ru/2013/03/01/poland-s-strategy-for-dealing-with-russia-s-human-rights-record/fn0t).

124. That said, Sikorski tried very hard to persuade the Maidan protesters to reach an accommodation with Yanukovych instead of insisting on his removal— "Ukraine Protests: Polish Minister Radoslaw Sikorski Warns Protest Leader 'You'll All Be Dead'" (https://www.youtube.com/watch?v=EiI5xozu6gg).

125. Accumulated Polish FDI into Russia at the end of 2011 was US$704 million— less than 0.5 percent of total FDI into Russia (US$347 billion), and barely 1.5 percent of total Polish FDI (almost US$45 billion). Maya Rostowska, "Investment in Russia: Risks and Opportunities," Bulletin 45 (398), April 30, 2013, Polish Institute of International Affairs (https://www.pism.pl/files/?id_plik=13523).

126. Andrew Monaghan, "The UK and Russia—Towards a Renewed Relationship?," *Russian Analytical Digest* 130, July 1, 2013, p. 9.

127. In exchange for selling its 50 percent stake in TNK-BP in 2013, BP received 18.5 percent of Rosneft shares plus US$12.5 billion in cash. Counting its pre-deal holding of shares (1.25 percent), this meant that it now held 19.75 percent of Rosneft stock (http://www.bp.com/en/global/corporate/about-bp/bp-worldwide/bp-in-russia.html).

128. James Kirkup, "Russia Mocks Britain, the Little Island," *The Telegraph*, September 5, 2013 (http://www.telegraph.co.uk/news/worldnews/europe/russia/10290243/Russia-mocks-Britain-the-little-island.html).

129. In November 2006, the former Russian spy Alexander Litvinenko fell seriously ill after a meeting with Andrei Lugovoi, a member of Russia's Federal Protective Service. Litvinenko died in great agony less than a month later, accusing the Russian intelligence services of poisoning him. There ensued a diplomatic standoff between London and Moscow, resulting in the mutual expulsion of diplomats and a complete freeze on security cooperation. In fact, the political relationship had been in trouble well before the Litvinenko affair, following the British government's decision in 2003 to grant asylum to the exiled tycoon Boris Berezovsky and Chechen "foreign minister" Ahmed Zakayev.

130. Ewen MacAskill, "NATO to Announce 4,000-strong Rapid Reaction Force to Counter Russian Threat," *The Guardian*, September 5, 2014 (http://www.the-guardian.com/world/2014/sep/05/nato-4000-rapid-reaction-force-baltics-russia).

131. Andrew Monaghan, "Litvinenko Inquiry Another Blow to UK-Russia Relations," Chatham House Expert Comment, July 23, 2014 (http://www.chatham

house.org/expert/comment/15234?dm_i=1TYG,2NVKV,BI05S2,9QNL5,1). Home Secretary Teresa May had previously resisted a public inquiry, acknowledging that "international relations" had been a factor in her decision.

132. Igor Ivanov, "Russia, Turkey and the Vision of Greater Europe," RIAC, January 12, 2015 (http://russiancouncil.ru/en/inner/?id_4=5055#top); Igor Torbakov, "Europe's Twin Sisters," Open Democracy, June 14, 2013 (http://www.opendemocracy.net/od-russia/igor-torbakov/europe%E2%80%99s-twin-sisters). I witnessed this sense of identification between Russia and Turkey at first hand after delivering a lecture on "Russia and Europe" at Istanbul's Bogazici University in 2007. A member of the audience suggested that I could have been speaking, almost verbatim, about the dynamic between Turkey and Europe.

133. Christopher Stone, cited in Igor Torbakov, "Europe's Twin Sisters."

134. "Putin Sees New Opportunities for Turkey-Russia Economic, Trade Ties," Anadolu Agency, November 28, 2014 (http://www.hurriyetdailynews.com/putin-sees-new-opportunities-for-turkey-russia-economic-trade-ties.aspx?pageID=238&nID=74975&NewsCatID=344); Natalia Ulchenko, "What Is So Special about Russian-Turkish Economic Relations," *Russian Analytical Digest* 125, March 25, 2013, p. 7. Turkey's share of Russian gas may increase considerably as a result of Putin's decision to terminate the South Stream project.

135. "Russian Tourists Flooding into Turkey," Anadolu Agency, October 31, 2014 (http://www.hurriyetdailynews.com/russian-tourists-flooding-into-turkey-.aspx?pageID=238&nID=73719&NewsCatID=349).

136. Lally Weymouth, "Turkish President Abdullah Gul: Assad Must Go," *Washington Post*, September 24, 2012 (http://www.washingtonpost.com/opinions/turkish-president-abdullah-gul-assad-must-go/2013/09/23/ffc45d7a-246e-11e3-b75d-5b7f6 6349852_story.html).

137. Dimitar Bechev, "Putin and Erdogan: Partnership of Convenience?," *Al-Jazeera*, December 2, 2014 (http://www.aljazeera.com/indepth/opinion/2014/12/putin-erdogan-partnership-conven-20141227165377730.html).

138. Lamiya Adilgizi, "Putin's Visit to Turkey to Keep Bilateral Relations Strong," *Zaman*, December 9, 2012 (http://www.todayszaman.com/news-300580-putins-visit-to-turkey-to-keep-bilateral-relations-strong.html).

139. "The Eastern Blockage," *The Economist*, May 17, 2014 (http://www.economist.com/news/europe/21602277-new-europe-divided-about-russia-old-europe-bad- consequences-all-eastern).

140. "The Czechs and Russia—Spy versus Politician," *The Economist*, October 29, 2014 (http://www.economist.com/blogs/easternapproaches/2014/10/czechs-and-russia).

141. Cas Mudde, "Russia's Trojan Horse," Open Democracy, December 8, 2014 (https://www.opendemocracy.net/od-russia/cas-mudde/russia%27s-trojan-horse).

142. "Hungary's Foreign Policy—between Brussels and Russia," *The Economist*, July 19, 2014 (http://www.economist.com/news/europe/21607862-prime-minister-seeks-play-east-and-west-between-brussels-and-russia).

143. "Monument to Russian Czar Nicholas II Unveiled in Central Belgrade," ITAR-TASS, November 16, 2014 (http://en.itar-tass.com/world/759997).

144. Spasskiy, "The Decline of Europe and Russia's Future."

145. In the 2014 Russian Military Doctrine, as in the 2010 version, NATO tops the list of "main external military dangers" (http://www.scribd.com/doc/251695098/Russias-2014-Military-Doctrine#scribd).).

146. See comments by NATO Secretary-General Rasmussen—note 39 above.

147. Vyacheslav Nikonov, head of the Russkii Mir Foundation: "A course has been taken aimed at maximally weakening Russia's position in the world and dealing maximal [*sic*] economic, political, moral and other damage with the aim of triggering an economic crisis in the country and, preferably, conditions for regime change, with its replacement being pro-American"—Russkii Mir press release, July 23, 2014 (http://www.russkiymir.ru/en/news/146499/).

148. Patrick Donohue and Ilya Arkhipov, "Merkel, Putin Clash over Human Rights at Kremlin Meeting," Bloomberg, November 16, 2012 (http://www.bloomberg.com/news/2012-11-16/merkel-putin-meet-in-moscow-amid-rising-criticism-in-germany.html).

149. As Andrew Wood has remarked, "Putin has consistently seen the United States as Russia's necessary counterpart"—"Russia: Cold Shadows and Present Illusions," Chatham House Program Paper, March 2013, p. 2. Ed Lucas in *The Economist* (February 16, 2013) puts it even more starkly: "If America did not exist, Russia would have to invent it." "Russia and America: the Dread of the Other" (http://www.economist.com/news/europe/21571904-leading-role-played-anti-americanism-todays-russia-dread-other).

150. According to a former Western diplomat: "The traditional Russian style of negotiation is . . . zero/sum: a contest of trial and strength. It has winners and losers. The objective is to use all of the strength and cunning at your disposal to achieve victory (ideally total victory) and the maximum possible short-term advantage. Concern for reputational damage is minimal: the reputation that matters is to be strong and successful. . . . Consequently the style tends to be confrontational, unyielding and highly opportunistic. . . . In this adversarial style of negotiation, two results are seen as acceptable: either total victory or a deal which entails direct and visible trade-offs . . . the 'principle of reciprocity.'"

151. In fact, perhaps the problem Russians face in dealing with the Chinese is that the latter have a similar negotiating mentality to their own. For all the talk about "win-win outcomes," a leading Chinese trade diplomat once told a friend of the author that "win-win just means you haven't negotiated hard enough."

152. Remarks by Anatoly Chubais at the 2012 United States–Russia Business Council (USRBC) Annual Meeting, Atlanta, Georgia, October 23, 2012.

153. Chrystia Freeland, "The Russians are Coming—to Silicon Valley," Reuters, May 27, 2011 (http://blogs.reuters.com/chrystia-freeland/2011/05/).

154. While Russians adhere to the idea of a "strong leader," polls have shown consistently high support for an independent judiciary, fair elections, and uncensored media. It is striking that despite the Ukraine crisis (and the painful impact of sanctions

on their everyday lives), most Russians still favor closer ties with the West. A Levada poll from March 2015 found that 60 percent of respondents supported "increasing economic, political, and cultural ties [and] policies that are more closely aligned with the West" versus 29 percent who favored "cutting off ties and relations [and] distancing Russia from the West." See "Russia's Role in the World," Levada Center press release, March 25, 2015 (http://www.levada.ru/eng/russia%E2%80%99s-role-world).

155. Rilka Dragneva and Kataryna Wolczuk, "Russia, the Eurasian Customs Union and the EU: Cooperation, Stagnation or Rivalry?," Chatham House Briefing Paper, August 2012, pp. 2, 14–15.

156. Andrey Ostroukh, "Russia's Capital Outflows at Whopping $63 Billion in 2013," *Wall Street Journal*, January 17, 2014 (http://blogs.wsj.com/emerging europe/2014/01/17/russias-capital-outflows-at-whopping-63-billion-in-2013/); Alexander Kolyandr, "Russia's Capital Flight Surges in First Quarter, Fueled by Ukraine Crisis," *Wall Street Journal*, March 24, 2014 (http://online.wsj.com/news/articles/SB10001424052702303725404579459320826557770).

157. Andrew Kramer, "Putin Trumpets Economic Strength, but Advisors Seem Less Certain," *New York Times*, October 2, 2014 (http://www.nytimes.com/2014/10/03/world/europe/putin-russia-economy.html?_r=0).

158. Angela Stent, "Reluctant Europeans: Three Centuries of Russian Ambivalence toward the West," in Robert Legvold (ed.), *Russian Foreign Policy in the Twenty-First Century and the Shadow of the Past* (New York: Columbia University Press, 2007), pp. 399, 421.

159. See Putin's annual address to the Federal Assembly, December 4, 2014 (http://eng.kremlin.ru/news/23341).

160. Lilia Shevtsova notes that "this [ruling] class's dependence on, and personal incorporation into, the West [has] proved no hindrance to the task of rebuilding an anti-Western regime in Russia"—in Lilia Shevtsova and Andrew Wood, *Change or Decay: Russia's Dilemma and the West's Response* (Washington: Carnegie Endowment for International Peace, 2011), p. 49.

161. Igor Ivanov, "What Diplomacy Does Russia Need in the 21st Century?," *Russia in Global Affairs*, December 29, 2011 (http://eng.globalaffairs.ru/number/What-Diplomacy-Does-Russia-Need-in-the-21st-Century-15420).

162. 2013 Russian Foreign Policy Concept.

163. Ibid.

164. Konstantin Eggert, "Due West: Putin's Campaign Platform: Echoes of Prince Gorchakov," RIA-Novosti, January 18, 2012 (http://sputniknews.com/analysis/20120118/170828395.html).

## Chapter 7

*Epigraph*: Lao Tzu, *Tao Te Ching* (Harmondsworth: Penguin, 1986 [1963]), p. 81.

1. See remarks by Dmitry Suslov and Andrei Tsygankov in "Russia's Foreign Policy: Total Success or Utter Failure?," Russia Direct, November 13, 2012

(http://www.russia-direct.org/content/russia%E2%80%99s-foreign-policy-total-success-or-utter-failure); also Sergei Karaganov, "A Lop-Sided Power," *Russia in Global Affairs*, December 26, 2013 (http://eng.globalaffairs.ru/number/A-Lop-Sided-Power-16279).

2. If one counts the Putin-Medvedev tandem as a de facto presidency, then the period 2018–24 would be Putin's fifth term.

3. For an interesting discussion of the disjunction between the formulation and implementation of "strategy," see Andrew Monaghan, "Defibrillating the *Vertikal*? Putin and Russian Grand Strategy," Chatham House Research Paper, October 2014 (http://www.chathamhouse.org/sites/files/chathamhouse/field/field_document/2014 1024DefibrillatingVertikal.pdf).

4. This phrase first appeared in Nikolai Chernyshevsky's novel *What Is to Be Done?*, published in 1863 in response to Ivan Turgenev's *Fathers and Sons*. Lenin later took it up in a 1902 pamphlet of the same title.

5. Dmitri Trenin, "Hold Off on Champagne: Hard Slog Lies Ahead," Carnegie Moscow Center, September 19, 2013 (http://carnegie.ru/eurasiaoutlook/?fa=53040).

6. Lilia Shevtsova, *Lonely Power: Why Russia Has Failed to Become the West, and the West Is Weary of Russia* (Washington: Carnegie Endowment for International Peace, 2010).

7. Witness the long (if fruitless) campaign by Brazil, India, Japan, Germany, and many others to change the composition and rules of the UNSC. See also Kishore Mahbubani, *The Great Convergence: Asia, the West, and the Logic of One World* (New York: PublicAffairs, 2013), pp. 227–46.

8. Tony Paterson, "A New Russian Revolution: the Cracks are Starting to Appear in Putin's Kremlin Power Bloc," *The Independent*, July 27, 2014 (http://www.independent.co.uk/news/world/europe/a-new-russian-revolution-the-cracks-are-starting-to-appear-in-putins-kremlin-power-bloc-9631894.html).

9. Mikhail Gorbachev, *Perestroika: New Thinking for Our Country and the World* (London: Fontana, 1988).

10. Giuseppe Tomasi de Lampedusa, *The Leopard* (London: Everyman's Library, 1998 [1958]), p. 22. He was writing about the advanced decay of Sicilian society at the beginning of the Italian *risorgimento* (unification) in May 1860.

11. Although there has been a partial demographic recovery in recent years owing to increases in fertility and life expectancy, Russia's population is set to decline significantly over the next few decades. The main reason is the much smaller cohort of women born in the 1990s and now reaching child-bearing age, relative to numbers in other decades. Just as serious is the decline in the working-age population. In 2011 Rosstat (the government statistics agency) estimated this would decline from 102 million to 91 million by 2030—Philip Hanson, "The Russian Economy and Its Prospects," in Philip Hanson, James Nixey, Lilia Shevtsova, and Andrew Wood, *Putin Again: Implications for Russia and the West*, Chatham House Report, February 2012, p. 22. Other forecasts are even more pessimistic. A 2014 Higher Economic School report speaks of a decline of 15 million by 2030—see Olga Tanas, "Russia Takes Double

Punch as Vanishing Workers Fan Prices," Bloomberg, September 17, 2014 (http://www.bloomberg.com/news/2014-09-16/russia-takes-double-punch-as-vanishing-workers-fan-prices.html).

12. Richard Weitz, "The Rise and Fall of Medvedev's European Security Treaty," German Marshall Fund Paper, May 2012.

13. 2013 Concept of Participation of the Russian Federation in the BRICS.

14. During the 1990s this was exemplified by its opposition to the nascent GUUAM (Georgia, Ukraine, Uzbekistan, Azerbaijan, Moldova) grouping.

15. In its Soviet version, the culture of envy was reflected in the satirical slogan of "equal poverty for all." A twenty-first-century international relations version might read "equal frustration for all."

16. Fyodor Lukyanov argues that in the 1990s "Russia sought to pursue a consistent and independent policy, but objective circumstances . . . forced it to adjust to the situation all the time, weighing its goals against real possibilities"—"'Vigor, Toughness and Tolerance,'" *Russia in Global Affairs*, March 27, 2011 (http://eng.globalaffairs.ru/ number/Vigor-Toughness-and-Tolerance-15152).

17. Marie Mendras, in debate with Fyodor Lukyanov, "Talking Point: the Logic of Russian Foreign Policy," Open Democracy, December 13, 2012 (http://www.opendemocracy.net/od-russia/oliver-carroll-fyodor-lukyanov-marie-mendras/talking-point-logic-of-russian-foreign-policy).

18. See John Stephan, *The Russian Far East: A History* (Stanford University Press, California, 1994), pp. 84–86.

19. The bridge to Russkii ostrov ("Russian island") was especially controversial. It cost more than US$1 billion, and suffered many construction delays and mishaps. It was also dubbed the "bridge to nowhere" because it serves only 5,000 people. "Vladivostok's New Iconic 'Golden Gate' Bridge Opens to Ordinary Traffic," *Siberian Times*, August 1, 2012 (http://siberiantimes.com/business/others/news/vladivostoks-new-iconic-golden-gate-bridge-opens-for-ordinary-traffic/).

20. Alexei Lossan, "Rosneft to Sell 10 Percent Stake in Largest Oil Field to Chinese Company," Russia Beyond the Headlines, September 8, 2014 (http://rbth.com/ business/2014/09/08/rosneft_to_sell_10_percent_stake_in_largest_oil_field_to_ chinese_com_39607.html).

21. Karaganov, "A Lop-Sided Power."

22. Academic Ranking of World Universities 2014 (http://www.shanghairank ing.com/ARWU2014.html). The Times Higher Education World University Rankings 2014–15 come up with a very similar result, with the exception that Novosibirsk State has replaced St. Petersburg as Russia's second entrant in the top 400 (http://www.timeshighereducation.co.uk/world-university-rankings/2014-15/world-ranking).

23. This was highlighted by the awarding of the 2010 Nobel Prize in Physics to Andrei Geim and Konstantin Novoselov for their work on graphene. When asked what it would take for him to return to work in Russia, Geim answered: "reincarnation." Howard Amos, "Nobel Winners Tell Why Russia Lacks Allure," *Moscow Times*,

October 21, 2010 (http://www.themoscowtimes.com/news/article/nobel-winners-tell-why-russia-lacks-allure/420700.html).

24. This is very different from the situation with Chinese students. Although huge numbers study overseas, the majority return to China, sometimes after a stint at a Western company or international organization. For example, an acquaintance of the author went to America to pursue a PhD at Stanford, and later spent five years at the World Bank, before taking up a senior position in the Shanghai Municipal Government and then at the Shanghai Stock Exchange.

25. "Disenchanted with Putin, Some Russians Vote with Their Feet," Reuters, July 24, 2014 (http://www.reuters.com/article/2014/07/24/russia-putin-emigration-idUSL6N0PI4TH20140724).

26. Exacerbated by such infamous *oeuvres* as the Marquis de Custine's 1839 travelogue, *Empire of the Czar: A Journey through Eternal Russia.*

27. Indeed, it could be argued that the Sochi Olympics lowered Russia's reputation in the developed world. Western media coverage focused, in particular, on the massive corruption surrounding the games and Russian hostility toward gay and lesbian rights.

28. A 2014 Pew Global Attitudes survey gives the following ratings for Russia in the Middle East: Egypt (24 percent favorable versus 71 percent unfavorable), Jordan (22–75), and Turkey (16–73). Curiously, perceptions of Russia have become somewhat more favorable in both Israel (up from 21–77 in 2013 to 30–68 in 2014) and the Palestinian Territories (from 29–57 to 41–46)—"Russia's Global Image Negative amid Crisis in Ukraine," July 9, 2014 (http://www.pewglobal.org/2014/07/09/russias-global-image-negative-amid-crisis-in-ukraine/).

29. Ibid. See also "Global Opinion of Russia Mixed," Pew Global Attitudes survey, September 3, 2013 (http://www.pewglobal.org/2013/09/03/global-opinion-of-russia-mixed/).

30. Contrary to the trend elsewhere, the Ukraine crisis boosted Putin's popularity in China; in 2013 Russia's favorable versus unfavorable rating there was only 49–39—"Global Opinion of Russia Mixed."

31. The former journalist Angus Roxburgh worked for the Kremlin as part of the U.S. public relations agency Ketchum. He discovered to his dismay that "the Kremlin wanted us to distribute the message, not change it"—*The Strongman: Vladimir Putin and the Struggle for Russia* (London and New York: I. B. Tauris, 2012), p. 191.

32. See chapter 2, note 86.

33. Thomas Frear, Lukasz Kulesa, and Ian Kearns, "Dangerous Brinkmanship: Close Military Encounters between Russia and the West in 2014," European Leadership Network Policy Brief, November 2014.

34. According to Yan Xuetong, China has a cooperative relationship with Russia, a competitive relationship with the United States, and a confrontational relationship with Japan. Comments at the Carnegie-Tsinghua Global Dialogue meeting in Beijing, December 4, 2013 (attended by author).

35. Author's conversations with EU policymakers.

36. The phrase was originally a response to the execution in 1804 of the Duc d'Enghien for his part in a plot to assassinate Napoleon.

37. At the 2013 Valdai Club meeting, Putin declared that Russians and Ukrainians were "one people," and that Ukraine was "part of our greater Russian, or Russian-Ukrainian world" (http://eng.kremlin.ru/transcripts/6007).

38. Military-industrial cooperation has been one of the main casualties of the conflict so far—see Julian Cooper, "Sanctions Will Hurt Russia's Rearmament Plans," *Moscow Times*, August 12, 2014 (http://www.themoscowtimes.com/opinion/article/sanctions-will-hurt-russia-s-rearmament-plans/505006.html).

39. Nursultan Nazarbaev, cited in "Eurasian Economic Union: Searching for Agreement," *Astana Calling*, No. 338, January 10, 2014, p. 4.

40. Eurasian Economic Commission website (http://www.eurasiancommission.org/en/act/chairman/paos/Pages/default.aspx, accessed April 6, 2015).

41. Comments by Nargis Kassenova, in "Discussing the Eurasian Customs Union and its Impact on Central Asia," *Central Asia Policy Forum* 4, February 2013, p. 2.

42. It is worth recalling that the Soviet Union was able to do business with Western European gas customers even at the height of the cold war.

43. According to the UN, Russia is the final destination for 21 percent of Afghanistan's annual opium crop of 375 tons—Amie Ferris-Rotman, "In Russia: a Glut of Heroin and Denial," Reuters, January 25, 2011 (http://www.reuters.com/article/2011/01/25/us-russia-heroin-idUSTRE70O22X20110125). See also "8.5 Million Russians, or 6 Percent of the Population, Are Drug Addicts," UPI, September 17, 2013 (http://www.upi.com/Top_News/World-News/2013/09/17/85-million-Russians-or-6-percent-of-the-population-are-drug-addicts/31811379422389/).

44. Arnold Toynbee, in *A Study of History*, identified suicidal statecraft as the ultimate cause of imperial collapse.

45. Exemplified by the angry reaction of U.S. Republicans to Obama's comment to Medvedev that he would have more "flexibility" on missile defense after the 2012 U.S. presidential elections—see chapter 6, note 69.

46. Dmitry Suslov, "Cancellation of the Chicago Summit Suits Russia, U.S. Interests," April 19, 2012 (http://valdaiclub.com/usa/41380.html).

47. The sanctions included denial of access to European capital markets for Russian state-owned banks; an embargo on new arms sales; and restrictions on the sale of advanced technology and equipment for the Russian oil industry.

48. Clifford Gaddy and Barry Ickes, "Can Sanctions Stop Putin?," Brookings, June 3, 2014 (http://www.brookings.edu/research/articles/2014/06/03-can-sanctions-stop-putin-gaddy-ickes).

49. See "Russians Back Protest, Political Freedoms," Pew Global Attitudes survey, May 23, 2012 (http://www.pewglobal.org/2012/05/23/russians-back-protests-political-freedoms-and-putin-too/).

50. Lilia Shevtsova and David Kramer, *Crisis: Russia and the West in the Time of Troubles* (Carnegie Moscow Center, 2013), p. 138.

51. James Sherr, *Hard Diplomacy and Soft Coercion: Russia's Influence Abroad* (London: Chatham House, 2013), pp. 125–26.

52. "Russia 'to Alter Military Strategy towards NATO,'" BBC News, September 2, 2014 (http://www.bbc.co.uk/news/world-europe-29026623).

53. Pekka Sutela, "Ukraine Spared the EU and Itself," Bloomberg, December 6, 2013 (http://www.bloomberg.com/news/2013-12-06/ukraine-spared-the-eu-and-itself.html).

54. Samuel Charap argues that "there are no winners in the geopolitical tug of war between Russia and the West." Or rather the winner is "the dysfunctional, deeply corrupt political-economic system [that] depends for its very survival on the absence of Russia-Western substantive exchanges about Ukraine policy"—in "Ukraine's False Choice," *Foreign Policy*, February 7, 2014 (http://www.foreignpolicy.com/articles/2014/02/07/ukraines_false_choice_russia_eu).

55. As Roderic Lyne observed soon after the annexation of Crimea, "If the West is not prepared to make that commitment, it should not have got so deeply involved in Ukraine in the first place." See "When Is the Right Time to Negotiate with Russia over Crimea?," Chatham House Expert Comment, March 24, 2014 (https://www.chathamhouse.org/media/comment/view/198437).

56. An embarrassing example was the debt ceiling standoff between the White House and Congress in October 2013, which forced Obama to cancel—for the second time—a four-nation tour of Southeast Asia. Predictably, this provoked considerable debate in Asia about the sincerity of Washington's so-called "pivot" or "rebalancing." Jane Perlez, "Cancellation of Trip by Obama Plays to Doubts of Asia Allies," *New York Times*, October 4, 2013 (http://www.nytimes.com/2013/ 10/05/world/ asia/with-obama-stuck-in-washington-china-leader-has-clear-path-at-asia-conferences. html?_r=0).

57. The five countries are Greece (2.5 percent), Turkey (2.3), the UK (2.2), France (2.2), and Portugal (2.1)—World Bank, "Military Expenditure (% of GDP)" (http://data.worldbank.org/indicator/MS.MIL.XPND.GD.ZS).

58. "Stability" was the main theme of Putin's speech accepting the presidential nomination from United Russia—"Putin Nominated as Presidential Candidate," CBC News, November 27, 2011 (http://www.cbc.ca/news/world/putin-nominated-as-presidential-candidate-1.983075).

## Chapter 8

*Epigraph*: John Galsworthy, *Over the River* (1933), chapter 1 (https://ebooks.adelaide.edu.au/g/galsworthy/john/over/chapter1.html).

1. Although there is no exact timeline for the era of *zastoi*, it dates approximately from the slowing of Soviet growth (around 1973) to the death of Brezhnev in 1982.

2. Jim O'Neill, the originator of the BRICs concept, argues that Russia is no longer an emerging economy, but emerged some years ago as a developed economy—presentation at the Oxford Analytica Annual Conference, September 2012.

3. In theory, the tension between external power projection and economic prudence could be resolved through top-down, authoritarian modernization. But in

practice the latter has proved an oxymoron. China's socioeconomic transformation in the post-Mao era has owed much more to change from below than direction from above, while in Russia authoritarianism has acted as a direct check on "technological" as well as liberal modernization. Vested interests and the fear of losing control have trumped all other considerations. See Bobo Lo and Lilia Shevtsova, *A 21st Century Myth: Authoritarian Modernization in Russia and China* (Carnegie Moscow Center, 2012, http://carnegieendowment.org/files/BoboLo_Shevtsova_web.pdf).

4. Putin has always regarded Western companies as useful sources of political as well as economic support. As noted in chapter 6, the business lobby in Germany has played an important role in softening Berlin's responses to Russian domestic and foreign policy, although its influence has diminished considerably as a result of the Ukraine crisis.

5. This is not an unreasonable hope. For example, the U.S. government has adopted an indulgent attitude toward human rights abuses in Uzbekistan, motivated by the desire to engage Tashkent more closely in counterterrorism and counterinsurgency efforts. Catherine Fitzpatrick, "Did Clinton Go Soft on Human Rights during Uzbekistan Visit?," *The Atlantic*, November 1, 2011 (http://www.theatlantic.com/international/archive/2011/11/did-clinton-go-soft-on-human-rights-in-uzbekistan-visit/247643/).

6. One of the more assiduous proponents of the "China threat" in the past has been Dmitry Rogozin, currently first deputy prime minister in charge of the defense and space industries. Although Rogozin's anti-Chinese rhetoric has subsided, in keeping with the Kremlin's pro-Beijing line and his own official responsibilities, it would be unsafe to assume that he has completely changed his views.

7. The Weimar Republic lasted from the establishment of semi-presidential democracy in 1919 to the swearing-in of Adolf Hitler as chancellor of Germany in January 1933.

8. Margot Light, "Foreign Policy Thinking," in Neil Malcolm, Alex Pravda, Roy Allison, and Margot Light, *Internal Factors in Russian Foreign Policy* (Royal Institute of International Affairs and Oxford University Press, 1996), pp. 44–70; also Bobo Lo, *Russian Foreign Policy in the Post-Soviet Era: Reality, Illusion and Mythmaking* (Basingstoke: Palgrave Macmillan, 2002), pp. 40–65.

9. Lo, *Russian Foreign Policy in the Post-Soviet Era*, pp. 154–55.

10. The connection between economic insecurity and the rise of nationalism was crucial to the appeal of Hitler and national socialism in 1930s Germany.

11. Under the "unequal treaties" of Aigun (1858), Peking (1860), and Tarbagatai (1864), the Qing empire lost much of the present-day Russian Far East as well as vast territories in Central Asia.

12. One is reminded of Winston Churchill's quip that "democracy is the worst form of government, except for all those other forms that have been tried from time to time."

13. The original phrase attributed to Deng Xiaoping was "socialism with Chinese characteristics"—meaning a planned socialist economy, but with commodity (that is, capitalist) features.

14. The early Yeltsin years (1992–93) marked the first wave of post-Soviet Russian liberalism.

15. Dmitri Trenin, *Post-Imperium: a Eurasian Story* (Washington: Carnegie Endowment for International Peace, 2011), p. 242.

16. It has been suggested that authoritarian regimes in the ex-Soviet republics would be uncomfortable with a liberal Russia, in particular fearing the effects of a democratic "contagion." This is possible, but much would depend on whether Moscow felt inclined to promote democracy among its neighbors. The experience of the Yeltsin years suggests it would be unlikely to go down this path.

17. This is already apparent in relation to China in Central Asia, where there is a dichotomy between welcoming elite attitudes and popular xenophobia.

18. Ivan Krastev, "Would Democratic Change in Russia Transform Its Foreign Policy?," Open Democracy, February 7, 2013 (http://www.opendemocracy.net/od-russia/ivan-krastev/would-democratic-change-in-russia-transform-its-foreign-policy).

19. This was recognized by the father of modern Russian liberalism, Yegor Gaidar—"Rossiya zainteresovana v stabilnom razvitii Kitaya" [Russia Has a Vested Interest in the Stable Development of China], May 2002 (www.gaidar.org/otvet/may02_01.htm, accessed in 2007—link has since expired).

20. The prospect of a more dynamic future may also encourage the return of Russia's "lost generation" from abroad—a process that occurred in several central and east European countries after the fall of communism.

21. "It could be that, as happened in 1991–1992, the present will start to unravel before an institutionally robust alternative can be built to replace it"—remarks by Lilia Shevtsova, in Lilia Shevtsova and Andrew Wood, *Change and Decay: Russia's Dilemma and the West's Response* (Washington: Carnegie Endowment for International Peace, 2011), p. 238.

22. Vladimir Putin, remarks to the Valdai Club, September 19, 2013 (http://eng.kremlin.ru/transcripts/6007); also address to the Federal Assembly, December 12, 2013 (http://eng.kremlin.ru/transcripts/6402).

23. Sergei Karaganov, "Lucky Russia," *Russia in Global Affairs*, March 29, 2011 (http://eng.globalaffairs.ru/pubcol/Lucky-Russia-15154).

# Index

Abe, Shinzo: relationship with Putin, 153; role in Japan–Russia rapprochement, 152–53

Abkhazia, 89, 96, 104; attitude toward Tbilisi, 92; independence of, 63, 117, 118, 124, 173, 266nn38–39, 290n83; military agreement with Moscow, 118–19. *See also* "Frozen conflicts"

"Active measures" (*aktivnye meropriy-atiya*), 41, 256n12; disinformation (*disinformatsiya*), 215, 256n12; hybrid warfare, 57, 235; information war (*informatsionnaya voina*), 256n12

Afghanistan, 14, 45, 58, 59, 60, 64, 88, 98, 106, 114, 121, 125, 128, 134, 137, 149, 155, 168, 211, 217, 222, 225, 230, 265n37, 272n110, 315n43; Northern Distribution Network (NDN), 91, 92, 173, 178, 277n48, 280n95; Russian assistance to government of, 91, 222; Russia-U.S. cooperation, 92, 169, 171–72, 173, 176, 290n83

Ahmadinejad, Mahmoud, 93

Akhmetov, Rinat, 109–10

Aliyev, Ilham, 120, 279n83

Americacentrism, 98, 196, 226

Andijon massacre (May 2005), 121, 280n95

Angola, 146

Anti-Americanism, 15, 24, 25, 33, 37, 155, 159, 179, 188, 193, 211, 230, 310n149. *See also* Anti-Westernism

Anti-Ballistic Missile (ABM) treaty, U.S. withdrawal from, 15

Anti-trust suit, European Commission's, 29, 87, 183

Anti-Westernism, 14, 32, 235, 238, 311n160

APEC (Asia-Pacific Economic Cooperation), 85, 212; Bali summit (2013) appeasement, 160, 295n135; Russian attitudes toward, 50, 78, 136, 159–60; Vladivostok summit (2012), 52, 143, 159, 161, 177, 214, 296n146

Arab League, 94

Arab Spring, 11, 16, 175, 187, 204; Russian reaction to, 94, 95, 230

Arctic issues, 5, 87, 197; Barents Sea agreement, 87; Northern Sea Route (NSR), 88; Rosneft-CNPC agreement, 147, 174

Armenia, 106, 120, 127, 130, 282n123; diaspora, 127; economic dependence on Russia, 306n123; relations with Russia, 106, 127, 184

Arms control. *See* Disarmament

Arms sales, 120, 294n128, 298n16; to China, 144, 287n46, 292n104; to